THE SAGEBRUSH STATE

FIFTH EDITION

Wilbur S. Shepperson Series in Nevada History

Series Editor, Michael Green (UNLV)

Nevada is known politically as a swing state and culturally as a swinging state. Politically, its electoral votes have gone to the winning presidential candidate in all but two elections since 1912 (it missed in 1976 and 2016). Its geographic location in the Sun Belt; an ethnically diverse, heavily urban, and fast-growing population; and an economy based on tourism and mining make it a laboratory for understanding the growth and development of postwar America and postindustrial society. Culturally, Nevada has been associated with legal gambling, easy divorce, and social permissiveness. Yet the state also exemplifies conflicts between image and reality: It is a conservative state yet depends heavily on the federal government. Its gaming regulatory system is the envy of the world but resulted from long and difficult experience with organized crime. And its bright lights often obscure the role of organized religion in Nevada affairs. To some who have emphasized the impact of globalization and celebrated or deplored changing moral standards, Nevada reflects America and the world; to others, it affects them.

This series is named in honor of one of the state's most distinguished historians, author of numerous books on the state's immigrants and cultural development, a longtime educator, and an advocate for history and the humanities. The series welcomes manuscripts on any and all aspects of Nevada that offer insight into how the state has developed and how its development has been connected to the region, the nation, and the world.

Charcoal and Blood: Italian Immigrants in Eureka,
Nevada and the Fish Creek Massacre
Silvio Manno

A Great Basin Mosaic: The Cultures of Rural Nevada
James W. Hulse

The Baneberry Disaster: A Generation of Atomic Fallout
Larry C. Johns and Alan R. Johns

THE
SAGEBRUSH
STATE

NEVADA'S HISTORY, GOVERNMENT, AND POLITICS

FIFTH EDITION

MICHAEL W. BOWERS

UNIVERSITY OF NEVADA PRESS *Reno & Las Vegas*

University of Nevada Press | Reno, Nevada 89557 USA
www.unpress.nevada.edu
Copyright © 2018 by University of Nevada Press
All rights reserved
Cover photographs: (*background*) iStock/FierceAbin and iStock/btgbtg;
   (*inset*) iStock/DenisTangneyJr; (*bottom*) Allen Leo Svec

LIBRARY OF CONGRESS CATALOGING-IN-PUBLICATION DATA
Names: Bowers, Michael Wayne, author.
Title: The Sagebrush State : Nevada's history, government, and politics / Michael Wayne
   Bowers.
Other titles: Nevada's history, government, and politics
Description: Fifth edition. | Reno, NV : University of Nevada Press, [2018] | Series: Wilbur S.
   Shepperson series in Nevada history | Includes bibliographical references and index. |
Identifiers: ISBN 978-1-943859-74-0 (pbk. : alk. paper) | ISBN 978-1-943859-75-7 (e-book) |
   LCCN 2018004689 (print) | LCCN 2018005551 (e-book)
Subjects: LCSH: Nevada—History. | Nevada—Politics and government.
Classification: LCC F841 .B593 2018 (print) | LCC F841 (e-book) | DDC 979.3—dc23
LC record available at https://lccn.loc.gov/2018004689

The paper used in this book meets the requirements of American National Standard
for Information Sciences—Permanence of Paper for Printed Library Materials,
ANSI/NISO Z39.48-1992 (R2002).

FIRST PRINTING

Manufactured in the United States of America

Contents

Preface to the Fifth Edition ix

Preface xiii

Chapter 1. Nevada—Origins and Early History 3

Chapter 2. Nevada Territory and Statehood 19

Chapter 3. Civil Rights and Liberties in Nevada 34

Chapter 4. Political Parties and Elections 56

Chapter 5. Interest Groups and Lobbying 75

Chapter 6. The Nevada Legislature 84

Chapter 7. The Nevada Executive 99

Chapter 8. The Nevada Judiciary 115

Chapter 9. City and County Governments 134

Chapter 10. State and Local Finance 141

Chapter 11. Nevada—Past, Present, and Future 155

Appendix. The Constitution of the State of Nevada 177

Notes 289

Selected Bibliography 297

Index 301

Illustrations and Tables

Figures

2.1. Territory and State of Nevada   29
3.1. Racial Diversity in Nevada, 2010 Census   35
3.2. Asian Population of Nevada, 2010 Census   39
3.3. Hispanic and Latino Population of Nevada, 2010 Census   47
8.1. Structure of the Nevada State Judicial System   121
10.3. Nevada General Fund Revenue, Adjusted Economic
      Forum Forecast, 2015–2017 Biennium   153
10.4. Nevada General Fund, Legislature-Approved
      Appropriations, 2015–2017 Biennium   154

Tables

4.1. Voter Registration in Nevada by Party in Presidential
      Election Years, 1960–2016   58
5.1. Lobbyist Growth in the Nevada Legislature, 1975–2017   79
6.1. Party Control of the Nevada Legislature, 1961–2017   92
6.2. Standing Committees in the Nevada Legislature, 2017   94
6.3. The Nevada Legislature, Famous Firsts   96
7.1. Governors of Nevada, 1864–2018   102
7.2. Party Control of the Executive Branch, State of Nevada,
      1864–2017   106
7.3. The Nevada Executive, Famous Firsts   113
8.1. Judicial Districts in Nevada, 2018   126
8.2. The Nevada Judiciary, Famous Firsts   131
9.1. Nevada Counties   136
9.2. Nevada's Incorporated Cities   138
10.1. Nevada General Fund Revenues by Source, 1977–2017   144
10.2. Nevada General Fund Appropriations by Type, 1977–2017   152
11.1. Population of Nevada, 1860–2016   167

Preface to the Fifth Edition

Since the publication of the fourth edition of *The Sagebrush State* in 2013, the state of Nevada has undergone an incredible recovery from what were in some cases debilitating changes politically and economically. At the same time, many other good changes have occurred as well. In addition to the elections that have taken place since the fourth edition and the new officeholders who have taken their seats, there have been two regular and four special sessions of the legislature.

In the preface to the third edition, I noted that "the Democrats appear to be quickly losing ground in the Sagebrush State," given electoral successes by the Republicans in the 1990s and early 2000s. But in the fourth edition, I remarked that "it is the case that the Republicans seem to be on the ropes, with Tea Party, Libertarian, and more traditional factions battling for the soul of the party." Although the latter part of that statement remains true in 2018, it is the case that the Republicans made stunning victories in the 2014 elections, capturing both houses of the legislature and all six constitutional offices. And although the Democratic Party organization put together by now-retired Harry Reid continues to dominate that party's politics, it is arguably not as strong as it was now that Reid is no longer majority leader of the U.S. Senate. In 2016, the Democrats won back both houses of the state legislature and Hillary Clinton won the state's six electoral votes. All of that says that (1) the author is perhaps not the seer he believed himself to be and that (2) both major parties remain competitive in the state with election outcomes very much dependent upon individual candidates and voter turnout. The state senate remains closely divided, as it has for several years (with Democrats holding a two-seat majority), but the state assembly appears to be almost permanently in Democratic hands with the loss in 2014 a rare anomaly likely resulting from low turnout.

As most observers know, the state of Nevada was among the hardest hit by the Great Recession of 2007–2011. Unemployment rates and home foreclosures were the highest of any state. When the housing bubble burst, the bottom fell out of the construction industry, and many of these workers left the state to find jobs elsewhere. With national unemployment high and job security nonexistent in virtually every sector of the economy, tourists either did not have dollars to spend in Nevada or were too cautious to do so. As a result, the economy in the Sagebrush State tanked. Politically, the bad economy led to multiple special sessions of the legislature to balance the budget, conflict over raising taxes and cutting spending, and difficult relations between Governor Jim Gibbons and the legislature. In 2010 Gibbons became the first governor in Nevada to be denied renomination by his party. Since publication of the fourth edition, the state has come roaring back. Tourism has returned to and even exceeded levels prior to the Great Recession; airport traffic is up; unemployment is at a low five percent compared to over twelve percent in 2011; construction is booming; the economy is diversifying; and major sports leagues have come to the state in the National Football League (Raiders, set for 2020), the National Hockey League (Golden Knights), Major League Soccer (Lights), and the Women's National Basketball Association (Aces).

On a further positive note, the U.S. Court of Appeals for the Ninth Circuit and, later, the U.S. Supreme Court declared laws banning same-sex marriage (such as the one in the Sagebrush State) unconstitutional in 2015, thus allowing gay and lesbian couples to marry, entitling them to all the same rights as straight married couples had always been given. And in 2013, the legislature added transgender Nevadans to the list of hate crimes for which enhanced penalties may be given. In 2017, the legislature added "sexual orientation" and "gender identity or expression" to all of the state's anti-discrimination laws.

In addition to the economic recovery in the state, perhaps the biggest change since the fourth edition has been the increasing political power of the Sagebrush State's Hispanic population. As that population continues to grow, register to vote, and participate in various ways in numbers unseen before, Hispanics have become an important political force and one that officeholders cannot ignore.

I am very pleased to provide this updated version of a book that first came out in 1996. I hope the reader will find it to be educational and, if not entertaining, well, then, at least not boring. I am, as always, tremendously grateful to Brian Davie, formerly of the Legislative Counsel Bureau, for his assistance in tracking down even the most elusive and obscure information. This book is certainly the better for his efforts.

And, of course, I must once again thank all of the great folks at the University of Nevada Press for their helpfulness, cheerfulness, and assistance in creating all five editions of this work.

Preface

When I first began discussing this book with Nicholas Cady and Thomas R. Radko of the University of Nevada Press some years ago, I had in mind a relatively short work that would provide readers with an overview of Nevada history and government. I thought then, as I do now, that many Nevadans and non-Nevadans would be interested in a concise work that would allow them to understand Nevada's intriguing past and its effects on the present and future direction of the state. A work of that type could be utilized as a supplementary text in the state's universities and community colleges and would, perhaps, also find a niche among high school students and members of the general public.

These thoughts and discussions brought about *The Sagebrush State*. Throughout the writing of this book I have attempted to be true to my original intent to provide a concise work that could be revised on a regular basis to reflect changes in the state and its politics. Certainly this work does not pretend, nor was it ever intended, to be a comprehensive volume on every detail of Nevada history and politics; for that degree of thoroughness, the reader is directed to the bibliography. A great debt is owed by this author and all others in the field to those pioneering historians and political scientists who have taught us what we now know about the state: Hubert Howe Bancroft, Eleanore Bushnell, Don Driggs, Russell Elliott, James Hulse, Effie Mona Mack, William Rowley, Elmer Rusco, and many others too numerous to mention.

In addition, I would like to specifically thank Eugene Moehring of the History Department at the University of Nevada, Las Vegas, and Michael Green of the Community College of Southern Nevada for their assistance and counsel during the research and writing process. Were it not for their insights, this book would be the poorer. Brian Davie of the Legislative Counsel Bureau and Sidney Watson of the Government Documents Division of the James L. Dickinson Library at UNLV provided regular assistance in my quest for obscure facts and figures. I would also like to thank Leonard E. "Pat" Goodall for providing me with a draft of his forthcoming omnibus book with Don W. Driggs, *Nevada Politics and Government: Conservatism in an Open Society*. I am grateful to Trudy McMurrin of the University of Nevada Press for her unflagging devotion to seeing this work in print and her regular phone calls to ask, "So, how's the book coming?"

I would also like to thank Dean Guy Bailey of the College of Liberal Arts and the staff of the Dean's office (Joyce Nietling, Leslie Marsh, Judy Ahlstrom, Jeremy Wirtjes, and Mike Comstock) for all they have done to ease my burdens as an administrator. Without them, I would be unable to pursue the joys of research, writing, and teaching.

Any errors to be found within these pages must, of course, remain mine alone.

THE SAGEBRUSH STATE

FIFTH EDITION

CHAPTER ONE

Nevada

Origins and Early History

Early Exploration

Although recent archaeological excavations indicate the migration from Asia of prehistoric peoples to the area now known as Nevada as early as 15,000 years ago, the state's written history can be said to have begun in 1776, the same year the American colonists in the East launched their war for independence against the British Crown. In the spring of that year, a Spanish Franciscan missionary, Father Francisco Garcés, and two Indian guides broke off from the second expedition of Captain Juan Bautista de Anza at the present-day site of Yuma, Arizona, to discover a shorter, more direct route between Santa Fe and the Spanish military presidio at Monterey (on the central coast of what is now California). During the course of his exploration, it is believed, Father Garcés crossed the southernmost tip of what is today the state of Nevada.[1] It is also possible that a Spanish expedition of fifty-five soldiers led by Gabriel Morara entered the southern portion of what we now call Nevada in 1819. Morara's aims, however, were not quite so benevolent as those of Father Garcés. Morara's party set out to the northeast from the San Gabriel Mission (what is now present-day Los Angeles) in an unsuccessful attempt to wreak revenge against a band of Mojaves who had raided one of the Los Angeles–area missions.[2]

The Spanish, however, had little interest in exploring and developing the vast, barren region that eventually came to be identified as the Great Basin. In 1822 the area was transferred to Mexican possession when Mexico gained independence from its Spanish conquerors, thus following the earlier course of the American revolutionaries in throwing off the yoke of European imperialism. Within five years, however, British and American commercial interests were routinely violating Mexico's sovereignty in the furtherance of fur trapping and trading, concomitantly beginning the first serious explorations of the Great Basin. As one noted Nevada historian has observed, "Nevada's written history [began] with a struggle to exploit the resources of land as rapidly as possible. . . . [It is a] struggle [that] has recurred several times throughout Nevada's history."[3]

In 1826 two fur-trapping expeditions entered the Great Basin, one American and the other British. Although the two parties entered the region from different directions, they both had the same goals: to trap as many fur-bearing animals as they could and lay claim to the area for their own companies. The first English-speaking person known to have crossed into the Great Basin was the leader of the British expedition, Canadian-born Peter Skene Ogden. Ogden and his party, representing the Hudson's Bay Company, most likely ventured slightly into the northeastern corner of Nevada in the spring of 1826. Ogden's major explorations of Nevada, primarily in the north, did not occur until his later ventures into the territory in 1828 and 1829. He is generally credited as the first Anglo to discover and explore the Humboldt River.

The first American expedition, which started out in present-day Utah in August 1826, was a fifteen-member team led by twenty-seven-year-old Jedediah Smith, one of three co-owners of the Rocky Mountain Fur Company. Smith's party entered the area from the east and traversed present-day Clark County, in the south, reaching San Gabriel Mission in November. Mexican authorities, understandably anxious about new colonial threats so soon after they had gained independence from Spain, requested that Smith leave Mexican territory by the same route on which he had entered. Instead, he turned north, taking his party to an area along the American River in central California. The inhospitable nature of the snow-covered Sierra mountains made Smith decide to leave most of his party in California and attempt the mountain passage with only two other members of his expedition. Smith's three-person party successfully crossed not only the Sierras but also central Nevada, eventually reaching the Great Salt Lake. Smith's place in history is secure as the first Anglo to actually cross the hostile Nevada landscape. Although he retraced his original path through southern Nevada in 1827 to meet up with the members of his expedition whom he had left behind in California, Smith did not afterward return to the Great Basin.

The Ogden and Smith expeditions were the first to explore the region now known as Nevada, but they were most assuredly not the last. Other fur-trapping parties, originating in Santa Fe and traversing the southern part of the state, were led by Ewing Young (1829), Antonio Armijo (1829–1830), and William Wolfskill and George C. Yount (1830–1831). The path blazed by these hardy trappers eventually established an overland route known as the Old Spanish Trail.

One of the last fur-trapping expeditions, and one of the most famous and significant, was the Walker-Bonneville party of 1833 to 1834.[4] Although the group was putatively on a fur-trapping expedition, some evidence suggests that its leader, U.S. Army Captain Benjamin L.E. Bonneville, sent some members of the party, led by Joseph Walker, on an excursion into California to spy on the Mexicans.[5] During their trek through central Nevada, Walker's party killed thirty to forty Native Americans, establishing an unfortunate precedent that would haunt later relations between the region's oldest and newest inhabitants. Walker is perhaps best known for the "discovery" of the Yosemite Valley in California and Walker Pass over the Sierra Nevada, although native inhabitants had clearly known of these for many years.

Explorers and Immigrants

Spurred by the desire for land and the American creed of Manifest Destiny (that is, that the United States had a duty and an obligation to inhabit all land lying between the Atlantic and Pacific Oceans), emigrants on their way to California began to cross, but not settle in, the Great Basin. Unlike their forebears, who traveled in this region to pursue fur trapping, these individuals were interested in establishing a new life for themselves and their families in the Far West. The first group to do so was the Bidwell-Bartleson party in 1841. As head of the Western Emigration Society, twenty-year-old-schoolteacher John Bidwell organized the six-month journey from Missouri to California's San Joaquin Valley; John Bartleson served as the group's captain. In addition to its distinction as the first of the emigrant parties, the Bidwell-Bartleson party is noteworthy for including Nancy Kelsey and her young daughter, the first Anglo woman and child to cross the Great Basin. While the Bidwell-Bartleson party crossed the Nevada frontier in the north, a second emigrant party in 1841, the Rowland-Workman party, traveled through the Las Vegas Valley, following the Old Spanish Trail and the 1826 route of Jedediah Smith from Santa Fe to San Gabriel.

The hardship of the terrain and desert conditions along the Old Spanish Trail, however, led later emigrant parties to cross the Great Basin through the north along what became known as the Humboldt Trail. The discovery of the latter trail is credited to the aforementioned Joseph Walker, who led the 1843 Walker-Chiles party along the northern Nevada route he had discovered during his 1834 journey out of California. Other emigrant parties followed that route through the Great Basin over the next several decades, including one in 1844 led by Elisha Stevens, Martin Murphy, and John Townsend—an expedition famed for its successful crossing of the forbidding and deadly summit that would tragically become known a few years later as Donner Pass.

The Donner party left Missouri in the spring of 1846 to pursue dreams of land ownership in California. Following generally the path of the Humboldt Trail, the party took an ill-advised cutoff in northeastern Nevada that put them woefully behind schedule. Their tardiness caused them to reach the Sierras in October after winter storms had dumped snow on the mountains, which were difficult to cross even under better weather conditions. Trapped at Donner Lake, slightly more than half—forty-seven—of the eighty-seven people who began the trip survived, but only by allegedly cannibalizing the remains of their less fortunate companions. The misfortune of the Donner party caused a temporary slowdown in emigration to California, a hiatus that would end with the discovery of gold in California in January 1848 and the February 1848 cession of what is now the southwestern United States by Mexico at the end of the Mexican War.

In addition to the informal and unofficial explorations of the Great Basin area by fur trappers and immigrants to California, a number of official expeditions were launched by the U.S. government in the early 1840s into what was then still Mexican territory. The leader of these expeditions was a member of the U.S. Army's Topographical Engineers, Captain John C. Frémont, whose destiny was most assuredly not harmed by the fact that his wife, Jessie, was the daughter of influential Missouri senator Thomas Hart Benton, one of the most fanatical of the Manifest Destiny zealots. Frémont headed two expeditions into present-day Nevada, the first from 1843 to 1844 and the second in 1845. The former traversed the western edge of northern Nevada to central California and back along the Old Spanish Trail in the south. The latter expedition, on which he was accompanied by Joseph Walker and Kit Carson, explored the central portions of the state. The lasting significance of the Frémont expeditions can be seen to this day. Although Frémont "discovered" little that had not already been explored by others, his parties, unlike their predecessors, painstakingly and accurately mapped the area and gave names to its features, names that adhere today: the Humboldt River, the Walker River, the Carson River, Pyramid Lake. Indeed, it is Frémont who first identified this vast area of interior drainage as "the Great Basin."

Settlement of Nevada

The fur trappers, California immigrants, and explorers who visited the Great Basin in the 1820s, 1830s, and 1840s had no intention of settling in the region now known as Nevada. To them it was merely a place where they hunted or passed through on the way to a new land or to an adventure, respectively. Permanent settlement of Nevada would not come until the latter part of the 1840s. Political scientists Eleanore Bushnell and Don Driggs, among others, have noted that the settlement of Nevada came as a result of three contemporaneous events:

> (1) the cession by Mexico of vast territories to the United States in the Treaty of Guadalupe Hidalgo in 1848; (2) the migration of the Mormons into the Salt Lake area and later into much of the region that now comprises Nevada; and (3) the discovery of gold in California.[6]

None of these momentous events had much to do initially with Nevada. No Mexican War battles were fought here, the Mormons first settled in what is now Utah, and the first discovery of gold came in California. Like the fur trappers, California immigrants, and explorers who had traveled the land before, few among the next groups of travelers through the Great Basin saw it as an area of inherent desirability. Yet these three milestones ultimately conjoined to lead to the permanent settlement and eventual statehood of Nevada.

The Church of Jesus Christ of Latter-day Saints (the Mormons) was founded in western New York State in April 1830 by Joseph Smith, who claimed to have received from the angel Moroni a set of golden plates containing scripture and the Urim and Thummim to interpret them. Conflict with and persecution by more traditional Christian groups led Smith to move the Mormons to Ohio, Missouri, and Nauvoo, Illinois. The murder of the Mormon prophet in a Carthage, Illinois, jail led his successor, Brigham Young, to move the group once more. The journey, from 1846 to 1847, of 15,000 men, women, and children eventually came to rest at the Great Salt Lake, an area still within the sovereignty of Mexico. By March 1849 Young had proclaimed the independent State of Deseret, a region encompassing present-day Utah, Nevada, southern California, and parts of Arizona, New Mexico, Idaho, and Colorado.

While the Mormons were on their way to the Great Salt Lake, the United States was engaged in a war with Mexico for control of California and what is today the southwestern United States. Following the doctrine of Manifest Destiny to its logical, if bloody, conclusion, President James K. Polk launched the war in 1846, a war that ended successfully for the Americans in 1848 with the Treaty of Guadalupe Hidalgo. The treaty gave the United States control over California, Utah, Nevada, and portions of Arizona, New Mexico, Wyoming, and Colorado. The Great Basin was now firmly and legally ensconced in the hands of the United States.

Simultaneous to the end of the Mexican War, gold was discovered in California at Sutter's Mill on the American River near Sacramento. Beginning in 1849, thousands traveled from the east to California in search of riches; some came by sea around South America (the Panama Canal was yet to be built), while others traveled overland along the routes used by earlier California immigrants through the northern Great Basin.

As already noted, none of these three events initially had anything to do with Nevada. However, each in its own way contributed to the region's development. After 1848 the Great Basin was no longer foreign territory, the Mormons aggressively moved into its northern and southern regions to proselytize and establish settlements, and the influx of California gold seekers through the region created a need for supply stations along the overland route, including the area now known as Nevada.

The cession of California and the southwestern United States in 1848 by Mexico forced the U.S. government to deal with political issues of statehood and territorial boundaries. Rejecting Brigham Young's massive State of Deseret, Congress approved the Compromise of 1850 to establish some order in its newly acquired territory. That act, debated by Congress for two years over the heated issue of slavery, established California as a free, that is, nonslave, state (even though it had, unlike other states added after the original thirteen colonies, never been a territory) and divided the remainder of the Mexican Cession of 1848 into the territories of New Mexico and Utah, which could, upon statehood, determine for themselves whether to allow slavery. New Mexico Territory included not only New Mexico but also most of Arizona and the southern 10 percent of present-day Nevada. The newly created Utah Territory included all of present-day Utah, small parts of Colorado and Wyoming, and the northern 90 percent of present-day Nevada. Congress thus not only changed the name of the Mormon territory from Deseret to Utah but also included only half of the area Young and his followers had earlier claimed. It is doubtful that the Mormons would have achieved even that but for the death of President Zachary Taylor in July 1850. Taylor opposed the Mormon cause and was unsympathetic to state or territorial status for them. His successor, Millard Fillmore, however, was favorably impressed by the Mormons and their representative, Dr. John M. Bernhisel, who had been dispatched to Washington, D.C., in 1849 to lobby (unsuccessfully) for congressional recognition of the much larger State of Deseret. Not surprisingly, Fillmore appointed the Mormon leader, Brigham Young, as Utah's first territorial governor.[7]

Mormon settlement in the western Utah Territory (now Nevada) began that same year, 1850, when a party led by Joseph DeMont established a temporary trading post in Carson Valley near Utah Territory's western border with California.[8] The post, named Mormon Station, served the needs of emigrants and gold seekers crossing the Great Basin on their way to California. Although abandoned with the onset of winter, the post became a permanent settlement the following year when a party led by John Reese sought to establish a farming and trading community and fort. In 1856 the name of this first permanent settlement in Nevada was changed to Genoa.

Once the Mormons had established the feasibility of survival, agriculture, and commercial enterprise in the Carson Valley, they were joined by non-Mormons ("gentiles") who also opened trading posts in Carson, Eagle, and Jacks Valley and Truckee Meadows. Gentile population in the area was augmented by the discovery in 1850 of gold in Gold Canyon just east of the California border. Gold miners from California and new gold seekers from the East soon established residence in the region as well, although they generally had no intention of making the place a permanent home. The combination of Mormons and non-Mormons in the Carson Valley was from the beginning a volatile one and was partially responsible for Nevada's eventual separation from Utah Territory in 1861.

The area that is now southern Nevada was also being settled during this time. Although the development of the south did not have the same profound effects on Nevada's becoming a territory and, later, a state that the development of the north did, the settlement of both areas exhibited many of the same characteristics. Settlement of the Las Vegas Valley (part of New Mexico Territory since 1851) began in 1855, when Brigham Young sent a group of Mormons led by William Bringhurst to establish the Las Vegas Mission. The mission was to serve a dual purpose: establish supply stations along the Old Spanish Trail (just as Mormon Station had in the north) and convert the Native Americans, primarily Southern Paiutes, to Mormonism. Their task was, in many ways, a hard and thankless one, performed in a hostile environment. One of the missionaries, John Steele, observed in an 1855 letter that "the country around here looks as if the Lord had forgotten it."[9] Later in that same letter he noted that there was a "general weakness" among the Mormon missionaries because

> the weather is very hot; and not having light, suitable clothing fit for the season; and the last and principal reason is, they have nothing (with a very few exceptions) to eat but dry bread, as the cows are mostly dry. But we still are not discouraged, for we hope for better times ahead; and if we don't live to see it, maybe our children will.[10]

The Las Vegas Mission eventually was abandoned as a result of a split in the community between Bringhurst and Nathaniel V. Jones, whom Brigham Young had sent to the mission in 1856 to mine lead ore in the area. This division was part of a larger conflict within the Mormon community over whether its primary purpose was to proselytize or mine. By 1858 most of the missionaries had returned to Utah, leaving only a small band under the authority of Benjamin R. Hulse. Hulse's group soon followed, and the Las Vegas Valley was left to its Native American inhabitants until 1861, when small traces of silver were found in the old Mormon lead mine and a large gold strike was made near the current site of Hoover Dam. A permanent settlement in Las Vegas (named Los Vegas Rancho) did not take root until 1865, when Octavius Decatur Gass took ownership of the Old Mormon Fort and established a station to supply Las Vegas Valley miners and the settlers passing through to California.[11]

Establishing a Government

From the first moments of their arrival in the Carson Valley in 1851, the settlers agitated for separation from the Mormon-dominated Utah territorial government. Separated as they were by five hundred miles from the territorial capital, first in Fillmore City and later in Salt Lake City, and ignored by Brigham Young, who concentrated on organizing that part of the territory that was nearest to him, the western settlers were left with no established government and no protection from bandits and Indian attacks. In response to this lack of law and order and Utah's *de facto* policy of benign neglect, settlers held three meetings in Mormon Station on November 12, 19, and 20, 1851, to establish order.

During the course of these meetings, the settlers created a squatter government to establish bylaws and regulations for the community and to create public offices. Ten resolutions were adopted dealing with the survey and recording of land claims, while an eleventh established a committee of seven officers to act as the region's governing board. In addition, a magistrate's court, made up of a justice of the peace and four others, was to serve as the area's judicial body; appeal could be taken to a court of twelve citizens who had final say on matters brought to them. Notably, the group also adopted a petition to Congress seeking "a distinct Territorial Government" for the western Utah Territory.[12]

Displeased by the Carson Valley settlers' petition, Brigham Young intervened and attempted, at last, to establish territorial control over the area. Seven Utah counties were extended to the California border in order to include the western Utah Territory. County seats remained in present-day Utah, however, and with such a distance between them, county officials persisted in their failure to exercise any authority over their newly acquired western lands. The ineffectiveness of the squatter government in achieving law and order, combined with the objections by many non-Mormons to the possibility of control by Salt Lake City, led forty-three settlers in 1853 to sign a petition to the California Legislature requesting annexation by California "for judicial purposes until congress [sic] should provide otherwise."[13]

Although the settlers' petition was ignored by California, Utah took great note of it and attempted once more to bring its western territory into the fold. In January 1854 the territorial legislature created Carson County, an extremely large new county in the western Great Basin. It encompassed what is today Carson City, Washoe, Douglas, Storey, Lyon, and Mineral Counties and parts of Nye, Esmeralda, Churchill, and Humboldt Counties. Once again, however, no immediate attempts were made by the Utah authorities to exercise control over their newest creation.

Utah's lack of action led the squatters to once more endeavor to establish an organized government in what was now Carson County. In 1854 they hired attorney William A. Cornwall to write a constitution for the Carson Valley. Very little is known about the Cornwall Constitution, and most Nevada history books fail even to mention it. What we do know is that the powers of government were to be exercised by an elected group consisting of a sheriff, a president, a secretary, and a three-member court. The Cornwall Constitution was, apparently, never adopted, and "there seems to be no evidence that it was ever presented for a vote."[14]

In January 1855 the Utah Legislature took several actions that indicated a serious desire to maintain territorial control over the Carson Valley. It established Carson County as Utah's Third U.S. Judicial District, and George P. Styles was assigned as presiding judge. Orson Hyde, a member of the church's governing board, the Twelve Apostles, was appointed as probate and county judge to organize the county. In response to the settlers' complaints that they were without representation in the territorial legislature, Carson County was also given one vote in the Utah Territorial Assembly.

In May, Hyde, Styles, and thirty-eight others left Salt Lake City to once and for all establish territorial (and Mormon) control over Carson County. In those terms, Hyde was incredibly successful. Arriving in Carson Valley in June, Hyde first commissioned a survey to ensure that Mormon Station and Carson County were within the boundaries of Utah. Determining that they were, he called for county elections to be held at Mormon Station on September 20. All but one of the victorious candidates in the 1855 contest were Mormon, thanks to the immigration of Mormons into the area.

Not surprisingly, non-Mormons in the area were displeased with the now-realized Mormon domination of the Carson County government. The gentiles were convinced that the law was not administered fairly to Mormon and non-Mormon alike and were particularly dissatisfied with the practice of polygamy exercised by Hyde and others. They looked "with disgust upon the prospect of raising their daughters among such associates, and they ardently desired that their homes in their pleasant valley shall not be 'defiled' by the horrible favoritism and deception of Mormonism."[15]

Mormon domination of the Carson County government led non-Mormons in the area to petition once more, in November 1855, for annexation to California. Unlike its February 1853 predecessor, this petition was looked upon favorably by the California Legislature. Unfortunately for those seeking annexation, Congress failed to act on their plea. Hearing of the settlers' continued attempts at secession, Brigham Young ordered fifty to sixty more Mormon families into the Carson Valley. "By the middle of 1856 Carson County was organized politically, economically, and socially in the firm and able hands of the Mormons."[16]

Territorial and Mormon control over the western territory, however, was not destined to last. Probate Judge Hyde left Carson County to return to Salt Lake City in November 1856; whether he was frustrated with his position or recalled by Young is open to dispute. In January 1862 he illustrated his contempt for the people of the Carson Valley when he wrote to seek compensation for the sawmill he had left behind in his hasty departure:

> You shall be visited of the Lord of Hosts with thunder and with earthquakes and with floods, with pestilence and with famine until your names are not known amongst men, for you have rejected the authority of God, trampled upon his laws and his ordinances, and given yourselves up to serve the god of this world; to rioting in debauchery, in abominations, drunkenness and corruption. You have chuckled and gloried in taking the property of the Mormons, and withholding from them the benefits thereof. You have despised rule and authority, and put God and man at defiance. If perchance, however, there should be an honest man amongst you, I would advise him to leave; but let him not go to California for safety, for he will not find it there.[17]

Hyde's departure from Carson County left the area once more bereft of organized government and law and order. He was followed to Salt Lake City by a large party of Mormons in July 1857, and all of the faithful were officially called back to Salt Lake City by Brigham Young in September of that year to fend off what Young believed was an imminent invasion of Utah by federal troops in what became known as the Utah War. Although characterized by some historians as a series of

misunderstandings and miscommunications,[18] there were real causes for
the federal government to be concerned with goings-on in the territory,
including antagonism between Mormons and gentiles in the Carson
Valley and an incident in 1856 in which a federal judge had been "driven
from the bench" in eastern Utah by "an armed mob of Mormons."[19]

The official beginning of the Utah War came in July 1857 when President James Buchanan removed Brigham Young as territorial governor
and appointed a new, non-Mormon government headed by Alfred Cumming. The anticipated arrival of the new territorial government, accompanied as it was by 2,500 federal troops led by General Albert Sidney
Johnston, struck fear into the hearts of the Mormons. It was then that
Young called upon all Mormons, including approximately 1,000 in the
Carson Valley, to return to the capital to fend off the anticipated federal
invasion. In addition, Young issued an order prohibiting an armed force
from entering the Salt Lake Valley and declared martial law. The Mormons prepared for war, but the federal forces eventually were allowed
to enter the valley peacefully after successful negotiations between
Young and Buchanan's representative, Colonel Thomas L. Kane, who
had made friends with the Mormons when they had lived in Nauvoo. In
April 1858 the Utah War, such as it was, officially ended when Buchanan
granted amnesty to all who swore allegiance to the Union. Although the
returnees were, thus, not ultimately needed, they did not go back to the
Carson Valley, and the land, homes, and businesses they had spent years
building into profitable enterprises were often simply taken by the remaining settlers—a situation that led to Hyde's curse upon them.

In apparent anticipation of the September call by Young for all adher-
ents to return to the Salt Lake Valley, the Utah Legislature in January
1857 repealed the act creating Carson County and put the area under the
nominal control of Great Salt Lake County, headquartered in Salt Lake
City. Although no doubt happy to see the Mormon exodus, the western
settlers were once more left without any organized government, and the
Carson Valley was again in the grip of the same lawlessness it had suffered prior to the Mormons' arrival in large numbers in 1856.

The period between 1857 and 1861 has been described as an "era of
anarchy and confusion." The phrase is an apt one. In 1857, after the Utah
Legislature's dissolution of Carson County and Judge Hyde's return to
Salt Lake City, the settlers held a series of mass meetings in which they
once more petitioned Congress for status as a separate territory within

the shortest time possible. The settlers' representative to Washington, D.C., James M. Crane, predicted in a letter to his constituents that Congress would act favorably on the petition in order "to compress the limits of the Mormons and defeat their efforts to corrupt and confederate with the Indian tribes."[20] Crane's optimistic prediction was wrong. A bill granting territorial status, which included a change of name from Sierra Nevada to Nevada, passed the House Committee on Territories, but the full Congress adjourned before acting on the petition. The congressional failure to act was based in part on the pre–Civil War sectional strife over slavery that was even then dividing the nation: the territorial bill was held up in the House by Speaker James L. Orr of South Carolina, who feared that the new territory would not support slavery and who had a strong personal dislike for the bill's sponsor, Representative William "Extra Billy" Smith of Virginia. Of lesser, but still significant, importance, the federal government hoped that the newly appointed non-Mormon government of Alfred Cumming would resolve the antagonism in the western territory between Mormons and gentiles.

In addition to petitioning for separate territorial status, the settlers attempted to establish a more immediate mechanism for protecting law and order in the region. A committee of twenty-eight men was created during the 1857 squatters' meetings to serve as a provisional government. The committee proved ineffectual, and in March 1858 the settlers met again, this time to establish a vigilante committee to maintain law and order. The vigilantes were equally unsuccessful in holding the criminal element in check, although they did try, and sentence, several people. One of those, the ironically named William "Lucky Bill" Thorrington, was a prominent member of the community who had served on the twenty-eight-member provisional committee of 1857. Thorrington was hanged for being an accessory after the fact to murder, although substantial evidence supports his innocence.[21] Thorrington's hanging had the unfortunate consequence of creating a serious rift in the Carson Valley community between those convinced of his guilt and those who believed him innocent.

Once again, Utah Territory attempted to establish control over its wayward western province, this time by appointing, in 1858, John S. Child as probate judge to reorganize local government in the Carson Valley. Child called for new elections in October, elections noted for such intense conflict and voter fraud that the results in four of the six precincts were discarded because of charges of fraudulent voting. In January 1859 Utah officially reestablished Carson County, gave it a single representative in the territorial legislature, and combined it with two other counties to form the Second U.S. Judicial District. John Cradlebaugh was appointed as the district's judge.

The failure of Judge Child to effectively reorganize Carson County led the settlers to call for a mass meeting in Carson City on June 6, 1859, to take up once more the issue of separate territorial status. At that meeting an election was called for July 14 to choose a delegate to represent the interests of the Carson Valley in Washington, D.C., and to select fifty delegates to attend an unauthorized constitutional convention.

Nevada Territory

James M. Crane was again elected to serve as the settlers' representative to the nation's capital, although his election was surrounded by more charges of voter fraud. The convention delegates met in Genoa on July 18, 1859. Again, support for separation from Utah Territory appeared to be based primarily upon a desire to be freed from the Mormon authorities, who, according to the settlers, "so [mixed] together church and state that a man [could not] obtain justice in any of its courts."[22] Illustrating the point was a letter written in January 1859 by Crane to Representative William Smith in which he opined that

> The only remedy for this unnatural war, now raging between the Mormons and the Anti-Mormons in Utah, is to be found in the immediate separation of these people under two distinct governmental organizations. One thing is inevitable,—the Mormons and Anti-Mormons will never, and can never live together in peace, under one government.[23]

A nine-day convention, presided over by Colonel John J. Musser, voted to secede from Utah Territory, produced a territorial constitution modeled upon that of the state of California, and adopted the name Nevada. A ratifying election was held on September 7 concurrent with elections for a governor and territorial legislature.

Support for the 1859 constitution was substantial. The election returns were not preserved, but "there is evidence that the majority for the constitution was about four hundred, . . . although the board of canvassers failed to meet to canvass the votes, and the certificate of the president of the board, J.J. Musser, alone testified to the result."[24] Musser's certificate of election did not issue until December, three months after the election, leading to doubts about the veracity of the reported results. In any event, Isaac Roop was elected territorial governor and the legislature was to meet on December 15. The legislature did meet on that date but was unable to act for lack of a quorum; only four members attended. After an address by "Governor" Roop, the group adjourned, never to meet again. Roop, however, did continue to act as governor for some time.

Undeterred by the unauthorized actions of the settlers, U.S. District Court Judge John Cradlebaugh arrived in Genoa in the summer of 1859. Although not a Mormon, Cradlebaugh was a representative of the Utah territorial government, and Carson County residents refused to work with him. In yet one more attempt to establish control over the western settlers, Probate Judge Child attempted unsuccessfully to hold court in September and also called for new elections on October 8. In protest, only three of the county's ten precincts opened for the election. Under those rather disconcerting and unsupportive circumstances, the winning candidates refused to take office. Child could finally enjoy some sense of achievement in August 1860 when elections were successfully held to select various officeholders, including a representative to the Utah Territorial Assembly.

Attempts by the western settlers to achieve separate territorial status and some measure of law and order were exacerbated by three significant, contemporaneous events. In September 1859 James M. Crane, the settlers' delegate to Washington, D.C., died of a heart attack in Gold Hill. He was replaced by the aforementioned John J. Musser, who was unable to persuade Congress during its 1859–1860 session to establish an independent territory in Carson County. Complicating matters further was President Buchanan's appointment of R.P. Flenniken as the new judge of the Second U.S. Judicial District to replace Judge Cradlebaugh—and Cradlebaugh's refusal to leave his position. Thus was created the unworkable situation of two federal judges attempting to enforce the law. Conflict between the two only increased the judiciary's impotence in the face of escalating lawlessness. The ineffectiveness of any government authority to maintain law and order was further exacerbated by a third event: the discovery of gold and silver in what became known as the Comstock Lode. The Comstock Lode brought with it a huge tide of humanity, including miners and the tradespeople who sought to supply them. New towns sprang up overnight, and thousands of people rushed to make their fortunes. In addition to dealing with the general lawlessness to be expected with the sudden, unplanned influx of so many fortune seekers, the western territory now had a new problem with which to cope: conflict between various parties over ownership of lucrative mining claims.

Thus, the years 1857 to 1861 were marked by anarchy and confusion, without any strong authority to establish law and order and without an effective government. Confusion was at an all-time high, with at least three governments in operation: the provisional government of Isaac Roop, the Utah territorial government of Probate Judge John S. Child, and the divided federal court authority exercised by warring U.S. District Judges John Cradlebaugh and R. P. Flenniken. A San Francisco newspaper of the time noted that

> There is no government. Nominally the Mormon government bears sway over that portion of the territory as well as over Salt Lake City. But practically Mormon laws are a nullity, they are not enforced, nor could they be. Should a Mormon judge or justice of the peace attempt to hold his court at Carson City or Virginia City, he would not only find that he possessed no power to execute the mandates of his court, but also that all attempts to do so would endanger his personal safety.... Politically, the people are in a chaotic state, without law and without a Constitutional [sic] government.... The present position of the people is deplorable. The evils to which they are exposed are terrible to contemplate and the coming season it is to be feared, will witness scenes of anarchy and bloodshed, fearful to behold, as the rich silver mines will attract thither a large crowd of desperate and abandoned men, who, in the absence of law and a well-established government will give full scope to their vicious inclinations.[25]

CHAPTER TWO

Nevada Territory and Statehood

In 1861, the settlers' representative, John J. Musser, finally persuaded Congress to establish a separate territory in western Utah. Musser was aided by the election of Abraham Lincoln as president and the resulting secession from the Union of the southern states. With the pro-slavery states no longer represented in Congress and unable to block the territory bill, passage was virtually guaranteed. And it certainly did not hurt the settlers' cause that the influx of population and the increase in lawlessness in Carson County as a result of the discovery of the Comstock Lode had shown that the non-Mormon territorial government of Governor Cumming was no more effective than Brigham Young had been in assuring law and order and in quelling the desire for separate territorial status among the western Utah residents. On February 26, 1861, the U.S. Senate passed legislation entitled An Act to Organize the Territory of Nevada; the House of Representatives followed suit on March 2, and President Buchanan signed it into law later that day. Thus, after ten years of uninterrupted pleas and petitions, the western Utah settlers achieved their goal: the establishment of Nevada Territory.

Two days after Buchanan signed the act establishing Nevada Territory, Abraham Lincoln was sworn in as president of the United States. So it was his responsibility to name the territory's first officers. On March 22, President Lincoln announced the appointment of James W. Nye of New York as territorial governor and Orion Clemens (brother of Samuel, better known as Mark Twain) as territorial secretary. Both were patronage appointments: Nye was a good friend of Lincoln's secretary of state, William H. Seward, and the two had campaigned in the West for Lincoln during the 1860 election; Clemens had studied law in the St. Louis law offices of Edward Bates, Lincoln's attorney general.

Governor Nye arrived in Nevada on July 7, 1861. He chose Carson City as his site of operation and later instructed the first territorial legislature to meet there, indicating the town's ascendance in the territory over the previously dominant Genoa. Nye soon issued three proclamations: the first named his appointees to various territorial offices (July 12); the second announced the creation of a judiciary (July 17), and the third called for elections to be held on August 31 for the purpose of selecting a delegate to Congress and members of the territorial legislature (July 24).

Nye's July 17 proclamation establishing a judiciary was one of the most important actions he took in this early organizational period. The lawlessness that characterized Nevada demanded the creation of courts to enforce law and order; indeed, aside from the Mormon question, the absence of legal authority was the major reason the settlers had lobbied for separate territorial status. Following the dictates of Section 9 of the Territorial Act of 1861, Nye established a supreme court, three district courts, probate courts, and justices of the peace. Three Lincoln-appointed territorial judges each heard cases on original jurisdiction in one of the district courts, and all three sat *en banc* as the supreme court to hear appeals. The lower-court judges were appointed by Nye until such time as elections could be held. In a letter to Secretary of State Seward, Nye confirmed the importance of establishing a judiciary in the territory when he noted that there was "no such thing as law or order existing in the Territory" and that there was, in particular, a great need for a court system to establish mining rights.[1]

In the August election, Judge Cradlebaugh was chosen to serve as the territory's first delegate to Congress. Also elected were nine members to serve in the Council and fifteen to serve in the House of Representatives, the upper and lower houses, respectively, of the territorial legislature. The legislature met only three times: in 1861, 1862, and 1864. The first session convened on October 1, 1861, at Abe Curry's Warm Springs Hotel two miles outside of Carson City, a site purchased later by the territorial government for $75,000 that served as the Nevada State Prison until 2012. During this first session the legislature passed 107 pieces of legislation organizing the territory. Some of the more noteworthy acts were those adopting the common law of England, forming nine counties in the territory to be governed by three-member boards of commissioners, and establishing a system of common schools. And in marked contrast to what Nevada's future would hold, some of this early legislation made divorce difficult except under the most extreme circumstances and prohibited gambling, which Governor Nye had referred to in his address to the legislature as "the worst" of "all the seductive vices," which "captivates and ensnares the young, blunts all the moral sensibilities and ends in utter ruin."[2]

Two of the most controversial issues facing this first legislative session were the permanent location of the capital and the generation of revenue for supporting the territorial government. The question of where to locate the territorial capital was, apparently, a difficult and emotional one, resulting in charges of underhanded dealing and a barroom brawl in the Ormsby House Hotel between a Virginia City councilman and a Carson City representative. By a vote of 15 to 9, it was decided that Carson City, and not Virginia City, would be the capital. The issue of how best to raise revenue in the territory was a precursor of the events that would disrupt and derail later attempts to write a state constitution. Governor Nye proposed a tax on the gross proceeds of mines, at that time the major source of the territory's wealth. The mining-dominated legislature vehemently objected and eventually passed a general property tax measure of forty cents per one hundred dollars valuation on property in the territory. Counties could, in addition, adopt a levy of up to sixty cents more per one hundred dollars valuation on all property within their jurisdictions. The mines and their products would be untaxed. This battle over the taxation of mining property was only the first of many to come, leading one Nevada observer to note, "The background of Nevada politics for thirty years was a fight of mine operators against paying taxes."[3]

Statehood

Although Nevada had been a territory for little more than a year when the second session of the legislature met in 1862, an election was called for September 1863 to determine support for statehood and, assuming support, the selection of thirty-nine delegates to a convention to draft a constitution for the State of Washoe. Support for statehood in the fledgling territory was overwhelming, with a vote of 6,600 in favor and 1,502 opposed.[4] Even though Congress had authorized neither the election nor statehood for the territory, a convention met in Carson City for thirty-two days in November and December of 1863 to draft a constitution for the state they chose to name Nevada rather than Washoe, as the 1862 legislature had wished, or Esmeralda or Humboldt, as some of the delegates had proposed.

The 1863 Constitution

The delegates to this unauthorized convention were optimistic not only that Congress would grant statehood but also that their handiwork would be as overwhelmingly supported by the citizens as the question of statehood had been in the September election. In that, they were sadly mistaken. Except for an unprecedented clause in which the state's citizens pledged "paramount allegiance" to the federal government, the constitution coming out of this body was itself rather unremarkable, based as it was on California's and New York's constitutions. This constitution's lack of originality is not surprising when one considers that of the thirty-nine delegates, "all but 5 had come from California, all but 5 were under 50 years of age, and all but 2 had been in the territory less than 5 years."[5] In addition, a plurality of the delegates listed New York as their place of birth. Although many issues divided the delegates during the course of their deliberations, two of the most controversial spelled overwhelming defeat at the polls for the constitution they had so carefully and painstakingly crafted.

Just as mine taxation had led to a dispute between Governor Nye and the 1861 legislature, so it disrupted the 1863 convention. The move from territorial to state status would eliminate the federal government's subsidy of the Nevada government, creating a need for additional revenue to support it. Indeed, the additional cost to be borne by a state government, as opposed to a territorial one, was a common concern among some members of various anti-statehood movements in the West during the later nineteenth century.[6] One faction, led by convention president John W. North, proposed that mines should be taxed the same as other property, arguing that "all property should bear alike the burdens of society."[7] A second faction, led by the powerful mining lawyer William M. Stewart, objected that such a tax would "mean the death of the mining industry" by "impos[ing] a burden upon the miners which would be heavier than they could bear. It would mean a tax on the shafts, drifts, and bedrock tunnels of the mines whether they were productive or not."[8] Stewart noted ominously that taxing unproductive mines, ninety-nine out of one hundred by his calculation, would stop the mining industry dead in its tracks and lead to economic disaster for the state. Instead the Stewart faction favored taxing only the net proceeds of the mines. The North faction prevailed, however, and the convention adopted a provision requiring the legislature to "provide by law for a uniform and equal rate of assessment and taxation and [to] prescribe such regulations as shall secure a just valuation for taxation of all property, both real and personal including mines, and mining property."[9]

The second issue responsible for the 1863 constitution's defeat at the polls involved the election of officeholders to serve in the new state government. Convention delegates decided to offer a single slate of officeholders on the ballot with the constitution; thus, in voting for the constitution, one would also vote for a particular slate of candidates. This proved deadly. Even though the mining-tax issue created a serious rift in the territory, it is possible that the constitution, voted on by itself, could have been ratified. Indeed, Stewart, defeated as he was in the convention on the tax issue, supported the constitution's adoption and fought mightily for ratification. But the slate of candidates, to the chagrin of many, had been handpicked by Stewart in a pair of rather nasty Union Party conventions, first in Storey County and later at the territorial convention in Carson City.[10] Stewart's domination of the Union Party proceedings led to a split in the party and the defeat of territorial supreme court justice John North, his nemesis from the constitutional convention, in his bid for the party's gubernatorial nomination. Much of Stewart's vigorous support for the 1863 constitution, including as it did the mining-tax provision he opposed, was a result of his desire to be rid of the territorial judges, including North, whom he hated as much as, if not more than, the mining tax, and his belief that his chosen candidates for "the First State Legislature would amend the new Constitution to provide taxation only of the net proceeds of productive mines."[11]

The split in the Union Party had a twofold, negative impact on the quest for ratification. First, North and his followers, who supported the constitution itself, were in no mood to vote for its ratification if that meant, as it did, the concurrent election of Stewart's slate of candidates. North and other disappointed office seekers, "and their names were legion, became hostile to [the constitution's] adoption."[12] Second, small mining companies were unwilling to take a gamble that the legislature would, in fact, repeal the mine tax, especially if that meant turning control of the state government over to Stewart and the large San Francisco mining companies he represented. As historian David A. Johnson has noted, much of the opposition to the 1863 constitution was "based upon a widespread conviction that Stewart intended to control the new state government as a means to further his own interests and those of the mining corporation officials he represented."[13]

The unlikely combination of disappointed Union Party office seekers, small miners, merchants, farmers, and a few Democrats residing in the territory—who supported the Confederacy and wished, therefore, not to become a Union state—was large enough to ensure the overwhelming defeat of the constitution in the January 1864 election. The four-to-one vote against the constitution, 8,851 to 2,157, was ironically similar to that which had favored statehood earlier. In a letter later that year to his old friend Secretary of State Seward, Governor Nye noted that the chief reason for the constitution's defeat was a "dissatisfaction with some of the State ticket, and the proceedings of some of the county conventions [that] caused its opponents to act in concert, and all combined they were strong enough to defeat it."[14] A delegate to the second constitutional convention in 1864, John A. Collins, shared Nye's belief and laid blame for the constitution's defeat on "efforts to introduce a certain set of delegates into the State Convention."[15] Yet there were those who disagreed, including Charles E. DeLong, also a delegate to the 1864 convention, who noted colorfully that the mining-tax provision, which had "stunk in the nostrils of the people," was the true cause for the failure of the 1863 constitution to be ratified.[16]

The defeat of the 1863 constitution, however, did not entirely quell Nevadans' desire for statehood; the four-to-one vote in favor of statehood in the September 1863 special election was evidence enough of its force in the territory. But for the mining-tax provision and the Union Party split engendered by Stewart's political legerdemain, the 1863 constitution might well have been ratified. Nonetheless, as will be discussed later, the mining depression that gripped Nevada Territory in mid-1864 reduced statehood desires within the territory itself. What ultimately provided the impetus for Nevada's statehood came quite outside the young territory's borders; national issues were quickly coming to a confluence that would give Nevada its cherished prize. Within twenty days after the defeat of the 1863 constitution, a bill was introduced into Congress allowing the territories of Nevada, Colorado, and Nebraska to hold constitutional conventions and establish state governments. The bill, introduced on February 8, 1864, by Senator James R. Doolittle of

Wisconsin, a Republican, easily passed both houses of Congress and was signed by President Lincoln on March 21.

The driving force behind Doolittle's bill had four components. First, Lincoln desired additional votes in Congress to assure the two-thirds vote he needed in both houses for passage of the Thirteenth Amendment, which would abolish slavery and thereby place a constitutional imprimatur on his Emancipation Proclamation. Second, Lincoln expected that he would need Nevada's three electoral votes to win the 1864 presidential election. Third, the Radical Republicans, already at odds with their own party's president over the coming Reconstruction of the southern states, had their own reasons for supporting Nevada statehood: they sought additional Republican votes in Congress to support congressional, rather than presidential, policies on such matters. Finally, with the third-party candidacy of John C. Frémont, it was thought (until his withdrawal in September) that the 1864 presidential election might be so close that no candidate would win a majority in the Electoral College and the decision would thus be thrown into the House of Representatives; an additional Republican vote from Nevada in that body would help to assure selection of Lincoln, the Republican nominee.

The 1864 Constitution

Acting quickly, Governor Nye on May 2 called for an election to be held on June 6 for the purpose of choosing thirty-nine delegates to attend a second constitutional convention. Unlike the gathering in 1863, this convention was legally authorized by Congress and, ultimately, successful.

The convention, presided over by J. Neely Johnson, former governor of California, met in Carson City on July 4 and concluded its work on July 27; thirty-five of the thirty-nine elected delegates attended. The demographic makeup of the convention was similar to that of its predecessor: ten members had served in the 1863 convention; most were from California; lawyers and mining interests dominated; and all but one, Francis Proctor, a Democrat from Nye County, were Union Party members. Unlike the 1863 convention, antagonists John W. North and William M. Stewart were not delegates.

The Nevada Enabling Act established a number of limitations on the type of constitution the convention delegates could draft. Those restrictions, to which the delegates faithfully adhered, included the following:

(1) The new State Constitution must be republican in nature and not repugnant to the Federal Constitution or the Declaration of Independence; (2) there shall be no slavery or involuntary servitude other than for punishment of crimes, without the consent of the United States and the people of Nevada; (3) the Constitutional Convention must disclaim all rights to unappropriated lands in Nevada; (4) land owned by U.S. Citizens outside Nevada must not be discriminated against in taxation; and (5) there must be no taxation of federal property in the state.[17]

There were a great many areas of dispute among the delegates at the 1864 convention; some of the most interesting and significant included the naming of the state and the ever-present issue of mine taxation.[18] The convention as a whole supported the move to statehood but debated vigorously the state's name. Among the suggested appellations were Washoe, Humboldt, and Esmeralda, all of which had also been proposed at the 1863 convention, and Bullion, Oro Plata, and Sierra Plata. Because the territory's name was Nevada and the area was, therefore, known throughout the nation by that designation, and because the congressional Enabling Act had used that name, the convention agreed to call the new state Nevada. The delegates also agreed early in their proceedings to use the failed 1863 constitution as the basis for its new draft. Although some of the members had urged abandoning the rejected document and starting anew, utilizing the California Constitution as a base, it was agreed that the 1863 constitution "owed much of its substance to the California Constitution, [so] there was no point in starting all over again."[19] In addition, by using the 1863 document as a starting point, the convention saved considerable time and expense, since several hundred copies of it were already in print.

A statistical analysis of twenty-eight significant issues voted upon in the 1864 convention has shown that, to no one's surprise, the delegates' voting behavior was much the same as it had been in the 1863 convention. The chief division among them came along "economic and geographical lines," particularly in regard to variations in voting between mining and agricultural/ranching interests. Given that all except Francis Proctor were members of the Union Party, party affiliation was "largely meaningless" in explaining any of the divisions among the delegates.[20]

The 1864 constitution differed in two major respects from its failed 1863 predecessor. On the divisive issue of mine taxation, the delegates had apparently learned their lesson. Delegates from the non-mining "cow counties" continued to support the language of the 1863 constitution that allowed for the taxation of mines at the same rate as other property. Their strong feelings on the question were generated by at least two complementary issues: equity and colonization. In regard to equity, the cow-county delegates thought it unfair that mines be taxed only on the basis of their net proceeds, as some had suggested, while all other types of property were taxed on their assessed value. George A. Nourse, an attorney from Washoe County, argued that if mines were to be taxed solely on their net proceeds, then the constitution should also provide that "farms, and sawmills, and other property shall be taxed only on their net proceeds", only then would there be "some degree of fairness."[21] In pursuing an exemption from taxation, the mining interests were clearly exhibiting one of history's oldest political axioms: additional costs are fine (in this case, the higher expenses of statehood)—as long as someone else picks up the check.

On the issue of colonization, resentment had festered for some time in Nevada over the fact that large, wealthy mining companies from California controlled most of the area's mineral wealth. The *Virginia City Territorial Enterprise*, for example, had editorialized in 1862 that "the interests of no parent country and colony could possibly be more closely united than are those of California and Nevada. The colony has untold wealth of gold and silver, and the mother country manages...to get it all as fast as it is dug out."[22] This resentment was echoed at the 1864 convention by A. J. Lockwood, a mechanic from Ormsby County, who noted, "I am in favor of taxing the mines, because I want to make those gentlemen who are rolling in wealth in San Francisco, pay something for the support of our government, for the support of our common schools, and for the support of our courts."[23] Indeed, even now, San Francisco is still referred to by some as the "city Nevada built."

At the other end of the spectrum were those who did not want the mines taxed at all. E. F. Dunne, a lawyer from mining-dominated Humboldt County, warned that a tax on mines would "encumber the mining interest, which shall destroy it, or thwart its development, and...strike a ruinous blow" to the state's other economic interests.[24] More explicitly, delegate Charles E. DeLong from Storey County threatened that "but for the mines, all your stores would be removed, your farms would dry up, and be abandoned, and your wagons would stop in the streets or be turned elsewhere."[25] In addition to their superior numbers at the convention and the ghost of the 1863 constitution's failure, the miners held one other important card: the legality of taxing mining property. As noted above, the Enabling Act passed by Congress prohibited the state's taxation of unappropriated public lands within Nevada. Convention president Johnson, a lawyer from Ormsby County, concluded that this provision of the Enabling Act rendered the state powerless to tax the mines, which were situated on unappropriated federal lands.

The mining-tax debate was a long, divisive one in the convention; several proposals were offered and rejected by both sides. The unlikely alliance of small miners, farmers, and disappointed office seekers who had defeated the 1863 constitution now fell apart, victim of its own internal disagreements.[26] Eventually, however, in order to prevent the total collapse of the convention, the delegates agreed by a vote of 23 to 10 to a compromise proposal stating that "the legislature shall provide by law for a uniform and equal rate of assessment and taxation,...excepting mines and mining claims, the proceeds of which alone shall be taxed."[27] It was left to the legislature to determine whether these taxable "proceeds" would be net or gross. The compromise was not without cost, however. The mining exemption from taxes marked a turning point in the convention; thereafter, the small miners, who had previously supported positions taken by the cow-county delegates, began voting uniformly on the side of the large mining interests.[28] At the end of the convention, the "odious and unjust discrimination between different kinds of property" led George A. Nourse and Israel Crawford, an editor from Ormsby County, to vote against the constitution.[29]

The second significant distinction between the 1864 constitution and its 1863 predecessor was in the election of the state's first officers. This time the constitutional ratification vote and the election for state officials would take place separately, the former on September 7 and the latter on November 8. Thus, in the 1864 ratification election, the voters would be free to support statehood and the constitution without necessarily voting for a particular slate of candidates they might find unacceptable.

Support for the 1864 constitution was overwhelming. At the convention it received a positive vote of 19 to 2, and in the September 7

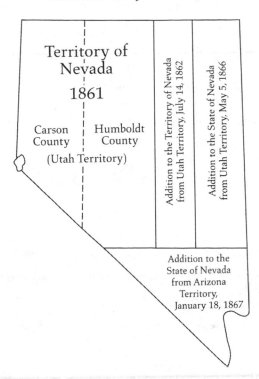

FIGURE 2.1. Territory of Nevada formed in 1861 from Carson and Humboldt
Counties of Utah Territory. In 1862 Nevada Territory enlarged by extension
eastward one degree into Utah Territory. Enlarged Territory, and State as created
in 1864, coextensive in size. Additional extension eastward one degree into Utah
Territory in 1866 by State of Nevada. Extension south into Arizona Territory
to the Colorado River by State of Nevada in 1867. Nevada Territory existed in
two different sizes; Nevada as a state in three different sizes. Courtesy of Dean
Heller, *Political History of Nevada*, 2006, 11th ed. Reprinted with permission.

election it was decisively supported by a popular vote of 10,375 to 1,284,
a margin of more than eight to one.[30] In its haste to admit Nevada as a
state before the 1864 national elections, Congress, in the Enabling Act,
waived the right to inspect and approve the constitution and allowed
Nevada Territory to become a state upon acceptance of the constitution
by President Lincoln. On October 17 the territorial government wired
the entire text of the state constitution to the nation's capital at a cost of
$4,303.27, making it the "longest and most expensive telegram ever dis-
patched in the United States up to that time."[31] Finding the constitution
acceptable, on October 31, 1864, President Lincoln issued the proclamation making Nevada the thirty-sixth state in the Union.

Thus, in the course of approximately one year, the residents of Nevada had made a complete turnaround from rejecting to accepting a state constitution. Clearly the 1864 convention's decisions to tax only the proceeds of the mines and to separate the ratification ballot from that for state officers are critical in explaining this reversal. Two other issues, however, bear brief mention here. The first of these was a mining depression that hit the territory hard in 1864. It had two effects on the acceptance of the 1864 constitution. The depression's impact upon the region's economy was so immense that six of the eight delegates at the convention who had also served in the 1863 convention and who had previously voted against the tax exemption for mining property supported it in 1864. With the mining economy now fallen upon hard times, the tax-exemption compromise was more acceptable to them, since "concern over economic survival supplanted [their] fear of domination by outside interests."[32] In short, Nevadans had come to believe, accurately, that the day of the solitary miner was over and that mining could survive only with the infusion of capital from other places and the "corporatization" of what had previously been an individual labor. The California capital they had so feared and distrusted in 1863 had come to be seen as crucial to the mining industry's, and thus the state's, survival.[33] The depression also had the effect of strengthening statehood desires among the general populace. This sentiment was evidenced by an editorial in the *Territorial Enterprise*: "The only hope we have of effecting a speedy and absolute cure of our crushing ills is in the adoption of a state government. . . . Better to pay even double taxes, if by doing so we can make our property ten times more productively valuable, than to pay even less and let property continue to depreciate. . . . If we should have flush times again, we must vote for the State Constitution."[34]

The second issue, to be noted again in chapter 8, was the sad and disreputable state of the territorial judiciary. The residents of Nevada Territory were now as resolute in ridding themselves of the federally appointed territorial judiciary as they had been in 1858 in ridding themselves of the Mormon-dominated judiciary emanating from Utah. Indeed, DeLong noted at the 1864 convention that "many are going to vote for the Constitution in order that we may be released from the present judiciary system."[35] The territorial judges were accused of being corrupt and of worsening the mining depression by failing to move mining cases along quickly enough. Although the judges had behaved in a sometimes-unprofessional manner, much of the opposition to them was politically motivated and engineered by William M. Stewart. As historian Hubert Howe Bancroft has noted:

> Probably the first federal judges would have been able to hold their own against the criminal element in Nevada; but opposed to the combined capital and legal talent of California and Nevada, as they sometimes were, in important mining suits, they were powerless. Statutes regarding the points at issue did not exist, and the questions involved were largely determined by the rules and regulations of mining districts, and the application of common law. Immense fees were paid to able and oftentimes unprincipled lawyers, and money lavished on suborned witnesses.[36]

Stewart could certainly be counted among the "unprincipled" lawyers to whom Bancroft referred. At a time when "cases were to be won through the bribing and browbeating of witnesses, juries, and justices," it has been observed, "Stewart had no equal on the [Comstock] lode."[37]

Stewart's attacks on the alleged corruption of the territorial judges disguised in a cloak of good government his continuing desire to control the state government and to remove from the bench his old enemy, John North. Stewart's dispute with North, which had begun over the mining-tax provision in the 1863 convention, had now reached a boiling point with Judge North's decisions in several mining cases that were adverse to the financial interests of Stewart's California clients.

On August 22, 1864, North and the other two territorial judges, Powhatan B. Locke and Chief Justice George Turner, resigned, giving (unwarranted) credence to Stewart's claims of corruption and bribe taking. That they did so was in no small part due to attacks upon them and a petition signed by more than 3,500 voters in Virginia City and Gold Hill demanding their resignations.[38] Stewart and his supporters took the opportunity to push for ratification of the constitution on the grounds that statehood would be the only remedy to ensure justice in the region. The *Nevada Transcript* editorialized, for instance, that "[Nevada] can never prosper while the judiciary is suspected. Capital will refuse to go there for investment unless at heavy premium for risk, and men of families will decline to make a spot for their homes where vice instead of virtue reigns."[39] Although there is no proof the three judges were corrupt, it is hard to imagine that the intense campaign impugning their integrity had no effect on those voting on the constitution slightly more than two weeks after their mass resignation. As Robert M. Clarke, Nevada's second attorney general, later observed, "Nevada became a state to escape the deadfall of her Territorial courts. Her Temple of Justice had been transformed into a den of iniquity."[40]

After their territory became a state on October 31, Nevadans' first duty was to hold elections for state officials and for their representative to the U.S. House of Representatives (at that time, prior to the Seventeenth Amendment, U.S. senators were selected by the state legislatures). "Battle Born" and loyal to Lincoln and the Republicans who had given them the statehood they had desired, Nevada voters lived up to congressional expectations. Republicans won the presidential ballot, all executive and judicial seats, and all but two of the legislative contests. Republican H.G. Worthington was elected to the House, and when the legislature met in December, Republicans William Stewart and James Nye were selected as the state's first U.S. senators. Worthington voted in favor of the Thirteenth Amendment, but Stewart and Nye were not sworn into office in time to join him; the state ratified it in 1865. Nevada's three federal representatives were not needed, however, to ensure Lincoln's reelection; the 1864 presidential and vice-presidential elections were not, as had been widely expected, thrown into the House and Senate, respectively. (Of perhaps minor interest is the fact that only two of Nevada's three electors voted in the 1864 Electoral College; the third, A.S. Peck, was stuck in a snowstorm in Aurora and could not attend the convocation to vote.) Thus, the state's first elections not only put Nevada firmly in the Republican fold but also began the domination of the state's politics for years to come by the victorious William M. Stewart.

The Nevada State Constitution

The State of Nevada continues to function under its 1864 constitution, although that document has been amended over 150 times since. Its contents are not particularly remarkable or unique, based as they are on the constitutions of California and New York. What does distinguish it most of all, perhaps, is that it is the culmination of a series of five "constitutions" proposed, sometimes ratified and sometimes rejected, that sought to govern the area. From the 1851 squatters' compact to the Cornwall Constitution of 1854, the ineffective constitution of 1859, and the rejected 1863 state constitution, Nevadans have shown an abiding interest in and respect for constitutional government. The 1864 constitution must, then, be seen as the successful product of those other attempts at constitution making and as the ultimate will of the state's people.

The Constitution of the State of Nevada consists of nineteen articles that perform the functions of all such documents: creation of an organized government, distribution of government power among its divisions, and the protection of individual rights from government infringement. Because the Tenth Amendment of the U.S. Constitution reserves to the states all powers not delegated to the federal government or prohibited by it to the states, state constitutions do not grant powers but seek to structure and limit those powers reserved to the states. Therefore, like the constitutions of the other forty-nine states, the Nevada Constitution tends to be longer and more specific than the federal Constitution, particularly in regard to express limitations on the power of the state. Daniel J. Elazar, the nation's most prominent scholar of federalism, cites Nevada's constitution as an example of the "Frame of Government" type of constitution, a type that is "found exclusively among the less populated states of the Far West" and characterized as a "business-like" document of moderate length reflecting "the relative homogeneity of the states themselves."[41]

By the way of comparison, the U.S. Constitution contains 240 provisions and consists of only 7,500 words. The Nevada Constitution, on the other hand, has more than twice that number of provisions and more than three times as many words. Although lengthy by reference to the federal Constitution, the Sagebrush State's constitution is actually shorter than the "average" state constitution, which encompasses 828 provisions and 34,000 words.[42]

In the chapters that follow, we shall examine various provisions of the state's constitution in more detail as they relate to particular topics in Nevada's post-1864 political history.

CHAPTER THREE

Civil Rights and Liberties in Nevada

Civil rights are generally defined as those "positive acts of government designed to protect persons against arbitrary or discriminatory treatment by government, or individuals."[1] Civil rights include those we deem necessary for equality to prevail among and between citizens: the right to vote, for example, and the right to equal employment and housing regardless of sex, sexual orientation, gender identity, race, color, creed, or religion. Civil liberties, on the other hand, refer to "negative restraints" upon the government in its exercise of power.[2] Included here would be those rights normally found in a bill of rights, such as the freedoms of speech, press, and religion. In this chapter we shall examine the past and present of Nevada's record on civil rights and liberties, a record that is at times sad and at other times cause for jubilation.

Civil Rights

Nevada, like most states, has a mixed and sometimes pitiful historical record in protecting the civil rights of its citizens. Indeed, for many years, the state was referred to as "the Mississippi of the West." Although that sobriquet was neither entirely justified nor entirely wrong, the state's treatment of minorities does not, unfortunately, always suggest the actions of an enlightened populace or government.

The roots of discrimination against ethnic, religious, and other minorities run deep in Nevada history. The Declaration of Rights that forms the first article of the Nevada Constitution states that "all men are by Nature free and equal and have certain inalienable rights." Yet even the men who wrote those words did not necessarily believe that they applied to all men, and most assuredly not to women. For example, delegates to the 1864 constitutional convention, the very convention at which those awe-inspiring words were written and adopted, also agreed upon Article 2, which gave the right to vote to white males only. Indeed, Nelson E. Murdock, one of these delegates, noted during the

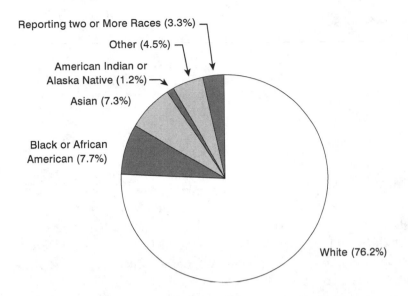

Reporting two or More Races (3.3%)
Other (4.5%)
American Indian or Alaska Native (1.2%)
Asian (7.3%)
Black or African American (7.7%)
White (76.2%)

FIGURE 3.1. Racial Diversity in Nevada, 2010 Census. Note that Hispanics constitute 26.5 percent of the state's population but are not indicated separately on this chart because they may be of any race. *Source*: U.S. Census Bureau, 2010. Percentages compiled by author.

convention's deliberations over the issue of voting rights that "I think the Anglo-Saxon, the Celtic, or any other of the White or Caucasian races, is a far superior race of men to the Indian, the Negro, or any of the colored races.... Why should we condescend to make any of the inferior races our equals?"[3] The irony of the convention's actions on the issue of voting rights in the face of both its previous high-sounding rhetoric and the fact that Nevada was born in the midst of a civil war over the issue of slavery apparently occurred only in passing to the delegates. For instance, in that same discussion over voting rights George Nourse suggested striking the word "white" from the suffrage article; his motion received neither a second nor discussion.

Although politically incorrect by today's standards, Murdock's speech before the convention delegates represented nothing more than a continuation of the attitudes that had existed in the territory for some time. In one of its first acts, the Nevada Territorial Legislature, meeting in 1861, provided that "no black person, or mulatto, or Indian, or Chinese" would be allowed to give evidence in court either in favor of or against any white person, presumably because they were considered untrustworthy.

Similarly, the legislature prohibited cohabitation with "Indians, Chinese, or negroes [sic]" and made a breach of that law punishable by either a fine or a jail term. Things were little better after the granting of statehood, when the state legislature amended the law to allow blacks, but not Indians or Chinese, to testify against a white person.

Native Americans

Although virtually all minorities in the United States have been discriminated against at one time or another, Native Americans have arguably been the only group targeted for genocide. As noted in chapter 1, prehistoric peoples entered the Great Basin as early as 15,000 years ago via a land bridge between Asia and North America at the present site of the Bering Strait near Alaska. Those who settled in present-day Nevada eventually came to be known as the Northern Paiutes (in northern and western Nevada), Southern Paiutes (in southern Nevada), Shoshones (in northern and eastern Nevada), and the Washos (in a small area of western Nevada).

One of the first encounters between these Native Americans and whites, as noted earlier, came in 1833, when at least thirty of them were killed by members of Joseph Walker's trapping party; unfortunately for the Indians, it would not be the last hostile meeting between the natives and the new immigrants. The influx of new settlers and treasure seekers to the Great Basin led to numerous conflicts with the various tribes. One of the most noteworthy was the Pyramid Lake War of 1860. That episode involved Bannock Indians who were temporarily staying at Pyramid Lake after leaving their homes farther north for the winter. The Bannocks killed either three or five whites (accounts differ) at Williams Station after two Indian girls had been kidnapped by the men and reportedly held in a cave near the station. In retaliation, more than one hundred white settlers moved, mistakenly, against the Northern Paiutes, who had, in fact, refused the Bannocks' invitation to join their raid on Williams Station. Prepared for the assault they knew would come, the Paiutes, led by Chief Sequinata, also known as Chiquito ("Little") Winnemucca, killed seventy-nine whites and wounded another twenty-six before the defeated settlers-turned-militiamen returned to Carson City. More battles ensued, with the now-outnumbered Paiutes receiving the worst of it. The U.S. Army was called in to build a garrison at Fort Churchill, and thirteen military outposts were eventually established in Nevada to "control" the Native American population. The influx of troops and the coming of the railroad eventually made it clear to all that the Native Americans could not stop the increasing tide of white settlers and miners. Ultimately most of their land was taken and treaties with the federal government were routinely broken. In the 1870s, reservations were created to house these, Nevada's first inhabitants: the Pyramid Lake Reservation and the Walker River Reservation in 1874 for the Northern Paiutes, the Moapa Reservation in 1875 for the Southern Paiutes, and the Duck Valley Reservation in 1877 for the Shoshones.

During the period after white settlement in Nevada, Native Americans quickly became foreigners in their own land, the object of both social and legal discrimination. Through various laws, first the territory and then the state of Nevada prohibited the sale of alcohol, firearms, and ammunition to the Indians, prohibited intermarriage between the tribes and whites, controlled fishing on the Walker River Reservation, sought to diminish the size of reservations in order to secure prime timber property, and prohibited Indians from attending public schools. During this early period of Nevada's history, the Native Americans were exiled to live on the fringes of white society, performing unskilled labor. At one point, legislators went so far as to suggest that any Indians who could not be "subjugated" should be "exterminated."[4]

In the 1920s, Indian children were allowed to attend public schools, and in the 1940s Native Americans began to see somewhat better legislation as the state recognized the validity of Indian marriages, repealed laws prohibiting the sale of alcohol to Indians, and allowed the use of peyote in Native American religious ceremonies. In 1965 an Indian Affairs Commission was created by the legislature to study and make recommendations to the state government on issues relating to Nevada's Native American population.[5] At the federal level, Congress established the Indian Claims Commission in 1946 to place a monetary value on, and pay compensation to the tribes for, the lands taken. Although the amounts to be paid were in the millions of dollars, some tribes, most notably the Western Shoshone, refused the moneys. However, in lopsided votes in 1998 (1,130 to 53) and 2002 (1,703 to 230), tribal members voted to accept the money which, as a result of interest had by 2005 grown from $26.1 million to more than $145 million. Distribution of these funds began in 2011. Nonetheless, many of the tribe's members challenge the decision and continue to lay claim to the lands, approximately one-third of the state of Nevada, which were promised to them in the Treaty of Ruby Valley in 1863.

In two separate cases during the Clinton administration the federal government turned over land to the Washo and Timbisha Shoshone tribes. In the former case, the Washo Tribe of Nevada and California is leasing 350 acres of U.S. Forest Service land on the California side of Lake Tahoe and has access to ninety additional acres near the lake, land upon which it built a cultural center for tribal ceremonies. Although the leases will run for only thirty years, the tribe hopes to make their status permanent before the expiration date of 2027. And, in 2000 the Timbisha Shoshone were granted a permanent homeland in the Mojave Desert consisting of 5,800 acres in Nevada and 1,900 acres in California. At one time, the Timbisha Shoshone occupied 15,000 square miles in the area around Death Valley.

The Chinese

Chinese immigrants began arriving in Nevada after 1849 for the same reason their white counterparts had come: to find wealth in the area's mines. Discrimination against them began almost immediately, and what the law could not accomplish, physical violence often did. Apparently not satisfied that the Chinese were prohibited by state statute from owning property, whites singled out Chinese miners as the subjects of frequent attack, and they were soon driven out of the industry and relegated to service occupations such as laundering and cooking.

The greatest increase in the Chinese population occurred from 1867 to 1869, during the construction of the Central Pacific Railroad across the state. Because they were willing to work hard in dangerous situations for little pay, the Chinese were prized workers for the railroads. However, in spite, or perhaps because, of this, they were despised by the local inhabitants, who saw them as a threat to their own livelihoods. Mining unions saw them as threats "to the union against the bosses" and "as tools of corporate monopolists."[6] They were excluded from union membership and thus were denied employment in the mines, which at that time were closed union shops. Discrimination against the Chinese was so intense that most left the state after the railroad's completion. Various federal acts in 1882, 1907, 1921, and 1924 established strict immigration quotas and regulations, slowing to a trickle any further Chinese emigration to the United States.

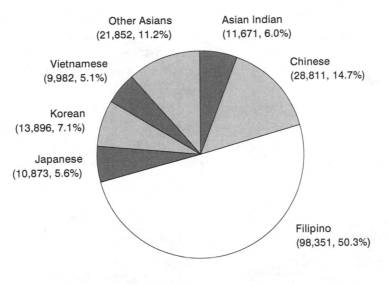

Other Asians
(21,852, 11.2%)

Asian Indian
(11,671, 6.0%)

Vietnamese
(9,982, 5.1%)

Chinese
(28,811, 14.7%)

Korean
(13,896, 7.1%)

Japanese
(10,873, 5.6%)

Filipino
(98,351, 50.3%)

Total Asian Population: 195,436

FIGURE 3.2. Asian Population of Nevada, 2010 Census. *Source*: U.S. Census Bureau, 2010. Percentages compiled by author.

Although the Chinese were allowed after 1881 to give testimony in court against whites, jurors often disregarded that testimony. In a case tried in 1903, more than twenty Chinese witnesses testified to the guilt of five white men who had beaten and killed two elderly Chinese laundry-men in Tonopah's Chinatown. All five were acquitted.[7] Various anti-Chinese organizations were created in the state, including one in Virginia City that passed a resolution stating that "the presence of the Chinese in Nevada 'was injurious to the welfare of the State and a danger to the Republic.'"[8] And in one of the most blatant and egregious acts of violence against the Chinese, most of Reno's Chinatown, including private homes, was burned to the ground in 1908 by a mob acting upon the instructions of local officials.

Beginning in the 1940s, the federal government relaxed its laws limiting Chinese immigration to the United States. Employment prohibitions against the Chinese were repealed by the state legislature in 1959. In addition, as we shall see later, various anti-discrimination laws enacted by the federal and state governments in the 1960s and 1970s worked to free the Chinese, as well as other minorities, from much of the discrimination that had impeded their progress over the years.

Of course, the Chinese are not the only Asians to have settled in Nevada. One will also find those whose heritage can be traced to India, Pakistan, Japan, the Koreas, Thailand, and a host of other nations, although the largest single group of Asians living in the Sagebrush State is Filipinos. In the decade of the 2000s, the Asian population in Nevada grew at a faster rate than did the state as a whole. In 2000 there were only 90,266 Asians in the state, approximately 5.7 percent of the population. By 2010 that number more than doubled to 195,436 or 7.24 percent of the statewide population. By comparison, during that same time, Nevada's population grew by 32 percent.

African Americans

The existence of a sizable community of African Americans in Nevada is a relatively recent phenomenon. Even though African Americans lived in the state in the latter nineteenth and early twentieth centuries, their numbers were small. Fewer than 40 blacks lived in Las Vegas at the time of the 1910 census, and only 134 lived in the entire state at the turn of the century. African Americans in Nevada were discriminated against in various ways and never treated as full equals, but the worst discrimination against them did not begin in earnest until Nevada's black population began to rise in the 1930s and 1940s. In the early period of statehood, Nevadans, like the inhabitants of other western states, expressed a "paternalistic—if condescending—interest in the few blacks who migrated to [the] state."[9] Indeed, Nevada, as a Republican-dominated state, easily and eagerly ratified the Thirteenth and Fourteenth Amendments and was the first state to ratify the Fifteenth Amendment to the U.S. Constitution, which prohibited denial of the right to vote on the basis of race.

Discrimination against African Americans certainly existed from the beginning, with prohibitions on their testimony against whites and their exclusion from public schools. A significant number of African Americans came to the Las Vegas area in the 1930s and 1940s as a result of the federal government's construction of Hoover Dam and the creation of war-related industries and military bases. Perhaps because of the growing African-American population in the state at that time, discrimination against blacks began to increase in 1931 when the companies constructing the Hoover Dam near Las Vegas refused to hire them. Unlike the southern states, where statutes existed mandating separate and unequal treatment for blacks, Nevada had no laws requiring segregation; nonetheless, African Americans found themselves increasingly discriminated against by private segregation in housing and employment. In addition to their relegation to only menial jobs, they were not allowed to gamble, eat, drink, or attend shows in casinos and restaurants; the state's business owners did not want to offend their white clientele, many of whom were Californians who had migrated west from the southern states. Indeed, African-American entertainers such as Sammy Davis Jr. and Lena Horne were not even allowed to stay in the hotels in which they played.

With the looming threat by NAACP leader Dr. James McMillan of massive demonstrations and sit-ins such as those that had occurred in the South, Las Vegas mayor Oran Gragson announced in March 1960 that segregation in public accommodations in the city would end; the businesses on the Strip, outside city limits, soon followed suit. The state's crisis in race relations, however, did not end there. A sit-in at Reno's Overland Hotel and demonstrations at various Reno casinos and the state capitol building in Carson City occurred in 1961 to protest unequal treatment and to support creation of a state Equal Rights Commission. In 1969 and 1970, several riots occurred at Las Vegas schools over the race issue.

Even though discrimination against and segregation of African Americans in Nevada was the result of private actions, the federal and state governments were forced to come to grips with the issue, just as they had in the states of the former Confederacy. The U.S. Congress responded by passing the Civil Rights Act of 1964, the Voting Rights Act of 1965, and the Fair Housing Act of 1968. In Nevada, the state legislature moved more slowly. At the urging of Governor Grant Sawyer, who had supported civil rights legislation since at least his election in 1958, the state legislature in 1965 passed a civil rights bill outlawing discrimination in public accommodations and employment on the basis of race, creed, national origin, or color (a prohibition on sex discrimination was not added to the law until 1971). Discrimination in employment did not end with the passage of civil rights legislation, however. Hotels and casinos continued to discriminate until 1971, when a consent decree was signed in Las Vegas in which the hotels and unions, without admitting that any discrimination had occurred, agreed not to engage in discriminatory practices.[10] Also in 1971, under the threat of federal court action and with the support of Governor Mike O'Callaghan, the state legislature finally passed a fair housing act ending residential segregation.

Much more recently, attention has focused on disparities between blacks and others in education, employment, and the justice system. In the area of education, for example, the rate of failure on Nevada's high school proficiency exams is higher for African Americans than for any other group of students. According to the State of Nevada Department of Education Annual Reports of Accountability for 2009–2010, statewide only 50 percent of blacks taking the mathematics exam were graded as "meets" or "exceeds" the standard. For whites that number was 82 percent, Native Americans 66 percent, and Hispanics 62 percent. According to the National Center for Education Statistics, statewide graduation rates show that same unfortunate trend. For the Class of 2015, 78 percent of white seniors graduated while only 56 percent of black seniors and 67 percent of Hispanic seniors achieved that distinction. For Asian/Pacific Islanders it was 83 percent. Although it is unclear exactly why these disparities exist, many believe that they are the result of a lack of equal access to the classes necessary to learn these skills.

Although African Americans can no longer be legally discriminated against, it is the case that they are scarce in management and executive positions in the state. A March 2001 survey, for example, found that all twenty-one of Station Casinos' (now Red Rock Resorts) top executives were white; these results are neither unique to Station Casinos nor are they surprising. As a result, many gaming companies, including MGM Resorts International, Red Rock Resorts, Caesars Entertainment Corporation, and others, have pledged to increase their attempts to diversify their executive suites and to patronize minority-owned suppliers and contractors. In a 1997 breakthrough, Hilton Hotels Corporation named the first African-American director of a major gaming corporation when Robert Johnson, founder of the Black Entertainment Network, took his seat on the board. In December 2001 Don Barden became the first African American to wholly own a casino in Nevada when he took the reins of Fitzgeralds (now The D Las Vegas) in downtown Las Vegas while, in 2002, Lorenzo Creighton took the helm of the Flamingo, becoming the first African-American president of a Las Vegas Strip hotel-casino. Still, U.S. Census Bureau data show that, although the percentage of African Americans in Nevada rose from 6.8 percent in

2000 to 7.7 percent in 2010, the percentage of black-owned businesses stands at only 3.9 percent.

African Americans also tend to fare poorly in the state's justice system. A report in 1996 by the Nevada Supreme Court Task Force for the Study of Racial and Economic Bias in the Justice System found disturbing trends in the judicial system's treatment of minorities. For example, based on 1994 data from the Clark County Family and Youth Services Division, the panel found that, in spite of their relatively low numbers in the population, 54 percent of detentions, 84 percent of transfers, and 62 percent of commitments involved minorities. The panel also found that black youths were more likely to face stiff penalties and transfer of their cases to adult court than were whites. According to a report by the Sentencing Project, nationally in 2005 blacks were nearly six times as likely to be incarcerated as whites and Hispanics nearly double the white rate. In Nevada Hispanics were incarcerated at the rate of 621 per 100,000, while whites came in slightly higher at 626 and the black rate for incarceration was 2,916 per 100,000. It is difficult to know whether these statistics are the result of racism or broader socioeconomic factors such as poverty and urbanization that hit minorities particularly hard (that is, minorities tend to have higher levels of poverty and live in cities, factors that correlate to criminal activity).

On an optimistic note, a study by the University of Georgia found that, between 1990 and 1997, the buying power of African Americans increased 54.2 percent. Nevada placed third in terms of its increase with a rise of 103.6 percent in the seven-year period. It was outpaced only by Idaho (160 percent) and Utah (136.9 percent). Although Nevada's relatively small African-American population easily allows for such large increases, it is significant nonetheless that the state's increase was only slightly less than double the national average. In a follow-up study the UGA researchers found that black buying power nationally rose 98 percent between 2000 and 2016.

Also on an optimistic note, African Americans have generally fared well in Nevada's more recent elections. In the 2017 legislative session, for example, there were four African-American members of the state assembly, including the speaker of the assembly and the chief deputy majority whip. There were three African-American members in the state senate, including the majority leader and the assistant majority leader, the most powerful individuals in that body. Thus, at a time when African

Americans made up 7.7 percent of the state's population, they held seven out of sixty-three seats in the legislature, or 11.1 percent.[11]

The African-American population in Nevada is growing faster than the state as a whole, but at a smaller rate than other minority groups. Between 2000 and 2010 the state's population grew by 35.1 percent. While the Hispanic population grew by 77.8 percent and the Asian population by 93.6 percent, the African-American population grew only 49.6 percent, to a total of 202,700.

Hispanics

To speak of Hispanics as a single group can be somewhat misleading; in fact, Hispanics trace their roots to any number of Spanish-speaking countries and territories, including Mexico, Puerto Rico, Cuba, and the various nations of Central and South America. It is important to bear in mind that these different groups often have disparate cultures, backgrounds, and political and social ideologies. Similarly, although some are new immigrants to the United States, others are native-born citizens whose families have lived in this country for many years. Some of the immigrants, such as the Cubans, have come to escape political oppression, while others, such as the Mexicans, have fled poverty and poor economies in their native homelands. Nonetheless, for purposes of simplicity, in this section we shall speak of Hispanics generally while observing those areas in which the various groups differ.

As noted in chapter 1, the Spanish and, later, Mexicans were the first nonnative explorers of the area now known as Nevada, although they did not settle here in large numbers. During the pre-statehood period of gold and silver mining, however, Hispanics were represented in large and important numbers; indeed, the Comstock mine was first discovered by Ignacio Paredes of Sonora, Mexico, who abandoned it prematurely. Miners from northern Mexico not only were responsible for the discovery of many of Nevada's ore sources but also taught Anglos the methods of panning, placer mining, dry digging, and ore reduction.[12] As was the case with other minorities on the western frontier, however, Hispanics were frequently treated as second-class citizens, receiving less pay than did their Anglo counterparts.

Hispanics began migrating to the state in large numbers in the 1860s for the same reason that other groups did: opportunity. They worked in the mines, in service occupations, and as sheep and cattle ranchers. In this early period, most of Nevada's Hispanic population resided in the north. Hispanic migration into southern Nevada began in the early twentieth century with the construction of a railroad line between Los Angeles and Salt Lake City that passed through the Las Vegas Valley. Along with the Chinese, Mexican laborers performed much of the work on this and other railroads in the state. In the American Southwest as a whole, including Nevada, Mexicans made up 70 percent of the section crews and 90 percent of the extra gangs on the principal railroad lines.[13]

The most significant migration of Hispanics to the state began after World War II. Federal investment in the state in the form of capital and military expenditures brought Hispanics to Nevada in large numbers as construction workers and soldiers and to fill a number of other occupations. As had been the case with other minorities, however, these new residents frequently found themselves the victims of discrimination. In Las Vegas, for example, Hispanics, like African Americans, were concentrated on the Westside or in North Las Vegas as a result of restrictive covenants by white homeowners prohibiting the sale of property in most parts of Las Vegas to anyone other than whites.

Virtually all Hispanics residing in Nevada prior to the 1960s were of Mexican descent, that pattern changed somewhat with the communist revolution of Fidel Castro in Cuba. With casino experience derived from the gaming halls of Havana, many of these exiles settled in Nevada to continue the occupations they had known in their homeland. Many Hispanics from the East Coast, primarily Puerto Ricans, also began to migrate to the state during this period.[14] As had African Americans, Hispanics in the 1960s began to demand equality in housing, employment, and education. The changes noted above in the discussion of African Americans in Nevada apply equally to Hispanics in the state. Civil rights laws passed during the 1960s did much to make Nevada a more egalitarian state for all minorities.

Unlike African Americans, however, Hispanics have often been at odds with one another over even the most basic issues. As sociologist Jim Frey has noted,

> Cubans were class conscious and tended to look condescendingly at lower-class Mexicans and Chicanos, while some Chicanos viewed the Cubans as aggressive, arrogant, materialistic, overly rational, and motivated totally by self-interest and greed. These personality

traits, combined with prior experience in Cuba's pre-Castro gaming and tourism, helped them to gain employment in highly paid positions in gaming and tourism. Mexicans and Chicanos, on the other hand, continued to be relegated to low-paying jobs in the service industry, some blue collar positions, and general laborers.[15]

Although the late twentieth and early twenty-first centuries have seen unity among Hispanic groups on some issues, the community frequently remained divided. This division and the small percentages of Hispanics who register and vote had the effect of marginalizing their political power even though they constituted the state's largest minority. Historically few public officeholders in Nevada were of Hispanic origin. Prominent members of the Nevada Hispanic community, however, have been and are attempting to remedy this situation by recruiting quality candidates, actively participating in reapportionment to design districts friendly to Hispanic candidates, and registering new voters, especially in Clark County where three-fourths of the Sagebrush State's Hispanic population reside. Clearly, these efforts have paid off in recent elections. In January 2011 Nevadans swore in the first and, to date, only Hispanic governor in the state's history. And in the 2017 legislative session, two of the twenty-one senators (9.5 percent) were Hispanic, as were six of the forty-two members of the assembly (14.3 percent). Overall, then, 12.7 percent of the state legislature was of Hispanic origin, a better representation than in past sessions but still well below the 26.5 percent in the state's population as a whole. However, of particular note was that the president pro tempore and majority floor leader of the assembly were Hispanic, thus ensuring that population a voice in the legislative leadership.

Continued growth in the Hispanic population of Nevada, as well as the United States in general, is likely to continue for some time. As anthropologist Tony Miranda has noted, Hispanics are on average younger than most of the state's other residents, which means that they are approaching or have reached childbearing age. Thus, as a natural consequence of birthrates, there will be more Hispanics in the state in the years to come. A 2008 Census Bureau report noted that although the average U.S. woman produces 1.9 children, that number is 1.7 for Asian Americans, 1.8 for whites, 2.0 for blacks, and 2.3 for Hispanics. Also, Hispanic immigration is likely to continue as many Hispanics flee from California

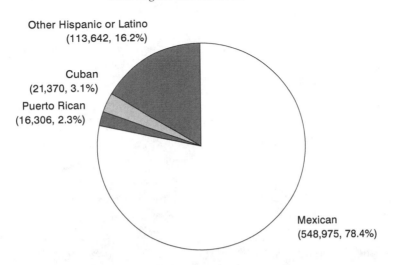

Other Hispanic or Latino
(113,642, 16.2%)

Cuban
(21,370, 3.1%)

Puerto Rican
(16,306, 2.3%)

Mexican
(548,975, 78.4%)

Total Hispanic or Latino Population: 700,293

FIGURE 3.3. Hispanic and Latino Population of Nevada, 2010 Census.
U.S. Census Bureau, 2010. Percentages compiled by author.

to Nevada. Additionally, many Hispanics outside the United States who speak little English find Nevada's gaming and tourist economy one in which they can thrive in unskilled but relatively well paying jobs. Those who are bilingual can find higher-paying jobs and are much in demand as Nevada markets itself to an increasingly international community.[16]

It should come as no surprise, therefore, to discover that while Hispanics made up only 6.8 percent of the state's population in 1980 (54,130 out of 800,493) by 2010 they comprised 26.5 percent (700,293 out of 2,643,085). The difference between 1980 and 2010 represents an increase of an eye-opening 1,194 percent. The largest single group responsible for this growth is Mexicans and Mexican Americans, making Nevada one of the fastest-growing Mexican communities in the country. In 1990, Mexicans and Mexican Americans constituted 68.5 percent of the state's Hispanic population; in 2010 that figure had grown to 78.4 percent. At the same time, the Puerto Rican community in the Sagebrush State was also one of the fastest-growing in the nation.

Although, to date, Nevada's Hispanics have historically been less successful in the political arena than other groups, they have made gains economically. The University of Georgia study noted earlier found that Hispanic buying power is growing nationally at three times the rate of inflation. The 2016 update conducted by UGA researchers found that between 2000 and 2016, Hispanic buying power had risen by 181 percent. According to a 2004 study by the Progressive Leadership Alliance of Nevada (PLAN), Hispanics generated as much as $20 billion annually of Nevada's gross state product, or approximately one out of every four dollars in the state.[17] One area in which gains have been slow is in business ownership. A survey of Hispanic-owned businesses in the Sagebrush State between 2002 and 2007 found that such businesses had increased from 9,741 to 18,029, an increase of 85.1 percent. And between 2007 and 2012 that number jumped another 86.7 percent. Although this does represent growth, it is not at all reflective of the Hispanic community's explosive growth during that period. On the other hand, the Census Bureau's 2007 Survey of Business Owners shows Nevada ranking eighth in the nation in the percentage of businesses owned by Hispanics, at 8.1 percent.

Clearly the Hispanic population will continue to grow in the state; what remains to be seen, however, is whether these numbers and the increased buying power that comes with them will continue to translate into a concomitant increase in political and economic power as they have in California, Arizona, New Mexico, and Texas.

Women

As in most other states, discrimination was applied in Nevada to virtually all minorities, in addition to those already discussed. It was noted earlier that women were not allowed to vote under the 1864 constitution. Unlike the state's lag in guaranteeing equal rights for racial minorities, however, Nevada was among the first to grant women the right of suffrage. Whereas the Nineteenth Amendment to the U.S. Constitution granting women the right to vote was not added until 1920, women in Nevada had had suffrage rights since 1914. Women's success in Nevada, at least on this issue, was due in no small part to the efforts of the untiring Anne Martin, president of the Equal Franchise Society in Nevada.

Economically, however, the struggle for equal rights for women was a different matter. Although women were sometimes employed in the lucrative fields of dealing and bartending in northern Nevada casinos, that was not true in southern Nevada. Indeed, the Las Vegas City Commission recommended as late as 1958 that women not be hired as dealers for fear that their lower salaries would undercut the men; only one of the city's many dealers schools would even permit women to enroll. In 1959 the North Las Vegas City Council prohibited women from being hired as bartenders. Instead, women were more often to be found in the lower-paying jobs of waitress, cashier, and keno runner. Only a few southern Nevada casinos would hire women as dealers and bar-tenders. It was not until 1981 that Las Vegas's casinos and unions signed an agreement to end discrimination against women in employment-related matters.[18]

In spite of legal protections against discrimination, women still often found themselves in a second-class position economically and politically in both the nation as a whole and in Nevada. Although women made up 49.1 percent of Nevada's population in 2000, a Nevada Personnel Department study discovered that they held only 35.5 percent of administrative jobs, but 91 percent of lower-paid support, or secretarial, positions in state government. No doubt as a result of women's predominance in these lower-paying positions in both the public and private sectors, a 2009 Census Bureau survey found that for every dollar earned by Nevada men, women earned only eighty-two cents. However, that was better than the national average of seventy-seven cents.

Women have, however, made some notable advances economically and politically. In spite of the differences in median pay between men and women, as of 2016 Nevada ranks as the eleventh best state in wage disparities. The national figure indicates women make only seventy-six cents to every dollar made by a man whereas in the Sagebrush State that figure is eighty-four cents. Statewide, in 2016 women owned a majority stake in over 75,000 privately held businesses generating billions in sales and employing thousands of people. U.S. Census Bureau data show that between 1997 and 2011, the number of women-owned enterprises grew from 33,311 to 62,500, an increase of 87.6 percent, second highest in the United States, behind only Georgia, at 97.5 percent.[19] In 2016 that number stands at 75,600. In addition, the percentage of women in poverty has historically been lower than the national rate. Whereas the national rate for women in poverty in 2009 was 13.9 percent, in Nevada it was 12.3 percent, tying the state of Washington for thirty-eighth place in the country. According to the National Women's Law Center, in 2016, after the Great Recession, Nevada ended up worse than the national average with a U.S. rate of 12.8 percent of women in poverty while in Nevada that figure was 13.8 percent, tying for twenty-fifth place with Montana and Oregon. In other words, the Sagebrush State fell into the middle of the pack for the rate of women in poverty.

Women have also made strides politically. In 2005, a Reno resident, Cindy Kirkland, was named the first female adjutant general of the Nevada National Guard. In 1998, women held five out of seven seats on the Clark County Board of Commissioners, although by 2017 that number had fallen to three. In 2017 the Washoe County Board of Commissioners saw a majority of women, three out of five, serving. In the 2017 session of the state legislature, eight of the twenty-one senators were women (38.1 percent), as were seventeen of the forty-two assembly members (40.5 percent). At 39.7 percent total women legislators, Nevada's 2017 legislature came in second only to Vermont (40 percent) in the percentage of women in the state house. Also of some note is that in the senate, two women served as co-majority whips and two served as co-caucus policy coordinators. In the assembly, women served as the speaker pro tempore, majority floor leader, minority whip, and both assistant majority whips. Although these figures are not proportionate to the percentage of women in Nevada's population—49.1 percent, according to the 2010 census—they do represent gains over previous decades, especially in the number of women holding leadership positions. Also worth noting is that after the 2010 elections, women held exactly half of the six constitutional officer positions in the state's executive branch (treasurer, controller, and attorney general) although by the 2014 elections that number had dropped to one (secretary of state). It is also notable that in 2017 the mayors of Nevada's three largest cities were women: Carolyn Goodman in Las Vegas, Debra March in Henderson, and Hillary Schieve in Reno.

Nevada is also noteworthy as one of only 15 states that failed to ratify the proposed Equal Rights Amendment to the federal Constitution by the 1982 deadline imposed by Congress. Proposals to ratify the ERA were defeated in the state senate in 1973 and 1975 and in the state assembly in 1977. Wishing to avoid the heat and controversy created by the ERA issue, the legislature washed its hands of the affair and submitted the ratification issue to the voters. After heavy lobbying against the proposal by conservative women, some business interests, and the Mormon Church, the measure failed in a 1978 election by a two-to-one margin. However, in 2017 the legislature voted to ratify the ERA on the forty-fifth anniversary of its having been sent to the states by Congress in 1972. Even if Congress accepts that Nevada is the thirty-sixth state to ratify the ERA (in spite of the 1982 deadline), two additional states would be needed before it could be added to the U.S. Constitution.

LGBT

The changes wrought by the state's 1965 civil rights legislation worked to the benefit of all minorities in the state, not only African Americans. Asians, Native Americans, and Hispanics likewise have benefitted from its liberalization of employment, public accommodations, and housing. Several groups historically excluded from such civil rights protection, however, have been the lesbian, gay, bisexual, and transgender (LGBT) communities. Until recently, the state's estimated 200,000-plus LGBT individuals could be discriminated against solely because of their sexual orientation or transgender status. However, over the past two decades Nevada has shown a more enlightened perspective on issues surrounding discrimination against gays and lesbians. In 1993, the state legislature repealed its antiquated anti-sodomy law, a law aimed specifically at the state's homosexual minority, and in 2013 it equalized the age of consent at 16 for both opposite sex and same sex couples. In 1995 the legislature added sexual orientation to the state's hate crime statute that enhances penalties for crimes committed against an individual due to that person's race, religion, color, nationality, or disability. And in 2013 gender identity and expression was also added to the list of hate offenses. The 1999 session of the legislature passed legislation that outlaws employment discrimination on the basis of sexual orientation. The law applies equally to homosexuals, heterosexuals, and bisexuals. In 2011 gender identity and expression was added to the list of characteristics for which one cannot be discriminated against. In 2003 the legislature unanimously passed a statute allowing hospital patients to designate who their visitors could be. Although the law is applicable to everyone in the state, its primary intent was to serve as a means to grant gay partners hospital visitation privileges that they were frequently denied on the basis that they were not a family member, no matter how long the two had been in their relationship. And, in the 2005 session the legislature passed a bill declaring it state policy that services provided by private establishments such as casinos, restaurants, movie theaters, hotels, and other places of public accommodation should not be denied to anyone on the basis of sexual orientation. Although the law did not provide penalties for discriminating, it did allow the Nevada Equal Rights Commission to investigate complaints. In 2009 the legislature expanded upon the law by allowing individuals to bring a civil suit for damages against any business or other place of public accommodation that discriminates based on sexual orientation.

With the passage of three bills, the 2011 legislative session was a particularly good one for those supporting the rights of transgender individuals. Those three bills essentially protected rights that had previously been protected for gays and lesbians: protection against discrimination in public accommodations, protection against discrimination in housing such as the sale and rental of homes and property, and protection from workplace discrimination based on gender identity or expression. A fourth bill that would have added transgender people to the state's hate-crimes protections failed to pass, but, as noted above, was successful in 2013. In an omnibus one-fell-swoop way, the 2017 legislature passed and the governor signed a law that added "sexual orientation" and "gender identity or expression" throughout all instances of Nevada statutes next to race, sex, religion, age, etc. In keeping with the notion of equality of treatment, Nevada in 2017 became the eighth state to ban conversion therapy for minors.

As with the other groups discussed in this chapter, legal protections alone have not ended all forms of discrimination and inequality for the LGBT community. A survey by the Gay, Lesbian and Straight Education Network in 1997 and again in 1998 gave the state's largest school district, Clark County, an "F" for failing to protect the rights of gay, lesbian, and bisexual students. And, of course, marriage between same-sex couples is also prohibited by state statute. In the 2000 and 2002 general elections a ballot initiative to install this ban into the state constitution passed overwhelmingly. It is ensconced as a part of Article 1 of the Nevada Constitution, an article that is, quite ironically, the state's "Declaration of Rights." However, in a significant victory for supporters of LGBT rights, in 2009 the state legislature overrode the veto of Governor Jim Gibbons to establish domestic partnerships in Nevada. Under the law, gay, lesbian, and straight couples could register as domestic partners with the state and are entitled to all the same rights as married couples. The law passed not only because of support for equal rights but also with substantial lobbying by major gaming companies such as Harrah's (now Caesars), MGM Mirage (now MGM Resorts International), and Wynn Resorts, which heavily market to gay and lesbian customers and their typically larger-than-average discretionary income.[20]

At the time of the 2010 Census, Nevada had over 9,000 same-sex couples listed as "head of household." No doubt given the closeted nature of some in the LGBT community, that number is likely higher.

The largest and most significant victory for the LGBT community came when first various U.S. Courts of the Appeals and then the U.S. Supreme Court struck down as unconstitutional bans on same-sex marriage such as those in Nevada. As a result of those rulings Nevada's ban could no longer be enforced and marriage was opened to same-sex couples in Nevada in 2015. In response to that, the state legislature in the 2017 session began the lengthy process to repeal the state constitutional ban on same-sex marriage.

Civil Liberties

As noted at the beginning of this chapter, civil liberties are those "negative restraints" upon government that define what it cannot do to its citizens. In general, these liberties are of the type found in the U.S. Constitution's Bill of Rights: freedom of speech, freedom of the press, freedom of assembly, the rights to counsel and a jury trial, and so on. In 1833, however, the U.S. Supreme Court held in the landmark case *Barron v. Baltimore* that none of the twenty-three provisions in the Bill of Rights applied to the states.[21] That is, although the Bill of Rights prohibited the federal government from engaging in any of these violations of civil liberties, the state governments were not bound in any way by these provisions. Thus, the only protections that an individual had from the state government were those in his or her own state constitution's bill of rights.

In light of that, the framers of Nevada's 1864 constitution included as the document's first article a Declaration of Rights to protect the state's citizens from an overzealous state government. Included within Article 1 are the standard civil liberties protections we have come to know in the United States: freedom of speech, press, and assembly; trial by jury; religious freedom; habeas corpus; a prohibition on excessive fines and bails, cruel and unusual punishment, bills of attainder, ex post facto laws, unreasonable searches and seizures, and double jeopardy; and the right to just compensation for property taken by the government through its power of eminent domain.

   The Nevada Constitution's Declaration of Rights was far more significant in 1864 than it is today. At that time, it constituted the sole protection the state's citizens had against intrusions into civil liberties by the
state government. However, in a series of cases from the 1920s through
2008, the U.S. Supreme Court, in a process known as incorporation, held
that virtually all of the provisions in the U.S. Bill of Rights apply to the
states via the due process clause of the Fourteenth Amendment. Thus,
today the state governments are held to the same federal constitutional
standards as the federal government has always been; even if Nevada's
Declaration of Rights did not exist, Nevadans would now be protected
in their civil liberties from both federal and state intrusion by the U.S.
Constitution's Bill of Rights.
   The process of incorporation, however, does not render state bills of
rights obsolete. In some states (California, Oregon, Washington, and
Hawaii), state courts have held that their state bills of rights grant civil
liberties protections to their citizens even greater than those in the U.S.
Constitution. The Nevada courts, however, have not followed the lead
of their western counterparts and have traditionally interpreted civil
liberties protections in the state's Declaration of Rights to be parallel
to similar clauses in the federal Bill of Rights. For that reason, any
student familiar with the rights embodied in the Bill of Rights will also
be knowledgeable about the rights protected by Nevada's Declaration of
Rights. Nonetheless, there are a couple of areas in which the Declaration
of Rights differs from the Bill of Rights, and they are worth discussing.
   Although juries in both civil and criminal trials at the federal level
must be unanimous, that is not the case in Nevada. Article 1, Section 3,
of the Nevada Constitution allows a jury in civil cases to reach a decision
by a three-fourths vote of its members (nine of twelve jurors). The ra-
tionale for what at the time was a departure from tradition and practice
in the country can be found in Nevada's unfortunate history with juries
during the territorial period. During that period many a jury was unable
to reach a unanimous verdict, and civil cases often ended in a mistrial
with a split vote (a hung jury)—the result of the bribing of at least one
juror by the mining companies that stood to win or lose fortunes, depending upon the verdict. Apparently believing that it was more difficult
to bribe four jurors than one, the framers of the constitution, over the
objections of the cow-county delegates, agreed upon the three-fourths

requirement. Like their federal counterparts, however, juries in criminal cases in Nevada have always been required to reach unanimous verdicts.

A second distinction between the two constitutions is in the area of eminent domain. The Nevada Constitution, like the federal Constitution, allows the government to take private property for government use if it provides "just compensation" to the property owner. Unlike the U.S. Constitution, however, the Nevada Constitution requires that the compensation be made prior to the taking unless the property owner waives that right. As a result of an initiative in the 2006 and 2008 elections, the state constitution was amended to define fair-market value of such property as the highest price the property would garner on the market. This initiative further prevents the state, county, or city government from taking private property in order to transfer it to another private party; that is, the taking must be by the government and for the government's use, not, for example, a private commercial developer. And, finally, the 2006–2008 initiative mandates that if the government has not used the property within five years for the original purpose it was taken, the original property owner has a right to the property upon repayment of the government's purchase price.

CHAPTER FOUR

Political Parties and Elections

Nevada has traditionally been a competitive, two-party state in which elections are fought more on the basis of personalities and issues than parties. Nevadans are notorious ticket splitters who take pride in the fact that they vote for the "person" and not the "party." Nonetheless, it is possible to divide Nevada's political history into five distinct periods of voting patterns.[1]

From the granting of statehood in 1864 until 1890, the Republicans dominated the state's elections. That they did so is chiefly explained by the support of the national Republican Party for Nevada statehood and the lingering effects of the Civil War, which had been fought against the Democratic-dominated, proslavery states of the South. As noted in chapter 2, all of Nevada's state and federal officers selected in 1864, with the exception of two legislators, were Republicans. Of the elections held during the twenty-six years of this period, Republicans won six of seven presidential races, eight of ten for the U.S. Senate, ten of thirteen for the House, four of seven for governor and lieutenant governor, seven of seven for secretary of state, five of seven for state treasurer, seven of seven for state controller, and five of seven for attorney general.

During the second period, 1892 to 1906, the state's voters turned to the Silver Party for leadership. During that time, the national issue of free coinage of silver dominated the politics of Nevada and the other western mining states. In the first two elections of this period, the Silver Party won all but two statewide positions.[2] In 1896 the Silver Party joined with the Democrats to become the Silver Democrats and dominated the state's political landscape until 1908.

Between 1908 and 1930, electoral victories in the state were roughly equal between the Democrats and Republicans, with the Democrats winning more positions but the Republicans winning the top spots at the presidential, congressional, and gubernatorial levels. The fourth period

56

of electoral dominance began in 1932 with the election of Franklin D. Roosevelt to the presidency. From 1932 until the mid-1980s, Democrats tended to dominate state politics with an overwhelming number of registrants and control of the legislature and most of the executive offices.

Starting in the 1980s the Republican Party began a resurgence in the state that lasted through the 1990s and into the twenty-first century. During this fifth period, no one party has dominated the state's elections. As of 2017, for instance, elective positions in the state were fairly evenly divided. Although all six executive officers were Republican, Nevada's federal delegation was split with one Democratic and one Republican U.S. Senator and three Democratic and one Republican members of the U.S. House of Representatives. The 2017 state senate and the state assembly were majority Democratic. The resurrection of the Republicans in the state to the point that they were competitive with the previously dominant Democrats was due to several factors: increased voter registration activity by the Republicans, the popularity of Ronald Reagan, and the pattern of migration by upper-middle and upper-class retirees to the state.

By the end of 1995, Republican registrants had overtaken Democrats for the first time since 1930. As table 4.1 shows, this continued to be true in the presidential elections of 1996, 2000, and 2004 when Republicans had more registrants than did the Democrats. The pendulum swung back again, however, after 2004 as a result of a significant push by the Democrats, led by Senator Harry Reid, to register more voters to support Barack Obama's campaign for president in 2008 and Reid's reelection campaign in 2010. As a result of that push and the recruitment of many young or minority voters who might not otherwise have registered, the Democrats went from 40 percent of registered voters in 2004 to more than 43 percent in 2008, percentages they had not seen since 1992. It appears that 2008 may have been an anomaly. Democratic voter registration went down from 43.2 percent in 2008 to 42.3 percent in 2012 and, by the 2016 presidential election, it had declined to 39.7 percent.

At the same time, the split of the state's congressional delegation in 2017 and the mix of parties in the constitutional, legislative, and local offices suggest that ticket splitting and the fact that most Nevada Democrats tend to be fairly conservative mean that elections, especially nonpresidential ones, will likely continue to be highly competitive between the two parties.

TABLE 4.1. Voter Registration in Nevada by Party in Presidential Election Years, 1960–2016

Year	Democrats	Republicans	Other*	Total	Percent (%) Democrats
1960	81,682	41,357	5,858	128,897	63.4
1964	104,630	50,462	8,383	163,475	64.0
1968	111,390	65,302	12,119	188,811	58.9
1972	133,278	80,199	17,568	231,045	57.6
1976	149,397	83,374	18,182	250,953	59.5
1980	158,617	115,182	23,519	297,318	53.3
1984	184,199	146,553	25,632	356,384	51.7
1988	209,048	188,571	47,314	444,933	47.0
1992	295,111	255,897	98,905	649,913	45.4
1996	324,283	325,098	122,780	772,161	42.0
2000	372,889	374,196	151,262	898,347	41.5
2000	372,889	374,196	151,262	898,347	41.5
2004	429,808	434,239	207,054	1,071,101	40.1
2008	625,134	513,629	307,775	1,446,538	43.2
2012	635,419	504,974	360,425	1,500,818	42.3
2016	666,222	547,429	465,603	1,679,254	39.7

Source: Secretary of State's Office.
*The "Other" category includes independent (nonpartisan) voters and those registered in minority parties (e.g., Libertarian, American Independent).

One of the most interesting facets of Nevadans' voting patterns is their almost unerring ability to vote for the winner in presidential elections. Of the thirty-nine presidential elections in which Nevadans have participated between 1864 and 2016, the state voted for the winning candidate thirty-two times; of the seven instances in which Nevadans voted for the losing candidate, they had supported the free-silver crusader William Jennings Bryan three times (1896, 1900, 1908) and had one time (1892) voted for the candidate of the People's Party, who had been endorsed by the Silver Party. Since 1908 the state has voted for the eventual winner in all presidential elections except in 1976, when Nevadans voted for the Republican ticket of Gerald Ford and Robert Dole instead of Democrats Jimmy Carter and Walter Mondale, and in 2016 when the Sagebrush State went with Democrat Hillary Clinton instead of eventual winner Republican Donald Trump (although in Nevadans' defense, Clinton did win the national popular vote by almost three million). Thus, in the twenty-seven presidential elections between 1912 and 2016, Nevadans have gone with the winner in twenty-five instances. Perhaps those figures indicate that Nevada is much more like the rest of the country than we have traditionally wanted to believe.

Political Parties

Political parties in the United States have traditionally been much weaker than those in other parts of the world. That is particularly true in Nevada, where political-party labels have little meaning. Democrats and Republicans in the state tend to be rather conservative, and there exist few in either party who would describe themselves as liberal, much less radical. Nonetheless, it is possible to say that, *as a general rule*, Democrats are more supportive of education and labor issues, while Republicans support business and the conservative social agenda to a greater degree. Worth watching is that more recently the Sagebrush State seems to have followed the national trend and become more politically polarized. A study by the Guinn Center for Policy Priorities, for example, found steadily declining levels of bipartisanship in the state legislature.

European political parties are "responsible" parties. That is, members of the party, once elected to office, are expected to support the party platform, defer from publicly criticizing party leaders, and vote with their party on each issue that may come forward. Failure to do so could lead to drastic consequences, including the loss of one's position. In Nevada, and in the United States generally, elected officials win or lose based on their own personalities and stands on the issues, regardless of party affiliation. The parties have few measures available to discipline errant members and have little ability to keep them off the ballot. Candidates raise their own campaign funds, run their own campaigns, and owe little to the party with which they are nominally affiliated.

The chief function of political parties in Nevada and elsewhere is to select candidates to run in a general election against an opponent from the other party. Prior to the election of 1910, the method of selecting candidates was a generally close-knit affair. Members of the party would gather in precinct meetings to select delegates to county party conventions that in turn would select a smaller number of delegates to a state party convention. Party nominees would then be chosen by the state convention of each party. Typically, only a few party activists would participate in such meetings, leaving the vast number of voters out of the process. In 1909, the state legislature adopted a direct primary law mandating that parties select their candidates in primary elections held in September (now June) of each year in which a general election is to be held. Primary elections give the average party member more control over who his or her party's nominees will be than did the old system. At the same time, however, primaries have reduced whatever hold the party's leadership may have once exercised on its party's slate of nominees; candidates now rely upon the voters, not the party elite who attend the precinct meetings and party conventions, for their place on the general election ballot.

Elections in Nevada
Eligibility to Vote

As it was originally ratified in 1864, the state constitution allowed only white males of the age of twenty-one or older to vote. Even though Nevada, in 1869, was the first state to ratify the Fifteenth Amendment to the U.S. Constitution (1870) prohibiting the denial of the right to vote on account of race, the word *white* was not removed from this part of the state constitution until 1880. In 1914, six years before the Nineteenth Amendment to the U.S. Constitution gave women the right to vote, Nevadans amended their state constitution to extend the right of suffrage to them; nonetheless, Nevada was one of the last western states to do so. In 1971, the state's voters barely approved (51–49 percent) a referendum to amend state law to reduce the voting age in the state to eighteen. Interestingly, the Nevada legislature never voted on ratification of the Twenty-sixth Amendment, which made this same change to the U.S. Constitution. That amendment, however, was ratified within one hundred days and did not require Nevada's vote.

Today, the chief requirements one must meet in order to vote in the state are age, residency, and registration. In addition to the minimum age of eighteen, one must be a U.S. citizen and have resided in the state for at least thirty days. Actually, the state constitution requires a six-month residency period, but when the U.S. Supreme Court declared such lengthy residency requirements unconstitutional in 1972, that provision became unenforceable. The state legislature subsequently adopted the thirty-day requirement; but for reasons unexplainable, the voters refused in 1976 and again in 2008 to amend the constitution with parallel language. The state legislature has also adopted registration provisions requiring one to register in order to vote. One may register as a member of a political party or as an independent, or nonpartisan.

Specifically excluded by the constitution from voting are those who have been judged mentally incompetent and those who have been found guilty of treason or a felony, unless they have had their civil rights restored. In Nevada voting rights are automatically restored in a nonviolent felony case once the sentence has been completed. Violent felonies and second-time felonies, however, require a court to restore these rights. The 1864 constitution also prohibited anyone who had borne arms against the United States or who had served in an office of the Confederacy from voting. That the framers included this provision is not surprising, given the state's entrance into the Union during the Civil War. This prohibition was removed by constitutional amendment in 1914 at the same time that suffrage was extended to women.

The 1864 constitution also provided for payment of a poll tax in order to vote. All males between the ages of twenty-one and sixty, "uncivilized American Indians excepted," were required to pay the tax. White males had to pay the tax in order to vote; minorities were also required to pay the tax even though they were not allowed to vote. In 1910 that section of Article 2 was amended to remove the connection between paying the tax and voting, and the proceeds of the poll tax were earmarked for public roads. In 1966, the entire poll tax provision was eliminated by an amendment to the state constitution.

Today anyone may vote who is at least eighteen years of age, a U.S. citizen, a resident of the state for at least thirty days, registered to vote, and neither mentally incompetent nor a felon whose rights have not been restored. Although these requirements are quite minimal, Nevada has one of the lowest percentages of voters in the nation. In the very competitive presidential election of 2008, which also included contests for all three seats in the U.S. House of Representatives, all forty-two seats in the state assembly, half of the state senate positions, and a variety of other local offices and ballot questions, only 80 percent of registered voters in the Sagebrush State exercised their right to do so. This ranked Nevada forty-second in voter turnout in the fifty states.[3] Turnout has not increased in more recent presidential elections, settling in at 81 percent in 2012 and 77 percent in 2016. Although these percentages might sound high, they include only those who are registered to vote and not the large number of citizens who do not even register. In part these

lower-than-national-average figures reflect Nevada's transient population, distrust of politicians, and a generalized feeling that it makes little
difference who is elected given the power of the gaming industry to control the state's various governments. One group, however, that continues to turn out in large numbers, thus making them a serious force to
be dealt with, is senior citizens. In spite of age and health problems faced
by some, they register to vote and, in any given election, approximately
three-quarters of those registered actually vote, compared to approximately half of all other registered voters in the state who choose to do so.

Primary Elections

The Direct Primary Law of 1909, as noted earlier, opened the process of
candidate selection to the average party member, who could now simply
show up at the ballot booth and cast a vote within a few minutes rather
than attend a lengthy precinct meeting or party convention. The law also
provided, four years before ratification of the Seventeenth Amendment
to the U.S. Constitution, that party nominees for U.S. Senate seats would
also be selected in the primary.

State primary elections in Nevada occur on the second Tuesday of
June in even-numbered years. It is here that each party will select its
nominees to run in the November general election. Nevada primaries
are "closed," which means that only those who are registered to vote in
a particular party may vote in that party's primary election. Republicans
and Democrats cannot cross over to vote in the other party's primary
election, and independent voters cannot vote in party primaries at all,
although they can vote in primary elections for nonpartisan seats such
as the supreme court.

In the November general election, the candidate who wins the most
votes (a plurality) is declared the winner, regardless of whether he or she
actually receives a majority. Thus, unlike some other states, particularly
those in the South, Nevada does not have runoff elections when no one
receives a majority of the vote in the general election.

Prior to the presidential election of 1976, Nevada's delegates to the
national parties' presidential conventions were selected in the traditional
manner of precinct meeting, county convention, and state convention, as
discussed earlier. However, in 1973 the legislature approved a law allowing the parties to hold presidential primaries for the purpose of choosing
each party's delegation to the national conventions. That process was

followed in the 1976 and 1980 elections for president. In 1981, however, the legislature rescinded that legislation, and national party convention delegates in 1984, 1988, and 1992 were once again selected by state party conventions. The 1995 legislature approved a compromise proposal allowing each party to decide whether it would use presidential primaries or state conventions to choose delegates to represent the state at future national conventions. Should a party choose the presidential primary option, it may also determine whether to allow only party members to vote or to open the election to independent voters. Unlike the 1973 statute, the 1995 version attempts to cut costs by mandating the use of mail-in ballots in presidential primaries rather than opening the polls. Nevada's mail-in primary process was first used in the 1996 election by the Republicans, who chose Bob Dole as their candidate. The process was generally successful with a turnout rate of 51 percent of registered Republicans returning their ballots. Less positively, however, this first-of-its-kind primary in the state cost over $555,000, almost three times the $200,000 appropriated by the state legislature. With an incumbent president running for reelection and no serious opposition to him, the Democrats in 1996 opted for the traditional state party convention method. In the 2000, 2004, 2008, 2012, and 2016 presidential elections, both parties relied upon state conventions rather than mail-in primary elections for selecting their delegates to the national party conventions. A proposal to eliminate the caucus system and adopt a secret-ballot primary failed to get a vote in the 2015 legislative session.

One of the unique aspects of Nevada elections is the availability of the "none of these candidates" option. In both primary and general elections for statewide offices (e.g., governor, U.S. Senate) the voter may choose to vote for one of the candidates or for none of them. Thus, rather than simply not voting in a particular race, voters can now show their dissatisfaction with the slate by voting for "none of these candidates." Even if the "none" option receives the most votes, as occurred in the 1976 Republican primary for Congress and the 2014 Democratic primary for governor, the actual candidate who receives more votes than his or her opponent(s) is declared the winner. In 2012, shortly before the election, a U.S. District Court judge in Nevada declared the "none of these candidates" option unconstitutional. The option had been challenged in a lawsuit financed by the Republican National Committee on the basis that because "none of these candidates" could not win the election, these votes essentially would not count. The judge agreed with that argument. However, because the decision had come so close to the election and left little time for the secretary of state to prepare ballots, a three-judge panel of the U.S. Court of Appeals for the Ninth Circuit issued an injunction staying the order. Consequently, voters in 2012 were allowed to vote for "none of these candidates." Subsequently in 2013, the Ninth Circuit held that the plaintiffs in the case did not have standing to sue (i.e., they could show no personal stake in the outcome of the case) and dismissed it. An appeal taken to the U.S. Supreme Court was denied a hearing.

Campaign Finance

In 1974, Congress passed the Federal Election Campaign Act, which now limits individual donations to no more than $2,700 per year to any candidate for federal office; all donations of $100 or more must be reported to the Federal Election Commission. These regulations apply to all candidates running in presidential, U.S. Senate, and House elections in Nevada.

In 1975, the Nevada Legislature followed suit and passed limitations on spending in state races and required candidates to disclose the sources of contributions. Following the lead of the U.S. Supreme Court,[4] the Nevada Supreme Court upheld the disclosure requirement but declared the spending limitations to be unconstitutional as a violation of freedom of speech.[5]

Although the state's campaign finance laws are designed to inform the voters of the source of a candidate's campaign funds and to prohibit any single person or individual from having too much influence in the election process, they have been criticized by proponents of more openness in government. Prior to 1997, contributors of $499 or less to individual candidates did not have to be identified. Further, political parties and their caucuses were not required to disclose the source of any donation, no matter how large. These groups were then able to "bundle" these contributions and give an unlimited amount to their party's candidates without disclosing to whom it was given. The secretary of state has estimated that the sources of only $2 million out of more than $5 million donated to candidates and parties in the 1994 legislative campaigns were required to be disclosed. The Senate Republican Leadership Conference, for example, received almost $400,000 in donations from individuals and groups; neither the donors' names nor the names of the candidates receiving funds from the SRLC were required to be made public. A report by the Progressive Leadership Alliance of Nevada found that six dollars out of every ten given to state legislative candidates who won in 1994 and 1996 were unidentified, either because they fell under the $500 limit or because they came from party caucuses. The parties and caucuses were seen by many individuals and corporations as an effective method for hiding the source and amount of their contributions to candidates. For example, in the 1994 legislative elections, four of the top five contributors were the Senate Republican Leadership Conference (1), the Senate Democratic Caucus (2), the Republican Assembly Caucus (3), and the Assembly Democratic Caucus (5). The fourth-ranked contributor was Bizpac, the political action committee of the Las Vegas Chamber of Commerce.[6]

Campaign finance was a major issue in the 1995 legislature when Secretary of State Dean Heller's proposals for reform were defeated by his Republican brethren in the state senate. Heller came back in 1997, however, and with bipartisan support from Governor Bob Miller, Attorney General Frankie Sue Del Papa, and the public, the state legislature adopted Heller's recommendations. Under current law, candidates must report the source of contributions over $100 and political action committees and political parties must also disclose the source and amount of all contributions.

Voters also had an opportunity to be heard on campaign finance. In the 1994 and 1996 general elections, the state's voters approved Question 10, which amended the state constitution to define campaign contributions and to limit them to $5,000 in a primary and $5,000 in a general election per candidate whether individual, corporate, or a political action committee. That is a steep reduction from the previous law, which allowed candidates to accept up to $20,000 from individuals and $40,000 from corporations. The provision adopted by the voters applies to all candidates for state or local, but not federal, office and it applies to individuals and organizations seeking to support or oppose ballot questions. However, in a 1998 decision, U.S. District Court Judge Philip Pro held that the restriction on campaign contributions to groups supporting or opposing ballot questions was a violation of freedom of speech protected by the First Amendment of the U.S. Constitution. Thus, although other provisions of the law are valid and enforceable, that portion of it is not.

Although the new campaign finance laws are better at informing the public than they were in the past, they still have gaping holes. For example, under the law each corporate entity may donate up to $5,000 in both the primary and the general elections to each candidate, for a total of $10,000 per individual. However, if a casino owner, developer, or other entity controls several corporations, each may donate up to the maximum, thereby exerting great influence on the electoral process. For example, in the 2014 gubernatorial election Barrick Gold Corporation was able to use its subsidiaries to legally donate $55,000 to Governor Sandoval's reelection campaign while Wynn Resorts and MGM Resorts International each legally contributed $120,000 and Caesars Entertainment legally offered up $215,000 to Sandoval through its subsidiaries. Worse, however, is the case of limited liability corporations (LLCS). Those entities may donate the maximum $10,000 per candidate and, under state law, are not required to divulge the names of their owners. Consequently, an individual or a small group of individuals could create a number of these LLCS, and each of the LLCS could donate the maximum $10,000. Not only would these individuals be exerting a great deal of influence over the electoral process (donating potentially hundreds of thousands of dollars), their names would be undisclosed to the public. A proposal in the 2005 state legislature to require LLCS to identify their owners was defeated. A similar situation occurs in the case of political action committees or PACS. Each PAC is allowed to donate the maximum $10,000. A corporation or individual could create several of these PACS and each could contribute the maximum.

At the urging of Secretary of State Ross Miller, the 2011 legislature passed three laws to increase the transparency of who is contributing to campaigns. The first of these requires candidates to file their contribution reports electronically through the secretary of state's office. Unlike the paper reports that were previously filed at different locations, such as county clerks' offices, these electronic reports will be in one place and in a searchable database. A second change in 2011 was that contribution and expense reports must be filed four days before early voting begins. Thus, voters will be able to examine who is contributing to which candidates. And, finally, any advertisement such as a radio spot or billboard on behalf of a candidate by a third party that costs more than $100 must identify who paid for it, and the third party must register with the secretary of state and file expense reports.

At the urging of Senate Majority Leader William "Bill" Raggio, the state legislature added to Heller's 1997 campaign finance reform legislation an amendment requiring the State Ethics Commission to investigate complaints by political candidates that their opponents lied about them. In spite of charges that the amendment was designed to kill the reform bill and that it violated freedom of speech, it was passed by both the Republican senate and the Democratic assembly. In 2005, the "truth squad" law was declared unconstitutional by a U.S. district court in Las Vegas and the state legislature repealed the law.

Direct Democracy Elections

In the late nineteenth and early twentieth centuries, the United States, especially the western states, was swept up in a wave of reform and a move toward greater democratic participation by the individual in government. The Progressive Era, as this period was known, resulted in the direct primary and civil service reform. It also led to the creation in Nevada and elsewhere of three special types of elections: initiative, referendum, and recall. The three are generally referred to as "direct democracy" elections. They allow the voters to bypass the legislature and directly initiate and approve laws and constitutional amendments, approve or reject laws passed by the legislature, and remove elected officials prior to the expiration of their terms.

Initiative

The state constitution's provisions on initiative were added in 1912 and have been amended several times over the intervening years. Prior to 1912, only the legislature could enact laws and propose constitutional amendments. The initiative allows the citizens of the state to propose and enact constitutional amendments and legislation, independent of the legislature.

In order to propose a statute or constitutional amendment through the initiative process, a petition must be signed by 10 percent of the number of those who voted in the previous general election. According to the state constitution, a petition must receive the signatures of 10 percent of the voters from at least thirteen counties who voted in the previous general election. This requirement prohibited the state's two most populous counties (Clark and Washoe) from putting an initiative on the ballot without the support of at least eleven other counties. The

"13-counties" rule was declared unconstitutional in 2004 by a U.S. district court judge whose decision was upheld by the U.S. Court of Appeals for the Ninth Circuit in 2006, and, thus, it is unenforceable. In response, the 2007 state legislature passed and Governor Jim Gibbons signed into law a requirement that signatures must be gathered from all seventeen counties based on the percentage of the state's population in each of the counties. Thus, if a county had 5 percent of the state's population, then 5 percent of the total number of signatures required would have to come from that county. In 2008 that law, too, was declared unconstitutional by Judge Philip Pro of the U.S. District Court.

The problem with both laws was that they violated equal protection in favoring residents of sparsely populated counties over residents of densely populated counties. That is, the signature of a voter in a less populated county counted more under this scheme than that of a voter in a more populated county, thus violating the "one person, one vote" mandate in the U.S. Constitution. The issue was revisited by the state legislature, which voted to require that the signatures come from 10 percent of voters who participated in the previous election in each congressional district. Given that, unlike counties, theoretically each congressional district has the same number of residents, this requirement has been upheld by the federal courts as constitutional.

If the initiative petition proposes a *statute*, the proposed legislation goes to the next session of the legislature, which then has forty days to act. If the legislature approves and the governor signs, the proposed statute becomes law. If the legislature or governor disapproves or does nothing, the proposal goes on the next general election ballot for approval or disapproval by the voters. If the voters approve, the measure becomes law and cannot be changed by the legislature for at least three years. Should the legislature wish, it has authority to propose an alternative measure that would go on the same general election ballot as the initiative proposal. Should both measures pass, the one winning the most affirmative votes would become law.

If the initiative petition proposes a *constitutional amendment*, the proposal does not go to the legislature. Instead it must be put directly on the ballot and must be approved by a simple majority at the next two general elections. Should the measure fail to pass either election, it is defeated.

Referendum

The referendum process was added to the state constitution in the election of 1904 and has been amended twice since then. The referendum allows voters to approve or disapprove any law passed by the legislature. A law may be referred to the voters by the legislature itself, or the voters may demand a referendum election by petition. A referendum petition requires the signatures of at least 10 percent of the number of voters who participated in the state's last general election. Unlike the initiative petition, these signatories are not required to be dispersed among the state's congressional districts.

Should the appropriate number of signatures be acquired, the law in question is put on the ballot for a vote by the people. If the law is supported by a simple majority, it remains on the statute books; if it is not, the law is repealed and no longer in effect. A law that is approved by a referendum initiated by the voters cannot be repealed or amended by the legislature; it can be changed or repealed only through another direct vote of the people. This fact led pro-choice forces in Nevada to refer the state's abortion statutes to a vote of the people in 1990. These statutes, generally along the guidelines approved by the U.S. Supreme Court in *Roe v. Wade*,[7] were approved. Therefore, even if the Supreme Court were to someday overturn *Roe*, pro-life forces could not repeal or change the state's abortion laws without another time-consuming and costly referendum election. This immunity from legislative change, however, applies only in those cases where the referendum has been called by petition; laws approved through legislatively mandated referendum elections can be amended or repealed by the legislature at its discretion.

Recall

State constitutional provisions on recall were added in 1912. Recall allows the voters to remove any state or local, but not federal, official from office prior to the expiration of his or her term. No statewide official has ever been recalled in Nevada, and the process has generally been unsuccessful at the local level as well. Only a few local officials have been successfully recalled in the state, most recently in 2009 when Fernley voters removed a city council member.

Recall elections can be held only after a petition seeking recall has been signed by the requisite number of registered voters. As amended in 1996, the recall provision of the state constitution requires that 25 percent of the number of voters who voted in this officeholder's most recent election must sign the petition. If, for example, the governor or a supreme court justice is targeted for recall, the petition must have the signatures of at least 25 percent of the number of people who voted statewide in that official's most recent election. Should a mayor be the target then the figure would be taken from the number of people who voted in that city in the mayor's most recent election. It is important to note that the number of signatures is based on that officeholder's most recent election and not simply the most recent election in that jurisdiction. Some confusion was thrown into the signature process in 2008 when Secretary of State Ross Miller opined that in order to sign a recall petition, the state constitution requires that one must have actually voted in the election in which the targeted official was elected to office. Although there was no prior decision on this issue, it was generally the practice prior to that time that anyone who was a registered voter within that election district could sign a recall petition. Miller's decision had the expected effect of making recall elections more difficult to call. In response, the state legislature passed a law in its 2009 session rejecting Miller's interpretation and allowing any registered voter living within the jurisdiction to sign a recall petition. However, in 2010 the Nevada Supreme Court held unanimously that only the signatures of voters who actually voted in the prior election could be counted. In 2015 the state legislature codified that into the statutes. Thus, in order to sign a recall petition in the Sagebrush State one must have voted in the most recent election for that officeholder.

Once the required number of signatures has been obtained, the official has five days to resign. If he or she refuses to do so, a recall election is held within thirty days. At that election, both sides have the opportunity to state their case on the ballot. Other candidates may run against the targeted official, and the candidate winning the most votes serves the remainder of the term. Should no other candidates file, the voters simply vote to recall or not to recall. If the official is recalled, the seat is declared vacant and is filled as for any other midterm vacancy.

Officeholders are protected by the constitution from harassment by their losing campaign opponents and their opponents' supporters in two ways. First, the official must have been in office for at least six months before being subject to a recall. The sole exception is for members of the legislature, who may be recalled after ten days from taking office.

Second, those wishing to promote a second recall effort against an official must first pay the costs of the first recall election.

Constitutional Amendment and Revision

There are two ways to amend the state constitution: initiative and legislative proposal. The initiative process, discussed previously, has been available for amending the constitution only since 1912. Prior to 1912, the sole method for amending the constitution was by legislative proposal; that process still exists today. The legislative proposal method of amending the constitution is a multistep process requiring (1) the approval of a proposed constitutional amendment by two consecutive sessions of the legislature and (2) ratification by the voters at an election. Just as is the case with other legislation, the proposal must be passed by a majority of the total membership of each house and not simply a majority of those present. In the ratifying election, a simple majority of those voting on the amendment is needed to formally add the amendment to the constitution.

There is also a provision in the state constitution (Article 16) allowing for its revision, that is, for writing an entirely new constitution rather than simply adding amendments. There have been four attempts, all occurring in the late nineteenth century, to revise the constitution; none were successful. Not surprisingly, the process of revision is more difficult than that for mere amendment. A convention to revise the constitution can be called only with the approval of two-thirds of the total membership of each house of the legislature and a majority of the voters at a general election. If the voters give their approval, the convention must occur within six months of the election. The number of delegates to the convention cannot be less than the total number of legislators in both houses of the legislature (currently sixty-three). There is no provision in the state constitution for selecting these convention delegates; presumably those details would be included in the legislature's proposal to call a convention. Also not included in the revision provisions of the state constitution is a requirement that the proposed constitution coming out of the convention be ratified by the voters. The issue was not discussed at the 1864 constitutional convention. However, since the Enabling Act allowing Nevada to form a state required a ratification vote on the 1864 constitution, it is probable that the revised constitution would have to be approved by the state's voters if, as required by the U.S. Constitution, the state is to have a "republican" form of government. Furthermore, it would be strange indeed for a constitutional amendment to require voter ratification, while an entirely new constitution would not.

Term Limits in Nevada

Riding the national wave of popularity for term limits that hit in the late 1990s, Nevada voters also enacted term limits on the state's executive, legislative, and local officials. Prior to 1996 only the governor was limited in the number of terms he or she could serve. Now, however, an initiative passed in 1994 and 1996 has amended the state constitution such that all elected state and local officials except judges have their service eligibility limited.

Although the original initiative to impose term limits included Nevada's U.S. Senators and House members, the U.S. Supreme Court held in a case out of Arkansas that such limits violated the U.S. Constitution, which already established the criteria for election to the federal Congress.[8] Since an identical amendment to the state constitution in Nevada would, therefore, be invalid at its inception, the portion of the term-limits initiative relating to members of Congress was removed from the ballot by Nevada's secretary of state.

The original initiative included all state and local officials except the governor in its term-limits provisions. However, the Nevada Supreme Court held that the sections limiting the terms of judges were to be listed as a separate question on the ballot from those sections limiting other officeholders. The provision limiting executive, legislative, and local officials was passed with 54 percent of the vote while the question relating to judges failed, garnering only 41 percent of the vote. Consequently, judges are not limited in the number of terms they may serve. Members of the state legislature, on the other hand, may not serve more than twelve years (six terms for members of the assembly or three terms for senators) and members of the executive branch other than the governor and lieutenant governor (i.e., attorney general, secretary of state, treasurer, controller) may not serve more than eight years or two terms. Furthermore, all other nonjudicial state officeholders, including the lieutenant governor, and local officials are limited to no more than twelve years in a particular office. Any partial term that may be filled by appointment is counted as a full term. In a surprising ruling in 2014 the state supreme court held in a case out of Reno that time spent as a member of the city council counted for purposes of eligibility to serve as mayor. That is, if a person had served for twelve years as a city council member, he or she would be ineligible to then run for mayor; if a person had served eight years on the council, he or she could serve only one term as mayor before hitting the limit. The governor was not included in the term-limits initiative because that office was already subject to a limited term of no more than ten years.

Exactly when the term-limits clock began to tick was a matter of some contention. A 1996 opinion by Attorney General Frankie Sue Del Papa held that term limits would not apply to those elected in the 1996 election since the ballot measure imposing these limits would not be effective until election results were officially certified three weeks after the election. This led many officeholders to believe that the term-limits clock would not start until the 1997 municipal elections and 1998 statewide elections. However, in 2008, Secretary of State Ross Miller informed several Nevada System of Higher Education regents, county school board members, and county commissioners who were elected in November 1996 that they were not eligible to run for reelection because they were term limited, having reached their twelve-year mark. Miller's logic was that because these 1996 election winners did not take office until January 1997, they were affected by the term-limits measure that was certified in late November 1996. However, state legislators who were elected in November 1996 were considered to have started their terms as soon as they were elected. Therefore, their terms would have started in early November 1996, prior to the certification of the term-limits measure in late November. The case eventually wound up in the state supreme court, where the justices unanimously upheld Miller's reading of the law and ruled twenty-one incumbents across the state ineligible to run for reelection in 2008.

Those in favor of term limits argue that they will allow more people to serve in government and will put limits on career politicians. Those who oppose such limits respond that they will result in less experienced officeholders who will more easily be manipulated by lobbyists. These arguments will be proved or disproved only by the passage of time; the first officials to bump against the term limits' wall did not do so until the elections of 2008. However, one likely outcome of legislative term limits is that they will increase the power of southern Nevada in the legislature. Historically, turnover among the southern delegation in the legislature was high, primarily a result of the hardship imposed by having to give up one's business interests and family for four months every other year in order to move to Carson City for the biennial sessions. This turnover has allowed northern Nevada's longer-term legislators who could continue to live a more normal life and go home at night during the sessions, to build seniority and, thus, control the leadership positions in the legislature. Now that northern legislators will also be required to rotate out of office periodically, it is the case that turnover rates between northern and southern legislators have become more comparable.

By 2011, the first session after term limits kicked in for the state legislature, northern and rural Nevada lost substantial seniority through the loss of legislative giants such as Randolph Townsend, Bernice Mathews, Maurice Washington, John Carpenter, John Marvel, Sheila Leslie, and Mark Amodei. That trend continued in succeeding sessions when legislative stalwarts from outside Clark County such as Dean Rhoads, Bonnie Parnell, Mike McGinness, and others reached the twelve-year mark. As in 2011, the 2013, 2015, and 2017 legislative leadership teams were dominated by legislators from Clark County.

CHAPTER FIVE

Interest Groups and Lobbying

Introduction

While political parties are concerned with ensuring that their members are elected to various governmental positions, interest groups are more interested in seeing that the policies they favor are enacted into law, regardless of which party controls the government. Thus, parties tend to be more personnel oriented, while interest groups are more issue oriented. Of course, those lines are often blurred by the fact that some interest groups are more likely to support one party over another, since that party and its members are, in turn, more likely to favor a group's interests than is the other party (e.g., mining and ranching interests are likely to find that working with Republicans is easier for them than attempting to persuade Democrats, who are more often sympathetic to environmental causes). The decline in the importance of political parties in the United States that was noted in chapter 4 has been accompanied by a rise in the power of interest groups. A study of Nevada politics and history, therefore, would not be complete without an examination of the interest groups that have affected the state since its inception.

Political scientist Don W. Driggs has argued that the dominance of various interest groups in the state has changed over time.[1] Not unexpectedly, the first fifty years of statehood found railroad and mining interests dominating the political landscape. Chief among the lobbyists for those groups were Charles "Black" Wallace of the Central Pacific Railroad and various agents of the big California banks (the "Bank Crowd") that owned the most lucrative mines in the state. In addition to using the usual forms of political activity, Wallace and his counterpart with the Virginia and Truckee (V & T) Railroad, H.M. Yerington, ensured their success through bribery, vote buying, and intimidation.

For the next fifty years, from roughly 1908 to 1958, the chief forces in the state were those representing Nevada's powerful political machines.

75

From 1908 until he lost most of his wealth in the Depression, George Wingfield controlled the state's politics through a bipartisan, but predominantly Republican, machine. He was replaced by the machine of Senator Pat McCarran, a Democrat, and his allies, John Mueller and Norman Biltz. The McCarran-Mueller-Biltz machine was dominant until McCarran's death in 1954, when he was replaced by E. L. Cord, inventor of the Cord automobile. The Cord-Mueller-Biltz machine, however, suffered a staggering blow in 1958 when Grant Sawyer defeated the machine's candidate for governor. Driggs notes that Sawyer's 1958 victory spelled the end of machine politics in the state.

Since that time, no one group has dominated the state's politics in the way that the railroads and the Bank Crowd had done. That is not to say, however, that some groups and individuals are not more successful than others. Since 1958, three groups in particular, three organized and one not, have been highly successful in influencing state politics. Not surprisingly, gaming interests have been extremely powerful in the state. As the state's chief industry and primary campaign contributor, gaming has been extraordinarily successful in getting its preferred candidates elected to office in large numbers. Although they do not have the financial resources of the gaming industry, the various state teachers' organizations have also been successful in obtaining their goals in Nevada. The teachers' unions are unable to contribute monetarily to campaigns to the same degree as gaming; however, they have thousands of volunteers at their disposal to walk districts, stuff envelopes, and engage in other forms of campaigning that candidates depend upon to win elections. After the boom-and-bust cycles of mining in the late 1800s and early 1900s, the industry made a comeback in the late 1960s after the discovery of heap leaching, which allowed small amounts of gold to be economically taken from large amounts of ore through the use of cyanide. In 2011, compared to the $10.7 billion in gaming revenue, mining brought to the Sagebrush State $9.6 billion, $8.8 billion of which came from silver and gold.[2] Yet in spite of that figure, the mining industry has generally been out of the minds of those Nevadans not employed or dependent upon it. "Out of sight, out of mind" has historically allowed the industry to maintain its privileged place in the state constitution. However, as mineral prices, particularly gold, began to dramatically increase in the first and second decades of the twenty-first century, the industry organized to protect its interests and to prevent increased taxation and a change to the state constitution. Much of this lobbying has been through public relations campaigns promoting mining's contributions to the state.

Unorganized but still highly effective have been the media power brokers in the state. Through their endorsements and decisions over what stories to run in their newspapers and on their television and radio stations, these individuals have shaped the state's politics in significant ways. Jack McCloskey of the *Mineral County Independent,* Walter Cox of the *Mason Valley News,* Hank Greenspun and (former governor) Mike O'Callaghan of the *Las Vegas Sun,* and Donald Reynolds of the *Las Vegas Review-Journal* have certainly had a great influence on the state. Indeed, O'Callaghan's columns on the 300 percent pension increase that legislators gave themselves in 1989 and the public outcry that resulted are partly responsible, along with television editorials by Las Vegas newsman George Knapp and the actions of Common Cause of Nevada, for the legislature's repeal of the provision in a special session later that year. Whether the media will continue to have the same degree of influence since the deaths of media giants Greenspun, McCloskey, O'Callaghan, and Reynolds remains to be seen. However, it is likely that as the state grows and voters become more removed from direct contact with state government officials in the years to come, the influence of the media will become even more significant. This would seem to be particularly likely in the area of the electronic and social media, which most citizens rely upon for news and information.

Lobbying in Nevada

Interest groups and the lobbyists who work for them have a wide array of tools at their disposal with which to affect governmental policy. They may provide campaign contributions to candidates they favor, testify for or against bills at the legislature, seek to persuade executive-branch officials to adopt or reject certain rules and regulations, encourage writing campaigns to officeholders, organize protest marches, endorse candidates, or attempt to influence the appointment of judges and other officials who are outside the electoral arena. The appropriateness of a particular method in a given situation will depend upon the goals to be achieved, the interest group's available resources, and the venue in which the lobbying takes place.

Interest groups attempt to influence officials at all levels and in all branches of state government. At the executive level they will, for instance, contribute to and campaign for favored candidates and lobby executive-branch officials, both elected and appointed, to enact regulations and rules that they favor. In the judiciary, interest groups will attempt to influence the selection of judges either by lobbying the governor to appoint a particular judge or by contributing to the campaigns of judicial candidates they support. In addition, they may bring test cases, that is, lawsuits challenging the constitutionality or application of state laws with which they disagree. Or they may file *amicus curiae* (friend of the court) briefs in cases brought by others in an attempt to convince a judge to rule in a particular way that is favorable to the group's interests.

By far the most visible lobbying activities of interest groups, however, occur at the biennial sessions of the state legislature. During these sessions, Carson City becomes a beehive of lobbyists intent on persuading the legislators to pass laws favorable to them or to defeat laws they find unpalatable. That the actions of the legislature are of growing importance to the state's organized interests can be seen in the fact that about 350 lobbyists registered for the 1975 session, 519 registered in 1985, 642 were registered in 1995, and 883 were registered in 2011. A study in 1991 concluded that the Nevada legislature was the sixth "most lobbied" legislature in the country, with nine lobbyists for every legislator;[3] the 2011 session surpassed that mark with an average of over fourteen lobbyists per legislator. The national average is seven per legislator. An examination of Table 5.1 shows that, with few exceptions, the number of lobbyists continues to grow each year. In the 2017 session, the absolute number exceeded, for the first time, one thousand and the average per legislator exceeded sixteen.

Because the Nevada State Legislature is a part-time body, legislators are especially reliant upon lobbyists for information regarding bills that are pending before them. Although, as we shall see in chapter 6, they have the expertise of professional lawyers, auditors, and researchers in the Legislative Counsel Bureau available to them, the legislators are, by virtue of their part-time status and the press of time, dependent upon lobbyists for information regarding the potential effects of legislation. A survey of legislators and lobbyists at the 1971 session found general agreement between the two groups that a major purpose of lobbyists is to provide information to the legislators.[4]

That same survey indicated that lobbyists and legislators agreed on the five most effective lobbying techniques in the state legislature:

TABLE 5.1. Lobbyist Growth in the Nevada Legislature, 1975–2017

YEAR OF SESSION	NUMBER OF LOBBYISTS	RATIO OF LOBBYISTS TO LEGISLATORS
1975	350	5.83
1985	519	8.24
1995	642	10.19
1997	667	10.59
1999	803	12.75
2001	802	12.73
2003	842	13.37
2005	807	12.81
2007	882	14.00
2009	912	14.48
2011	883	14.02
2013	872	13.84
2015	960	15.24
2017	1,048	16.63

Source: Legislative Counsel Bureau, Research Division.

personally presenting arguments, presenting research results, testifying at hearings, initiating contacts by constituents, and contributing or withholding a contribution to a candidate.[5] It is doubtful that those conclusions have changed in the years since the survey was taken.

Regulation of lobbyists in Nevada began only in 1973. Prior to that time, lobbyists were not required to register, they did not have to identify the group or groups for whom they were lobbying, and in some cases they were actually permitted to sit on the floor with legislators. As one observer has noted, "Nevada legislators have been traditionally very friendly toward lobbyists."[6]

In 1973, when it appeared that a more stringent initiative supported by Common Cause of Nevada might qualify for the ballot, the legislature reluctantly passed a bill requiring lobbyists to register with the secretary of state. Spurred by the same fears in 1975, the legislature required lobbyists to report monthly on their expenditures during the session for entertainment, gifts, and loans to legislators. In 1979, lobbyists were further required to wear identification badges while in the halls of the legislature, and the registration site was moved from the secretary of state's office to the Legislative Counsel Bureau.

One of the most important pieces of legislation to regulate lobbyists was enacted during the 1993 session. The legislators passed a law requiring not only that lobbyists list their expenditures for the session, as they had done since 1975, but that beginning with the 1995 session they specify the individual legislators on whom the expenditure was made and the amount of that expenditure. The law has had a significant effect on lobbyist spending on legislators. Not wanting to find themselves on a list of those frequently wined and dined by lobbyists, a distinction that election opponents would surely use against them, many legislators simply avoided the gifts and free meals they had so willingly accepted in past sessions. To no one's surprise, spending by lobbyists on legislators dropped by more than 90 percent between the 1993 and 1995 sessions, when this new law took effect. In recent years, however, lobbyist expenditures on legislators have begun to creep up although still comparatively low.

Winners and Losers

Interest groups and their lobbyists have always been controversial in the United States. On the one hand are those who argue that they serve an important function in a democratic system by allowing people to band together and make their wishes known to their elected representatives; interest groups simply serve to communicate to officials what their constituents want. On the other hand are those who abhor the increased importance of interest groups and their money in the governmental process and who note that what is in the best interests of these organized groups is often not in the best interests of either the state or its citizens. As noted earlier, some groups are more successful in obtaining their wishes than others. As with any aspect of politics, there are winners and losers. The winners, not unexpectedly, are often those with the greatest resources: money, organization, effective leadership, and a cadre of dedicated members who campaign for and against candidates. The losers, not infrequently, are those without such resources.

By far the most frequent winner in Nevada politics is the gaming industry. Although it has not dominated the issues to quite the same degree as banking and railroad interests did in the nineteenth century, the gaming industry is clearly the biggest winner in the state. That it finds itself in this position is the result of several factors.

First, gaming is the single most important industry in the state. Nevada has typically been a one-industry state, first with mining and now gaming. As a result, the economic health of the industry is of vital concern to the state's officials, who must protect jobs and encourage economic growth if they are to remain in office. Proposals that affect gaming are sure to result in close inspection by the state's officials. With the "corporatization" of casinos in the 1960s and the declining influence of organized crime in the industry, gaming has succeeded in establishing for itself a clean reputation and a legitimacy that, with its economic dominance, gives it influence beyond that of other groups.

Second, gaming is a significant contributor to election campaigns in Nevada. A 1993 study by the Western States Center, comparing seven western states, found that gaming gives more to political candidates in Nevada than the primary industries of the six other states give to their preferred candidates. The study also found that of disclosed contributions in the 1990 state and legislative elections, gaming provided 18 percent, mining 2 percent, organized labor 3.7 percent, and resource development industries 2.8 percent. Although gaming and other contributors frequently give to both candidates (just in case), the industry has a knack for choosing winners: "winning candidates got 41.5 percent of their traceable funds from gambling, while losers got just 13.5 percent."[7] In addition to channeling funds toward favored candidates, gaming also "freezes out" those who pose a challenge to them by ensuring that potential candidates cannot raise sufficient funds to run a serious campaign. An example is that recounted by political columnist Jon Ralston in his book *The Anointed One*. In his book, Ralston examined how gaming (and other interest groups) anointed Kenny Guinn governor by starving for funds and forcing out potential challengers such as Attorney General Frankie Sue Del Papa.[8]

Third, gaming has been successful as a result of its high-quality, well-connected lobbyists. For many years, gaming interests were represented by the powerful and hugely talented Jim Joyce. A survey of the 1983 legislature indicated that the three most effective lobbyists were all from the gaming industry: Jim Joyce, Harvey Whittemore, and Sam McMullen.[9] Joyce died in 1993, but the influence of gaming has been continued by Richard Bunker and other lobbyists, including Joyce's son, Robin. It has also been the case that the gaming industry has achieved an amazing degree of access to government officials through its hiring of lobbyists who also run the election campaigns of state and legislative officials. In 2010, for example, two of the most important and successful lobbyists in the state, Pete Ernaut and Greg Ferraro, served as key campaign advisers for Brian Sandoval as he ran for governor. After Sandoval's election, both returned to their primary job, lobbying the governor and legislature on behalf of gaming, tourism, and mining. Such arrangements are not novel in the state; in 1998 Ernaut, backed by Ferraro, Sig Rogich, and Billy Vassiliadis, together arguably the four most significant and powerful lobbyists in Nevada over the past several decades, ran Kenny Guinn's campaign. Interestingly, after guiding Guinn's election to the governorship, Ernaut served as his chief of staff, an incredibly powerful position in any administration.

For different reasons, the Nevada State Education Association has also been a frequent winner in state politics. The association does not have the economic clout and deep pockets of the gaming industry, but the tremendous growth in the state's population has vastly increased the number of schoolteachers, giving NSEA thousands of volunteers willing to walk precincts to campaign for or against electoral hopefuls.

Other groups have also had success in lobbying state government. Organized labor and the State of Nevada Employees Association, as a result of their cadres of volunteer campaign workers, have been successful on occasion, particularly with Democrats. The Chamber of Commerce and the Nevada Taxpayers Association have been more influential with Republicans. One of the quieter winners continues to be the mining industry, which not only has the constitutional protection of paying taxes only on net proceeds, but over the years has also convinced policy makers to define very broadly the expenses that could be deducted in defining "net" proceeds for taxation purposes. In spite of broad public opinion that mining pays too little in taxes, the industry has been able to fend off attempts to require it to pay more. In 2011, however, the legislature reduced some of the deductions that mining companies could take prior to determining "net" proceeds. Nonetheless, the additional $24 million in tax levies the mining industry paid was less than the $38 million it would have had to pay had the legislature stuck with a law passed in a 2010 special session.

Some of the "losers" in Nevada politics tend to vary over time, finding themselves victorious in one era but not in another. Yet others seem to find themselves chronically defeated and disappointed. Mothers Against

Drunk Driving (MADD) had some successes in the 1980s and early 1990s but was soundly defeated by the gaming industry when it worked for legislation to lower the legal intoxication level from .10 to .08 and to make bars and casinos legally liable for accidents caused by drivers who had been drinking at their establishments. The state legislature did eventually lower the legal intoxication level to .08 but only after the U.S. Congress passed a statute denying federal transportation funds to states that did not adopt the lower limit.

Welfare recipients and their advocates have regularly found themselves among the state's lobbying underdogs. As far back as 1955, a study of social welfare policies found Nevada's services for the poor were in such dreadful condition that they fell "below those of many of the poorest states" and the state consistently "turn[ed] a cold poormaster's eye to its poor, its sick, and its socially misshapen."[10] In the six decades since, services have gotten better, but the state continues to rank near the bottom of any national list assessing state-provided social services. Because the poor tend to vote less often than others, because they are unorganized, and because they are often seen by the public and officials as architects of their own condition, they simply do not achieve the victories that gaming, mining, the Chamber of Commerce, and any number of other groups in the state do.

CHAPTER SIX

The Nevada Legislature

Introduction

Like the federal government, the state government of Nevada consists of three branches that oversee one another through a series of checks and balances. The state legislature is the first of these. Unlike the federal Constitution, which merely implies the separation of powers, the state constitution establishes this separation explicitly in Article 3. That separation of power is maintained by the constitution through a separation of duties and a separation of personnel. In terms of the former, Article 3 specifically prohibits any branch from exercising the powers of another. And in terms of the latter, no person may serve in more than one branch simultaneously.[1]

As noted in chapter 2, the Tenth Amendment to the U.S. Constitution reserves to the states all powers not delegated to the federal government or prohibited to the states. Consequently, the framers of the 1864 constitution sought to incorporate into that document limitations and exclusions on the legislature's vast reserve of power. The Declaration of Rights, discussed in chapter 3, is one example of that effort, as are the various provisions in the constitution limiting the power of the legislature in areas such as taxation, borrowing, and spending. The constitutional convention delegates of 1864 feared the possibility of an all-powerful legislature run amok. During the convention's debates, E. F. Dunne of Humboldt County noted, "The fact is, that whenever the Legislature is in session, the people wait with fear and trembling for it to adjourn, and then they thank God that it is over."[2]

Apportionment

Nevada's legislature, like that of all other states except Nebraska, is bicameral; the lower house is called the Nevada State Assembly and the upper house is the Nevada State Senate. Currently there are forty-two members in the assembly and twenty-one in the senate. Although those numbers are not constitutionally mandated and have been altered over the years, Article 15 does limit the total number of legislators to seventy-five and Article 4 requires that the number of senators be no more than one-half or less than one-third the number of members of the assembly.

During the 2001 and 2011 reapportionments northern and rural legislators hoped to increase the size of the senate and the assembly. On account of the explosive growth of Clark County, if the membership remained at twenty-one and forty-two, northern and rural areas of the state would not only lose representatives to Clark County, but also some incumbents from the same party in these areas would be forced to run against each other in upcoming elections. The battles between North and South were not resolved in favor of the status quo. Unlike the Civil War that gave Nevada its "Battle Born" motto, the South won and the senate and assembly will remain at twenty-one and forty-two, respectively, until at least 2023.

For fifty years the senate was wildly malapportioned, with representation not commensurate with population. From 1915 to 1965 the state senate was apportioned on the basis of one senator per county. In addition, each county, no matter how sparsely populated, was given at least one assembly member. This scheme had the effect of overrepresenting the rural counties while underrepresenting the urban areas of the state. For instance, prior to 1966, the districts representing the state's most populous areas, Reno and Las Vegas, contained 75 percent of the population but had only twenty-one of thirty-seven seats in the assembly (57 percent) and two of seventeen seats in the senate (12 percent). The fourteen least populous counties, on the other hand, had only 21 percent of the population but controlled 37 percent of the assembly seats and 82 percent of the senate seats. The remaining population and representatives were to be found in Elko County, which was slightly overrepresented in the legislature.[3]

From the beginning, this arrangement was of dubious constitutionality, since Articles 1 and 15 of the state constitution require that legislative apportionment in both houses be based on population. Nonetheless, it was not until 1964, in *Reynolds v. Sims*,[4] that the U.S. Supreme Court interpreted the federal Constitution to require that both houses of all state legislatures be apportioned on the basis of population. The failure of the 1965 legislature to fairly apportion legislative seats led Flora Dungan, a member of the assembly from Las Vegas, to file suit in federal court. A three-judge federal court held that Nevada's apportionment scheme was unconstitutional, and they ordered the governor to call a special session of the legislature for the purpose of reapportionment.[5] The governor called the session in 1966, and the legislature, dominated by the rural counties, grudgingly reapportioned its seats on the basis of population. The effect of that reapportionment, and the succeeding ones that occur after the census every decade, has been to shift legislative power from the rural counties to the populous urban counties, especially Clark County, which now has a majority in both houses.

Structure and Function of the Legislature
Qualifications, Sessions, Salary

Article 4 of the state constitution requires only that members of the legislature be "duly qualified electors in the respective counties and districts which they represent." Under the constitution, an "elector" is not necessarily the same as a "registered voter." Any U.S. citizen who is eighteen years of age or older, who has not been convicted of a felony, and who has resided in the state for thirty days is considered a qualified elector, regardless of whether he or she is registered to vote. However, the legislature has also required by statute that a legislator be at least twenty-one years old at the time of election and have resided in the state for at least one year prior to the election. And the courts have held that although candidates running in a nonpartisan election do not have to be registered to vote, political parties can require that candidates in party primaries be registered to vote in that party.

Members of the state senate serve four-year, staggered terms; members of the assembly serve terms of two years. Thus, every two years all seats in the assembly and approximately half of those in the senate are up for election. This structure parallels that in the U.S. Congress and guarantees some continuity, at least in the senate, at each legislative session. Although originally the constitution required that vacancies occurring between sessions be filled by election, amendments adopted in 1922 and 1944 now allow county commissioners to fill them. In doing so, however, the commissioners must select an individual who is of the same party as the legislator vacating the seat and who lives in the district to be represented. These interim appointments may be made only if there is to be no regular election prior to the next legislative session and are valid only until such time as a regular election does occur, at which time the remaining term, if any, is up for election.

The sixty-three members of the state legislature meet in regular session biennially, that is, every other year for a period of approximately four months. These regular sessions begin on the first Monday of February in odd-numbered years and are required to conclude within 120 calendar days. The 1864 constitution originally placed a limit of sixty days on regular sessions and twenty days on special sessions. These limits were removed by constitutional amendment in 1958 as it became clear that the state's growing and complex business could not be conducted in so short a time. With the limitation removed, the length of sessions progressively increased after 1958. Whereas the 1973 session lasted 102 days at a cost of slightly more than $1 million, the 1997 session, the longest in state history, went on for 169 days at a cost of approximately $15.5 million.

The growing length and escalating cost of these biennial sessions eventually led to the adoption in 1998 of another constitutional amendment establishing the current limit of 120 calendar days in a regular session. In addition to saving time and millions of dollars in legislative expenses, it is hoped that a shorter session will encourage more people to serve in Nevada's citizen legislature. At the same time, however, there is legitimate concern that many good bills might fall between the cracks of an expedited schedule and that legislators will not have the time or opportunity to examine complicated bills upon which they are expected to vote. During the 2001 session, for example, at one point the assembly passed nine bills in seven minutes; it is doubtful that the members knew exactly what was contained in each of them.

In order to conduct its business within this shortened time period, the legislature adopted new rules and procedures to expedite legislation. These rules impose time limits on when legislation can be introduced by lawmakers, approved by committees, and voted on in each house so that action can be taken in the other. In addition, members of the money committees, Senate Finance and Assembly Ways and Means, begin their hearings on the governor's budget two weeks prior to the official start of the session.

In the first session to occur under the 120-day limit, in 1999, everything ran fairly smoothly, with the legislature adjourning sixteen minutes early, 11:44 p.m. on the 120th day. Although there were some concerns that citizens had not had an opportunity to testify on bills that were pushed quickly through the committees and that the committees themselves had little time to explore the complexities of legislation pending before them, most legislators and observers seemed content with the outcome.

During the 2001 session, however, the wheels fell off. The legislature not only did not finish its business by midnight on the 120th day, based upon an opinion by the Legislative Counsel Bureau it continued to pass legislation until 1:00 a.m. In addition, the governor was forced to call a special session in order to conclude reapportionment deliberations. At this special session, the governor requested that the legislature reapprove legislation that it had previously approved between midnight and 1:00 a.m., in order to avoid any question of their legitimacy, and to pass a reapportionment plan. Although the houses did ultimately agree upon a reapportionment plan, the fifteen Republicans in the assembly were unhappy with it and voted against two bills in the special session that they had previously voted for in the regular session, thus denying them the majority needed to pass. The two bills sat in limbo for several weeks until the Nevada Supreme Court held that they had been legitimately passed in the regular session (that is, because the state constitution specified adjournment by midnight Pacific Standard Time, and because the legislature was operating on Daylight Savings Time at that point, they could continue to meet and pass bills until 1:00 a.m.). Therefore, the two bills did not need to be repassed in the special session, and they were transmitted to the governor who then signed them.

Since 2001 the ability of the legislature to complete its business on time has only worsened. Two special sessions had to be called after the 2003 regular session ended in order to deal with tax issues. And yet another special session was called after the 2005 regular session ended in order to work on Millennium Scholarship and Canadian prescription-drug importation issues. In addition, a special session was called in 2007 after the regular session ended, and special sessions were called in 2008 (twice) and in 2010. No special sessions were called immediately after the 2009 through 2017 legislatures adjourned (although there were special sessions called in 2013, 2014, 2015, and 2016). That did not mean, however, that the legislature had concluded its business, only that the governor found no reason to expect that a special session would result in a successful outcome. For example, by the end of the 2011 legislature, a new reapportionment plan for the state had still not been passed and signed by the governor; Governor Brian Sandoval had vetoed two redistricting plans favored by the Democrats, and they did not have the votes to override him. Ultimately, reapportionment fell to a state district court judge in Carson City, working with a panel of three electoral experts from the state. A two-hour special session was called at the end of the 2013 session to conclude business.

The embarrassment and disgust many feel as a result of the 120-day limit has led to calls by some to adopt annual sessions, or at least to establish a limited session in even-numbered years to deal with budget issues. In 1958 the voters approved an amendment to the constitution allowing for annual sessions but promptly repealed it in 1960. Although biennial sessions have created significant problems for the legislature, particularly in its attempts to accurately predict revenues and then budget for a two-year cycle, further proposals to adopt annual sessions have died in the legislature. For example, a proposal in the 2001 legislature to amend the state constitution to provide for a 120-day session in odd-numbered years and a forty-five-day session in even numbered years passed in the assembly but was once again defeated in the senate, where it was opposed by the powerful majority leader, Bill Raggio. Likewise, attempts in the 2013, 2015, and 2017 sessions to provide for annual sessions all failed. The single post-1960 proposal that did manage to get through the legislature died at the hands of the voters by an almost two-to-one margin in the 1970 elections. To date, Nevada is one of only four states continuing to mandate biennial sessions. The others are Montana, North Dakota, and Texas.

In addition to these regular biennial sessions, the legislature may meet in special session. Prior to 2013, the state constitution allowed only the governor to call the legislature into special session, and he or she was given authority to determine what business the legislators could conduct; no business other than that called by the governor could be conducted. Special sessions called by the governor since 1958 have had no constitutional limit placed upon their length. An opinion by the state attorney general, however, determined that the governor can limit the length of a special session that he has called either at the time that he calls it or by simply rescinding his call at any point once the special session has begun.

As noted, until 2013 only the governor could call the legislature into special session. However, after defeating a constitutional amendment in 2006, the state's voters in 2012 approved allowing the state legislature to call itself into special session without relying upon the governor. The legislature may now call itself into special session upon the written request of at least two-thirds of the members of each house. A special session called by the legislature may last no more than 20 days. In making this change, Nevada joined thirty-four other states that also allow legislatively called special sessions. Although there was little campaign either for or against this constitutional change, it is thought by many that the troubled tenure of Governor Jim Gibbons (2007–2011) had much to do with the public's desire to remove this monopoly power from the hands of the state's chief executive and put the legislature on a more level footing. During Gibbons's tenure, there was at least some discussion of impeaching the man some have referred to as the worst governor in Nevada history. However, no governor would call the legislature into special session for the purpose of impeaching himself and possibly removing himself from office. Arguably, it is with this history in mind that the voters approved in 2012 what they had disapproved only six years earlier, prior to Gibbons's governorship.

By the time of the 2017 regular session, there had been thirty special sessions of the legislature, fourteen of them since the 120-day limit on regular sessions was imposed in 1999. Because most special sessions prior to 1969 had been called by the governor for the purpose of dealing with revenue and appropriation shortfalls between sessions, the creation of the Interim Finance Committee in 1969 decreased the need for special sessions, at least for a while. That committee, made up of the members of the Senate Finance Committee and the Assembly Ways and Means Committee, has authority between regular sessions to appropriate additional funds to agencies experiencing shortfalls or to allow them to move funds from one pool to another. However, the trend away from special sessions appears to have ended with the 120-day limit on regular sessions. Prior to the special session in 2001, the most recent special session had been in 1989 to repeal a 300 percent pension increase the legislators had voted for themselves in that year's regular session. As noted above, in the period between 2001 and 2017, the legislature met in fourteen special sessions to deal with various measures, budgetary and otherwise, that were left incomplete after 120 days or which arose after they were out of session.

Until 2005, legislators received $130 per day for salary and a per diem for living expenses plus telephone and travel expenses. The state constitution provides that the salary figure may be paid only for the first sixty days of a regular session and the first twenty days of a special session. The per diem for expenses, however, is paid for the entirety of the session. An attempt in 2006 to allow legislators to receive compensation for every day of regular and special sessions that they work went down to a massive defeat by the voters. Since that time, however, state statute has incrementally increased legislative pay by the same percentage as other state employees' pay. Consequently, in the 2017 regular session, legislators were paid $8,777.40 in salary ($146.29 per day for the first sixty days only), $17,040 in per diem expenses, up to $10,000 for travel and living expenses, and the constitutionally mandated cap of $60 for postage and stationery (Article 4, Sec. 33).

Organization of the State Legislature

The presiding officer of the senate, the president of the senate, is the lieutenant governor, one of the few instances in which the constitution allows an individual to serve in two branches simultaneously. In that sense, the lieutenant governor is like the vice president of the United States, who serves as president of the U.S. Senate. In this capacity, the lieutenant governor has the authority to interpret rules and has the power to exercise a "casting vote" in case of a tie. In the absence of the lieutenant governor, the senate is presided over by the president pro tempore, an elected position held by a member of the majority party.

The real power of the senate, however, is held by the majority leader and, to a lesser extent, the minority leader. These individuals are chosen by their party caucuses at the beginning of each session. Each is considered the leader of his or her party in the senate and in that capacity makes committee assignments for his or her party's members; in addition, the majority leader chooses the chairs of each senate committee and controls floor debate. The power of the majority leader is tremendous, and no better example of that can be found than Republican senator William "Bill" Raggio of Reno, who served in that position for ten sessions. As majority leader, Raggio managed to advance Republican issues and protect the interests of northern Nevada by delaying, forcing compromises, and killing bills in the senate, in spite of Clark County's majority in that body. Because of his power and persuasiveness, Raggio had an unerring and somewhat baffling ability to keep his fellow Republicans in line, even when that meant Clark County Republicans were voting against the interests of the southern portion of the state. After the 2001 session, however, the long-term majority leader had difficulty keeping his troops

TABLE 6.1. Party Control of the Nevada Legislature, 1961–2017

Year of Session	Majority Party Senate	Majority Party Assembly
1961	R	D
1963	R	D
1965	D	D
1967	D	D
1969	D	R
1971	D	R
1973	D	D
1975	D	D
1977	D	D
1979	D	D
1981	D	D
1983	D	D
1985	D	R
1987	R	D
1989	R	D
1991	D	D
1993	R	D
1995	R	Split*
1997	R	D
1999	R	D
2001	R	D
2003	R	D
2005	R	D
2007	R	D
2009	D	D
2011	D	D
2013	D	D
2015	R	R
2017	D	D

Source: Compiled by the author from data on legislative membership.
*1995 assembly split evenly (21–21) between Democrats and
Republicans. D = Democrat, R = Republican.

in line and was not quite the power he was in past sessions. In the 2010 election, Raggio endorsed incumbent Democrat Harry Reid for the U.S. Senate over Republican and Tea Party favorite Sharron Angle. Shortly thereafter, the Republican caucus in the state senate removed him as majority leader, and he resigned from that body entirely. Raggio died in February 2012 at the age of eighty-five, after having served longer than anyone else in the history of the state senate, with nineteen regular and twelve special sessions to his credit. With legislative term limits now in place, no one will ever come close to Raggio's mark.

In the assembly, the presiding officer is the speaker of the assembly. The speaker, who is selected by the majority party caucus, not only presides over the assembly but also serves as his or her party's leader. In that capacity, he or she appoints the majority party's members to the various committees and selects the majority leader, the speaker pro tempore, and the committee chairs. Unlike the senate majority leader, who typically serves for many sessions, assuming his or her party controls the upper house, only four speakers of the assembly have served two or more consecutive terms. The record is held by Democrat Joe Dini of Yerington, who held the speaker's position in 1977, 1987, 1989, 1991, 1993, 1997, and 1999 and was co-speaker in 1995. The assembly minority leader makes committee assignments for his or her party members.

No one party has dominated Nevada politics, and that is true also for the legislature. In the senate, the Republicans have been the majority party forty-eight times; the Democrats, twenty-five. In the assembly, Democrats have reversed that trend and been the majority party forty-seven times, compared to twenty-six for the Republicans.[6] In an odd turn of events in 1994, the Democrats and Republicans each won twenty-one seats in the 1995 assembly. After substantial maneuvering, legal and political, it was determined that co-speakers and committee co-chairs would be appointed and would alternate their service on a daily basis. That is, the Republican co-chair would preside over a given committee on Monday, the Democratic co-chair on Tuesday, and so on.

Lawmaking in the Legislature

The process of making laws in the Nevada legislature is quite similar to the process in the U.S. Congress, but with some important distinctions. Unlike the U.S. Constitution, which leaves such matters up to congressional discretion, the Nevada Constitution quite specifically lays out the

TABLE 6.2. Standing Committees in the Nevada Legislature, 2017

SENATE	ASSEMBLY
Commerce, Labor, and Energy	Commerce and Labor
Education	Corrections, Parole, and Probation
Finance	Education
Government Affairs	Government Affairs
Health and Human Services	Health and Human Services
Judiciary	Judiciary
Legislative Operations and Elections	Legislative Operations and Elections
Natural Resources	Natural Resources, Agriculture, and
Revenue and Economic Development	Mining
Transportation	Taxation
	Transportation
	Ways and Means

Source: Guide to the Nevada Legislature: 2017–2018.

procedures that must be utilized by the state legislature in passing a bill into law.

Although the importance of committees in Congress cannot be overstated, their importance in the state legislature is even more significant. Because the members of the legislature are part-time legislators and meet for only four months every other year, the level of expertise developed in various policy areas may often be less than that of members of Congress who serve as full-time legislators in a full-time legislature. Consequently, members of the state legislature are more dependent upon the specialization developed by committee members and more compelled by the press of time to complete their business before the end of the 120-day session. It is, therefore, relatively rare that a committee recommendation on a bill is rejected by the full house.

A second difference from the U.S. Congress comes in the types of bills that may be introduced. The U.S. Constitution, for example, mandates that all revenue (i.e., taxation) bills originate in the House of Representatives. The Nevada Constitution makes no similar distinctions, so a bill of any type may originate in either house.

Yet a third difference arises in the time-honored practice of attaching nongermane amendments to legislative proposals. In Congress it is common practice to attach an unrelated amendment (or "rider") to a popular bill in order to ensure the amendment's passage. For example, a controversial welfare proposal might be attached to a popular crime-control bill that members of Congress would have a hard time voting against. Nongermane amendments in the Nevada legislature are prohibited by Article 4 of the state constitution, which requires that all bills "embrace but one subject."

The majority necessary to approve a bill in the state legislature also differs from that at the federal level. The framers of the 1864 constitution were fearful that a handful of legislators, in the absence of others, would pass obnoxious legislation. Consequently, whereas in the U.S. Congress a bill needs only a positive vote by a majority of those present to pass, the Nevada Constitution requires a majority of the *elected* members of each house to vote for passage of a bill. Thus, for a bill to pass it must have eleven votes in the senate and twenty-two in the assembly, regardless of how many legislators are actually present and voting on the proposal.

Some bills, however, are required to have a supermajority in order to be passed. In 1996 Nevada's voters approved an amendment to the state constitution known as the Gibbons Tax Restraint Initiative, named after its primary sponsor, Jim Gibbons. The amendment requires that tax increases be passed by a two-thirds majority in both houses of the legislature. Thus, a tax increase now requires the votes of twenty-eight members of the assembly and fourteen in the senate. Conversely, a minority of fifteen assembly members or eight senators could stop any tax increase from passing. It is this supermajority requirement that allowed the fifteen Republicans in the assembly to put into question the passage of the two bills at the 2001 special session discussed previously in this chapter. A similar situation brought the legislature to a standstill in 2003 when assembly Republicans refused to go along with Republican Governor Kenny Guinn's proposed tax increases, thus requiring two special sessions that summer. It is probable that future bills to fund state government and its programs in education, transportation, and many others will likewise be in jeopardy as a result of the Gibbons Initiative, which allows a minority of either house to subvert the will of the majority.

Two final differences in the lawmaking process occur once a bill has been passed by both houses and is transmitted to the governor. In order for a bill to become a law, the governor must sign it or his veto must be overridden. Once a bill is transmitted to the governor, he has five days (Sundays excepted) to consider the bill if the legislature is in session and

TABLE 6.3. The Nevada Legislature, Famous Firsts

First Hispanic to serve in the assembly	Pablo Laveaga (1875)
First Nevada–born assembly member	Frank P. Langan (1889)
First Nevada–born state senator	George D. Pyne (1889)
First woman to serve in the assembly	Sadie D. Hurst (1919)
First woman to serve in the state senate	Frances G. Friedhoff (1935)
First Native American to serve in the state legislature	Dewey Sampson (1939)
First Basque to serve in the state senate	Peter Echeverria (1959)
First African American to serve in the assembly	Woodrow Wilson (1967)
First African American to serve in the state senate	Joe Neal (1973)
First Hispanic to serve in the state senate	Bob Coffin (1987)
First woman to lead a party in the state senate	Dina Titus (1993)
First openly gay member of the legislature	David Parks (1997)
First woman to serve as assembly majority leader	Barbara Buckley (2001)
First African American to serve as senate majority leader	Steven Horsford (2008)
Youngest person to serve as senate majority leader	Steven Horsford (35)
Longest serving member of the legislature	Bill Raggio (38 years)
First openly lesbian member of the legislature	Patricia Spearman (2013)
First Hispanic to serve as senate majority leader	Moises "Mo" Denis (2013)
First African American to serve as speaker of the assembly	Jason Frierson (2017)
First Latina to serve in the state senate	Yvanna Cancela (2017)

Source: Secretary of State's Office and the Nevada State Library and Archives.

ten days (Sundays excepted) if the legislature has adjourned. By the end of that period the governor must sign or veto the entire bill (in Nevada, unlike forty-three other states, the governor does not have the power of line-item veto and thus cannot pick and choose parts of the bill to sign or veto). If the governor does nothing the bill automatically becomes law. Unlike the president, then, the governor of Nevada does not have a pocket veto, whereby a bill may be vetoed by inaction.

To override a gubernatorial veto, the legislature must obtain a two-thirds majority of the *elected* membership of each house (fourteen in the senate, twenty-eight in the assembly) and not, as in the Congress, simply two-thirds of those present and voting. Bills that are vetoed by the governor after the session has adjourned are returned to the legislature for

any override action at the beginning of the next regular session two years later.

Modernization

Over the past several decades, concomitant to the state's tremendous population growth, the legislature has attempted to modernize its proceedings in order to deal with the ever-increasing complexity of state government. As noted above, the Interim Finance Committee was established in 1969 to deal with appropriations issues between regular sessions and reduce the need for additional special sessions. With the opening of a new legislative building in 1971, each legislator got an office, something that had not happened during previous sessions when legislators met in the cramped confines of the State Capitol Building. In the late 1990s, the legislative building was given a $20 million remodeling that added 80,000 square feet and a new facade, a welcome addition for those who found the old building one of the least attractive structures in the state.

In addition to providing laptop computers for all legislators, the legislature has entered the twenty-first century by utilizing the internet and television to allow citizens to keep abreast of their activities. Interested parties can view bills and bill-draft requests, and committee hearings can be heard on the legislature's website at www.leg.state.nv.us. Those who wish to participate in hearings without traveling to Carson City can do so through videoconferencing that is available.

Perhaps the most important step toward modernization, however, has been the creation and expansion of the Legislative Counsel Bureau (LCB). The LCB was established in 1945 and has been essential to the success of Nevada's citizen legislature. The bureau is overseen by the Legislative Commission, which is made up of six members from each house and which meets monthly between sessions. The Legislative Commission has the authority to appoint the director of the Legislative Counsel Bureau. The director in turn is responsible for hiring the LCB's staff, including four of the five division heads.

The Legal Division of the LCB is of primary importance. It provides legal advice to the legislature and drafts bills requested by legislators. As citizen legislators, members of the assembly and senate rarely possess the knowledge and skills necessary to draft complex legislation without the assistance of the professionals in the Legal Division.

The Legal Division also possesses the authority to issue advisory legal opinions, although like those of the attorney general they are not binding upon the courts in any later litigation.

Not as well known or as visible as the Legal Division, but equally important, are the four other divisions of the LCB: Administrative, Audit, Fiscal Analysis, and Research. The Administrative Division provides accounting, information systems, police protection, maintenance, purchasing, and other operational support for the other divisions and for the legislature. The director of the LCB also serves as director of this division. The Audit Division performs legislative audits on the various agencies of the executive branch in order to provide the legislature with the information it needs to ensure that appropriated funds have been expended properly and efficiently. The Fiscal Analysis Division is responsible for providing the legislature with information on the fiscal effects of various spending and revenue proposals by the executive branch. In that sense, then, they too assist the legislature in its ability to check and balance the governor and other members of the executive branch. The Research Division provides necessary research and background information to the legislature on a multitude of issues confronting it. For example, with the even party split in the assembly in 1995, the Research Division was assigned the task of determining what legislatures in other states had done when faced with the same dilemma.

CHAPTER SEVEN

The Nevada Executive

Introduction

In general, the executive power can be defined as one that enforces and implements the laws passed by the legislature as interpreted by the courts. The area now known as Nevada has been governed by an executive throughout its recorded history. During the period of Spanish colonialism, the area was governed by a provincial governor. After the Mexicans overthrew their Spanish conquerors, what is now Nevada was governed by the Mexican governor of the Province of Alta California (headquartered in Monterey). From the time of the Compromise of 1850 until Nevada became a separate territory in 1861, the northern 90 percent was under the formal authority of the Utah territorial governor, while the southern 10 percent was controlled by the governor of the vast New Mexico Territory. James W. Nye served as the only territorial governor of Nevada Territory from its inception in 1861 until statehood was granted in 1864.

Since 1864, when Republican Henry G. Blasdel was elected the state's first governor, Nevada's chief executive has continued to be its governor. As in all other states, the governor may be considered the "chief" executive, but in Nevada he or she is not the only member of the executive branch to be elected by the voters. Nevada has what is called a "plural executive." Under this system, voters elect six executive-branch officers: the governor, lieutenant governor, attorney general, secretary of state, treasurer, and controller. Under the 1864 constitution the surveyor general and the superintendent of public instruction were also elected executive officers; the former was eliminated entirely and the latter was made an appointive office through constitutional amendments approved by the voters in 1954 and 1956, respectively.

In some states, these five other executive branch officers are appointed by the governor and are responsible solely to him or her. The framers of the Nevada constitution, although on good relations with territorial Governor Nye, were generally distrustful of concentrating too much power in the hands of any single officer or branch. The incorporation of a plural executive in the constitution was, therefore, a purposeful effort on their part to diffuse the executive power among the six officers. Because these five other officers are all elected by the voters, they owe their allegiance to them and not the governor; the governor cannot command them to do anything, nor can he or she remove them. This provides for a system of multiple constitutional checks upon the executive branch: the governor is prevented from absolutely controlling the entire executive branch, the other five executive officers are held accountable to the voters and not to the governor, and executive power is made less dangerous by its diffusion into the hands of six officers instead of one.

Eligibility, Election, and Removal

All six elected members of the executive branch must meet the same eligibility requirements for office. They must be at least twenty-five years of age, qualified electors, and residents of the state for the previous two years. Each serves a term of four years, and all are chosen at the same general election; that is, their terms are not staggered like those in the state senate.

The failed 1863 constitution had included a term of only two years for the governor. For reasons not indicated in the published debates, the framers of the 1864 constitution increased it to four years. Under the original 1864 constitution, all six officers could serve an unlimited number of four-year terms. However, in 1970 the voters approved a constitutional amendment, similar to the Twenty-second Amendment to the U.S. Constitution, limiting the governor, but not the other five officers, to no more than two full terms and up to two years of his or her predecessor's unexpired term. Even before passage of the 1970 amendment, however, no governor had ever been elected to a third term and none of the three who had attempted to do so (Lewis R. Bradley, Charles H. Russell, and Grant Sawyer) were successful. At the end of his term in January 1999, Governor Bob Miller became the longest-serving governor in Nevada history, having served two full terms and the last two years of Governor Richard Bryan's term, which came vacant upon Bryan's move to the U.S. Senate in January 1989.

As noted in chapter 4, in 1996 Nevada's voters once more amended the state constitution, this time to impose term limits on all other state and local officials, except judges. Consequently, starting with the election of

1998, the secretary of state, treasurer, controller, and attorney general can serve no more than two terms in office. Furthermore, any partial term (e.g., appointment to fill a midterm vacancy) is counted as a full one for term-limit calculation; thus, anyone appointed to fill such a vacancy would be allowed to run for the office only once more. Perhaps because the office of lieutenant governor is a part-time one with little power, the 1996 amendment limits that officeholder to twelve years, or three terms, in the position.

The six elected officers of the executive branch are all subject to removal through recall by the voters or impeachment by the legislature. Article 7 of the state constitution provides for the sanction of impeachment for reasons of misdemeanor or malfeasance in office. The process of impeachment is similar to that at the federal level: the lower house, the assembly, votes on articles of impeachment, which require a simple majority to be approved, and the upper house, the senate, conducts the trial. A two-thirds majority in the senate is needed for conviction and removal from office. One important difference between the federal and state procedures for impeachment, however, is the state constitution's provision that these majorities be based on the number of *elected* members of each body and not, as in Congress, on the number of those present and voting. Thus, impeachment in Nevada requires at least twenty-two votes in the assembly, and conviction requires at least fourteen votes in the senate, regardless of how many legislators actually vote.

As noted in chapter 6, the lieutenant governor serves as the president of the senate. Consequently, he or she would preside in an impeachment trial. However, in the case of an impeachment trial involving the governor, the chief justice of the Nevada Supreme Court has been designated by Article 7 as the presiding officer. The framers of the constitution thought it inappropriate for the lieutenant governor to preside over the impeachment trial of the governor, since the lieutenant governor would become acting governor if the governor were to be convicted and removed from office. To have the lieutenant governor preside over the governor's impeachment trial would constitute a clear conflict of interest, and every decision that he or she made in that capacity would be questioned. The difficulties that an acting governor would have in establishing his or her own legitimacy to the office after having presided over the preceding governor's removal led the framers to follow the federal constitutional model, which provides that the chief justice of the United

TABLE 7.1. Governors of Nevada, 1864–2018

Name	Party	Years
James W. Nye, acting governor	R	Oct. 31–Dec. 5, 1864
Henry Goode Blasdel	R	1864–1871
Lewis Rice Bradley	D	1871–1879
John H. Kinkead	R	1879–1883
Jewett W. Adams	D	1883–1887
Charles C. Stevenson*	R	1887–1890
Frank Bell, acting governor	R	Sept. 1, 1890–1891
Roswell K. Colcord	R	1891–1895
John E. Jones*	S	1895–1896
Reinhold Sadler, acting governor	S	April 10, 1896–1899
Reinhold Sadler	S	1899–1903
John Sparks*	SD	1903–1908
Denver S. Dickerson, acting governor	SD	May 22, 1908–1911
Tasker L. Oddie	R	1911–1915
Emmet D. Boyle	D	1915–1923
James G. Scrugham	D	1923–1927
Fred B. Balzar*	R	1927–1934
Morley Griswold, acting governor	R	March 21, 1934–1935
Richard Kirman Sr.	D	1935–1939
Edward P Carville**	D	1939–1945
Vail M. Pittman, acting governor	D	July 24, 1945–1947
Vail M. Pittman	D	1947–1951
Charles H. Russell	R	1951–1959
F. G. "Grant" Sawyer	D	1959–1967
Paul Laxalt	R	1967–1971
D. N. "Mike" O'Callaghan	D	1971–1979
Robert List	R	1979–1983
Richard H. Bryan**	D	1983–1989
Robert J. "Bob" Miller, acting governor	D	Jan. 3, 1989–1991
Robert J. "Bob" Miller	D	1991–1999
Kenny Guinn	R	1999–2007
Jim Gibbons	R	2007–2011
Brian Sandoval	R	2011–

Source: Dean Heller, *Political History of Nevada*, 2006, 11th ed., 188–89. Reprinted with permission.

*Disabled and/or died in office and succeeded by lieutenant governor.

**Resigned governorship to take a seat in the U.S. Senate; succeeded by lieutenant governor.

D = Democrat, R = Republican, S = Silver, SD = Silver Democrat.

States presides over an impeachment trial of the president. Should an officeholder be impeached and convicted, the legislature has authority to remove him or her from office and to disqualify that person from other state office in the future. If the removed officeholder has committed any crimes, he or she could also be subject to a trial in the courts and any appropriate penalties that might ensue; this does not constitute double jeopardy. To date, only one executive official in Nevada has ever been impeached: State Controller Kathy Augustine. In a 2004 special session of the legislature, the assembly voted unanimously to impeach Augustine on three articles relating to her use of state employees and state resources to run her 2002 reelection campaign. In an odd ending to Augustine's impeachment, the state senate voted 20–0 to convict her on one of the articles of impeachment but did not remove her from office. Consequently, although impeached and convicted by unanimous votes in both houses of the state legislature, she would have thus been able to finish out the final two years of her term as controller had she not been murdered by her husband in August 2006.

The Governor

Between 1864 and 2018, the state of Nevada will have had thirty governors: fifteen have been Republicans, eleven have been Democrats, and the remaining four were members of either the Silver Party or the Silver Democrat Party. These four governors served from 1895 to 1911, when the issue of free coinage of silver was an important one in Nevada and other western mining states. Democrats dominated the governor's office for most of the twentieth century, with Republicans holding that office for only twenty-eight years between 1895 and 1999. However, in spite of the Harry Reid–Barack Obama juggernaut and increased Democratic registration in the twenty-first century, all governors elected between 1998 and 2014 were Republicans (Kenny Guinn, Jim Gibbons, and Brian Sandoval).

Other patterns can also be found among the men, and they have all been men, holding the office. During the first twenty-four years of statehood, when mining and ranching were the state's chief industries, all ten of the state's governors had backgrounds in mining, cattle ranching, or both. Since 1959, seven of the nine have been attorneys and four of those have previously served as county district attorney. Six have been graduates of the University of Nevada, Reno (Emmet D. Boyle, Charles H. Russell, Grant Sawyer, Richard Bryan, Jim Gibbons, and

Brian Sandoval), none have been graduates of the University of Nevada, Las Vegas, and only eight have been native-born Nevadans (the most recent being Jim Gibbons, who served from 2007 to 2011). Eight had served in the legislature prior to becoming governor, three (Richard Bryan, Robert List, and Brian Sandoval) had served as attorney general, and other than those six who became acting governor upon the vacation of the office by their predecessors, only one (Laxalt) had previously served as lieutenant governor.[1]

Should the office of governor become vacant, Article 5 of the constitution provides that the lieutenant governor becomes acting governor. Should both offices be vacant, that section provides for the president pro tempore of the senate to exercise gubernatorial powers. In the rare chance that all three offices are vacant, the legislature has provided by statute that the line of succession be continued with the speaker of the assembly and the secretary of state. Permanent succession to the office of governor by the lieutenant governor has occurred six times in Nevada. One of those instances involved the disability (and later death) of the governor, three were cases in which the governor died in office, and two involved resignations by the governor to serve in the U.S. Senate.

Chief Executive

Although only one of six elected executive officers, the governor is considered the chief executive of the state. In this capacity it is his or her duty to see that the laws of the state are faithfully executed. In order to achieve that goal, he is imbued with the power to appoint a substantial number of executive-branch officials. Currently the governor appoints about 80 heads and deputy heads of cabinet-level departments and the members of 200 boards, commissions, and committees. In addition, he is a member of several state boards and commissions.[2] Among the most important appointments the governor makes are the heads of the departments of Motor Vehicles, Public Safety, Human Resources, and Employment Security, and the members of the Gaming Control Board, the Gaming Commission, the Public Works Board, and the Parole Commission.

In making these appointments, the governor is more powerful than the president of the United States and the governors of many other states because he or she is not required to solicit the approval of the state legislature. Although, as we have noted earlier, the framers were distrustful of a strong executive and sought to limit its power, the irony of their giving the governor sole power to appoint these officials was no doubt related to the fact that they were also realists who knew that the legislature would be in session for only a few months every other year and thus in no position to approve or disapprove the governor's appointments.

Even though it would be unwieldy for legislators to attempt to approve gubernatorial appointments, they have attempted to assert power over the governor's appointees by granting themselves the authority to overturn regulations adopted by agencies of the executive branch. The voters defeated a ballot question giving the legislature this power in 1988, and a similar bill passed by both houses of the state legislature in 1995 died when the assembly failed to override Governor Miller's veto. The legislature did ultimately get its way, however, when the voters approved a constitutional amendment granting it this power in 1996. This provision (Article 3, Section 1) gives the legislature the power (1) to review proposed executive branch regulations before they become effective, (2) to suspend the regulations if they appear to exceed the agency's statutory authority, and (3) to reject the regulations entirely if the legislature deems them to exceed the agency's authority. Given that the legislature is out of session twenty months out of every twenty-four, the first two functions may be performed by a legislative agency delegated that task by the legislature while the third function, complete nullification of a regulation, can be accomplished only by a majority vote of a legislative body consisting of members of both the assembly and senate that is authorized to do so (e.g., the Legislative Commission.)

That the governor is more powerful in his discretion to select executive-branch appointees than are his counterparts in many other states is an anomaly in a system in which his power is generally quite limited. For example, as noted above, he is only one of six members of Nevada's elected plural executive. Not only is he without power over the actions of these other officers, they may be, indeed are likely to be, members of other political parties and may use their positions to actively oppose him and his policies at every turn. This often has the effect of reducing his ability to see that the laws are duly enforced. The governor's power over these other five constitutional officers is, as political scientist Richard Neustadt once noted concerning the power of the president of the United States, ultimately nothing more than the power to persuade them to do what he thinks is right. In only fourteen out of thirty-nine elections for state officers has a single party controlled all six executive

TABLE 7.2 Party Control of the Executive Branch, State of Nevada, 1864–2017

ELECTION YEAR	GOVERNOR	LIEUTENANT GOVERNOR	ATTORNEY GENERAL	SECRETARY OF STATE	TREASURER	CONTROLLER
1864	R	R	R	R	R	R
1866	R	R	R	R	R	R
1870	D	D	D	R	D	R
1874	D	D	D	R	D	R
1878	R	D	R	R	R	R
1882	D	R	R	R	R	R
1886	R	R	R	R	R	R
1890	R	R	R	R	R	R
1894	S	S	S	S	S	S
1898	S	S	S	S	SD	SD
1902	SD	SD	SD	R	SD	SD
1906	SD	SD	SD	R	SD	R
1910	R	D	D	D	R	R
1914	D	D	D	D	D	D
1918	D	D	D	D	D	D
1922	D	D	D	D	D	D
1926	R	R	D	D	D	R
1930	R	R	D	D	R	R
1934	D	D	D	D	D	D
1938	D	D	D	D	D	D
1942	D	D	D	D	D	D
1946	D	D	D	D	D	D
1950	R	D	D	D	D	R
1954	R	R	D	D	D	R
1958	D	R	D	D	D	D
1962	D	R	D	D	D	D
1966	R	R	D	D	D	R
1970	D	D	R	D	D	R
1974	D	D	R	D	D	R
1978	R	D	D	D	D	R
1982	D	D*	R	D	R	R
1986	D	D	R	D	R	R
1990	D	R	D	R	R	R
1994	D	R	D	R	R	R
1998	R	R	D	R	R	R
2002	R	R	R	R	R	R
2006	R	R	D	D	D	D
2010	R	R	D	D	D	D
2014	R	R	R	R	R	R

Source: Compiled by the author from general election returns.
*Lt. Governor Robert Cashell was elected as a Democrat but changed his affiliation to Republican during his term.
D = Democrat, R = Republican, S = Silver, SD = SilverDemocrat.

positions; the last couple of times this occurred was in 2002 and 2014, when Republicans swept all six constitutional offices. Prior to that time, no party had done so since 1946, when the Democrats had achieved the same feat.[3]

Consistent with their thoughts on limiting the power of the governor, the framers of the 1864 constitution also denied to him the sole power to issue pardons, a power held by the president and many state chief executives. In its debates on the issue, the convention's delegates stated that the power to issue a pardon for crimes against the state's citizens "should not rest upon one man alone."[4] Apparently, modern Nevadans agree: a constitutional amendment to grant the governor that power was defeated by the voters in 1960 by a 59–41 majority. Instead, the governor serves as one member of a nine-member state Board of Pardons Commissioners; the other members are the attorney general and the seven justices of the state supreme court. A majority of the board must vote to grant a pardon. However, even here the governor has some leverage, albeit negative. According to Article 5, he exercises a veto in that he must be one of those in the majority to grant a pardon; therefore, even if all eight of the board's other members were to vote in favor of a pardon and the governor did not, a pardon would not be granted.

As chief executive, the governor exercises other constitutional powers as well. He has the power to appoint officials to serve in some offices should a vacancy occur between elections; he may suspend a fine or forfeiture and grant a reprieve in a criminal conviction for up to sixty days from the time of judgment, and he must sign all grants and commissions from the state. In addition to his membership on the Board of Pardons Commissioners, the governor also serves on the Board of State Prison Commissioners, which oversees the state prison system, and the Board of Examiners, which reviews all claims against the state for money or property; no money can be appropriated by the legislature to pay a claim against the state unless it has first been submitted to the Board of Examiners, although the board's recommendation is merely an advisory one.

Chief of State

Like the president of the United States, the governor serves as chief of state. This is a ceremonial and symbolic function but an important one nonetheless. The governor serves as the state's chief goodwill ambassador, attending various state functions and representing the state to the world outside of Nevada. In this role, he or she will meet with the president and other governors and engage in more low-profile activities such as ribbon cuttings at new casinos and groundbreakings for important construction projects. In performing these noncontroversial functions the governor not only is able to meet with the people and hear their concerns but also is guaranteed generally positive media attention that will aid him in his reelection or in bringing his pet issues to the state's attention.

Chief Legislator

Although not a member of the legislature, the governor is deeply involved in its biennial sessions in a number of ways. The state constitution requires the governor to give a State of the State address to the legislature at every regular session. Through this address the governor is able, in part, to set the legislative agenda by proposing bills he would like to see adopted, supporting those proposed by others that he favors, and indicating those that he would be unwilling to sign into law should they be passed. The constitution requires a State of the State message only at each biennial session of the legislature; some modern governors, however, have seized upon the media's attention to this address and have sometimes given one in even-numbered years, when the legislature is not meeting.

The governor's chief method for shaping the legislative agenda, however, has not been with the State of the State address but through his budget proposals. The executive branch uses a system of "central clearance," which means that all budget requests by state agencies must be submitted to the governor prior to transmission to the legislature. The governor and his budget director may reduce or add to these requests before submitting them to the legislature. Woe be unto the agency head who attempts to subvert the governor by asking for more at the legislature than the governor has recommended, for his or her time in office may be short. Although the money committees in the legislature often consist of legislators who are seasoned in budget matters and who are aided by budget professionals in the Fiscal Analysis Division of the Legislative Counsel Bureau, the brevity of legislative sessions means that the governor's budget is usually adopted with only a few modifications by the legislature.

That the legislature generally adopts the governor's budget with few changes is probably to the good, as far as the governor is concerned, for he is held responsible by the voters for the state's economy despite the fact that it is often buffeted or bolstered by factors over which he has no control. For example, the Great Recession that hit the U.S. after 2007 reduced the number of tourists to Nevada and created a decline in revenue to the state's coffers. Unfortunately, there was little Governor Gibbons and, later, Governor Sandoval could do other than reduce state spending or raise taxes. Gibbons chose the former, causing a rift with the legislature, while Sandoval chose the latter, causing a rift within the state Republican Party.

As chief legislator, the governor has some limited power over the legislature's commencement and adjournment. He may call special sessions of the legislature, which are restricted to conducting only the business for which he has called them. (Although he no longer exercises exclusive power to call special sessions as the legislature may now do so as well.) Also, should the two houses of the legislature find themselves unable to agree upon a time of adjournment, Article 5 gives the governor authority to adjourn them at "such time as he may think proper."

The governor also exercises the power of the veto. All bills passed by the two houses of the legislature in the same form go to the governor for his action. In order for these legislatively approved bills to become law, the governor must sign them, do nothing, or have his veto overridden. In this respect, governors of Nevada have not fared as well as those nationally; whereas the national average is only 1 percent of gubernatorial vetoes overridden, Nevada's governors have been overridden 12 percent of the time.[5] In modern times, governors have typically vetoed a half-dozen or fewer bills passed by the legislature each session. However, a new record was set during the 2009 session when Governor Gibbons vetoed forty-eight bills, more than the five governors before him combined. Of this record number of vetoes, a record number were also overridden: twenty-five, or slightly more than half. The record number of vetoes came about in part because of the state's serious budget plight during the Great Recession that saw Gibbons seeking to cut budgets and services and Democratic legislators seeking to increase taxes to provide what they deemed necessary services. That Gibbons was generally disengaged during this time, rarely meeting with or talking to legislators, did not help an already fraught situation. Continuing this partisan divide in the 2011 session, Governor Sandoval vetoed twenty-eight bills, with the legislature taking no post veto action on any of them, knowing that they did not have the votes to override. Although Gibbons holds the record for the highest number of vetoes by a governor in a single session of the legislature, Sandoval holds the record for the highest number of vetoes by a governor during his tenure in office. In addition to the twenty-eight bills that he vetoed in 2011, he also vetoed seventeen in 2013, seven in 2015 (when Republicans held both houses of the legislature), and forty-one in 2017, for a total of ninety-three vetoes during his two terms in office.

Other Duties

Chief executive, chief of state, and chief legislator duties take up most of a governor's time and efforts, but he also engages in a number of other functions given to him by the constitution, statutes, or custom. Articles 5 and 12 of the state constitution make the governor commander-in-chief of the Nevada National Guard. As commander-in-chief, he has authority to call the guard into service during emergency situations such as riots or catastrophes of nature, and he appoints the functional head of the guard, the adjutant general.

By custom the governor is seen as the chief of his party in the state. It is considered his responsibility to ensure that members of his party are elected to various positions, especially in the legislature. Success in this area, of course, works to the governor's advantage, since he would prefer to see an executive branch and legislature dominated by his party rather than by the opposition. Just how sensitive this role can be is illustrated by an episode arising out of the 2000 general election. In a race for a seat on the Nevada Supreme Court, Governor Kenny Guinn endorsed the incumbent, Nancy Becker, for reelection. Although the race is nonpartisan and candidates are not identified by political party, it happened that Becker, a Democrat, was running against a Republican, Gary Backus. Guinn's endorsement of Becker brought forth condemnation from some of his Republican cohorts, including the Clark County Republican Central Committee. As chief of his party the governor is also expected to use his patronage power to reward members of his party by appointing them to important posts in the state government.

Lieutenant Governor

Unlike the situation at the federal level where the president and vice president run on a ticket and are, therefore, of the same party, the lieutenant governor in Nevada runs for office independently and may be of a different party from the governor. This has occurred only nine times out of a total of thirty-nine elections.[6] When it does occur, a problem could develop when the governor is out of state.

Under Article 5 of the state constitution, the lieutenant governor becomes acting governor not only through a vacancy but also in case of the governor's "absence from the state" for any reason. Exactly what *absent* means became a matter of some importance in 1965 during the governorship of Grant Sawyer, a Democrat, who was serving with a Republican lieutenant governor, Paul Laxalt. While Sawyer was out of the state for five hours, Laxalt requested that a state judge impanel a grand jury to investigate the Highway Department. When Sawyer returned, he rescinded the order.

The case eventually landed in the Nevada Supreme Court, where the justices voted to construe the constitutional language narrowly. In *Sawyer v. District Court*, the state's highest court held that in order for the lieutenant governor to serve as acting governor in the governor's absence, there must be an "effective absence" and a critical, emergency need for action; the governor's absence must be "measured by the state's *need* at a given moment for a particular act." Given that the grand jury impanelment was not critically needed during the governor's absence, the court held Laxalt's request for a grand jury constitutionally invalid.[7] The most recent event of this type occurred in 1996. While Democratic Governor Bob Miller was on vacation in the Caribbean, Republican Lieutenant Governor Lonnie Hammargren attempted to appoint a county commissioner to fill a vacancy in Lincoln County. Because there was no emergency need to do so, Secretary of State Dean Heller refused to notarize the appointment, in spite of Hammargren's personal pleas to do so. That a conflict of this type has not occurred since 1996 is at least partly due to the fact that the three governors elected since Governor Miller left office have all been Republicans with lieutenant governors of the same party.

Constitutionally, the lieutenant governor has few powers, and the position is considered a part-time one. He or she serves as president of the senate with a "casting vote" in case of ties and serves as acting governor when the governorship is vacant through death, disability, impeachment, or recall or when the governor is "effectively absent" from the state and emergency action must be taken. Should the lieutenant governor become acting governor, he or she holds both offices until the next general election, at which time a successor is chosen. Most recently this occurred between January 1989 and January 1991, when Lieutenant Governor Bob Miller also served as acting governor.

By statute, the legislature has given the lieutenant governor the chairship of the Commission on Tourism and he or she also serves as a member of the Board of Directors of the Department of Transportation and on the Board of the Governor's Office on Economic Development. The lieutenant governor may also serve as the governor's confidant and adviser when the two are close; but when they are not, the lieutenant governor is frequently left out of the executive "loop." Such was the case after the 1994 election with Governor Bob Miller, a Democrat, and Lieutenant Governor Lonnie Hammargren, a Republican. However, Republican Governor Sandoval and Republican Lieutenant Governor Brian Krolicki worked closely together after their elections in 2010 and that relationship continued with the 2014 election of Republican Mark Hutchison as lieutenant governor.

Attorney General

Next to the governor, the attorney general is probably the most visible member of the executive branch. Although chief legal adviser to the state, the attorney general is not legally required to be an attorney; it would, nonetheless, be improbable that a layperson could now be elected to the position. Constitutionally, the attorney general has few powers. He or she serves with the governor and secretary of state as a member of the Board of State Prison Commissioners and the Board of Examiners and with the governor and justices of the supreme court on the Board of Pardons Commissioners.

Other duties have been given to the attorney general by statute, including the obligation to provide legal advice to the various agencies of state government through advisory legal opinions. These advisory opinions serve only as guidelines to the agencies and are not binding upon the courts in any subsequent legal action that may arise. The attorney general is also responsible for defending the state or prosecuting cases at the Nevada Supreme Court and the U.S. Supreme Court. Technically,

TABLE 7.3. The Nevada Executive, Famous Firsts

First woman to serve as lieutenant governor	Maude Frazier (1962–1963)*
First woman elected state treasurer	Patricia D. "Patty" Cafferata (1983)
First woman elected secretary of state	Frankie Sue Del Papa (1987)
First woman elected lieutenant governor	Sue Wagner (1991)
First woman elected attorney general	Frankie Sue Del Papa (1991)
First Asian American elected secretary of state	Cheryl Lau (1991)
First woman elected state controller	Kathy Augustine (1999)
First Nevada executive to be impeached (and convicted)	Kathy Augustine (2004)
First Hispanic elected attorney general	Catherine Cortez Masto (2007)
First Hispanic elected state treasurer	Kate Marshall (2007)
First governor denied renomination by his party	Jim Gibbons (2010)
First Hispanic elected governor	Brian Sandoval (2011)
First African-American Adjutant General	Ondra Berry (2014)
First woman to chair the Gaming Control Board	Becky Harris (2018)

Source: Secretary of State's Office
*Frazier was appointed on July 13, 1962, to fill the unexpired term of Rex Bell and served until January 1963.

the attorney general also has authority to oversee the district attorneys in Nevada's seventeen counties. Since these district attorneys are popularly elected by the voters of their individual counties, however, the attorney general rarely involves his or her office in their affairs. He or she will do so, however, if a district attorney has a conflict of interest in a case or if it appears that out of favoritism or a lack of fortitude a district attorney has failed to pursue a case. Finally, the attorney general is required by statute to submit a biennial report to the governor on the condition of law enforcement in the state.

Secretary of State

The secretary of state is primarily a custodian of the state's records. Constitutionally, he or she is prescribed only three duties. First, the secretary of state, along with the governor, must sign all state grants and commissions. Second, with the governor and attorney general, he or she serves on the Board of State Prison Commissioners and the Board of Examiners. Third, the secretary of state is required by Article 5 to "keep a true record of the Official Acts of the Legislative and Executive Departments," which includes printing the official acts of government departments and the journals of the legislature and returning to the legislature at the beginning of each regular session any bills that may have been vetoed by the governor after the adjournment of the previous session.

The secretary of state is also responsible for issuing certificates of incorporation to Nevada businesses and regulating securities issued by these state-based entities. Statutorily, the secretary of state commissions notaries public in Nevada. Although Article 5 makes the Nevada Supreme Court the official canvasser of votes in the state, the secretary of state is responsible for preparing the official ballot, publishing official election results, and issuing certificates of election to the winners.

Controller and Treasurer

The offices of controller and treasurer are created by the state constitution, but that document assigns them no particular responsibilities. Consequently, whatever functions they do perform are prescribed in state statutes. In its 1999 session, the state senate voted to combine the offices of treasurer and controller, but they were blocked by the state assembly, which refused to go along.

In spite of attempts in 1995 and 1999 to combine the offices, today they remain separate and independent. Nonetheless, the two offices must work together closely. The treasurer receives all moneys paid to the state and disburses them upon receipt of a warrant from the controller. It is the responsibility of the treasurer to deposit all state funds and to ensure not only that they are not lost, as happened in Orange County, California, in the mid–1990s, but that they build the state's treasury by accumulating interest at the highest rate safely possible. In addition to issuing warrants to the treasurer, the controller serves as the state's chief bookkeeper, making an annual report of state expenditures to the governor and serving as the chief auditor in any claims against the state. In this latter capacity, the controller, along with the Board of Examiners, makes advisory recommendations to the legislature on appropriations to pay such claims.

CHAPTER EIGHT

The Nevada Judiciary

Introduction

In interpreting the meaning of various statutes and constitutional provisions, the judges of Nevada's courts engage in a form of policy making that affects not only the lives of the litigants in each case but also the lives and fortunes of all the state's citizens. It should come as little surprise, then, that the state's judges, especially the justices of the Nevada Supreme Court, have come under intense scrutiny and, on occasion, criticism for the decisions they have made. Two periods of Nevada history in particular illustrate the vigor of the courts' critics.

The early years of the judiciary in the Great Basin were not good ones. As noted in chapter 1, early settlers in the Carson Valley were eager to gain separate territorial status as early as 1851. This desire was based in part on their wish to rid themselves of the Utah territorial judiciary, Mormon judges who were accused by the settlers of "so [mixing] together church and state that a man [could not] obtain justice in any of its courts."[1] Even after separate territorial status was granted in 1861, however, the courts were not spared criticism of their actions. President Lincoln's three appointed territorial judges (Chief Justice George Turner, Associate Justice Horatio N. Jones, and Associate Justice Gordon N. Mott) and their successors were subjected to at least as much criticism as their Mormon predecessors, albeit for different reasons.

Although, as we will discuss, the Nevada territorial judges did behave in unprofessional and inappropriate ways, the primary factors undermining them were the overwhelming number of disputed mining claims they were forced to handle and the unbridled desire of William M. Stewart to control the territorial and state governments. The Nevada territorial courts were inundated with mining claims and did not have the staff to deal with them in a timely fashion. As one historian of the period has noted, "The first result of the opening of the Comstock mines was wild speculation, and the second almost endless litigation."[2] Chief among the reasons for this litigation was the question whether various lucrative ore veins were part of a single ledge and therefore the property of one company or whether they were separate ledges that would allow ownership by a number of individuals or companies.

A decision by the judges on behalf of either theory meant the gain or loss of tremendous fortunes to those involved. With such high stakes at issue, the judges were in a no-win situation and could not escape severe criticism regardless of how they decided. To make matters worse, there were virtually no statutes governing the issues at hand and the judges were forced to apply obscure mining-district regulations and common law, when those were available. As though the deck were not stacked enough against the judges, witnesses and jurors in these cases were often bribed by the mining companies, which stood to win or lose millions of dollars.

It is perhaps possible that the first territorial judges could have survived the controversy over mining claims, had it not been for Stewart's actions. As explained in chapter 2, Stewart was partly responsible for the failure of the 1863 constitution because he maneuvered control over the Union Party convention in Storey County and ensured that individuals allied with him were listed on the ballot for the state's first officers. The unwillingness of many in Nevada Territory to allow Stewart and his minions to control the new state government led them to defeat the proposed constitution and Stewart's handpicked slate of candidates by a four-to-one margin. Stewart, however, was not to be stopped. Politically and economically, Stewart had much to gain by destroying the territorial judges' legitimacy. As a well-paid attorney for wealthy California mining companies, he and his clients stood to win (or lose) vast riches depending upon the judges' decisions in these mining-claim cases. Politically, Stewart could achieve two goals important to him by undermining the territorial judiciary. He could, on the one hand, increase support for statehood and rid the area of its appointed territorial judges, replacing them with elected state judges, whom he believed would be more controllable. On the other hand, he could wreak revenge against his old nemesis, John North, who had replaced Justice Mott on the territorial bench.

Stewart's conflict with Justice North had begun at the 1863 constitutional convention over the issue of mine taxation; North had also opposed Stewart's stacking of the 1863 ballot with his allies. The relationship further deteriorated between 1863 and 1864 when North, serving in his capacity as a district court judge, ruled against several of Stewart's clients, including the Chollar Mining Company. Stewart appealed his Chollar loss to the territorial supreme court, where North and Justice Powhatan B. Locke, who had replaced Justice Jones, upheld the earlier decision against Stewart's client and in favor of the Potosi Mining Company. Politically and economically, then, North had stood in Stewart's way, and the latter was not a man to be denied.

By early August 1864 more than 3,000 people had signed a petition demanding that all three judges resign, and on August 22, Stewart had his revenge when he and his allies forced all three territorial judges to resign. That they did resign was due in no small part to their own unprofessional conduct. North himself had ascended to the bench under dubious circumstances. A newspaper of the time reported that the Potosi Company had paid Justice Mott a $25,000 bribe to resign so that he could be replaced by North, whom the company knew to favor their cause. North muddied the waters further when he accepted a loan from the Potosi Company to build a mill in Washoe City, even though he knew he might be assigned the Potosi-Chollar litigation. Stewart threatened Chief Justice Turner with an arrest warrant charging that he had accepted a $5,000 bribe in a previous mining case. Justice Locke, after deciding with North in favor of the Potosi Company, issued an addendum to the file, reopening the hearing of evidence. Besieged by that company, he then withdrew it, causing him to gain enemies from both sides. Thus, from August 22 until December 1864, when the state's first officials took office, Nevada Territory was without a judiciary. That fact certainly led many, as Stewart had surely hoped, to support statehood.

From 1864 until 1984 the Nevada courts enjoyed a period of relative calm, although there were various problems over the years. In the decades of the 1980s and 1990s, however, the Nevada Supreme Court was once again the subject of much criticism and debate. And like their territorial predecessors, the justices of that court were in no small part responsible for their own difficulties.

In 1984 two particularly nasty judicial elections dominated the state's attention. The race for district court judge in Clark County between Charles Thompson and Joe Bonaventure and the supreme court race between incumbent Noel Manoukian and challenger Cliff Young were rampant with charges of conflict of interest and unethical behavior on the part of the candidates and their supporters. Unfortunately, that pattern continued in the distasteful and expensive (more than $1 million) contest for an open supreme court seat between Thompson and Miriam Shearing in 1992. Eighteen percent of those voting in the Thompson-Shearing race were apparently so disgusted that they cast their votes for "none of these candidates." This trend continued in 1996 when a race between incumbent Justice Cliff Young and Clark County Family Court Judge Steve Jones took an undignified turn. Jones attacked Young for an inappropriate joke the justice had made about sexual assault victims, and Young bought media time to point out that Jones's wife had been arrested after a dispute with her husband. Another Young ad criticized Jones for signing a court order involving one of his former clients, while Jones attacked a dissent by Young in which the incumbent had voted for a new death-penalty hearing for a convicted murderer. Eventually, a mud-stained Young won reelection by the narrow margin of 41 to 38 percent with 21 percent of voters, apparently sickened by the whole affair, choosing "none of these candidates." Total costs for the campaigns by both men were almost $900,000. Supreme court elections between 1998 and 2016 were tame, but given the divisiveness, high costs, and interest group electioneering that have been occurring in high court races in other states this century, one doubts that future races will not mirror the embarrassments of 1984, 1992, and 1996.

It is perhaps to be expected that election campaigns, even for judgeships, will sometimes be too vigorously contested. However, the troubles of the supreme court have not ended there. In late 1991, three justices of the supreme court publicly attacked glaucoma-afflicted Chief Justice John Mowbray's proposed bid for reelection, claiming that he was unable to perform his duties and should step down. With charges and countercharges flying among the justices and their respective supporters over competency, conspiracy, and inappropriate telephone use, Mowbray eventually decided not to run, thus setting up the open seat that resulted in the 1992 Thompson-Shearing free-for-all.

In 1993 the supreme court involved itself in proceedings of the Commission on Judicial Discipline into the actions of Washoe County District Judge Jerry Carr Whitehead. Whitehead had been accused of attempting to intimidate attorneys who sought to have their cases removed from his court. The court's proceedings were held in secret and two of its members recused themselves from the case, one voluntarily (Cliff Young) and one by force (Robert Rose). In a series of decisions between 1993 and 1995, the supreme court removed the attorney general as the commission's legal adviser and dismissed the charges against Whitehead. Only Justice Shearing, the first woman to serve on the high court, dissented from these orders. Whitehead, in a bargain with federal authorities, eventually resigned from the bench in order to avoid prosecution for unspecified federal charges.

Whether it was true or not, many believed that the court was merely acting to protect one of the state's "good ol' boys," and the justices' standing among the public and the legal community declined even more. In a 1994 poll of three hundred attorneys conducted by the state's largest newspaper, the *Las Vegas Review-Journal*, 75 percent indicated that they had only "some" or "not much" confidence in the supreme court.

Since the end of the Whitehead matter, the state's high court has attempted to salvage its image in various ways. The court has opened to the public its meetings to discuss administrative rules changes that affect how the courts operate. In addition, it has determined that disciplinary proceedings against attorneys by the State Bar of Nevada are to be open once probable cause has been established. And in an addition to the Whitehead case, the justices unanimously agreed to open to the public the proceedings of the Commission on Judicial Discipline once a complaint is judged to have merit. Any sanctions against a judge by the commission must also be made public. Beginning in 2008, the Nevada Commission on Judicial Selection opened its hearings to the public so that members of the public and the media could examine the applications of those seeking appointment to the bench and attend the interviews and deliberation by the commission. Also in 2008, in a nod to more openness in the judicial process, supreme court justices unanimously ordered that all civil court records be opened to the public unless there was a compelling safety or privacy interest in sealing them. These rules limited the discretion of trial judges to seal cases for any reason and without explanation, which was occurring prior to that time.

Nonetheless, the court continues to find itself at the center of controversy. Because the state constitution prohibits elected state officials, including judges, from receiving a pay increase until after they have stood for election, some of the justices of the supreme court will, after a pay

raise, make more than others. For example, a pay raise given in 2008
could be collected by justices only after they have stood for reelection.
Two of the seven justices received the raise after their election in 2008,
two others after their election in 2010, and the remaining three after
2012. The justices attempted to equalize their salaries by including additional funds in a 1997 bill to study the family courts. The funds would
have augmented the salaries of three justices and seven district court
judges to make up for the fact that they were paid less than their col-
leagues. The provision led to accusations by the media that the justices
were attempting to sneak hidden pay raises into the legislation, although
members of the legislature claim that they had been informed by the
court about the purpose of the funds. As a result, the extra salary funding was pulled from the bill but not before further damaging the court's
reputation. Ironically, an identical bill to augment the salaries of justices not receiving immediate pay raises was passed by the legislature in
2001 with little critical attention except by Mike O'Callaghan of the *Las
Vegas Sun*. In 2007 these commissions were extended so that justices on
the supreme court not receiving a raise would receive $30,000 for serv-
ing on the Supreme Court Commission on Law Libraries. Family court
judges not receiving the raise would receive the same amount for serving on the District Court Commission on Law Libraries. In 2014, when
all family court judges were on the same election schedule, the latter
practice ended.

The state supreme court also spurred criticism when it stepped into
the 2003 controversy between Governor Guinn and the legislature.
As a result of the refusal by fifteen Republican assembly members
to approve the governor's tax proposals, the legislature was unable to
complete its budget, including funding for education, after the regular
session and two special sessions. Consequently, the governor filed suit
in the supreme court seeking a writ of mandamus to compel the legislature to fulfill its constitutional duty to pass a balanced state budget and
fund education. Although many assumed that the court would avoid the
issue by declaring it a "political question" to be resolved between the
other two branches, the court stepped into the controversy by nullify-
ing, in this case only, the supermajority rule applicable to tax increases
under the Gibbons Initiative discussed in chapter 6. The court's decision
was ultimately unnecessary when one of the fifteen Republicans voted
for the new taxes, thus providing the needed two-thirds supermajority

necessary. Nonetheless, the court was subject to considerable criticism for activism and overreaching by opponents of the decision. Three years later the court overturned its decision in the *Guinn* case.

Structure and Functions

The state court system of Nevada operates separately and independently of the federal court system. Its chief function is to interpret state statutes and state constitutional provisions and impose sanctions on those who violate them. State court decisions based entirely on state law cannot be appealed to the federal courts; however, should a state case also involve issues of federal law (e.g., a state drug case in which the defendant invokes the Fourth Amendment protection from unreasonable searches and seizures), it could be appealed to the U.S. Supreme Court.

The state court system is divided into four levels: court of last resort (Nevada Supreme Court), intermediate appellate court (Nevada Court of Appeals), courts of general jurisdiction (Nevada district courts), and courts of limited jurisdiction (justice courts and municipal courts). Until 2015 Nevada was one of only ten states not to have an intermediate court of appeals between its supreme court and trial courts. Proposed constitutional amendments to reduce the supreme court's increasing workload by adding an intermediate court to the state judicial system were defeated by the voters four times: 1972, 1980, 1992, and 2010. However, on the fifth attempt in 2014, voters in the Sagebrush State approved the creation of a court of appeals, judges were appointed quickly by Governor Sandoval, and the court became operational in 2015. In 2016 all three appointed judges were elected to full terms of office.

FIGURE 8.1 Structure of the Nevada State Judicial System.

Nevada Supreme Court

The Nevada Supreme Court is the court of last resort in the state judicial system. Except when a federal issue is involved, its decisions are final. Justices on the court are elected for six-year, staggered terms. Between 1864 and 1915, these elections were partisan; since 1915, however, candidates for the high court run in nonpartisan elections. Constitutionally, any "qualified elector" is eligible to run for election. By statute, however, one must also be at least twenty-five years of age, an attorney licensed to practice law in Nevada, and a two-year resident of the state. In 2005 the legislature further required by statute that candidates for a supreme court seat have at least fifteen years of legal experience with at least two of those in Nevada.

The 1864 constitution established a three-member supreme court. Given the perceived corruption of the territorial judiciary, there was great debate among the convention delegates on the issue. Some of the delegates favored a five-member court, believing that five justices would be harder to bribe than three, while others, including James A. Banks of Humboldt County, thought it impossible to find more than three "pure" and "able" justices to sit on the bench.[3] A compromise adopted in the convention established the number of justices at three and included the proviso that the legislature could increase the number to five without constitutional amendment. In 1967 the legislature exercised that option. In 1976 the voters approved a constitutional amendment removing the cap on the number of justices and leaving the matter solely to the discretion of the legislature.

As a result of the supreme court's ever-increasing workload and the failure of the voters to support establishment of an intermediate court of appeals, the legislature expanded the high court from five to seven, effective January 1999. The expansion of the court allows it to hear twice as many cases as before given that, instead of all justices sitting on all cases, the justices sit in two panels of three to hear appeals. The northern panel sits in Carson City and the southern panel in Las Vegas. The panels are randomly appointed, and membership rotates every twelve months. The chief justice does not normally sit on a panel but may do so if one of the panel's justices recuses himself or herself from a case due to a conflict of interest. All seven justices sit as a group (*en banc*) to hear only the most important cases, such as those involving ballot questions, direct appeals in death penalty cases, and contested cases involving attorney suspension or disbarment.

The expansion of the court's membership created a difficulty in selection of the chief justice. The chief justiceship is a rotating position held by the most senior justice, that is, the justice in his or her last two years of a term. When there were only three justices on the court, their staggered terms of office made the question who would serve as chief justice an easy one. However, now that there are seven justices, it is often the case that there will be two or three justices serving the last two years of their terms at the same time. In those cases, the constitution provides for the selection of the chief justice by lot, typically a coin toss. In some instances the justices have cooperated, with one of them serving as chief justice in the first year and the other in the second. The other would serve as vice-chief justice during the year in which he or she was not chief justice. In 1992 the voters rejected a constitutional amendment that would have allowed the court to select its own chief justice.

The supreme court exercises both original and appellate jurisdiction. However, the court decides few original jurisdiction cases; its appellate docket constitutes the vast majority of the court's workload. On original jurisdiction, the court has authority to issue various writs, including writs of mandamus, certiorari, prohibition, quo warranto, and habeas corpus. The legislature is prohibited from increasing or decreasing the court's original jurisdiction without a constitutional amendment.

The court hears appeals coming from the state's district courts but is restricted to hearing questions of law only (e.g., was a confession illegally obtained) and not questions of fact (e.g., is the defendant innocent or guilty). Like the U.S. Supreme Court, the court cannot give advisory opinions or hear cases involving moot issues. Its appellate jurisdiction includes power to issue the writs noted above and any other writs that may be necessary or proper in the exercise of its appellate duties.

The state's booming population has led to an increase in the court's workload. From 1955 to 1990, the number of cases filed increased by an astounding 2,000 percent.[4] In 1998, the last year that the court still had only five members, there were 2,521 cases carried over from the year before plus 1,928 new cases filed and 15 that were reinstated, for a total of 4,464. Through Herculean efforts, the court decided 2,299 of these cases but still carried 2,165 over to the 1999 term. Cases filed at that time could expect to wait at least two years for a decision. Growth in the supreme court's caseload and the backlog that it causes did not abate after the court grew from five to seven members. In fiscal year 2014, the last year before implementation of the court of appeals, the supreme court had 2,481 cases filed and made decisions in 2,372. However, because of the previous year's backlog of 1,879, at the end of the year the court still had 1,988 cases awaiting decision. Some cases would linger at the state supreme court for three years prior to a decision being rendered.

As is true in other appellate courts in the United States, the supreme court justices do not hear evidence, witnesses, or testimony. Instead, the attorneys for both sides submit written briefs to justices, indicating why they believe the proceeding in the district court was proper or improper. In some of these cases, the attorneys are allowed to present oral arguments to the justices in open court as well. The justices then meet in secret conference to discuss and vote on the case and write a majority opinion. In some cases, justices will also write concurring opinions (agreeing with the decision but for different reasons than the majority opinion) or dissenting opinions (disagreeing with the majority's decision).

Nevada Court of Appeals

As noted earlier, after four failed attempts the voters in 2014 approved creation of an intermediate court of appeals to reduce the overwhelming workload of the supreme court. Governor Sandoval appointed three judges to the court to serve until the 2016 election. In 2016 all three of these appointed judges ran unopposed and, thus, won election to full terms.

To be eligible to serve as a court of appeals judge, an individual must meet the same legal requirements as a supreme court justice. In addition to being a qualified elector, they must be at least twenty-five years old; be a licensed attorney in Nevada; have at least fifteen years' experience as an attorney, at least two of which are in Nevada; and be a resident of the state for two years preceding the election or appointment. Like supreme court justices the judges of the court of appeals are chosen in nonpartisan elections and serve six-year terms of office. Unlike supreme court justices, however, they do not serve staggered terms; all three come up for election at the same time.

The Nevada court of appeals is different from those in most states that have one. In most states with an intermediate court of appeals the court of appeals sits between the trial courts and the supreme court.

That is, appeals from the trial courts go directly to the court of appeals and, if one of the parties is dissatisfied, the case could then be appealed to the state supreme court. Nevada instead uses what is called a deflective or "push down" model for the court of appeals. In this model cases continue as in the past to be appealed from the trial courts directly to the state supreme court. The supreme court will then push down some of these cases to the court of appeals to resolve. The court of appeals will make a decision (it has no discretion as to which cases to hear) and at that point a dissatisfied party may appeal back to the supreme court. However, because the parties have received one appeal, the supreme court has discretion as to whether to hear the case or to let the court of appeals decision stand.

This system is unusual but not unique. Intermediate courts of appeals in Iowa, Idaho, and Mississippi are similar. In the fiscal year ending 2016 after the court of appeals was operational, the supreme court received 2,452 new appeals and sent 637 of those, about a quarter, to the court of appeals for decision. Of those decided by the court of appeals, sixty-one were appealed back to the supreme court with that court denying fifty-four of those, thus letting the court of appeals decision stand. The creation of the court of appeals has had the concomitant effect of increasing the number of cases heard and decreasing the number of cases waiting for decision. As noted above, in fiscal year 2014 (prior to establishment of the court of appeals) the state supreme court had 1,988 cases pending, whereas in fiscal year 2016 (after the first year of operation for the court of appeals) it had only 1,519.

Nevada District Courts

District court judges are, like supreme court justices, chosen in nonpartisan elections for six-year terms. They must meet the same eligibility requirements as members of the high court except that they need only ten years of prior legal experience, not fifteen. Unlike supreme court justices, however, they do not serve staggered terms; the state constitution mandates that all district court judges stand for election at the same time. In a 2008 case involving a man who ran for district court judge in Winnemucca but lived in Reno, the state supreme court held that he was eligible for the office. The justices unanimously held that district court judges, although elected by district, serve in statewide offices with statewide jurisdiction. Therefore, as a statewide officer (much like,

TABLE 8.1. Judicial Districts in Nevada, 2018

DISTRICT	AREA ENCOMPASSED	NUMBER OF JUDGES
First	Carson City and Storey County	2
Second	Washoe County	15*
Third	Lyon County	2
Fourth	Elko County	2
Fifth	Esmeralda and Nye Counties	2
Sixth	Humboldt County	1
Seventh	Eureka, White Pine, and Lincoln Counties	2
Eighth	Clark County	52**
Ninth	Douglas County	2
Tenth	Churchill County	1
Eleventh	Pershing, Lander, and Mineral Counties	1

Source: Nevada Revised Statutes (N.R.S.) Section 3.010 et seq.
*Six of these judges are statutorily required to serve in family court.
**Twenty of these judges are statutorily required to serve in family court.

for example, the governor), the candidate need live only in the state of Nevada and not in the district in which the court is located.

Although the number has varied over the years, since 2015 there have been eleven judicial districts in Nevada. It is the prerogative of the legislature to determine the number and boundaries of these districts and the number of judges serving in them. Some districts may have only one judge; others will have several. The Eighth Judicial District, comprising only Clark County, is the state's most populous and, consequently, has the largest number of judges; in 2018, it had fifty-two, twenty of whom served in the family court division. Regardless of the number of judges in a judicial district, however, district courts are single judge courts, meaning that cases are heard by a single judge and not by a panel as in the supreme court. In some civil cases and in all "serious" criminal cases, defined as those in which the defendant may receive a penalty of incarceration of more than six months, the U.S. Supreme Court has determined that the defendant is entitled to a jury trial. It is always within the discretion of the defendant, however, to waive a jury trial and be tried solely by the judge. As noted in chapter 3, criminal-trial juries must be unanimous to reach a verdict, while civil juries may do so with only a three-fourths decision.

The district courts exercise both appellate and original jurisdiction. Their original jurisdiction is broad and includes all cases in which the legislature has not granted jurisdiction to the courts of limited jurisdiction. These cases involve more serious criminal offenses (felonies and gross misdemeanors) and civil cases over $15,000. However, under a law passed by the state legislature to reduce the district courts' workload, all civil cases of less than $50,000 must first be submitted to non-binding arbitration. If no agreement is reached, the case proceeds to district court for a hearing. Original jurisdiction of the district courts also includes the authority to hear appeals from the final orders of state administrative agencies such as the Gaming Control Commission. In addition, the district courts have power to issue the same writs as the supreme court. Decisions made by the district courts in any cases that are part of their original jurisdiction are appealable to the state supreme court.

The appellate jurisdiction of the district courts is found in their authority to hear appeals from the decisions of the municipal and justice courts. At one time, justice and municipal courts were not required to record their proceedings. Since they were not courts of record, all appeals from them to the district courts were given a trial *de novo*, that is, an entirely new trial. The large number of appeals from the courts of limited jurisdiction led, by the late 1970s, to a tremendous workload on the district courts. In 1979, the state legislature mandated that all justice courts tape-record their proceedings, thereby transforming them into courts of record. To reduce the district courts' workload further, a 1991 statute allows municipal courts to record their proceedings as well. Appeals from the justice courts and the municipal courts that have chosen to tape trials are no longer mandatory upon the district courts, and the appellants must show that they did not receive a fair trial.

In 1990, the voters approved a constitutional amendment allowing the legislature to establish family court divisions within the district courts. The legislature exercised that authority in 1991 and created family courts to hear cases involving issues such as child support and custody and other civil, domestic law matters, including concurrent jurisdiction with the district courts over criminal charges of domestic violence.

Beyond the family courts, Nevada also has forty-two other specialty courts. These courts, hosted within the existing district and family courts, are designed to provide a coordinated response by the prosecution, defense, probation, mental health experts, social services and child

protection services to treat root causes of criminal behavior such as alcoholism and drug addiction. Twenty-seven are in urban areas, while
fifteen are rural. They include seventeen adult drug courts, three family
drug courts, four juvenile drug courts, six DUI courts, five hybrid DUI/
drug courts, one prostitution prevention court, one veterans treatment
court, and two habitual offender courts.

Municipal and Justice Courts

The lowest tier in Nevada's judicial system, the courts of limited jurisdiction, consists of the justice and municipal courts. They have original
jurisdiction only and hear minor criminal and civil matters, most notably
traffic violations.

Judges in the justice courts are referred to as justices of the peace and
are selected by the voters of the state's forty-three townships in nonpartisan elections for six-year, staggered terms. The only constitutional
requirement for office is that they be qualified electors; the constitution
does not require them to be attorneys. However, by statute the legislature has additionally mandated that all justices of the peace have a high
school diploma or its equivalent. The legislature has further required
that in a county whose population is 700,000 or more a justice of the
peace in a township whose population is 100,000 or more must be an
attorney for at least five years. Likewise, only attorneys of five years or
more may serve as justices of the peace in a county whose population
is less than 700,000 and the township is 250,000 or more. These rules
are designed to apply to the urban areas in Washoe and Clark counties
where the justice courts' business tends to be more complex and where
the scarcity of lawyers that exists in the rural townships is not present.
Justice courts have three major duties: to hear cases involving minor
criminal offenses (misdemeanors), to hear civil cases of $15,000 or less,
and to hold preliminary hearings in felony and gross misdemeanor cases
to determine if there is probable cause to hold the defendant over for
trial in a district court.

One special division of the justice courts is small claims court. These
courts hear claims for money only and the amount the plaintiff is seeking to recover cannot exceed $10,000. Although one can hire an attor-
ney to argue his or her case in small claims court, the parties typically
represent themselves (what is called "pro se" representation) and the
process tends to be less formal and more relaxed. And, one cannot be

awarded attorney's fees in small claims court; thus, the party hiring an attorney would be responsible for paying the attorney's fees.

The eighteen incorporated cities in Nevada must also have a municipal court. The chief function of these courts is to hear traffic cases, cases involving recovery for the city of $2,500 or less, and cases involving violations of city ordinances. Municipal court judges are selected either by nonpartisan election or city council appointment, as determined by the city council or city charter. Those who are elected, such as judges in Sparks and Las Vegas, serve four-year terms of office while those who are appointed, as those in Boulder City, serve at the pleasure of the city council. State statute requires only that these judges be citizens of the state, a resident of the city for one year, and a qualified elector. The cities may also add to these qualifications, such as requiring municipal court judges to be lawyers.

Judicial Discipline, Removal, and Vacancies
Nevada Commission on Judicial Discipline

In 1976 the voters of Nevada approved a constitutional amendment establishing a state Commission on Judicial Discipline. The commission consists of seven members: two judges or justices appointed by the supreme court, two members of the State Bar of Nevada selected by the bar's board of governors, and three laypeople appointed by the governor. The 1976 amendment gave the commission authority only to censure, retire, or remove supreme court and district court judges and retire or remove, but not censure, municipal and justice court judges.

In 1994, however, the voters amended the constitutional provisions regulating the commission to allow the supreme court to establish other sanctions against misbehaving judges. In 1995 the supreme court adopted new rules that allow the commission to fine judges, prohibit them from running again, require them to issue public apologies, and force them to enter counseling or training programs. In addition, the commission was authorized by the court to issue public reprimands, something less than censure, against wayward judges. Any discipline imposed by the commission can be appealed to the state supreme court.

At least partly in response to the Whitehead proceedings noted above, the court also directed that once the commission has decided that a complaint against a judge has merit, all further proceedings must be open to the public. Furthermore, any sanctions issued against a judge must be made public. Previously some judges avoided public knowledge of their misdeeds by agreeing to private sanctions from the commission. The supreme court clearly hopes that making such matters public not only will make judges more obedient to the code of judicial conduct but also will help the public maintain its confidence in the state's judicial system. It may be too soon to know, but such disclosures may also have the unintended consequence of increasing the supreme court's workload, since judges might feel compelled to appeal all sanctions, no matter how small, in order to clear their names.

The Commission on Judicial Discipline has been especially active and visible over the past decades. The first time the commission voted to remove a judge was in 1987—District Court Judge Paul Goldman, who had already left the bench. In 1995 the commission removed North Las Vegas Municipal Court Judge Gary Davis from office for misconduct, and, in 1998, it purged from the bench Family Court Judge Fran Fine for having had conversations with one side of a case without including the other (*ex parte* conversations), a practice for which she had previously been fined and reprimanded by the commission in other cases in 1995. Among various censures and reprimands handed out by the commission, three other judges have been removed involuntarily from the bench. In 2008 the commission removed Clark County Family Court Judge Nicholas Del Vecchio from the bench after he admitted to various sexual improprieties. In 2007 the commission suspended Clark County District Judge Elizabeth Halverson from the bench due to her inexperience with the law and as a judge and her poor judgment. She was permanently removed by the commission in 2008, and that decision was upheld by the supreme court in 2011. And in 2012, Clark County Family Court Judge Steven Jones was suspended by the commission after he was indicted in an alleged investment-fraud scheme. In 2016 the commission banned Jones from ever serving as a judge in Nevada again. In 2017 the commission reprimanded Las Vegas Justice of the Peace Melanie Andress-Tobiasson for violating professional ethics codes, censured Las Vegas Justice of the Peace Conrad Hafen for violation of judicial canons and also banned him from future judicial office, suspended Goodsprings Justice of the Peace Dawn Haviland for one year for breaking ethics rules (she later resigned), and suspended Clark County Family Court Judge William Potter for two months for inappropriate behavior in his election campaign and on the bench.

TABLE 8.2. The Nevada Judiciary, Famous Firsts

First Hispanic to serve on the district court	John Mendoza (1967)
First African American to serve on the district court	Dell Guy (1975)
First woman to serve on the district court	Miriam Shearing (1983)
First woman to serve on the state supreme court	Miriam Shearing (1993)
First woman to serve as chief justice on the state supreme court	Miriam Shearing (1999)
First Hispanic woman to serve on the district court	Valorie Vega (1999)
First African-American woman to serve as a judge	Karen Bennett-Haron, JP (2002)
First African American to serve on the state supreme court	Michael Douglas (2004)
First African American to serve as chief justice	Michael Douglas (2011)
First Asian American to serve as a state judge	Jerry Tao (2011)
First openly gay Nevada Supreme Court justice	Lidia S. Stiglich (2017)

Source: Secretary of State's Office and the Nevada State Library and Archives.

Judicial Removal

Although voters always have the option of not returning a judge to the bench at election time, judges in Nevada may also be removed from office prior to the expiration of their terms in three ways. Under the original Nevada Constitution, they could be recalled but the supreme court in *Ramsey v. City of North Las Vegas* (2017) held that judges were not "public officers" as required for recall and, even if they were, the constitutional amendment adding the Nevada Commission on Judicial Discipline eliminated that option. With that option eliminated, the three ways they may be removed are that they may be retired or removed from the bench by the Commission on Judicial Discipline, and, in the case of supreme court justices and district court judges but not justices of the peace, they may be impeached, or otherwise removed by the legislature.

Legislative removal provides a method short of impeachment whereby the state legislature may remove a supreme court or district court judge for "any reasonable cause." The majority necessary to do so (a two-thirds majority of the elected members in both houses) is more stringent than that required for impeachment, but this procedure dispenses with the need to bring formal charges and to conduct a trial in the senate. Many

at the constitutional convention feared that such a process would under-
mine the independence of the judiciary. Others, however, believed that
some sort of process was necessary for removing judges in an emergency
situation or for dealing with a judge who was behaving badly but had
not engaged in any misdemeanor or malfeasance sufficient to invoke
impeachment.

The legislative removal provision was widely supported by the mining
interests at the convention. Given, as noted above, the tremendous financial stakes involved in mining litigation, they wished to have at their
disposal a faster and less formal method than impeachment to remove
"unfavorable judicial opinion."[5]

It is unclear after the *Ramsey* case whether legislative removal remains a legally viable option for judicial removal. The court majority
explicitly accepted in its opinion that impeachment was still permissible
because the constitutional provision adding the commission on judicial
discipline specifically noted impeachment as a possible option for removing judges. The amendment did not mention legislative removal nor did
the court's majority opinion, although it did say after its discussion on
legislative impeachment and the authority of the commission to remove
errant judges that "no other method of removal is retained." Thus, until
the legislature attempts to use this option and the targeted judge challenges it, the answer remains murky.

Judicial Vacancies

Prior to 1976, a vacancy on the supreme court or district courts was
filled by gubernatorial appointment. In 1976, however, the voters chose
to limit the governor's sole power to fill vacancies by approving a constitutional amendment creating the Nevada Commission on Judicial
Selection. Under this system, when a vacancy occurs the commission
takes applications from interested parties and recommends three names
to the governor. The governor then selects one of these three individuals
to fill the vacancy; he or she cannot go off the list and must make a selection within thirty days or be prohibited from making any other appointments until such time as he has filled the judicial vacancy. Judges
selected in this way serve only until the next general election, when they
must run in a nonpartisan election for the remainder, if any, of the term.

Those who support the election of judges on the basis that the electoral process is more likely to hold judges accountable will, no doubt, be

unpleasantly surprised to find that since 1939, 67 percent of the justices who served on the supreme court were initially appointed to their positions to fill midterm vacancies. It has also been the case in Nevada that incumbent judges, even those appointed to fill vacancies, are rarely if ever defeated at the polls. Since the state adopted nonpartisan elections in 1915, 93 percent of incumbents running for reelection to the supreme court have won; 71 percent of these winners failed to even draw an opponent.[6] Interestingly, although judicial elections in Nevada are nonpartisan, the supreme court in 2000 amended the Nevada Code of Judicial Conduct to allow judicial candidates to identify themselves as a member of a particular party when asked. However, they cannot list their party affiliation on campaign literature and advertising. That does not, however, prevent the political parties from mailing their own literature identifying party affiliations of judicial candidates, which they do.

Should a vacancy occur at the supreme court level, the so-called "permanent commission" determines the three names to be submitted to the governor. The "permanent commission" consists of the chief justice of the supreme court or an associate justice designated by him, three members of the state bar appointed by the bar's board of governors, and three laypeople named by the governor. Should the vacancy be at the district court level, the list of nominees is developed by a "temporary commission" made up of the permanent commission plus one other member of the state bar and one other layperson residing in the district in which the vacancy has occurred. The members of the permanent commission serve four-year, staggered terms of office, and the terms of the two additional members of a temporary commission expire once the list has been submitted to the governor.

Vacancies in the justice courts are filled by the county commission with jurisdiction over the particular township in which the vacancy occurs. Municipal court vacancies are filled according to the rules and regulations embodied in the city charter, typically city council appointments.

CHAPTER NINE

City and County Governments

It is generally true that most citizens pay far more attention to the actions of the national and state governments than they do to local governments such as counties and cities. This is due in part to the nature of the issues dealt with by those larger entities, such as war and peace and economic policies; in part it is due to the microscopic attention paid by the mass media to their every move. Yet, the policies and concerns of local governments affect citizens' lives in significant ways: taxes, streets, sewage and garbage services, law enforcement, zoning, liquor licenses, schools, and a host of others. Indeed, on a daily basis, these governments may have a more profound effect on citizens than those at the national and state levels.

It is worth noting, however, that the powers exercised by local governments are highly circumscribed by the state. Under the U.S. Constitution, states are autonomous and independent of the federal government in many ways. The Tenth Amendment reserves to the states all powers not delegated to the federal government or prohibited to the states. Thus, states are generally free to exercise these reserved powers as they see fit, so long as they do not infringe upon federal power or the civil liberties of their citizens.

The same is not true for local governments. They are considered creatures of the state and have no independent power; as subdivisions of the state they may exercise only those powers given to them by the state constitution and statutes. In 1911, John F. Dillon defined the powers of local governments:

It is a general and undisputed proposition of law that a municipal corporation possesses and can exercise the following powers, and no others: first, those granted in express words; second, those necessarily or fairly implied in or incident to the powers expressly granted; third, those essential to the accomplishment of the declared objects and purposes of the corporation—not simply convenient, but indispensable. Any fair, reasonable, substantial doubt concerning the existence of power is resolved by the courts against a corporation, and the power is denied.[1]

Dillon's rule, as this formulation is called, continues to hold sway in Nevada in the twenty-first century. True local government independence is called "home rule," which the Sagebrush State does not have. However, in 2015 the state legislature approved and Governor Brian Sandoval signed a law giving counties a limited version of home rule called "functional home rule." Under this provision, counties are allowed to exercise powers over those "matters of local concern" so long as they do not infringe upon federal or state jurisdiction while doing so. The law does not give them any additional authority over cities as these continue to be subject to state authority and their city charters. One other point of interest that will become clearer below is that local governing boards (e.g., county commissions and city councils) are not required to abide by the separation of powers that characterizes the national and state governments. These boards exercise executive, legislative, and, on occasion, quasi-judicial powers.

Counties and Townships

When Nevada's first territorial legislature met in 1861, it established nine counties. Between 1861 and 1864, two additional counties were created so that, at the time of statehood, Nevada had eleven. During its first decade of statehood, four more were created and one of the original nine, Roop County, was folded into Washoe County. Today, the state has seventeen counties; the most recently established was Pershing County (1919), although in 1969 the legislature consolidated Carson City and Ormsby County into a single city-county. Given that the state constitution requires a majority of a county's voters to approve the abolition of their county, it is doubtful that further changes will take place.

Article 4 of the state constitution requires the legislature to establish a "uniform" system of county and township governments. This language means that the legislature may not arbitrarily single out a certain county for special treatment; all must be treated uniformly. However, the state may distinguish between counties based on reasonable and neutral criteria. For example, the state supreme court has upheld a statute

TABLE 9.1. Nevada Counties

COUNTY	YEAR OF CREATION	CURRENT COUNTY SEAT
Carson City	1969	Carson City
Churchill	1861	Fallon
Clark	1909	Las Vegas
Douglas	1861	Minden
Elko	1869	Elko
Esmeralda	1861	Goldfield
Eureka	1873	Eureka
Humboldt	1861	Winnemucca
Lander	1862	Battle Mountain
Lincoln	1866	Pioche
Lyon	1861	Yerington
Mineral	1911	Hawthorne
Nye	1864	Tonopah
Pershing	1919	Lovelock
Storey	1861	Virginia City
Washoe	1861	Reno
White Pine	1869	Ely

Source: Dean Heller, *Political History of Nevada*, 2006, 11th ed., 122.
Reprinted with permission.

allowing consolidation of city and county law enforcement agencies in county seats with populations of more than 200,000, even though at the time the law was passed few cities and counties in the state would qualify. This distinction was permissible because it was "prospectively applicable to all counties which might grow into it."[2]

The governing board of each county is the Board of County Commissioners. The state constitution requires the legislature to establish these boards as elective positions, although the number and salary of commissioners is left to legislative discretion. Clark County's board, with seven commissioners, is the largest; the smallest boards, found in the least populous counties, have three. All county commissioners in the state are chosen in partisan elections for terms of four years. Midterm vacancies are filled by the governor.

As creations of the state, county boards of commissioners have historically exercised only the powers specifically given to them by the state legislature or the constitution. However, the establishment of functional home rule in 2015 has expanded their authority to act without a specific grant of power by the legislature so long as they do not infringe on federal or state jurisdiction. Their primary role is to perform the duties delegated to them by the state, such as law enforcement and administering state statutes on health, marriage, divorce, child custody, and property. Some of the more populous counties have also hired professional county managers to assist them in managing the county bureaucracies that were created to fulfill these responsibilities.

In addition to limits put upon them by the state, county commissioners and managers also find their powers over county government circumscribed by the fact that many county department heads are independently elected to their positions. Thus, these individuals are autonomous and dependent upon the voters, not the commissioners, for their continuance in office. Among these officers are the county clerk, district attorney, county recorder, county assessor, sheriff, and public administrator.

The legislature has also established forty-three townships within the state's seventeen counties. Unlike in some eastern states, townships are not particularly important in Nevada except as legal subdivisions in which justices of the peace are elected.

City Governments

Article 8 of the state constitution requires the legislature to enact laws providing for the organization of cities and towns. Cities, referred to in the constitution as "municipal corporations," may be established by general or special charters. A general charter is a "standard form of city government drawn up by the legislature that permits creation of a municipal government under its terms," while a special charter, as the name implies, is "usually drafted by a city to reflect its particular requirements," but which must still be approved by the legislature. Examples of the former are Ely and Winnemucca, while Reno and Las Vegas illustrate the latter.[3] Currently, there are eighteen incorporated cities in the state: eleven established by special charter and seven by general charter.[4]

Cities perform the same general functions within their boundaries as counties do within theirs, although their powers have historically been broader than those of the counties, although that is likely to change as

TABLE 9.2. Nevada's Incorporated Cities

City	Type of Charter	Year of Incorporation
Boulder City	Special	1959
Caliente	Special	1943
Carlin	Special	1925
Elko	Special	1917
Ely	General	1907
Fallon	General	1908
Fernley	General	2001
Henderson	Special	1953
Las Vegas	Special	1911
Lovelock	General	1917
Mesquite	General	1984
North Las Vegas	Special	1946
Reno	Special	1903
Sparks	Special	1905
Wells	Special	1927
West Wendover	General	1991
Winnemucca	General	1917
Yerington	Special	1907

Source: Brian Davie, Nevada Legislative Counsel Bureau. Used with permission.

a result of the grant of functional home rule to counties in 2015. They are governed by a city council chosen in nonpartisan elections. Unlike county government, which is subject to the structure imposed by the legislature, cities are free to adopt the form of government most attuned to their needs. In some cities, such as Las Vegas and Reno, the mayor is elected by the voters. In others, the city council selects the mayor from among its members.

Like the counties, some of the larger cities have hired professionals, city managers, to administer the bureaucracy. City managers, like county managers, serve at the pleasure of the council or commission, respectively. Unlike in the counties, most department heads are chosen by the manager rather than elected by the voters. Thus, the city council and manager tend to have greater control over the structure and functioning of city government than their counterparts in the county have over county government.

Other Local Governments

In 1955, the state legislature consolidated the state's 167 school districts into 17, one for each county. The Clark County School District, largest in the state, is also the fifth largest school district in the country and educates almost seventy-five percent of all students in Nevada. The governing body of each school district is an elected school board. The board, in turn, appoints a superintendent to manage the day-to-day affairs of the district. The school boards have tremendous discretion to establish district policies governing attendance, curriculum, and many other facets of their educational mission. They are, however, subject to the dictates of the state Board of Education. Until 2013 the board consisted of ten members elected in nonpartisan elections for four-year terms. However, at the urging of Governor Sandoval, the state legislature approved legislation giving the governor more control (and accountability) over public education in the state by making some of the board's members appointees. Since 2013 the board consists of four elected members (one in each congressional district), one voting member appointed by the governor, one voting member appointed by the governor but nominated by the majority leader of the state senate, and one voting member appointed by the governor but nominated by the speaker of the state assembly, for a total of seven voting members. In addition, there are four nonvoting members appointed by the governor, but his selections are limited by the fact that one must be a member of a school district board of trustees nominated by the Nevada Association of School Boards, one must be a superintendent of schools nominated by the Nevada Association of School Superintendents, one must be a regent of the Nevada System of Higher Education nominated by the Board of Regents, and one must be a pupil in a Nevada public school nominated by the Nevada Association of Student Councils. Elected members serve four-year terms, appointed voting members serve two-year terms, and appointed nonvoting members serve one-year terms. In addition to this rather complicated arrangement, the statute passed by the legislature makes the state superintendent of schools a gubernatorial appointee rather than a board appointee, as had previously been the case. Higher education in the state is governed by the Nevada System of Higher Education's elected thirteen-member Board of Regents, chosen in nonpartisan elections for six-year staggered terms.

The state also has established more than one hundred noneducation special district governments. Indeed, nationwide such districts are the fastest-growing entities at the local level. These district governments are responsible for performing a single function and include fire districts, health districts, water districts, library districts, and so on. They are governed by boards, some elected and some appointed, and some of them have the power to tax. As local government entities, they are also creations of the state and exercise only the powers given to them by the state and they may be altered by the state legislature.

CHAPTER TEN

State and Local Finance

Supreme Court Justice Oliver Wendell Holmes once noted that taxes are the price we pay for a civilized society. Although most can agree with Holmes's sentiment, questions over who will pay taxes and how those funds will be spent inevitably invite disagreement. Indeed, revenue and appropriations questions are the epitome of what we call "politics." Deciding who does and who does not pay taxes and who benefits from these moneys is the quintessential method of determining the winners and losers in the world of politics and government.

As noted in chapter 2, political conflict over taxation began early in the state's history. Territorial governor Nye had battled with the legislature at its first session in 1861 over whether mines and/or their products would be taxed. The 1863 constitution had been defeated, at least in part, because it included a provision taxing mines at the same rate as all other property. That "indiscretion" was avoided in the 1864 constitution, which taxed only mining proceeds.

Mines, however, were not the only industry in the state attempting to benefit from sympathetic constitutional provisions. The failed 1863 constitution had also included a section allowing the state to issue up to $3 million in bonds to assist in building a railroad. Noting that Nevada would be a poor state, especially since the delegates decided to limit taxes on the state's major industry, the 1864 delegates rejected a similar proposal to aid the wealthy railroad companies and included a provision in Article 8 prohibiting the state from donating or lending money or its credit to any corporation other than those considered educational or charitable.

The state constitution requires the biennial budget to be balanced. With the exception of the Clinton years, the federal government has had deficit budgets in most years since 1969, but Nevada's officials must equalize revenue and appropriations with a surplus available to deal with any emergencies that may arise. That has been made difficult over the years for a number of reasons: population growth, economic downturns, a general anti-tax stance within the state, and biennial budgeting.

For several years, Nevada has been one of the fastest-growing states in the nation. That growth has meant unpredictability in budgeting for two-year cycles. In the 2010 census, Nevada's population was 2,700,551, an increase of over 35 percent from the 2000 census, and more than five times the 488,738 living here in 1970. Of these almost three million residents, 1,951,269, or 72.3 percent, lived in Clark County, which had an almost unbelievable growth rate between 2000 and 2010 of 41.8 percent in spite of a crippled economy for half that decade. Although these new residents pay taxes, those revenues are spread over their lifetimes, while their needs (schools, roads, hospitals, recreation) are immediate. For example, even before they have paid a penny in taxes, these newcomers require roads for their cars and schools for their children. The need for immediate services among one of the fastest-growing populations in the nation has put tremendous strain on the state's ability to meet its citizens' needs, especially when budgets must be approved for two years at a time.

Biennial budgeting is even more difficult when it is based on an unstable revenue base. Over half of Nevada's revenue is based on gaming and sales taxes. These taxes are the most unstable of all types and create a certain degree of unpredictability in estimating state income over a two-year period. In an economic downturn, such as the state faced in the 2007–2009, 2009–2011, and 2011–2013 biennia, and after the September 11, 2001, terrorist attacks fewer people were likely to visit the gaming tables or purchase big-ticket items. Thus, in a recession, when residents' needs for state services such as unemployment compensation, food stamps, and welfare are at their highest, the revenues coming into the state's coffers from gaming and sales taxes will be in decline.

It was once observed that the perfect legislator is one who "votes for all appropriations, and against all taxes."[1] Indeed, most citizens want the government to offer a multitude of services; they simply do not want to pay for them. That is equally true in Nevada, which has managed to shift much of the tax burden to the state's visitors in the form of gaming and sales taxes. The state may suffer the consequences of an unstable tax base in a recession, but it seems to be a chance Nevada's residents are willing to take. Nevada's anti-tax stance is illustrated by the fact that in a 2017 study of 2015 data the state was ranked thirty-third in the nation in taxes collected per person at a per capita average of $5,487; by comparison the highest state was North Dakota at $12,455 per capita, the lowest was Alabama at $5,299, and the national average was $6,768.[2]

As noted in chapter 5, Nevada's low tax burden has frequently meant low levels of service for the state's poor and disabled, who have generally been unsuccessful at the lobbying game. It is also noteworthy that the state's residents have not only a lower than average state and local tax burden, they also have a slightly lower than average income. In 2015 residents of the Sagebrush State had the twenty-ninth-highest median per capita income among the fifty states at $52,431. This compares to a U.S. average of $55,775.[3]

Revenue

The state receives its revenue from a variety of sources: taxes, fees, fines, and the federal government. Not all of these funds can be expended at the state's discretion. Some federal funds, for instance, are earmarked for airports, highways, or education; some taxes and fees must be spent on particular programs such as fuel taxes that must be spent on transportation projects. In all, about 52 percent of the state's revenues are earmarked for particular purposes;[4] the remainder is disbursed at the discretion of the legislature, which must appropriate any money expended from the state treasury.

Taxes

Two forms of taxes are prohibited by the state constitution. State income taxes have long been prohibited by statute, but in the 1980s many in the state feared that the legislature might approve them in order to stabilize the state's tax base. A successful citizens' initiative in 1988 and 1990 put the issue outside legislative discretion by amending the constitution to prohibit taxes on personal income.

A constitutional amendment passed in 1942 prohibits the state from collecting inheritance taxes on the estates of deceased residents. Unfortunately, that provision also precluded the state from picking up its share of the *federal* estate tax; Nevada was the only state not to do so and its share, sometimes in the millions, reverted to the federal treasury. An attempt in 1982 to allow the state to pick up its share of the federal

TABLE 10.1. Nevada General Fund Revenues by Source, 1977–2017 (in Percent)

Biennium	Gaming Taxes	Live Enter. Tax*	Sales & Use Tax*	Commerce Tax	Business License Tax**	Insurance Prem. Tax	Cigarette Tax	Mining Tax	Liquor Tax Transfer	Slot Tax Transfer	Tobacco & Other Taxes	Nontax Revenues ***
2015–2017	19.6	4.0	30.1	3.2	2.8	9.1	4.6	0.5	1.2	0.1	0.3	6.0
2013–2015	25.5	4.9	34.0	NA	9.3	9.4	2.7	1.5	1.4	0.2	0.4	7.8
2011–2013	27.0	4.8	30.3	NA	8.5	9.1	3.1	1.1	1.5	0.2	0.4	8.8
2009–2011	26.6	4.7	32.4	NA	9.6	9.1	3.6	0.9	1.5	0.2	0.3	7.7
2007–2009	27.6	4.0	32.8	NA	9.6	8.8	3.4	0.7	1.3	0.1	0.3	6.9
2005–2007	27.3	4.8	33.2	NA	0.7	8.3	3.9	0.5	1.3	0.2	0.3	6.3
2003–2005	29.4	5.8	31.7	NA	1.0	7.9	4.7	0.4	1.4	0.2	0.3	6.5
2001–2003	34.0	3.7	37.7	NA	4.5	8.4	2.5	0.6	0.8	0.3	0.3	7.0
1999–2001	34.8	3.2	38.5	NA	4.8	7.8	2.7	0.9	0.9	0.3	0.4	5.7
1997–1999	35.1	2.6	38.4	NA	4.9	7.5	2.6	1.1	1.0	0.3	0.3	6.2
1995–1997	37.9	2.9	35.4	NA	4.9	7.2	2.7	1.7	1.1	0.4	0.2	5.6
1993–1995	41.3	2.5	31.8	NA	5.3	8.3	2.9	1.7	1.2	NA	0.2	4.8
1991–1993	40.1	2.3	32.6	NA	5.7	6.5	3.6	2.1	1.3	NA	0.2	5.6
1989–1991	40.0	2.3	35.2	NA	NA	7.2	4.4	3.3	1.5	0.6	0.3	5.2
1987–1989	41.4	3.0	35.5	NA	NA	7.7	2.4	1.7	1.9	0.8	0.3	5.3
1985–1987	43.7	3.3	36.2	NA	NA	5.9	1.6	NA	2.3	1.0	0.4	5.6
1983–1985	42.3	3.5	33.8	NA	NA	7.2	1.3	NA	2.4	1.2	0.4	6.5
1981–1983	42.3	5.7	39.6	NA	NA	3.9	NA	NA	2.6	NA	NA	5.9
1979–1981	41.5	5.8	39.9	NA	NA	4.2	NA	NA	3.2	NA	NA	5.4
1977–1979	37.6	6.3	36.8	NA	NA	3.3	NA	NA	4.3	NA	NA	5.5

Source: Compiled by the author from the Legislative Counsel Bureau's *Nevada Legislative Appropriations Report* for each of the biennial periods.

*The Casino Entertainment Tax is now the Live Entertainment Tax and applies to all live entertainment in venues of 200 or more seats. Ninety percent of the revenue comes from casinos.

**In 2003 the state legislature eliminated the Business License Tax and replaced it with the Modified Business Tax (MBT). The later figures are for the MBT.

***Includes fees for licenses, fines, charges for services, use of money and property, and miscellaneous revenue.

Note: Rows will not always total 100 percent, since some revenue measures have been omitted.

estate tax was defeated by the voters; apparently they thought that the proposal would create additional taxes rather than simply give the state its share of federal taxes already collected. In the 1986 election, with assurances in hand that the proposal would not create any new or increased taxes, the voters approved amending the constitution. The 1986 amendment is important because many wealthy individuals, drawn to the state by its lack of an income tax and its generally low taxes, choose to live (and die) here. Nevada may now pick up its share of what is often a substantial federal estate tax. Proceeds of the tax credit are earmarked solely for education.

Until recently, gaming taxes made up the largest share of the state's revenue. There are four different types of gaming taxes in Nevada, and their distribution differs from type to type. The largest source of gaming taxes is on the gross gambling income of each casino. Proceeds from the tax go into the state's general fund to be appropriated by the legislature. The second source of gaming taxes is derived from an annual tax of $250 on each slot machine. Revenue from the slot machine tax is earmarked 80 percent for education and 20 percent to pay off bonds sold to construct and renovate the Thomas & Mack Center at the University of Nevada, Las Vegas, and the Lawlor Events Center at the University of Nevada, Reno. Third among the gaming taxes is the live entertainment tax, which is applied to live entertainment events in gaming and nongaming establishments; like the gross receipts tax, it is deposited into the general fund. The live entertainment tax, currently a 9 percent tax on admission, applies to all live entertainment in or out of casinos. However, 90 percent of this tax is generated in casino venues. Finally, the state levies a tax on each gaming table in Nevada, with the revenues being divided evenly among the seventeen counties. Without this tax, generated primarily in Clark and Washoe Counties, the less-populated counties in the state would have difficulty meeting their revenue needs.

One sort of gaming tax that will not be found is on lotteries. To the surprise of many outside the state, the Nevada Constitution prohibits lotteries. Until the constitution was amended in 1990, that provision also made it illegal to run a church raffle or other charitable lottery. Although the constitutional prohibition on charitable lotteries was frequently ignored, the voters decided that an exemption to the lottery ban was in order if for no other reason than to recognize actual practice. Attempts to amend the constitution to allow a lottery regularly fail in the legislature over the economic concerns of the gaming corporations and the moral concerns of those who fear lotteries will increase gambling addiction and hurt the poor.

Gaming taxes and sales taxes, as noted earlier, make up over half of the state's revenue and are popular in the state, since much of these taxes are paid, at least indirectly, by tourists. Sales taxes began in Nevada in 1955 at a level of 2 percent; proceeds go into the state's general fund. The tax was brought to a referendum vote by the people in 1956 and was approved. Because the 2 percent level was approved in a popularly initiated referendum, it is immunized from legislative change, as explained in chapter 4; it can be added to only by another vote of the people. In a special election in 1963, the voters refused to raise the tax to 3 percent.

In order to meet the state's dire need for additional revenue to fund the public schools, the legislature in 1967 added a 1 percent "school support tax," to be collected at the point of all sales. Because the 1 percent was earmarked for education and was returned to the county in which it originated, the Nevada Supreme Court held that it was not a "sales" tax and, thus, did not violate the constitution.[5] In 1969, the legislature further provided for an optional one-half cent city-county relief tax to aid those counties and cities in need of additional revenues; like the school support tax, these taxes do not go into the state's general fund and are not, therefore, considered "sales" taxes. As of 2017, those making purchases in the state pay a 2 percent sales tax, 2.60 percent school support tax, and 2.25 percent city-county relief tax for a total tax rate of 6.85 percent. However, the only counties that actually charge that rate are Esmeralda, Eureka, Humboldt, and Mineral. All other counties have exercised their option to charge additional taxes for specific purposes such as transportation, tourism, public safety, and water systems improvements. The highest rates are to be found in Washoe (8.265 percent) and Clark (8.25 percent) counties while the remaining counties range between 7.1 percent and 7.725 percent.

That Nevada currently has one of the highest "sales" taxes in the country is the result of a deliberate decision by the state to shift the tax burden away from property owners and onto tourists. In order to stave off a proposal similar to California's Proposition 13, Governor List and the 1981 legislature approved a shift that would reduce property taxes, paid almost entirely by Nevada residents, and raise sales taxes, paid by residents and tourists alike. That List's ploy was successful can be seen in the voters' rejection of Question 6 (Nevada's version of Proposition 13) in the 1982 election.

List's "success," however, must be measured against two important facets of reliance upon sales taxes rather than property taxes for state revenue. Sales taxes are less stable and more difficult to predict than are property taxes. Thus, as noted earlier, in an economic downturn when residents' needs for social services are highest, sales taxes will be in decline. Second, sales taxes are regressive. That is, unlike an income tax, which has rates that increase as income increases, the sales tax actually takes a higher percentage of one's income the lower his or her earnings. A 1982 study concluded that a family of four living in Las Vegas with an income of $17,500 would spend 2.4 percent of their income in direct state and local taxes; direct taxes would take only 1.2 percent of the income of the same family making $100,000.[6] A national study in 2000 found that the poorest 20 percent of Americans, those earning less than $25,700 per household, pay 3.5 percent of their income in sales taxes while the top 20 percent, those households making $75,000 or more, pay only 1.3 percent.[7] And a 2015 study by the Institute on Taxation and Economic Policy found that, in Nevada, the richest 1 percent pay a state and local tax rate of 1.4 percent, the middle 20 percent pay 6.6 percent, and the poorest 20 percent pay at a rate of 8.4 percent. In order to reduce the regressivity of the tax somewhat, Nevada's voters approved a constitutional amendment in 1984 exempting food from the sales tax. Nonetheless, a study by the Pew Center on the States in 2003 rated Nevada as the worst state in the U.S. for fairness of its tax system. The report, published by *Governing* magazine noted that Nevada's tax system is "regressive and dysfunctional" and that it "hits lower-income residents hardest."[8]

As a result of the tax shift of 1981, Nevadans pay one of the lowest property tax rates in the country. By statute, property is assessed at 35 percent of its market value. Thus, a $100,000 home is assessed at $35,000. A 1936 amendment to the state constitution limits the property tax to a maximum of 5 cents per every dollar of assessment. Thus, the maximum property tax that could be collected on a $100,000 home would be $1,750 ($35,000 × .05). In fact, the state's property tax rate comes nowhere near the maximum allowed by the constitution, and most of what is collected by the state in property taxes is returned to local governments.

Property taxes became a lively issue once again in the 2005 session of the state legislature. Although these taxes remain generally low by comparison to other states, rampant appreciation in the cost of housing and property in the Sagebrush State caused home valuations to rise dramatically, thus leading to the possibility of huge increases in property tax bills (amounting to 300 percent or more) for individual property owners. In order to spare homeowners that shock, and to stave off even more draconian measures, the legislature established a cap on property taxes. Under this 2005 law, property taxes cannot rise more than 3 percent per year on owner-occupied homes and no more than 8 percent on other types of property and businesses. Although this "split roll" would appear quite clearly to violate the Nevada Constitution's requirement that all property be taxed at a "uniform and equal rate," it is unlikely that it will be challenged in the courts. Were the litigants to win, their victory would be a Pyrrhic one as the entire cap would be declared unconstitutional and property taxes would rise quickly and by substantial amounts. And, given the incredible increases in property values in the state, even those whose property is capped at the higher 8 percent level receive substantial tax relief from the law. In 2005 alone, taxpayers in the Sagebrush State saved almost $300 million. The downside to this tax relief is that local and county governments will be more dependent upon unpredictable and fickle sales taxes to fund services to their citizens. Although property taxes tend to be more stable and predictable than sales taxes, the Great Recession that hit Nevada in 2007–2011 caused the housing bubble in the state to burst. When it did, property values took a nosedive, as did the concomitant collection of property taxes. Cities and counties, which are dependent upon these property taxes, found themselves in dire straits and began cutting millions of dollars and hundreds of employees from their budgets. Because of the 3 percent and 8 percent caps on increases in property taxes year over year, the cities and counties find themselves in a situation where property values are rising at substantially higher rates but property taxes cannot.

In 1991 the legislature approved a business tax of $100 per employee up to a maximum of $400,000. The $400,000 cap was criticized because it worked to the benefit of the state's largest casinos, and in 1993 the legislature removed it in favor of a flat rate per employee, no matter how large the enterprise. The business tax was repealed by the state legislature in 2003 and replaced with a Modified Business Tax (MBT). Although financial institutions such as banks and mines are taxed at a higher rate (2.0 percent) than non-financial institutions (1.475 percent), the latter pay more of these taxes due to their sheer numbers. During the 2015–2017 biennium, the MBT was expected to bring in about 14.7 percent of the state's revenue.

A new type of business tax was also created by the 2015 legislature at Governor Sandoval's urging. The Commerce Tax is a gross receipts tax on businesses in the Sagebrush State with gross revenue exceeding $4 million. The tax rate varies depending upon the type of business but, given that the first $4 million in revenue is exempt from the tax, it is expected that it will apply to less than 10 percent of the businesses in the state. Although the tax was and remains controversial, in the 2015–2017 biennium the Commerce Tax was expected to bring in only about 3.2 percent of state revenues.

Excise taxes are the final type of tax used in Nevada. Like sales taxes, they are collected at the time of purchase. Unlike sales taxes, they are collected only on selected items, such as fuel, cigarettes, alcohol, and insurance. Proceeds from fuel taxes and license fees are earmarked by Article 9 of the state constitution for purposes of "construction, maintenance, and repair" of public roads. Cigarette taxes, which in 2015 were raised to $1.80 per pack, are distributed to the counties and incorporated cities on the basis of population. During the 2015–2017 biennium, it is estimated, the cigarette tax will provide about 4.6 percent of the state's revenue and a tax on insurance premiums will make up another 9.1 percent.

In addition to taxes, state and local revenues are also derived from fines and fees. Parking and traffic fines add to the government's coffers as do fees on everything from marriage, hunting, and fishing licenses to motor vehicles. The federal government also provides various moneys to the state in the form of grants. Typically, the use of these funds is highly circumscribed and they may be used only for a designated purpose, such as education, highways, airports, and the like.

A close examination of table 10.1 shows some interesting trends in Nevada's tax base. Gaming taxes, which include the "Gaming Taxes" and "Live Entertainment Tax" categories, after 1977 regularly accounted for more than 40 percent of the state's revenue stream. However, beginning with the 1997–99 biennium, the contribution by gaming has just as regularly fallen into the 30 to 38 percent range. Nonetheless, even though gaming's share of tax contributions has dropped consistently, the gaming industry has been uniformly victorious in fending off attempts to raise what is currently the lowest gaming tax in the country

(6.75 percent compared to Maryland's top rate (for slot machines) of 67 percent). Table 10.1 also indicates that, with the exception of the 2011–2013 biennium, sales and use taxes supplanted gaming taxes as the largest single source of revenue for the state since the 1997–1999 biennium. In the 2015–2017 biennium, it was projected that sales and use taxes will contribute 30.1 percent of the state's revenue while gaming taxes (19.6 percent) and the live entertainment tax generated primarily by casinos (4.0 percent) will bring in a total of 23.6 percent. No doubt this is in large part due to the fact that the state's casinos, in their competition with Native American gaming and gaming in almost every state in the Union, are now advertising themselves not simply as houses of gambling, but as total destination resorts for shopping, spas, restaurants, and theme parks. As tourists come to the state for these amenities, they, of course, pay the sales taxes on them, thus driving up the percentages in this category. Also, of course, the state's tremendous gains in population translate into more residents purchasing more goods, thus paying more sales taxes. Of further note in table 10.1 is the decline of mining taxes as a percentage of the state's revenue, from a high of 3.3 percent in 1989–1991 to less than 1 percent in all but two biennia since 1999–2001. Although Nevada's mines continue to be among the most productive in the world, these figures are, at least in part, indicative of the comparative decrease in their importance to the state's economy compared to tourism and gaming.

Appropriations

As noted in chapter 7, the governor's budget proposals are usually accepted, virtually intact, by the legislature. The extent to which the legislature is willing to change the governor's proposals will vary from year to year but is always constrained by the fact that the legislature has only four months to review, revise, and approve a budget that has taken the governor two years to develop. In the 2017–2019 biennium, the state's general fund was approximately $7.9 billion.

In addition to using the funds it receives from the operating budget, which must be balanced, the state may finance its operations by borrowing money through bond sales. Revenue from these bonds is typically used to finance long-term construction projects such as highways and the new addition to the legislative building in Carson City. The bonds are paid off over a long period of time, thus freeing current taxpayers of the burden of paying the entire tab now for projects that will be used by future residents as well. The 1864 constitution established a bonding limit on the state of $300,000. That a specific numerical cap was injudicious quickly came to be realized when, in the early twentieth century, the state had difficulty making capital improvements out of current operating revenue. In 1916, the constitution was amended to establish a bonding capacity of 1 percent of the state's assessed valuation. After a defeat by voters in 1960, the bonding capacity was raised to 2 percent in 1989.

The state's budget is an excellent prism through which to view the needs and desires of the citizens of Nevada. By far the highest level of appropriations in the state is for education. During the seventeen biennial budget periods between 1977 and 2017, state spending on education has, with only eight exceptions, decreased as a proportion of state spending every cycle, in spite of the fact that the number of students has increased dramatically during the same period. From a high of 60.2 percent of the state's budget appropriations in 1979, education's share had, by the 2001–2003 biennium, fallen to 52.4 percent, the lowest level in at least three decades. During the Great Recession of 2007–2011, education spending by the state continued to hover in the 54 percent region. By the 2011–2013 biennium, such spending had dropped to nearly record lows again, coming in at only 52.8 percent although it has rebounded a bit in 2013–2015 to 53.8 percent and 2015–2017 to 53.2 percent. Although education at all levels in the state was victim to the bad economy, higher education was affected most seriously and disproportionately. Whereas funding for K–12 education went up from 34.7 percent to 39.2 percent of the state's budget between the 2003–2005 biennium and the 2013–2015 biennium, spending on higher education by the state dropped in that same period from 20.5 percent to 14.6 percent, a loss of a quarter of its previous funding ratio. In the 2017–2019 biennium the state added $131 million in general funds to support higher education for a total of $1.2 billion for all seven campuses.

Not only has the number of students at all levels increased rapidly, larger and larger numbers of these students are first-generation students, or students who face disabilities, or who come from homes where English is not the first language. Such factors further increase the need for adequate educational funding beyond even what the raw numbers suggest. In Clark County, for example, over 46 percent of students are

Table 10.2. Nevada General Fund Appropriations by Type, 1977–2017 (in Percent)

Biennium	Constitutional Officers	Finance and Admin.	Education	Human Services	Commerce and Industry	Public Safety	Infrastructure	Special Purpose Agencies
2015–2017	4.1	1.7	53.2	29.8	1.6	8.6	0.8	0.2
2013–2015	3.0	1.4	53.8	30.8	1.4	8.7	0.7	0.2
2011–2013	3.1	1.3	52.8	31.2	1.3	9.4	0.8	0.1
2009–2011	3.0	1.5	54.9	29.5	1.3	8.7	0.9	0.2
2007–2009	2.9	1.8	54.5	28.3	1.5	9.8	1.0	0.2
2005–2007	2.8	3.0	54.2	28.3	1.7	8.9	0.9	0.2
2003–2005	3.6	1.1	55.4	27.5	1.8	9.4	1.0	0.2
2001–2003	3.2	2.5	52.4	27.4	2.1	10.8	1.1	0.4
1999–2001	3.5	1.5	55.0	24.4	2.4	11.6	1.3	0.3
1997–1999	3.2	2.3	53.5	26.0	2.4	11.0	1.4	0.2
1995–1997	3.0	2.6	53.9	25.8	2.3	10.9	1.4	0.1
1993–1995	2.8	1.6	55.0	25.9	2.5	10.6	1.5	0.1

Biennium	General Government	Regulatory	Education	Human Resources	Conservation	Public Safety	Motor Vehicles and Highways	Misc.
1991–1993	4.6	2.6	54.9	23.7	2.1	10.8	0.5	0.8
1989–1991	4.5	2.7	56.7	22.6	2.0	10.2	0.3	1.0
1987–1989	5.0	3.0	57.7	21.2	2.2	9.7	0.3	0.9
1985–1987	5.2	3.2	57.7	20.2	2.2	8.6	0.5	2.4
1983–1985	5.8	3.5	55.2	23.2	2.1	9.0	0.4	0.8
1981–1983	5.5	3.4	52.6	23.3	2.4	7.8	0.5	4.5
1979–1981	5.4	3.0	60.2	19.3	2.4	6.1	0.5	3.1
1977–1979	6.5	3.0	56.3	21.9	2.9	6.0	NA	3.4

Source: Compiled by the author from the Legislative Counsel Bureau's Nevada Legislative Appropriations Report for each of the biennial periods.
Note: The break between the 1991–1993 and 1993–1995 biennial periods indicates the change in categories used by the Legislative Counsel Bureau.

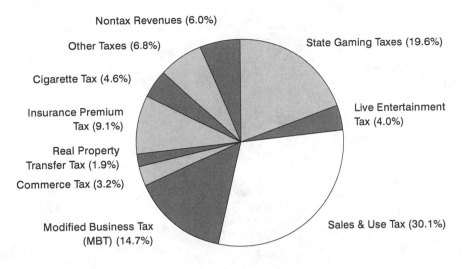

Nontax Revenues (6.0%)

Other Taxes (6.8%)

State Gaming Taxes (19.6%)

Cigarette Tax (4.6%)

Insurance Premium Tax (9.1%)

Live Entertainment Tax (4.0%)

Real Property Transfer Tax (1.9%)

Commerce Tax (3.2%)

Modified Business Tax (MBT) (14.7%)

Sales & Use Tax (30.1%)

Subtotal of all taxes: 94%

FIGURE 10.3. Nevada General Fund Revenue, Adjusted Economic Forum Forecast (by legislative action only), 2015–2017 Biennium. *Source*: "Forecast of Future State Revenues," State of Nevada Economic Forum (2014).

Hispanic, 64 percent receive free or reduced-cost meals, and 20 percent are English language learners. To assist with these needs Governor Sandoval proposed the legislature approve additional funds in the form of Zoom funding (2013) for schools with high ratios of English language learners and Victory funds (2015) for underperforming schools. In 2017 the weights used to distribute school funding were raised for special education and English language learners to provide additional funds for these students who require greater resources.

In contrast, state spending for human services has increased over the past three decades, constituting 21.9 percent of the total budget in 1977–1979 and 29.8 percent in 2015–2017. At least some of this increase is attributable to the increased need for these services in the face of a very bad economy during the Great Recession.

Education and human services accounted for 83 percent of the state's operating budget for the 2015–2017 biennium. The remaining amount was spent on prisons, highways, public safety, and the provision of other services in the state. That amount also includes various appropriations for special interest, or "pork barrel," projects favored by pow-

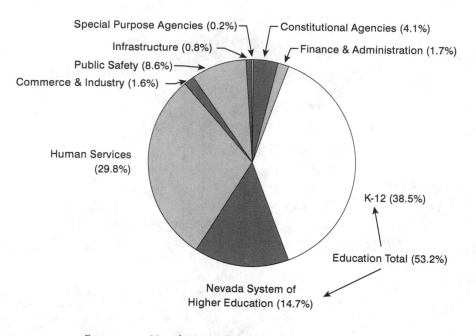

FIGURE 10.4. Nevada General Fund, Legislature-Approved Appropriations, 2015–2017 Biennium. *Source*: Legislative Counsel Bureau, *Nevada Legislative Appropriations Report, 2015–2017*.

erful legislators. An egregious example of pork barrel funding at its worst is when, at the same time it failed to provide funds for a Las Vegas woman's heart transplant, the 1995 legislature approved spending $3.2 million on the National Automobile Museum in Reno, $2.5 million for a railway between Boulder City and the Clark County Heritage Museum in Henderson, $5 million to rebuild the V & T Railroad between Carson City and Virginia City, and $250,000 for an animal pavilion at the Clark County Fairgrounds.

CHAPTER ELEVEN

Nevada
Past, Present, and Future

Chapters 1 and 2 examined the history of Nevada through 1864. The subsequent eight chapters outlined, within the context of individual topics, the state's historical and political path since it achieved statehood. It seems appropriate, therefore, in this final chapter to discuss and summarize in chronological sequence Nevada's leading historical and political epochs since 1864 and look forward to the state's future in the twenty-first century.

Nevada Since 1864

In a thoughtful work published in 1986, Nevada historian James Hulse suggested that the state's history tended to fall into three forty-year periods: 1859 to 1899, 1900 to 1939, and 1940 to 1980.[1] Hulse's timelines are certainly not the only ones extant; however, they offer the virtues of simplicity and brevity and constitute an excellent framework for an examination of Nevada history, with the addition of a period beginning in 1980.

The First Period: 1859–1899

The opening of a new frontier brings out the most adventurous and rapacious among a nation's population. That was certainly true in Nevada, where the first forty-year period was characterized by greed, avarice, and unbridled entrepreneurism. In the late 1850s, a California visitor to Nevada wrote in a letter home that

> I have seen more rascality, small and great, in my fairly brief forty days' sojourn to this wilderness of sagebrush, sharpers, and prostitutes, than in a thirteen years' experience in our not squeamishly moral State of California.... If I resided here six months I should turn out a consummate rascal.[2]

Organization of the territorial and state governments has been covered in some detail in chapter 2; it is unnecessary to discuss it further here. However, much of what occurred between 1859 and 1864 had a great influence on the first years of Nevada's statehood.

Issues related to mining economics dominated the period from statehood until the end of the nineteenth century, as had been the case prior to statehood. The major difference between the pre-statehood and post-statehood periods, however, was one of mine ownership. Prior to statehood, thousands of miners staked claims to the Comstock Lode. After statehood, ownership of the mines was concentrated in the hands of a wealthy few, the so-called Bank Crowd.

By 1864, it began to appear that the major mining lodes were depleted. In a move that well defines the era, the Bank of California, founded by William C. Ralston in that year, began lending money at discount rates to the state's ore mills. The idea to do so came from Ralston's Virginia City branch manager, William Sharon, about whom it "is probably impossible to find a really kind word that was ever said...and preserved in print."[3] Sharon's gamble paid off when the Depression continued and the mill owners could not repay the loans: the bank simply took over their mills. Eventually, the bank and its subsidiaries took control of mills and mines, the worth of which was far in excess of the value of the loans they had made. Their hold on the state's mining industry was made complete when in addition to monopolizing water and timber supplies the banks seized control of transportation by incorporating the Virginia and Truckee (V & T) Railroad Company to build a railway between the ore deposits and Carson City-Reno. Until 1875, the Bank Crowd dominated every aspect of Nevada's mining industry, and thus dominated the state's politics.

In 1875 a run on the Bank of California led to its failure when the bank, weighed down by unsafe investments, was unable to pay its depositors; Ralston responded by committing suicide. After 1875, the Bank of California and its subsidiaries were replaced in prominence by the Bonanza Firm of John W. Mackay, James G. Fair, James C. Flood, and William S. O'Brien. The Bonanza Kings, as these four were known, were responsible for discovering and exploiting the "Big Bonanza" gold and silver ore lode. Like the Bank Crowd before them, they solidified their economic power by coupling their mineral wealth with ownership in milling companies, water companies, and lumber resources.

Because of their economic power within the state, the Bank Crowd and the Bonanza Kings were also able to generally have their way in the political arena. At the federal level, Senator William Stewart did their bidding, and his lasting contribution was the National Mining Act of 1866, which allowed the mining companies to take public lands and water merely by using them. The mining law, still in effect today, also allows mining companies to "patent" (i.e., purchase) public land for five dollars or less an acre; in addition, the mines pay no royalties for the privilege of digging up and carting off the nation's mineral resources.

At the state level, the mining and banking interests were no less successful. In 1865 the first state legislature enacted legislation that would allow a property tax levy of $2.75 per $100 of assessed valuation. However, in its infamous Section 99 the law also provided that the levy on the proceeds of the mines would be limited to $1.00 per $100 of valuation. In addition, a $20 per ton deduction was allowed for working the ore and only three-fourths of the remaining amount could be taxed. As historian Russell Elliott has noted, "The mine owners got a three-way benefit in taxation, first in the state constitution, which specified that mines and mining claims were to be assessed on net proceeds only, and then in the revenue act of 1865, which allowed the deduction for working the ore and then taxed only a portion of the remainder."[4]

The revenue act was declared unconstitutional in 1867,[5] but the Bank Crowd had already convinced the legislature in 1867 and 1871 to pass substitute legislation that would continue preferential tax treatment for the mines. Legislation in 1875 ended that preference, and a series of setbacks in the courts and through gubernatorial vetoes established a more equitable taxation structure in the state. As discussed in chapter 10, the mines were not the only industry seeking to control the state's politics and economy. Indeed, the railroads were generally more successful than the Bank Crowd and the Bonanza Kings had been in having their way in the state and federal governments. Congress gave the railroads 5 million acres of land in Nevada. And it is beyond dispute that the Central Pacific and the V & T Railroads overcharged Nevada customers and avoided paying their just due in taxes. Nevada congressman Rollin Daggett, for example, noted in an 1881 speech that the cost of shipping a carload of coal oil from New York to San Francisco was $300; that same carload shipped from New York to Reno would cost $536 and $716 from New York to Winnemucca.[6] In comments reminiscent of those about the wealthy California mining companies that were made at the 1864 state constitutional convention, Daggett observed that "Nevada is an orange which for ten years these railroad vampires have been sucking in silence. We have been, and are still, bleeding at every pore."[7]

That the railroads were so successful in having their way can be attributed to their selection of astute political agents and a win-at-all-costs attitude. The "Big Four" of the Central Pacific Railroad (Leland Stanford, Charles Crocker, Mark Hopkins, and Collis P. Huntington) hired the services of Charles "Black" Wallace, and the V & T Railroad utilized the skills of its agent, H.M. Yerington, to control the state's government. They "literally bought legislators who promised to work for the railroad interest," they controlled delegations to the party conventions "obtaining favorable platforms," and they gave out free railroad passes and other favors to their allies.[8] Yerington gloated in an 1879 letter that

> during every Nevada legislature since 1869 bills have been introduced to regulate freight and fares, and many other matters connected with the working of railroads in this state, most of them have been of a blackmailing character requiring *Coin* to prevent them from being introduced or to get them out of the road after introduction. This Co. has put up the Coin in large sums every session and the result has been not one bill inimical to railroads has been passed during all these years.[9]

At the national level, the Big Four were able to influence Nevada's U.S. senators, especially William M. Stewart and John P. Jones, through various gifts and favors, including two hundred shares of Central Pacific Railroad stock given to Stewart in 1866.[10] They even managed to get one of their own elected to the Senate in 1875 when William Sharon of the V & T Railroad was chosen by the state legislature, a state legislature filled with men who were, in most respects, in office because of vote buying and the railroads' largess to their campaigns.

The purpose of all this activity on the part of the railroads was, of course, to defeat legislation at both the state and national levels calling for regulation of railroad freight rates. In that, they were generally successful until 1887, when Congress passed national railroad regulation in the form of the Interstate Commerce Act.

From the mid-1860s until the end of the first forty-year period in 1899, known ore deposits began to be mined out and the state suffered the blows of a serious mining depression exacerbated by federal monetary policies. In 1873 Congress passed the Mint Act, known in the western United States as the Crime of '73. The Mint Act put the United States on the gold standard and eliminated the minting of silver coins. With government demand for silver down and demand for gold rising, the price paid and the demand for Nevada's chief industrial product decreased dramatically. Attempts by the western states to convince Congress to return to bimetallism were defeated with the exception of a few minor, short-lived victories such as the Sherman Silver Purchase Act in 1890, which required the federal government to purchase 4½ million ounces of silver per month. It was repealed in 1893.

The Crime of '73 led to splits in both the Democratic and Republican parties and the eventual dominance in the state of the newly minted Silver Party. Democrats and Republicans alike fled their parties to join the Silver Party; and in the election of 1892, the Silver Party in Nevada won all three presidential electors, the race for the state's only congressional seat, and numerous seats in the legislature. That trend continued in state elections through 1906, when the Silver or Silver Democrat parties won virtually all major state and national elections in Nevada.

By 1900, however, the Silver Party was already in decline with the discovery of other silver and gold ore lodes in the state, the discovery and increased national and international importance of copper, and the decreasing significance of the silver issue at the national level. Before moving on to Nevada's second forty-year period, however, it is also worth noting that during this first period various movements for political and economic reform began to take hold in the state. Although their goals would not be achieved until the early twentieth century, supporters of women's suffrage, direct election of senators, western water projects, and railroad regulation began to see their issues seriously debated in the state during the silver period.

The Second Period: 1900–1939

The end of Nevada's mining depression came in 1900 when silver and gold were found near Tonopah and Goldfield in the southern part of the state. As had been the case in northern Nevada, mining towns in southern Nevada boomed and, eventually, busted. During that period of roughly a quarter century, however, various individuals in the state grew rich and powerful. Among the most influential were Key Pittman and

Tasker Oddie, who started their political careers, and George Wingfield, who made his fortune during the Tonopah-Goldfield boom.

By 1912, silver and gold were being replaced by copper, needed to supply the electrical industry of the early twentieth century's industrial revolution, as the state's chief mining export. In 1900 a large vein of copper was discovered in White Pine County near Ely, which accelerated the construction of company towns in the region to house the men who would mine it. These company towns often included stores, schools, and hospitals; they were planned communities, quite unlike the muddy, disorganized, and often-dangerous tent cities that had sprung up during the earlier mining period. What is also notable about the mines of the copper era is that unlike the gold and silver mines in the north, they were not dominated by California companies. Those who made their fortunes from the copper mines tended to stay in Nevada and contribute to the state's development. Demand for copper would continue to fuel the state's mining industry through the two world wars and the Korean War, until copper prices dropped in the 1970s.

By far the most important political and historical aspect of the first two decades of the twentieth century in Nevada was the state's support for Progressive Era reforms that gave the voters more control over their own government and reduced the power of the wealthy elite who often dominated the legislature and government officials. As noted in chapter 4, the state adopted the three direct democracy election methods of initiative, referendum, and recall between 1904 and 1912. In 1909 the legislature established the office of mine inspector to ensure mine safety for Nevada's working miners, and in 1911 a workman's compensation bill was passed to aid those injured on the job. In 1914, the efforts of Dr. Anne Martin, Dr. Jeanne Weir, and Ms. O. H. Mack paid off when women were given the right to vote. The Direct Primary Law was passed in 1909, establishing democratic primaries rather than backroom caucuses as the means for party selection of candidates and requiring that the state legislature abide by a popular vote in its appointment of U.S. senators. The ratification of the Seventeenth Amendment in 1913, providing for direct election of U.S. senators, put an end to vote buying in the state legislature by senate hopefuls.

The domination of the banks and railroads also began to falter during the Progressive Era. The legislature established the Railroad

Commission in 1907 to regulate rates and, in that same year, created the Board of Bank Commissioners to oversee the state's banks. In 1913 the Nevada Tax Commission was formed to ensure equity in the assessment of all property, especially railroad property, in the state. More than anything else, these boards and commissions brought an end to the freewheeling, unlimited laissez-faire attitude that had dominated the state's first half-century. Reflecting the moralistic components of the progressive tradition, the legislature also outlawed gambling in 1910. In 1918, the state's voters approved an initiative prohibiting the manufacture and sale of alcohol.

The state's economy staged a comeback during World War I, when demand for silver, gold, and copper increased dramatically. Demand and, consequently, prices for Nevada's agricultural and livestock products also rose during the war, making those marginal industries more profitable. At war's end, however, agricultural prices declined and the industry returned to its pre-war subsistence levels.

In the 1920s the bipartisan political machine of George Wingfield dominated the state's politics. Wingfield, never a candidate for major office himself, pulled the strings and supported Democrats, such as Pittman, and Republicans, such as Oddie. Wingfield's power, however, came crashing down in 1932 with the Depression-induced failure of his banking empire.

The 1930s brought about the dominance of the Democratic Party and the federal government in the state. After the Depression hit, Nevadans, like others in the nation, supported Democrats rather than Republicans, whom they blamed for bad economic conditions. As a result of the efforts of Nevada's congressional delegation, the state suffered less from the Depression than others did. Even before Franklin Roosevelt's New Deal benefited the state through tremendous federal investment, Nevada took advantage of various federal aid programs to the states, programs often initiated by the state's two U.S. senators. The Silver Purchase Act of 1934, introduced into Congress by Senator Pittman, aided Nevada's mining economy by providing for the increased purchase of silver by the federal government. In addition to utilizing federal highway assistance programs, Nevada also accepted federal aid that paid the entire cost of roads built through unappropriated federal lands and Indian reservations; with 87 percent of the state's land controlled by the federal government, this was no small matter. The act authorizing this massive road-building project, the Oddie-Colton Act of 1930, was co-authored by Senator Oddie.

The Naval Ammunition Depot opened in Hawthorne in 1930, and in 1931 construction began on Boulder (now Hoover) Dam near Las Vegas. The dam project, which employed five thousand workers at its peak in 1934, not only pumped millions of dollars into the local economy but also created what is today Boulder City. Millions more in federal dollars flowed into the state through FDR's various relief projects, including the Civilian Conservation Corps (CCC) and the Works Progress Administration (WPA), which built many of Nevada's streets, sewers, sidewalks, and parks. From 1933 to 1939, Nevada had the distinction among all states of the highest total per capita expenditures by the federal government.[11]

The state's economy was further aided during the Depression by two bills signed into law by Governor Fred Balzar on the same day in 1931. With one of those bills, the twenty-one-year-old ban on gambling was ended; the other, a divorce bill, allowed residency to be established in six weeks rather than six months, as had been the case since 1915. Both bills had the effect of bringing newcomers and their money to the state, even if only for a short time. Although the ramifications of the gaming bill would not be seen for a decade, the divorce bill had the immediate effect of creating a booming industry in the Reno area for dude ranches, hotels, boarding houses, and, of course, lawyers.

As noted earlier, the 1930s were a time of Democratic Party ascendance in the state. After twelve years in the U.S. Senate, Republican Oddie was defeated in the election of 1932 by Democrat Pat McCarran. In state elections of 1932, 1934, 1936, and 1938, Nevada Democrats won virtually every seat at the state and national level. The death of Nevada's senior senator, Key Pittman, in November 1940, brought McCarran to the forefront of state and national politics where he would stay until his own death in 1954.

The Third Period: 1940–1980

The beginning of World War II in Europe in 1939 increased not only demand for Nevada's copper but also federal investment in the state. Unlike federal funds in the second period, which had been directed almost exclusively to public works projects such as roads, dams, sewers, and sidewalks, these new federal moneys went toward the creation of military bases and industrial plants vital to the war effort.

In 1941, Camp Sibert was established in Boulder City to guard against sabotage at Hoover Dam, and an Army Air Corps gunnery school that would later become Nellis Air Force Base was created in the desert near Las Vegas. Stead Air Force Base near Reno was established in 1942, and a naval air station was situated in Fallon. In 1950, the Atomic Energy Commission began building what would become known as the Nevada Test Site (now the Nevada National Security Site). The Basic Magnesium plant was opened near Las Vegas in 1942 to manufacture magnesium needed for the war effort. All of these projects brought thousands of civilian and military workers to the state, and with them, their paychecks. In addition, the war created tremendous growth in the number and size of defense plants in southern California and a rising tide of California tourists to the state's gaming tables. Tourism and gaming were further aided by the federal government with passage in 1956 of the Interstate Highway Act, which would ultimately provide two major interstate highways through the state, routes by which tourists could travel easily and quickly to Reno and Las Vegas.

Mining continued to be important in the state during the war and post-war periods, but it was during this time that gaming and tourism began to supplant mining as the state's chief industry. It was also during this time that the state began to seriously regulate gaming. As had been the case with mining during the boom of the 1850s and early 1860s, gaming in the state had been the preserve of freewheeling entrepreneurs. Unlike mining, however, many of Nevada's gaming magnates had ties to organized crime. The state's 1931 statute allowing gaming put regulation into the hands of city and county officials who were less concerned with keeping out organized crime than with "fee collection and the control of drunks and cheaters."[12] In 1945 gaming control was transferred to the state Tax Commission, but this move did little to help, since those already holding licenses, many of whom had organized crime connections, were grandfathered in and allowed to keep their licenses with no further background checks.

That the state acted further had much to do with an effort to avoid federal control, or even prohibition, of gambling. Hearings held in 1950 and 1951 by Senator Estes Kefauver (D-Tennessee) confirmed the presence of organized crime in Nevada's casinos, and federal moves were afoot that would damage, if not eliminate, the state's major industry and source of revenue. In 1955, at the urging of Governor Charles Russell, the legislature established a three-member Gaming Control Board within the state Tax Commission to investigate gaming license applicants and recommend approval or disapproval of licenses.

In 1959 Governor Grant Sawyer proposed, and the legislature approved, a bill that removed the Gaming Control Board from the aegis of the state Tax Commission and made it the investigative arm of the newly created five-member Nevada Gaming Commission. The independent commission was given substantial control over licensing and regulation of all gaming in the state. The commission also created the state's official List of Excluded Persons, commonly known as the Black Book, that listed people with unsavory reputations and organized-crime ties who were not to be allowed in Nevada's casinos for fear that their presence would damage the industry's reputation. Allowing a person listed in the Black Book into gaming premises could result in substantial sanctions, including the loss of one's gaming license. This sanction was exercised in 1963 when Frank Sinatra, co-owner of the Cal-Neva Lodge in Lake Tahoe and the Sands Hotel in Las Vegas, had his license stripped from him when he allowed Black Book listee Sam Giancana to stay at the Lodge.

The increased regulation of gaming brought about by the efforts of Russell and Sawyer did not end federal scrutiny of the industry, however. In the 1960s U.S. Attorney General Robert F. Kennedy launched increased surveillance of Nevada gaming when it became clear that Jimmy Hoffa and the Teamsters were expanding their presence in the state through loans to various hotel-casinos from the Teamsters' pension fund. FBI investigations found sufficient evidence of skimming to acquire convictions of four associates of the Flamingo. Governor Sawyer's actions to clean up gaming staved off increased federal control, and in 1969 the state turned a corner when at the urging of Howard Hughes, who had bought the Desert Inn in 1967, the legislature passed the Corporate Gaming Act, which allowed corporations to invest in gaming without every single shareholder having to pass the rigorous background checks required by the state. That act encouraged normally conservative corporate and banking concerns to invest in gaming and led to an overall increased respectability of the industry throughout the country. Nonetheless, in the late 1970s and early 1980s, the state was rocked with charges of hidden organized-crime ownership and skimming at the

Tropicana, Aladdin, and Stardust casinos, events portrayed in Martin Scorsese's 1995 film *Casino*.

The Fourth Period: 1980 and the Future

In the 1980s Nevada saw a renaissance in the state's mining industry. As the price of gold in world markets increased and new methods for its recovery were developed, many of the "depleted" mines with small traces of gold returned to profitability. Nevada mines now account for approximately 83 percent of the country's gold and 27 percent of its silver production. If Nevada were a country, it would be the fourth largest gold-producing country in the world. In addition, the mining of other minerals, such as mercury and barite, has increased dramatically. The glory days of the 1980s went bust in the 1990s as prices for gold and silver declined dramatically and mining companies closed mines and laid off workers. However, in the early years of the twenty-first century, the industry boomed yet again. In 2002, with war in Iraq looming, currency exchange rates for the dollar low, oil prices high, the stock market down, and very few profitable investment vehicles available, the prices of gold and silver began to increase as did mining activity in the state, reversing a five-year trend. Mining continued its growth in Nevada as the economic downturn of 2007 and beyond led many investors to stock up on gold and silver. According to the Nevada Mining Association, the value of all minerals mined in Nevada in 2015 was almost $4.6 billion.

Since 1980, Nevada has been shaped by two primary forces: two-party competition and rapid population growth. For reasons explained in chapter 4, the once-dominant Democrats have found themselves in a competitive situation, similar to that existing prior to the New Deal, in which either party may win or lose any election in the state, depending upon the issues and candidates. Since 1980, the Republicans have won the state's presidential electors five out of ten times; the lieutenant governor and secretary of state races on seven of nine occasions; state treasurer and state controller in eight of nine elections; five of twelve U.S. Senate races; and U.S. House contests twenty-eight out of forty-nine times. At the state legislature, Democrats have been the majority party in the senate in eight of the past nineteen sessions and in the assembly sixteen times, with the Republicans the majority in 1985 and 2015 and an even split between the two parties in 1995. Even Democrats once thought invincible have fallen to the Republicans' newfound fourth-period vital-ity; in 1982, four-term incumbent senator Howard Cannon was defeated by the relatively unknown Chic Hecht, and in 1994, the year the Repub-licans recaptured both houses of the U.S. Congress, four-term congress-man James Bilbray was ousted by John Ensign. In a low-turnout election in 2014 Republicans took control of both houses of the state legislature and all six executive branch constitutional offices. Democrats came back in 2016 to win back the assembly and senate, although in the senate they were in the majority by only three votes, one of which was held by a former Republican turned Independent.

The state's tremendous growth in population began, not in the 1980s, but as far back as the 1940s, when federal investment in the state began to take off. Between the 1940 and 1950 censuses, Nevada's population increased more than 45 percent; by the time of the 1960 census, it had charged forward by another 78 percent; by the 1970 census, population had grown to almost half a million, an increase of more than 70 per-cent since 1960; and by 1980, the state was home to more than 800,000 people, an increase of more than 60 percent since 1970. At the time of the 2010 census, Nevada had almost 3 million residents, an increase of 35 percent since 2000.[13] Nevada had the distinction of being the fastest-growing state in the nation for two decades. That growth slowed consid-erably, however, in the wake of the Great Recession. As table 11.1 shows, the growth rate in the 2010 census was the lowest since 1940. The next census will not occur until 2020 but the Census Bureau estimates that in 2016 the Sagebrush State had 2,940,058 residents.

The effects of this phenomenal growth rate have been dramatic for the state. As noted in chapter 10, new residents require immediate ser-vices, and the state has been hard-pressed to keep pace with the need for new schools, roads, and other infrastructure required for a burgeon-ing population. Not surprisingly, the construction industry and its sup-pliers experienced a boom in the past few decades, building these public projects and providing the newcomers with houses, apartments, grocery stores, movie theaters, and other structural needs. The boom in construc-tion ended in the Great Recession as the housing bubble burst. With homes now worth substantially less than what people had paid for them prior to the bust, Nevada became the center of home foreclosures in the United States. And with all that inventory sitting empty, builders no longer were building and construction workers sat idle. However, events

TABLE 11.1. Population of Nevada, 1860–2016

CENSUS DATE	POPULATION	PERCENTAGE INCREASE OVER PRECEDING CENSUS
1860	6,857	NA
1870	42,491	519.7
1880	62,266	46.5
1890	47,355	−23.9
1900	42,335	−10.6
1910	81,875	93.4
1920	77,407	−5.5
1930	91,058	17.6
1940	110,247	21.1
1950	160,083	45.2
1960	285,278	78.2
1970	488,738	71.3
1980	800,508	63.8
1990	1,201,833	50.1
2000	1,998,257	66.3
2010	2,700,551	35.1
2016	2,940,058 (estimated)	NA

Source: Department of Commerce, Bureau of the Census.

in 2016 and 2017 have raised expectations that construction will make a comeback. The electric automobile manufacturer Tesla is building a huge battery factory in Reno, while Amazon, the largest online retailer in the nation, and Switch, a data storage company, are also constructing facilities in that area. In the southern part of the state, a practice facility for the Vegas Golden Knights of the National Hockey League and new stadiums for Las Vegas's minor league baseball team and for the soon-to-be Las Vegas Raiders National Football League team have been or are being constructed. The end of the Great Recession has seen completion of several gaming and commercial projects that were abandoned at the time, and the housing market has begun to recover at both ends of the state.

The state's gaming industry experienced some of its best times ever during this fourth period, although its good fortune was not necessarily tied directly to population growth. Gaming has taken off in hitherto unrecognized areas such as Laughlin and Mesquite as well as in the traditional centers of Reno and Las Vegas. In the decades of the 1980s and 1990s, Las Vegas megaresorts such as the MGM Grand, the Mirage, the Excalibur, the Luxor, Bellagio, Mandalay Bay, and Treasure Island were built and existing casinos such as Circus Circus, the Sahara (now SLS), the Golden Nugget, the Downtown Grand (formerly Lady Luck), Binion's Horseshoe, and others completed enormous expansion plans. In Reno, the Silver Legacy opened in 1995. Like housing and construction, the Great Recession hit the gaming and tourism industries hard. With unemployment nationally at record highs, those who might want to come to the Sagebrush State either did not have the resources to do so or were unsure enough of their own future employment that they stayed away in droves. This led to layoffs in the tourism and gaming industries, just as it had in construction, thus worsening not only individuals' futures but also the tax coffers of the state. Nonetheless, MGM was able to finish building the massive CityCenter structure, whereas other large projects such as the Fontainebleau and Echelon Place were shuttered without completion.

Gaming and tourism have also led to major expansions at the state's airports. McCarran International Airport in Las Vegas now serves as a hub for major airlines, including Southwest, and is the eighth busiest air terminal in the nation. Increasingly McCarran International is serving international travelers; fully one-fifth of all travelers to Nevada in 2017 were international. That the Las Vegas airport is named after Senator McCarran and the Reno airport was formerly named after Senator Cannon should come as no surprise; both men were at the forefront of aviation legislation that made airports and air travel more convenient and less expensive to the average American. Just as the Interstate Highway Act made travel to the gaming meccas of Las Vegas and Reno easier in its day, the actions of McCarran and Cannon have brought more tourists to the state's gaming tables by reducing travel time and making a weekend or week-long trip from anywhere in the country as convenient as a short plane trip.

Las Vegas, once a small railroad stop between Los Angeles and Salt Lake City, is now the state's commercial and population center. More than 75 percent of Nevada's population resides in Clark County. The transition of the state from one dominated politically and economically by Washoe and the rural counties to one living in the shadow of Las

Vegas has not been without its difficulties. In the mid–1980s, Clark County residents and their elected officials took on the issue of "fair share." As noted in chapter 10, the 1981 legislature approved a shift in the state's tax structure from a reliance on property taxes to sales taxes. Part of that sales tax came from a city-county relief tax that was returned to local governments in the state. Under the formula for distribution approved by the legislature, Washoe County, because it had lost more funds in the shift, received more of the city-county relief tax funds than it paid, whereas Clark County received less than it paid. After a great deal of turmoil, bickering, and name calling, the 1991 legislature approved a new formula that now returns to both Washoe and Clark counties approximately 97 percent of the amount each paid into the fund. The rural counties receive slightly more than their contribution.[14]

The "fair share" issue, however, did not end in 1991. During the 1995 legislature, the City of Las Vegas and Clark County went to war over distribution of sales tax revenues between them. In a successful eleventh-hour move, the county was able to convince the legislature to include the unincorporated town of Spring Valley and an area that has now become the unincorporated town of Summerlin South in the tax distribution formula. The move meant that Clark County gained and Las Vegas lost approximately $1.2 million annually. A similar struggle took place in the 2001 session when Speaker of the Assembly Richard Perkins proposed a bill transferring $4 million of sales taxes from Clark County and its incorporated cities to his hometown of Henderson. Perkins claimed that Henderson was not receiving its fair share because current formulas did not take into account the city's high level of growth. Although Clark County and the other cities tenaciously and loudly fought the move, Perkins was ultimately successful. The fight over fair share between the state and the counties came to a head in 2011 and 2012, with the counties, surprisingly, on the winning side. During the 2009 session of the state legislature, Governor Jim Gibbons and the legislators decided to take property taxes from the counties and funds from a clean-water coalition in order to fill the gaping hole in the budget caused by the economic downturn. In 2011 the state supreme court held that the state could not take money from a few counties in order to balance the state budget. As a result, the Clark County Clean Water Coalition was returned $62 million by the state, and Clark and Washoe counties received $103 million and $7.25 million, respectively.

A large number of Nevada's new residents are retirees, many of whom derive their support from government pensions, Social Security, and Medicare and require above-average medical care and social services. According to the U.S. Census Bureau, Nevada has one of the fastest-growing senior populations of any state in the country. By 2020 it is expected that the state's number of residents over the age of sixty-five will double from 2000. In other states where they have moved in large numbers, such as Florida and Arizona, they have been notorious for their refusal to support increased funding for government services they do not perceive as directly benefiting them. Whether this will also occur in Nevada remains to be seen. However, in recent years, voters in the southern portion of the state, where the vast majority of retirees live, have turned down one bond issue after another that would have gone to support more police, schools, parks, and libraries. Likewise Carson City voters turned down a sales tax hike that was earmarked for a new library and public plaza downtown; Lyon County voters rejected a property tax increase that was to improve emergency services; Nye County voters nixed a fuel tax increase to build and maintain highways; Washoe County voters turned down an increase in the vehicle registration fee that was to have paid for senior services, public safety, and infrastructure; and in Sparks the voters rejected an increase in the sales tax to fund the police.

To the extent that retirees living on government assistance exhibit hypocrisy in their failure to support these increased government services, they are merely reflecting an attitude long prevalent in the state. It is doubtful that any other state in the Union has been so dependent for its existence and survival on the federal government; yet Nevadans are among the most vociferous critics of the federal government and the first to tout themselves as "rugged individualists" who pulled themselves up by their own bootstraps. As we have noted in this chapter and others, Nevada came into existence as a result of the federal government's nurturing; it has grown and prospered as a result of vast federal investment in dams, roads, military bases, and industrial complexes. But for the federal government's largess, it is doubtful that Nevada would have achieved all that it has. Federal decisions not to regulate gaming have contributed to the state's prosperity and economic strength, too.

Yet, Nevada was in the forefront of the failed Sagebrush Rebellion in the 1970s, fomenters of which hoped to turn federal lands over to the states. It has also provided tremendous support for Sagebrush II and a county supremacy movement that claims control over all federal lands within county borders. Two court rulings in the late 1990s, however, have significantly set back the Sagebrush Rebels and the county supremacy movement. In 1996 U.S. District Court Judge Lloyd George held that the federal government holds jurisdiction over federally owned public lands in the state. His ruling had the effect of declaring unconstitutional Nevada's original 1979 Sagebrush Rebellion statutes and a Nye County resolution laying state and county claim to the lands. And in 1997 the U.S. Court of Appeals for the Ninth Circuit held in another case that federal public lands are owned by the federal government and not by the states or counties. That has not, however, stopped remnants of the past movements from pressing their case. In April 2014 members of the Cliven Bundy family and a large number of self-described militia members instigated an armed standoff between themselves and officers with the Bureau of Land Management and other agencies when the BLM sought to round up Bundy's cattle which, since 1993, had been illegally grazing on federal land. Indeed, it was estimated at the time that Bundy owed more than $1 million in grazing fees. Bundy, among others, argues that the federal government does not own the land and should return it to the states. However, as we noted in chapter 2, the congressional Nevada Enabling Act required residents to disclaim the rights to all unappropriated land as a condition of statehood, and the state did so in the third paragraph of the "Ordinance" section of the 1864 state constitution. Thus, as the courts have held repeatedly, the federal government is not required to give public lands "back" to the state in that they were never owned by the state.

Mining companies and livestock owners, with their representatives in Congress, have successfully fought off one attempt after another to raise the rents on grazing lands and the royalties on mining claims to something akin to their fair market value. Although the Bundy case is the most serious threat to date, it is the case that frequently officers with the Bureau of Land Management and the Forest Service have been threatened, and they sometimes even drive their own automobiles while working so as not to be targeted. This sentiment is not isolated: in 1995 the legislature passed a bill that would have required federal officers to seek the approval of state and local officials before they could enforce state laws on public lands. The bill died when Governor Bob Miller vetoed it and the assembly, which had previously passed it unanimously, came up a mere five votes short of an override.

Nevada residents' demand for low taxes and the state's increased urban population, however, may ultimately determine the political success of ranchers and mining companies in the state. Each year, the Bureau of Land Management pumps millions of dollars into the state in support of the 67 percent of Nevada's land under its stewardship. Turning this land over to the state would require Nevadans to pick up that tab with their own tax dollars or sell off the land to private interests. The vast majority of Nevada's new residents are moving into urban areas such as Las Vegas and Reno, and their concern for keeping these wilderness areas from being locked up by mining and grazing interests or sold off to private owners may ultimately prevail.

These urban residents also need water, which has already created conflict between Las Vegas and the surrounding rural areas. In addition to seeking additional water from the Colorado River in the 1990s, the Las Vegas Valley Water District proposed buying up water rights from ranchers and farmers and tapping into other water sources in the state. When that strategy resulted in protests from Nye, Lincoln, and White Pine counties, the District backed off and gave up some of its claims to unused groundwater in those three counties. The District's lust for water lying outside of Clark County has been quenched somewhat since reaching a unique agreement with the state of Arizona to "bank" Colorado River water. Under the agreement, Nevada will pay Arizona to store unused river water in aquifers underlying the Grand Canyon State. Nevada may then withdraw from this bank by having Arizona use the stored water while Nevada would take an equal amount of Arizona's allocation from Lake Mead. A similar deal was brokered with Mexico in 2012. In addition to the Arizona and Mexico compacts, southern Nevada bought the rights to a well in Coyote Springs Valley in northern Clark County and purchased water rights to the Muddy River. The various agreements are expected to provide southern Nevada sufficient water supply until at least 2037. As a result of an extended drought, northern Nevada is also feeling the strain of increasing population and decreasing water supplies; residents there, too, must seek additional sources of the vital liquid, and the rural areas seem the most likely target of opportunity.

Conclusion

Nevadans have a great deal of which they may be justly proud. In 150 years the state has gone from a Wild West, lawless region to a modern, urban one that offers opportunity to those willing to work for it. Nevada was among the first states in the nation to grant suffrage to women; to ratify the Thirteenth, Fourteenth, and Fifteenth Amendments to the U.S. Constitution; to provide for workman's compensation; to initiate a direct primary; and to put government in the hands of the people through initiative, referendum, and recall. It is a state that has dealt with astonishing growth over a short period of time, one that has passed statutes protecting its minorities from discrimination, and one that has established a community college and university system that is growing not only in numbers but in the quality of its students, faculty, and national reputation.

As Nevada makes its way through the twenty-first century many challenges lie on the horizon. Clearly the state must seek to diversify its economy to an even greater extent than it already has. Development of manufacturing and banking centers has already occurred to some degree; more must be done. If the state's history tells us nothing else, it surely informs us that reliance upon a single industry, whether mining or gaming, is a dangerous path. Gaming and tourism took significant hits in downturns in the 1980s and 1990s and after the September 11, 2001 attacks on the United States. However, the Sagebrush State seemed not to take the lessons to heart and continued to rely upon a continued influx of tourists and their dollars. The economic drubbing that the nation took in the Great Recession should have proved just how vulnerable a state relying on a single industry, especially one fueled by discretionary dollars, can be. The state also faces increased competition for gaming dollars from other states and nations, such as Singapore and Macao. The threat to Nevada's economy from Indian gaming is quite real and apparent. One report, by Applied Economics, estimates that the Sagebrush State could lose $24 million to $43 million per year in revenues and up to 16,000 jobs as a result of casinos on Indian reservations.[15] Although there is some debate about those figures, the state, especially Reno, clearly has cause to worry. In addition, members of the U.S. Congress continue to propose various bills that would harm Nevada's gaming revenue as well, including elimination of the federal income tax deduction for gambling losses.

Even if we could guarantee the perpetual solvency of gaming in the state, we must ask ourselves if a gaming-based economy is what we truly want. Do we truly want a tax base founded primarily on unstable and volatile gaming and sales tax revenues, or are we willing to raise other types of taxes in order to stabilize that base? Do we truly want a single industry that has the power to dictate to state government in the way that mining, the Bank Crowd, and the railroads once did? Do we truly want a state government so dependent upon the tax revenues of a single industry that it dare not tax or regulate it too much for fear that the state's budget may come crashing down? Are policies that are in the best interests of gaming corporations also in the best interests of the state? These are issues that will not go away; they will have to be addressed in the coming years.

Nevada must also come to terms once more with attempts at colonization and exploitation by outsiders. Just as California mining companies, railroads, and banks once sought to take what they could out of Nevada with little regard for the state's needs, new colonizers have arisen to take their place. Tons of precious gold, silver, and other metals are taken from the state every year by companies that pay the state little on these millions of dollars in net proceeds. That these companies are primarily owned by corporations outside the United States makes their colonialism and exploitation even more apparent. In 1994, for example, a Canadian-owned mining company, American Barrick Resources, Inc., paid only $10,000 to buy a mine with $10 million in gold deposits.[16] Within the United States, eastern politicians and nuclear power plant owners are single-minded in their goal to place a high-level nuclear waste repository at Yucca Mountain, just outside of Las Vegas; that Nevadans are almost unanimously opposed means little. To these corporations and politicians, Nevada seems a place good only for pillaging precious minerals and dumping unwanted and dangerous waste.

Nevada's prison system is also in a state of impending crisis. The state has one of the highest incarceration rates in the country, and its prisons are frequently overcrowded due to the actions of legislators and judges who need to show voters that they are tough on crime in order to be reelected. That overcrowding could be relieved by releasing nonviolent offenders on parole and probation. A Department of Corrections report in 2005 was critical of the Board of Parole Commissioners for turning inmates down for parole in a defensive move to avoid releasing a prisoner who might later re-offend, thus making the board look bad. According to the report, fewer than half of those eligible are paroled and, even though Nevada statute requires prisoners "to be released one year before the end of their sentence so they can be supervised on parole for a year," the parole board frequently invokes an exception to the law to keep them in prison.[17] Keeping inmates in prison who do not pose a threat to the state not only prolongs prison overcrowding and the need to spend precious tax dollars on new prisons but is also the most expensive option available to the state in dealing with those convicted of criminal behavior. At least part of the reason for the low percentage of paroled inmates, however, may be the result of actions taken by the 1995 legislature. In that session the legislature passed laws increasing the penalties for serious criminal offenses and allowing many nonviolent offenders to repay their debt to society without doing prison time. Consequently, those who are in prison and who are coming to the board with parole requests may be the most heinous and, therefore, least likely (and deserving) of parole. By 2007 the Sagebrush State's prison system was running 11 percent over its capacity. As a result, the legislature that year approved $300 million to build new prison space and also passed a law increasing prisoners' "good time" credits for good behavior and participation in educational programs. As a result, nonviolent offenders could be locked up for a lesser period of time if they behave while in prison.

Nevada must also come to terms in the next few years with its provision of social services. In virtually every national study, Nevada ranks at the bottom of those lists where a state wants to rank high and at the top of those lists where it's better to be at the bottom. Ranking near the bottom is consistent and longstanding for the state in the areas of per-pupil spending, teacher pay, percentage of high school graduates who go on to college, rate of high school dropouts, passage rates on proficiency examinations, funding for disability programs, ratio of nurses to population, and ratio of doctors to children. Although Nevada is among the lowest-ranked states in terms of education, welfare, and mental health spending, the state is among those with the highest rates of poverty, fatal domestic violence, infant mortality, high school dropouts, unwed mothers (and fathers), suicide, alcoholism, and gambling addiction in the nation. How and whether those figures will change are dependent upon Nevada's decisions over the next few years. The Great Recession served only to make these problems worse. As more and more of the state's citizens were unemployed, losing their homes, and in need of state services, the amount of money going into the state's coffers through gaming taxes, sales taxes, and property taxes plummeted. It will take vision and determination for the state to turn that around, when even in flush times it has generally been unwilling to provide these services. One bright spot is Governor Brian Sandoval's 2013 decision to expand Medicaid services to the poor of Nevada under the federal Patient Protection and Affordable Care Act and his successful push in 2015 to expand needed funding through the commerce tax and to avoid the sunsetting of taxes passed in 2011.

In short, Nevada is a state whose ability to prosper and continue as a land of dreams and opportunity rests in its own hands. Hard decisions—uncomfortable decisions—will have to be made on taxation, spending, government services, land and water use, and openness in politics. It is to be hoped that we will have the foresight, the skills, and the willingness to do what we must to ensure that all Nevadans enjoy the fruits of their labors and that all share equally the liberties and opportunities available in the Sagebrush State.

Appendix

The Constitution of the State of Nevada

[The Nevada constitution was framed by a convention of delegates chosen by the people. The convention met at Carson City on July 4, 1864, and adjourned on July 28 of the same year. On the 1st Wednesday of September 1864, the constitution was approved by the vote of the people of the Territory of Nevada, and on October 31, 1864, President Lincoln proclaimed that the State of Nevada was admitted into the Union on an equal footing with the original states.

The literal text of the original, signed copy of the constitution filed in the office of the secretary of state has been retained, unless it has been repealed or superseded by amendment. Where the original text has been amended or where a new provision has been added to the original constitution, the source of the amendment or addition is indicated in the source note immediately following the text of the amended or new section. Leadlines for sections have been supplied by the Legislative Counsel of the State of Nevada.]

[PRELIMINARY ACTION.]
ORDINANCE.
PREAMBLE.
ARTICLE   1. Declaration of Rights.
          2. Right of Suffrage.
          3. Distribution of Powers.
          4. Legislative Department.
          5. Executive Department.
          6. Judicial Department.
          7. Impeachment and Removal From Office.
          8. Municipal and Other Corporations.
          9. Finance and State Debt.
         10. Taxation.
         11. Education.
         12. Militia.
         13. Public Institutions.
         14. Boundary.
         15. Miscellaneous Provisions.
         16. Amendments.

    17. Schedule.

XVIII. [Right of Suffrage.] Repealed in 1992.

    19. Initiative and Referendum.

[ELECTION ORDINANCE.]

[PRELIMINARY ACTION.]
Whereas

The Act of Congress Approved March Twenty First A.D. Eighteen Hundred and Sixty Four "To enable the People of the Territory of Nevada to form a Constitution and State Government and for the admission of such State into the Union on an equal footing with the Original States," requires that the Members of the Convention for framing said Constitution shall, after Organization, on behalf of the people of said Territory, adopt the Constitution of the United States.—Therefore, Be it Resolved,

That the Members of this Convention, elected by the Authority of the aforesaid enabling Act of Congress, Assembled in Carson City the Capital of said Territory of Nevada, and immediately subsequent to its Organization, do adopt, on behalf of the people of said Territory the Constitution of the United States[.]

ORDINANCE

Slavery prohibited; freedom of religious worship; disclaimer of public lands. [Effective until the date Congress consents to amendment or a legal determination is made that such consent is not necessary.] In obedience to the requirements of an act of the Congress of the United States, approved March twenty-first, A.D. eighteen hundred and sixty-four, to enable the people of Nevada to form a constitution and state government, this convention, elected and convened in obedience to said enabling act, do ordain as follows, and this ordinance shall be irrevocable, without the consent of the United States and the people of the State of Nevada:

First. That there shall be in this state neither slavery nor involuntary servitude, otherwise than in the punishment for crimes, whereof the party shall have been duly convicted.

Second. That perfect toleration of religious sentiment shall be secured, and no inhabitant of said state shall ever be molested, in person or property, on account of his or her mode of religious worship.

Third. That the people inhabiting said territory do agree and declare, that they forever disclaim all right and title to the unappropriated public lands lying within said territory, and that the same shall be and remain at the sole and entire disposition of the United States; and that lands belonging to citizens of the United States, residing without the said state, shall never be taxed higher than the land belonging to the residents thereof; and that no taxes shall be imposed by said state on lands or property therein belonging to, or which may hereafter be purchased by, the United States, unless otherwise provided by the congress of the United States.

[Amended in 1956. Proposed and passed by the 1953 legislature; agreed to and passed by the 1955 legislature; approved and ratified by the people at the 1956 general election. See: Statutes of Nevada 1953, p. 718; Statutes of Nevada 1955, p. 926.]

Slavery prohibited; freedom of religious worship; taxation of certain property. *[Effective on the date Congress consents to amendment or a legal determination is made that such consent is not necessary.]* In obedience to the requirements of an act of the Congress of the United States, approved March twenty-first, A.D. eighteen hundred and sixty-four, to enable the people of Nevada to form a constitution and state government, this convention, elected and convened in obedience to said enabling act, do ordain as follows, and this ordinance shall be irrevocable, without the consent of the United States and the people of the State of Nevada:

First. That there shall be in this state neither slavery nor involuntary servitude, otherwise than in the punishment for crimes, whereof the party shall have been duly convicted.

Second. That perfect toleration of religious sentiment shall be secured, and no inhabitant of said state shall ever be molested, in person or property, on account of his or her mode of religious worship.

Third. That the people inhabiting said territory do agree and declare, that lands belonging to citizens of the United States, residing without the said state, shall never be taxed higher than the land belonging to the residents thereof; and that no taxes shall be imposed by said state on lands or property therein belonging to, or which may hereafter be purchased by, the United States, unless otherwise provided by the Congress of the United States.

[Amended in 1956 and 1996. The first amendment was proposed and passed by the 1953 legislature; agreed to and passed by the 1955 legislature; approved and ratified by the people at the 1956 general election. See: Statutes of Nevada 1953, p. 718; Statutes of Nevada 1955, p. 926. The second amendment was proposed and passed by the 1993 legislature; agreed to and passed by the 1995 legislature; and approved and ratified by the people at the 1996 general election, effective on the date Congress consents to amendment or a legal determination is made that such consent is not necessary. See: Statutes of Nevada 1993, p. 3136; Statutes of Nevada 1995, p. 2917.]

PREAMBLE.

We the people of the State of Nevada Grateful to Almighty God for our freedom in order to secure its blessings, insure domestic tranquility, and form a more perfect Government, do establish this CONSTITUTION.

ARTICLE 1.
Declaration of Rights

SECTION   1. Inalienable rights.

2. Purpose of government; paramount allegiance to United States.

3. Trial by jury; waiver in civil cases.

4. Liberty of conscience.

5. Suspension of habeas corpus.

6. Excessive bail and fines; cruel or unusual punishments; detention of witnesses.

7. Bail; exception for capital offenses and certain murders.

8. Rights of accused in criminal prosecutions; jeopardy; rights of victims of crime; due process of law; eminent domain. [Effective through November 26, 2018, and after that date unless the provisions of Senate Joint Resolution No. 17 (2015) are approved and ratified by the voters at the 2018 General Election.]

8. Rights of accused in criminal prosecutions; jeopardy; due process of law; eminent domain. [Effective November 27, 2018, if the provisions of Senate Joint Resolution No. 17 (2015) are approved and ratified by the voters at the 2018 General Election.]

8A. Rights of victim of crime. [Effective November 27, 2018, if the provisions of Senate Joint Resolution No. 17 (2015) are approved and ratified by the voters at the 2018 General Election.]

9. Liberty of speech and the press.

10. Right to assemble and to petition.

11. Right to keep and bear arms; civil power supreme.

12. Quartering soldier in private house.

13. Representation apportioned according to population.

14. Exemption of property from execution; imprisonment for debt.

15. Bill of attainder; ex post facto law; obligation of contract.

16. Rights of foreigners. [Repealed in 1924.]

17. Slavery and involuntary servitude prohibited.

18. Unreasonable seizure and search; issuance of warrants.

19. Treason.

20. Rights retained by people.

21. Limitation on recognition of marriage. [Effective through November 23, 2020, and after that date unless the provisions of Assembly Joint Resolution No. 2 (2017) are agreed to and passed by the 2019 Legislature and approved and ratified by the voters at the 2020 General Election.]

21. Recognition of marriage. [Effective November 24, 2020, if the

provisions of Assembly Joint Resolution No. 2 (2017) are agreed to and passed by the 2019 Legislature and approved and ratified by the voters at the 2020 General Election.]

22. Eminent domain proceedings: Restrictions and requirements.
23. Open, competitive retail electric energy market; granting of monopolies and exclusive franchises for generation of electricity prohibited; severability. [Effective November 27, 2018, if the proposed addition is approved and ratified by the voters at the 2018 General Election.]

SECTION 1. *Inalienable rights.* All men are by Nature free and equal and have certain inalienable rights among which are those of enjoying and defending life and liberty; Acquiring, Possessing and Protecting property and pursuing and obtaining safety and happiness[.]

SECTION 2. *Purpose of government; paramount allegiance to United States.* All political power is inherent in the people[.] Government is instituted for the protection, security and benefit of the people; and they have the right to alter or reform the same whenever the public good may require it. But the Paramount Allegiance of every citizen is due to the Federal Government in the exercise of all its Constitutional powers as the same have been or may be defined by the Supreme Court of the United States; and no power exists in the people of this or any other State of the Federal Union to dissolve their connection therewith or perform any act tending to impair[,] subvert, or resist the Supreme Authority of the government of the United States. The Constitution of the United States confers full power on the Federal Government to maintain and Perpetuate its existance [existence], and whensoever any portion of the States, or people thereof attempt to secede from the Federal Union, or forcibly resist the Execution of its laws, the Federal Government may, by warrant of the Constitution, employ armed force in compelling obedience to its Authority.

SECTION 3. *Trial by jury; waiver in civil cases.* The right of trial by Jury shall be secured to all and remain inviolate forever; but a Jury trial may be waived by the parties in all civil cases in the manner to be prescribed by law; and in civil cases, if three fourths of the Jurors agree upon a verdict it shall stand and have the same force and effect as a verdict by the whole Jury, Provided, the Legislature by a law passed by a two thirds vote of all the members elected to each branch thereof may require a unanimous verdict notwithstanding this Provision.

SECTION 4. *Liberty of conscience.* The free exercise and enjoyment of religious profession and worship without discrimination or preference shall forever be allowed in this State, and no person shall be rendered incompetent to be a witness on account of his opinions on matters of his religious belief, but the liberty of consciene [conscience] hereby secured, shall not be so construed, as to excuse acts of licentiousness or justify practices inconsistent with the peace, or safety of this State.

SECTION 5. *Suspension of habeas corpus.* The privilege of the writ of Habeas Corpus, shall not be suspended unless when in cases of rebellion or invasion the public safety may require its suspension.

SECTION 6. *Excessive bail and fines; cruel or unusual punishments; detention of witnesses.* Excessive bail shall not be required, nor excessive fines imposed, nor shall cruel or unusual punishments be inflicted, nor shall witnesses be unreasonably detained.

SECTION 7. *Bail; exception for capital offenses and certain murders.* All persons shall be bailable by sufficient sureties; unless for Capital Offenses or murders punishable by life imprisonment without possibility of parole when the proof is evident or the presumption great.

[Amended in 1980. Proposed and passed by the 1977 legislature; agreed to and passed by the 1979 legislature; and approved and ratified by the people at the 1980 general election. See: Statutes of Nevada 1977, p. 1697; Statutes of Nevada 1979, p. 1941.]

SECTION 8. *Rights of accused in criminal prosecutions; jeopardy; rights of victims of crime; due process of law; eminent domain.* [*Effective through November 26, 2018, and after that date unless the provisions of Senate Joint Resolution No. 17 (2015) are approved and ratified by the voters at the 2018 General Election.*]

1. No person shall be tried for a capital or other infamous crime (except in cases of impeachment, and in cases of the militia when in actual service and the land and naval forces in time of war, or which this State may keep, with the consent of Congress, in time of peace, and in cases of petit larceny, under the regulation of the Legislature) except on presentment or indictment of the grand jury, or upon information duly filed by a district attorney, or Attorney General of the State, and in any trial, in any court whatever, the party accused shall be allowed to appear and defend in person, and with counsel, as in civil actions. No person shall be subject to be twice put in jeopardy for the same offense; nor shall he be compelled, in any criminal case, to be a witness against himself.

2. The Legislature shall provide by law for the rights of victims of crime, personally or through a representative, to be:
   (a) Informed, upon written request, of the status or disposition of a criminal proceeding at any stage of the proceeding;
   (b) Present at all public hearings involving the critical stages of a criminal proceeding; and

(c) Heard at all proceedings for the sentencing or release of a convicted person after trial.

3. Except as otherwise provided in Subsection 4, no person may maintain an action against the State or any public officer or employee for damages or injunctive, declaratory or other legal or equitable relief on behalf of a victim of a crime as a result of a violation of any statute enacted by the Legislature pursuant to Subsection 2. No such violation authorizes setting aside a conviction or sentence or continuing or postponing a criminal proceeding.

4. A person may maintain an action to compel a public officer or employee to carry out any duty required by the Legislature pursuant to Subsection 2.

5. No person shall be deprived of life, liberty, or property, without due process of law.

6. Private property shall not be taken for public use without just compensation having been first made, or secured, except in cases of war, riot, fire, or great public peril, in which case compensation shall be afterward made.

[Amended in 1912 and 1996. The first amendment was proposed and passed by the 1909 legislature; agreed to and passed by the 1911 legislature; and approved and ratified by the people at the 1912 general election. See: Statutes of Nevada 1909, p. 346; Statutes of Nevada 1911, p. 474. The second amendment was proposed and passed by the 1993 legislature; agreed to and passed by the 1995 legislature; and approved and ratified by the people at the 1996 general election. See: Statutes of Nevada 1993, p. 3065; Statutes of Nevada 1995, p. 2880.]

SECTION 8. *Rights of accused in criminal prosecutions; jeopardy; due process of law; eminent domain. [Effective November 27, 2018, if the provisions of Senate Joint Resolution No. 17 (2015) are approved and ratified by the voters at the 2018 General Election.]*

1. No person shall be tried for a capital or other infamous crime (except in cases of impeachment, and in cases of the militia when in actual service and the land and naval forces in time of war, or which this State may keep, with the consent of Congress, in time of peace, and in cases of petit larceny, under the regulation of the Legislature) except on presentment or indictment of the grand jury, or upon information duly filed by a district attorney, or Attorney General of the State, and in any trial, in any court whatever, the party accused shall be allowed to appear and defend in person, and with counsel, as in civil actions. No person shall be subject to be twice put in jeopardy for the same offense; nor shall he be compelled, in any criminal case, to be a witness against himself.

2. No person shall be deprived of life, liberty, or property, without due process of law.

3. Private property shall not be taken for public use without just compensation having been first made, or secured, except in cases of war, riot, fire, or great public peril, in which case compensation shall be afterward made.

[Amended in 1912 and 1996. The first amendment was proposed and passed by the 1909 legislature; agreed to and passed by the 1911 legislature; and approved and ratified by the people at the 1912 general election. See: Statutes of Nevada 1909, p. 346; Statutes of Nevada 1911, p. 454. The second amendment was proposed and passed by the 1993 legislature; agreed to and passed by the 1995 legislature; and approved and ratified by the people at the 1996 general election. See: Statutes of Nevada 1993, p. 3065; Statutes of Nevada 1995, p. 2880.]—(Proposed amendment passed by the 2015 Legislature; agreed to and passed by the 2017 Legislature; effective November 27, 2018, if approved and ratified by the voters at the 2018 General Election. See: Statutes of Nevada 2015, p. 4074.)

SECTION 8A. *Rights of victim of crime. [Effective November 27, 2018, if the provisions of Senate Joint Resolution No. 17 (2015) are approved and ratified by the voters at the 2018 General Election.]*

1. Each person who is the victim of a crime is entitled to the following rights:

   (a) To be treated with fairness and respect for his or her privacy and dignity, and to be free from intimidation, harassment and abuse, throughout the criminal or juvenile justice process.

   (b) To be reasonably protected from the defendant and persons acting on behalf of the defendant.

   (c) To have the safety of the victim and the victim's family considered as a factor in fixing the amount of bail and release conditions for the defendant.

   (d) To prevent the disclosure of confidential information or records to the defendant which could be used to locate or harass the victim or the victim's family.

   (e) To refuse an interview or deposition request, unless under court order, and to set reasonable conditions on the conduct of any such interview to which the victim consents.

   (f) To reasonably confer with the prosecuting agency, upon request, regarding the case.

   (g) To reasonable notice of all public proceedings, including delinquency proceedings, upon request, at which the defendant and the prosecutor are entitled to be present and of all parole or other postconviction release proceedings, and to be present at all such proceedings.

   (h) To be reasonably heard, upon request, at any public proceeding, including any delinquency proceeding, in any court involving release or sentencing, and at any parole proceeding.

(i) To the timely disposition of the case following the arrest of the defendant.

(j) To provide information to any public officer or employee conducting a presentence investigation concerning the impact of the offense on the victim and the victim's family and any sentencing recommendations before the sentencing of the defendant.

(k) To be informed, upon request, of the conviction, sentence, place and time of incarceration, or other disposition of the defendant, the scheduled release date of the defendant and the release of or the escape by the defendant from custody.

(l) To full and timely restitution.

(m)To the prompt return of legal property when no longer needed as evidence.

(n) To be informed of all postconviction proceedings, to participate and provide information to the parole authority to be considered before the parole of the offender and to be notified, upon request, of the parole or other release of the offender.

(o) To have the safety of the victim, the victim's family and the general public considered before any parole or other postjudgment release decision is made.

(p) To have all monetary payments, money and property collected from any person who has been ordered to make restitution be first applied to pay the amounts ordered as restitution to the victim.

(q) To be specifically informed of the rights enumerated in this section, and to have information concerning those rights be made available to the general public.

2. A victim has standing to assert the rights enumerated in this section in any court with jurisdiction over the case. The court shall promptly rule on a victim's request. A defendant does not have standing to assert the rights of his or her victim. This section does not alter the powers, duties or responsibilities of a prosecuting attorney. A victim does not have the status of a party in a criminal proceeding.

3. Except as otherwise provided in Subsection 4, no person may maintain an action against this State or any public officer or employee for damages or injunctive, declaratory or other legal or equitable relief on behalf of a victim of a crime as a result of a violation of this section or any statute enacted by the Legislature pursuant thereto. No such violation authorizes setting aside a conviction.

4. A person may maintain an action to compel a public officer or employee to carry out any duty required by this section or any statute enacted by the Legislature pursuant thereto.

5. The granting of these rights to victims must not be construed to deny or disparage other rights possessed by victims. A parole authority shall extend the right to be heard at a parole hearing to any person harmed by the offender.

6. The Legislature shall by law provide any other measure necessary or useful to secure to victims of crime the benefit of the rights set forth in this section.

7. As used in this section, "victim" means any person directly and proximately harmed by the commission of a criminal offense under any law of this State. If the victim is less than 18 years of age, incompetent, incapacitated or deceased, the term includes the legal guardian of the victim or a representative of the victim's estate, member of the victim's family or any other person who is appointed by the court to act on the victim's behalf, except that the court shall not appoint the defendant as such a person.

(Proposed new section passed by the 2015 Legislature; agreed to and passed by the 2017 Legislature; effective November 27, 2018, if approved and ratified by the voters at the 2018 General Election. See: Statutes of Nevada 2015, p. 4073.)

SECTION 9. *Liberty of speech and the press.* Every citizen may freely speak, write and publish his sentiments on all subjects being responsible for the abuse of that right; and no law shall be passed to restrain or abridge the liberty of speech or of the press. In all criminal prosecutions and civil actions for libels, the truth may be given in evidence to the Jury; and if it shall appear to the Jury that the matter charged as libelous is true and was published with good motives and for justifiable ends, the party shall be acquitted or exonerated.

SECTION 10. *Right to assemble and to petition.* The people shall have the right freely to assemble together to consult for the common good, to instruct their representatives and to petition the Legislature for redress of Grievances.

SECTION 11. *Right to keep and bear arms; civil power supreme.*

1. Every citizen has the right to keep and bear arms for security and defense, for lawful hunting and recreational use and for other lawful purposes.

2. The military shall be subordinate to the civil power; No standing army shall be maintained by this State in time of peace, and in time of War, no appropriation for a standing army shall be for a longer time than two years.

[Amended in 1982. Proposed and passed by the 1979 legislature; agreed to and passed by the 1981 legislature; and approved and ratified by the people at the 1982 general election. See: Statutes of Nevada 1979, p. 1986; Statutes of Nevada 1981, p. 2083.]

SECTION 12. *Quartering soldier in private house.* No soldier shall, in time of Peace be quartered in any house without the consent of the owner, nor in time of War, except in the manner to be prescribed by law.

SECTION 13. *Representation apportioned according to population.* Representation shall be apportioned according to population.

SECTION 14. *Exemption of property from execution; imprisonment for debt.* The privilege of the debtor to enjoy the necessary comforts of life shall be recognized by wholesome laws, exempting a reasonable amount of property from seizure or sale for payment of any debts or liabilities hereafter contracted; And there shall be no imprisonment for debt, except in cases of fraud, libel, or slander, and no person shall be imprisioned [imprisoned] for a Militia fine in time of Peace.

SECTION 15. *Bill of attainder; ex post facto law; obligation of contract.* No bill of attainder, ex-post-facto law, or law impairing the obligation of contracts shall ever be passed.

SECTION 16. *Rights of foreigners* [Repealed in 1924.]
[Section 16 of the original constitution was repealed by vote of the people at the 1924 general election. See: Statutes of Nevada 1921, p. 416; Statutes of Nevada 1923, p. 407. The original section read: "Foreigners who are, or who may hereafter become Bona-fide residents of this State, shall enjoy the same rights, in respect to the possession, enjoyment and inheritance of property, as native born citizens."]

SECTION 17. *Slavery and involuntary servitude prohibited.* Neither Slavery nor involuntary servitude unless for the punishment of crimes shall ever be tolerated in this State.

SECTION 18. *Unreasonable seizure and search; issuance of warrants.* The right of the people to be secure in their persons, houses, papers and effects against unreasonable seizures and searches shall not be violated; and no warrant shall issue but on probable cause, supported by Oath or Affirmation, particularly describing the place or places to be searched, and the person or persons, and thing or things to be seized.

SECTION 19. *Treason.* Treason against the State shall consist only in levying war against it, adhering to its enemies or giving them Aid and Comfort. And no person shall be convicted of treason unless on the testimony of two witnesses to the same overt act, or on confession in open court.

SECTION 20. *Rights retained by people.* This enumeration of rights shall not be construed to impair or deny others retained by the people.

SECTION 21. *Limitation on recognition of marriage.* [*Effective through November 23, 2020, and after that date unless the provisions of Assembly Joint Resolution No. 2 (2017) are agreed to and passed by the 2019 Legislature and approved and ratified by the voters at the 2020 General Election.*] Only a marriage between a male and female person shall be recognized and given effect in this state.

[Added in 2002. Proposed by initiative petition and approved and ratified by the people at the 2000 and 2002 general elections.]

SECTION 21. *Recognition of marriage.* [*Effective November 24, 2020, if the provisions of Assembly Joint Resolution No. 2 (2017) are agreed to and passed by the 2019 Legislature and approved and ratified by the voters at the 2020 General Election.*]

1. The State of Nevada and its political subdivisions shall recognize marriages and issue marriage licenses to couples regardless of gender.
2. Religious organizations and members of the clergy have the right to refuse to solemnize a marriage, and no person has the right to make any claim against a religious organization or member of the clergy for such a refusal.
3. All legally valid marriages must be treated equally under the law.

[Added in 2002. Proposed by initiative petition and approved and ratified by the people at the 2000 and 2002 general elections.]—(Proposed amendment passed by the 2017 Legislature; effective November 24, 2020, if agreed to and passed by the 2019 Legislature and approved and ratified by the voters at the 2020 General Election. See: Statutes of Nevada 2017, p. 4558.)

SECTION 22. *Eminent domain proceedings: Restrictions and requirements.* Notwithstanding any other provision of this Constitution to the contrary:

1. Public use shall not include the direct or indirect transfer of any interest in property taken in an eminent domain proceeding from one private party to another private party. In all eminent domain actions, the government shall have the burden to prove public use.
2. In all eminent domain actions, prior to the government's occupancy, a property owner shall be given copies of all appraisals by the government and shall be entitled, at the property owner's election, to a separate and distinct determination by a district court jury, as to whether the taking is actually for a public use.
3. If a public use is determined, the taken or damaged property shall be valued at its highest and best use without considering any future dedication requirements imposed by the government. If private property is taken for any proprietary governmental purpose, then the property

shall be valued at the use to which the government intends to put the property, if such use results in a higher value for the land taken.

4. In all eminent domain actions, just compensation shall be defined as that sum of money, necessary to place the property owner back in the same position, monetarily, without any governmental offsets, as if the property had never been taken. Just compensation shall include, but is not limited to, compounded interest and all reasonable costs and expenses actually incurred.
5. In all eminent domain actions where fair market value is applied, it shall be defined as the highest price the property would bring on the open market.
6. Property taken in eminent domain shall automatically revert back to the original property owner upon repayment of the original purchase price, if the property is not used within five years for the original purpose stated by the government. The five years shall begin running from the date of the entry of the final order of condemnation.
7. A property owner shall not be liable to the government for attorney fees or costs in any eminent domain action.
8. For all provisions contained in this section, government shall be defined as the State of Nevada, its political subdivisions, agencies, any public or private agent acting on their behalf, and any public or private entity that has the power of eminent domain.
9. Any provision contained in this section shall be deemed a separate and freestanding right and shall remain in full force and effect should any other provision contained in this section be stricken for any reason.
[Added in 2008. Proposed by initiative petition and approved and ratified by the people at the 2006 and 2008 General Elections.]

SECTION 23. *Open, competitive retail electric energy market; granting of monopolies and exclusive franchises for generation of electricity prohibited; severability. [Effective November 27, 2018, if the proposed addition is approved and ratified by the voters at the 2018 General Election.]*

1. The People of the State of Nevada declare that it is the policy of this State that electricity markets be open and competitive so that all electricity customers are afforded meaningful choices among different providers, and that economic and regulatory burdens be minimized in order to promote competition and choices in the electric energy market. This Act shall be liberally construed to achieve this purpose.
2. Effective upon the dates set forth in Subsection 3, every person, business, association of persons or businesses, state agency, political subdivision of the State of Nevada, or any other entity in Nevada has the right to choose the provider of its electric utility service, including, but not

limited to, selecting providers from a competitive retail electric market, or by producing electricity for themselves or in association with others, and shall not be forced to purchase energy from one provider. Nothing herein shall be construed as limiting such persons' or entities' rights to sell, trade or otherwise dispose of electricity.

3. (a) Not later than July 1, 2023, the Legislature shall provide by law for provisions consistent with this Act to establish an open, competitive retail electric energy market, to ensure that protections are established that entitle customers to safe, reliable, and competitively priced electricity, including, but not limited to, provisions that reduce costs to customers, protect against service disconnections and unfair practices, and prohibit the grant of monopolies and exclusive franchises for the generation of electricity. The Legislature need not provide for the deregulation of transmission or distribution of electricity in order to establish a competitive market consistent with this Act.

(b) Upon enactment of any law by the Legislature pursuant to this Act before July 1, 2023, and not later than that date, any laws, regulations, regulatory orders or other provisions which conflict with this Act will be void. However, the Legislature may enact legislation consistent with this act that provides for an open electric energy market in part or in whole before July 1, 2023.

(c) Nothing herein shall be construed to invalidate Nevada's public policies on renewable energy, energy efficiency and environmental protection or limit the Legislature's ability to impose such policies on participants in a competitive electricity market.

4. Should any part of this Act be declared invalid, or the application thereof to any person, thing or circumstance is held invalid, such invalidity shall not affect the remaining provisions or application of this Act which can be given effect without the invalid provision or application, and to this end the provisions of this Act are declared to be severable. This Subsection shall be construed broadly to preserve and effectuate the declared purpose of this Act.

(Addition proposed by initiative petition and approved and ratified by the voters at the 2016 General Election; effective November 27, 2018, if approved and ratified by the voters at the 2018 General Election.)

ARTICLE 2.
Right of Suffrage

SECTION   1. Right to vote; qualifications of elector; qualifications of nonelector to vote for President and Vice President of United States.

1A. Rights of voters. [Effective November 24, 2020, if the provisions of

Senate Joint Resolution No. 3 (2017) are agreed to and passed by the 2019 Legislature and approved and ratified by the voters at the 2020 General Election.]

2. When residence not gained or lost.
3. Armed Forces personnel. [Repealed in 1972.]
4. Privilege of qualified electors on general election day.
5. Voting by ballot; voting in elections by legislature.
6. Registration of electors; test of electoral qualifications.
7. Poll tax: Levy and purpose. [Repealed in 1966.]
8. Qualifications of voters on adoption or rejection of constitution.
9. Recall of public officers: Procedure and limitations.
10. Limitation on contributions to campaign.

SECTION 1. *Right to vote; qualifications of elector; qualifications of nonelector to vote for President and Vice President of United States.* All citizens of the United States (not laboring under the disabilities named in this constitution) of the age of eighteen years and upwards, who shall have actually, and not constructively, resided in the state six months, and in the district or county thirty days next preceding any election, shall be entitled to vote for all officers that now or hereafter may be elected by the people, and upon all questions submitted to the electors at such election; *provided,* that no person who has been or may be convicted of treason or felony in any state or territory of the United States, unless restored to civil rights, and no person who has been adjudicated mentally incompetent, unless restored to legal capacity, shall be entitled to the privilege of an elector. There shall be no denial of the elective franchise at any election on account of sex. The legislature may provide by law the conditions under which a citizen of the United States who does not have the status of an elector in another state and who does not meet the residence requirements of this section may vote in this state for President and Vice President of the United States.

[Amended in 1880, 1886, 1914, 1970, 1971 and 2004. The first amendment was proposed and passed by the 1877 Legislature; agreed to and passed by the 1879 Legislature; and approved and ratified by the people at the 1880 General Election. See: Statutes of Nevada 1877, p. 213; Statutes of Nevada 1879, p. 149. The second amendment was approved and ratified by the people at the 1886 General Election, but no entry of the proposed amendment had been made upon the journal of either house of the Legislature, and such omission was fatal to the adoption of the amendment. See: State ex rel. Stevenson v. Tufly, 19 Nev. 391 (1887). The third amendment was proposed and passed by the 1911 Legislature; agreed to and passed by the 1913 Legislature; and approved and ratified by the people at the 1914 General Election. See: Statutes of Nevada 1911, p. 457; Statutes of Nevada 1913, p. 581. The fourth amendment was proposed and passed by the 1967 Legislature; agreed to and passed by the 1969 Legislature; and approved and ratified by the people at the 1970 General Election. See: Statutes of Nevada 1967, p. 1827; Statutes of

Nevada 1969, p. 1657. The fifth amendment was proposed and passed by the 1969 Legislature; agreed to and passed by the 1971 Legislature; and approved and ratified by the people at a special election held on June 8, 1971. See: Statutes of Nevada 1969, p. 1685; Statutes of Nevada 1971, p. 2263. The sixth amendment was proposed and passed by the 2001 Legislature; agreed to and passed by the 2003 Legislature; and approved and ratified by the people at the 2004 General Election. See: Statutes of Nevada 2001, p. 3469; Statutes of Nevada 2003, p. 3726.]

SECTION 1A. *Rights of voters.* [*Effective November 24, 2020, if the provisions of Senate Joint Resolution No. 3 (2017) are agreed to and passed by the 2019 Legislature and approved and ratified by the voters at the 2020 General Election.*] Each voter who is a qualified elector under this Constitution and is registered to vote in accordance with Section 6 of this Article and the laws enacted by the Legislature pursuant thereto has the right:

1. To receive and cast a ballot that:
   (a) Is written in a format that allows the clear identification of candidates; and
   (b) Accurately records the voter's preference in the selection of candidates.
2. To have questions concerning voting procedures answered and to have an explanation of the procedures for voting posted in a conspicuous place at the polling place.
3. To vote without being intimidated, threatened or coerced.
4. To vote during any period for early voting or on election day if the voter is waiting in line at a polling place at which, by law, the voter is entitled to vote at the time that the polls close and the voter has not already cast a vote in that election.
5. To return a spoiled ballot and receive another ballot in its place.
6. To request assistance in voting, if necessary.
7. To a sample ballot which is accurate, informative and delivered in a timely manner as provided by law.
8. To receive instruction in the use of the equipment for voting during any period for early voting or on election day.
9. To equal access to the elections system without discrimination, including, without limitation, discrimination on the basis of race, age, disability, military service, employment or overseas residence.
10. To a uniform, statewide standard for counting and recounting all votes accurately as provided by law.
11. To have complaints about elections and election contests resolved fairly, accurately and efficiently as provided by law.

(Proposed new section passed by the 2017 Legislature; effective November 24, 2020, if agreed to and passed by the 2019 Legislature and approved and ratified by the voters at the 2020 General Election. See: Statutes of Nevada 2017, p. 4589.)

SECTION 2. *When residence not gained or lost.* For the purpose of voting, no person shall be deemed to have gained or lost a residence solely by reason of his presence or absence while employed in the service of the United States, nor while engaged in the navigation of the waters of the United States or of the high seas; nor while a student of any institution of learning; nor while kept at any charitable institution or medical facility at public expense; nor while confined in any public prison.

[Amended in 1972. Proposed and passed by the 1969 legislature; agreed to and passed by the 1971 legislature; approved and ratified by the people at the 1972 general election. See: Statutes of Nevada 1969, p. 1695; Statutes of Nevada 1971, p. 2240.]

SECTION 3. *Armed Forces personnel.* [Repealed in 1972.]

[Amended in 1956. Proposed and passed by the 1953 legislature; agreed to and passed by the 1955 legislature; approved and ratified by the people at the 1956 general election. See: Statutes of Nevada 1953, p. 732; Statutes of Nevada 1955, p. 952. Repealed in 1972. Repealer proposed and passed by the 1969 legislature; agreed to and passed by the 1971 legislature; approved and ratified by the people at the 1972 general election. See: Statutes of Nevada 1969, p. 1695; Statutes of Nevada 1971, p. 2240. The section as amended in 1956 and repealed in 1972 read: "The right of suffrage shall be enjoyed by all persons, otherwise entitled to the same, who may be in the military or naval service of the United States; provided, the votes so cast shall be made to apply to the county and township of which said voters were bona fide residents at the time of their entry into such service; and provided further, that the payment of a poll tax shall not be required as a condition to the right of voting. Provision shall be made by law, regulating the manner of voting, holding elections, and making returns of such elections, wherein other provisions are not contained in this constitution."]

SECTION 4. *Privilege of qualified electors on general election day.* During the day on which any General Election shall be held in this State no qualified elector shall be arrested by virtue of any civil process.

SECTION 5. *Voting by ballot; voting in elections by legislature.* All elections by the people shall be by ballot, and all elections by the Legislature, or by either branch thereof shall be "Viva-Voce".

SECTION 6. *Registration of electors; test of electoral qualifications.* Provision shall be made by law for the registration of the names of the Electors within the counties of which they may be residents and for the ascertainment by proper proofs of the persons who shall be entitled to the right of suffrage, as hereby established, to preserve the purity of elections, and to regulate the manner of holding and making returns of the same; and the Legislature shall have power to prescribe by law any other or further rules or oaths, as may be deemed necessary, as a test of electoral qualification.

SECTION 7. *Poll tax: Levy and purpose.* [Repealed in 1966.]

[Amended in 1910. Proposed and passed by the 1907 legislature; agreed to and passed by the 1909 legislature; approved and ratified by the people at the 1910 general election. See: Statutes of Nevada 1907, p. 450; Statutes of Nevada 1909, p. 344. Repealed in 1966. Repealer proposed and passed by the 1963 legislature; agreed to and passed by the 1965 legislature; approved and ratified by the people at the 1966 general election. See: Statutes of Nevada 1963, p. 1421; Statutes of Nevada 1965, p. 1495. The section as amended in 1910 and repealed in 1966 read: "The Legislature shall provide by law for the payment of an annual poll tax of not less than two, nor exceeding four, dollars from each male resident in the State between the ages of twenty-one and sixty years (uncivilized American Indians excepted) to be expended for the maintenance and betterment of the public roads."]

SECTION 8. *Qualifications of voters on adoption or rejection of constitution.* All persons qualified by law to vote for representatives to the General Assembly of the Territory of Nevada, on the twenty first day of March A.D. Eighteen hundred and sixty four and all other persons who may be lawful voters in said Territory on the first Wednesday of September next following, shall be entitled to vote directly upon the question of adopting or rejecting this Constitution.

SECTION 9. *Recall of public officers: Procedure and limitations.* Every public officer in the State of Nevada is subject, as herein provided, to recall from office by the registered voters of the state, or of the county, district, or municipality which he represents. For this purpose, not less than twenty-five percent (25%) of the number who actually voted in the state or in the county, district, or municipality which he represents, at the election in which he was elected, shall file their petition, in the manner herein provided, demanding his recall by the people. They shall set forth in said petition, in not exceeding two hundred (200) words, the reasons why said recall is demanded. If he shall offer his resignation, it shall be accepted and take effect on the day it is offered, and the vacancy thereby caused shall be filled in the manner provided by law. If he shall not resign within five (5) days after the petition is filed, a special election shall be ordered to be held within thirty (30) days after the issuance of the call therefor, in the state, or county, district, or municipality electing said officer, to determine whether the people will recall said officer. On the ballot at said election shall be printed verbatim as set forth in the recall petition, the reasons for demanding the recall of said officer, and in not more than two hundred (200) words, the officer's justification of his course in office. He shall continue to perform the duties of his office until the result of said election shall be finally declared. Other candidates for the office may be nominated to be voted for at said special election. The candidate who shall receive highest number of votes at said special election shall be deemed elected for the remainder of the term, whether it be the person against whom the recall petition was filed, or another. The recall petition shall be filed with the officer with whom the petition for nomination to such office shall be filed, and the same officer shall order the special election when it is required. No such petition shall be circulated or filed against any officer until he has actually held his office six (6) months, save and except that it may be filed against a senator or assemblyman in the legislature at any time after ten (10) days from the beginning of the first session after his election. After one such petition and special election, no further recall petition shall be filed against the same officer during the term for which he was elected, unless such further petitioners shall pay into the public treasury from which the expenses of said special election have been paid, the whole amount paid out of said public treasury as expenses for the preceding special election. Such additional legislation as may aid the operation of this section shall be provided by law.

[Added in 1912, amended in 1970 and 1996. The addition was proposed and passed by the 1909 legislature; agreed to and passed by the 1911 legislature; and approved and ratified by the people at the 1912 general election. See: Statutes of Nevada 1909, p. 345; Statutes of Nevada 1911, p. 448. The first amendment was proposed and passed by the 1967 legislature; agreed to and passed by the 1969 legislature; and approved and ratified by the people at the 1970 general election. See: Statutes of Nevada 1967, p. 1782; Statutes of Nevada 1969, p. 1663. The second amendment was proposed and passed by the 1993 legislature; agreed to and passed by the 1995 legislature; and approved and ratified by the people at the 1996 general election. See: Statutes of Nevada 1993, p. 3135; Statutes of Nevada 1995, p. 2887.]

SECTION 10. *Limitation on contributions to campaign.*

1. As used in this Section, "contribution" includes the value of services provided in kind for which money would otherwise be paid, such as paid polling and resulting data, paid direct mail, paid solicitation by telephone, any paid campaign paraphernalia printed or otherwise produced, and the use of paid personnel to assist in a campaign.

2. The Legislature shall provide by law for the limitation of the total contribution by any natural or artificial person to the campaign of any person for election to any office, except a federal office, to $5,000 for the primary and $5,000 for the general election, and to the approval or rejection of any question by the registered voters to $5,000, whether the office sought or the question submitted is local or for the State as a whole. The Legislature shall further provide for the punishment of the contributor, the candidate, and any other knowing party to a violation of the limit, as a felony.

[Added in 1996. Proposed by initiative petition and approved and ratified by the people at the 1994 and 1996 General Elections.]

ARTICLE 3.
Distribution of Powers

SECTION   1. Three separate departments; separation of powers; legislative review
of administrative regulations.

SECTION 1. *Three separate departments; separation of powers; legislative review of administrative regulations.*

1. The powers of the Government of the State of Nevada shall be divided into three separate departments,—the Legislative,—the Executive and the Judicial; and no persons charged with the exercise of powers properly belonging to one of these departments shall exercise any functions, appertaining to either of the others, except in the cases expressly directed or permitted in this constitution.

2. If the legislature authorizes the adoption of regulations by an executive agency which bind persons outside the agency, the legislature may provide by law for:

   (a) The review of these regulations by a legislative agency before their effective date to determine initially whether each is within the statutory authority for its adoption;

   (b) The suspension by a legislative agency of any such regulation which appears to exceed that authority, until it is reviewed by a legislative body composed of members of the Senate and Assembly which is authorized to act on behalf of both houses of the legislature; and

   (c) The nullification of any such regulation by a majority vote of that legislative body, whether or not the regulation was suspended.

[Amended in 1996. Proposed and passed by the 1993 legislature; agreed to and passed by the 1995 legislature; and approved and ratified by the people at the 1996 general election. See: Statutes of Nevada 1993, p. 3082; Statutes of Nevada 1995, p. 2972.]

ARTICLE 4.
Legislative Department

SECTION   1. Legislative power vested in senate and assembly.

2. Biennial sessions of Legislature: Commencement; limitation on duration; void actions; submission of proposed executive budget.

2A. Special sessions of Legislature: Procedure for convening; precedence; limitations on business and duration; void actions.

3. Members of assembly: Election and term of office; eligibility for office.

4. Senators: Election and term of office; eligibility for office.

5. Number of Senators and members of Assembly; apportionment.

6. Power of houses to judge qualifications, elections and returns of

members; selection of officers; rules of proceedings; punishment of members.

7. Punishment of nonmember.
8. Senators and members of Assembly ineligible for certain offices.
9. Federal officers ineligible for state office; exceptions.
10. Embezzler of public money ineligible for office; disqualification for bribery.
11. Privilege of members: Freedom from arrest on civil process.
12. Vacancy.
13. Quorum; compelling attendance.
14. Journal.
15. Open sessions and meetings; adjournment for more than 3 days or to another place.
16. Bills may originate in either house; amendment.
17. Act to embrace one subject only; title; amendment.
18. Reading of bill; voting on final passage; number of members necessary to pass bill or joint resolution; signatures; referral of certain measures to voters; consent calendar.
19. Manner of drawing money from treasury.
20. Certain local and special laws prohibited.
21. General laws to have uniform application.
22. Suit against state.
23. Enacting clause; law to be enacted by bill.
24. Lotteries.
25. Uniform county and township government.
26. Boards of county commissioners: Election and duties.
27. Disqualification of jurors; elections.
28. Compensation of legislative officers and employees; increase or decrease of compensation.
29. Duration of regular and special sessions. [Repealed in 1958.]
30. Homesteads: Exemption from forced sale; joint consent required for alienation; recording of declaration.
31. Property of married persons.
32. County officers: Power of legislature; election, duties and compensation; duties of county clerks.
33. Compensation of members of Legislature; payment for postage, stationery and other expenses; additional allowances for officers.
34. Election of United States Senators. [Repealed in 2004.]
35. Bills to be presented to governor; approval; disapproval and reconsideration by legislature; failure of governor to return bill.
[36.] Abolishment of county; approval of voters in county.

37. Continuity of government in case of enemy attack; succession to
     public offices; legislative quorum requirements; relocation of seat of
     government.
37[A]. Consolidation of city and county containing seat of government into
     one municipal government; separate taxing districts.
38. Use of plant of genus Cannabis for medical purposes.

SECTION 1. *Legislative power vested in senate and assembly.* The Legislative
authority of this State shall be vested in a Senate and Assembly which shall
be designated "The Legislature of the State of Nevada" and the sessions of
such Legislature shall be held at the seat of government of the State.

SECTION 2. *Biennial sessions of Legislature: Commencement; limitation on
duration; void actions; submission of proposed executive budget.*
  1. The sessions of the Legislature shall be biennial, and shall commence
     on the 1st Monday of February following the election of members of
     the Assembly, unless the Governor of the State or the members of the
     Legislature shall, in the interim, convene the Legislature by proclama-
     tion or petition.
  2. The Legislature shall adjourn sine die each regular session not later
     than midnight Pacific time at the end of the 120th consecutive calen-
     dar day of that session, inclusive of the day on which that session com-
     mences. Any legislative action taken after midnight Pacific time at the
     end of the 120th consecutive calendar day of that session is void, unless
     the legislative action is conducted during a special session.
  3. The Governor shall submit the proposed executive budget to the Leg-
     islature not later than 14 calendar days before the commencement of
     each regular session.
  4. For the purposes of this section, "midnight Pacific time" must be deter-
     mined based on the actual measure of time that, on the final calendar
     day of the session, is being used and observed by the general popula-
     tion as the uniform time for the portion of Nevada which lies within
     the Pacific time zone, or any legal successor to the Pacific time zone,
     and which includes the seat of government of this State as designated
     by Section 1 of Article 15 of this Constitution. The Legislature and its
     members, officers and employees shall not employ any device, pretense
     or fiction that adjusts, evades or ignores this measure of time for the
     purpose of extending the duration of the session.
[Amended in 1889, 1958, 1960, 1998 and 2012. The first amendment was proposed and
passed by the 1885 Legislature; agreed to and passed by the 1887 Legislature; and approved and ratified by the people at a special election held February 11, 1889. See: Statutes of Nevada 1885, p. 151; Statutes of Nevada 1887, p. 165. The second amendment

was proposed and passed by the 1955 Legislature; agreed to and passed by the 1957 Legislature; and approved and ratified by the people at the 1958 General Election. See: Statutes of Nevada 1955, p. 946; Statutes of Nevada 1957, p. 793. The third amendment was proposed by initiative petition and approved and ratified by the people at the 1960 General Election. The fourth amendment was proposed and passed by the 1995 Legislature; agreed to and passed by the 1997 Legislature; and approved and ratified by the people at the 1998 General Election. See: Statutes of Nevada 1995, p. 2971; Statutes of Nevada 1997, p. 3725. The fifth amendment was proposed and passed by the 2009 Legislature; agreed to and passed by the 2011 Legislature; and approved and ratified by the people at the 2012 General Election. See: Statutes of Nevada 2009, p. 3285; Statutes of Nevada 2011, p. 3856.]

SECTION 2A. *Special sessions of Legislature: Procedure for convening; precedence; limitations on business and duration; void actions.*

1. The Legislature may be convened, on extraordinary occasions, upon a petition signed by two-thirds of the members elected to each House of the Legislature. A petition must specify the business to be transacted during the special session, indicate a date on or before which the Legislature is to convene and be transmitted to the Secretary of State. Upon receipt of one or more substantially similar petitions signed, in the aggregate, by the required number of members, calling for a special session, the Secretary of State shall notify all members of the Legislature and the Governor that a special session will be convened pursuant to this section.

2. At a special session convened pursuant to this section, the Legislature shall not introduce, consider or pass any bills except those related to the business specified in the petition and those necessary to provide for the expenses of the session.

3. A special session convened pursuant to this section takes precedence over a special session convened by the Governor pursuant to Section 9 of Article 5 of this Constitution, unless otherwise provided in the petition convening the special session pursuant to this section.

4. The Legislature may provide by law for the procedure for convening a special session pursuant to this section.

5. Except as otherwise provided in this subsection, the Legislature shall adjourn sine die a special session convened pursuant to this section not later than midnight Pacific time at the end of the 20th consecutive calendar day of that session, inclusive of the day on which that session commences. Any legislative action taken after midnight Pacific time at the end of the 20th consecutive calendar day of that session is void. This subsection does not apply to a special session that is convened to conduct proceedings for:

(a) Impeachment or removal from office of the Governor and other state and judicial officers pursuant to Article 7 of this Constitution; or

(b) Expulsion from office of a member of the Legislature pursuant to Section 6 of Article 4 of this Constitution.

6. For the purposes of this section, "midnight Pacific time" must be determined based on the actual measure of time that, on the final calendar day of the session, is being used and observed by the general population as the uniform time for the portion of Nevada which lies within the Pacific time zone, or any legal successor to the Pacific time zone, and which includes the seat of government of this State as designated by Section 1 of Article 15 of this Constitution. The Legislature and its members, officers and employees shall not employ any device, pretense or fiction that adjusts, evades or ignores this measure of time for the purpose of extending the duration of the session.

[Added in 2012. Proposed and passed by the 2009 Legislature; agreed to and passed by the 2011 Legislature; and approved and ratified by the people at the 2012 General Election. See: Statutes of Nevada 2009, p. 3284; Statutes of Nevada 2011, p. 3855.]

SECTION 3. *Members of assembly: Election and term of office; eligibility for office.*

1. The members of the Assembly shall be chosen biennially by the qualified electors of their respective districts, on the Tuesday next after the first Monday in November and their term of Office shall be two years from the day next after their election.

2. No person may be elected or appointed as a member of the Assembly who has served in that Office, or at the expiration of his current term if he is so serving will have served, 12 years or more, from any district of this State.

[Amended in 1996. Proposed by initiative petition and approved and ratified by the people at the 1994 and 1996 General Elections.]

SECTION 4. *Senators: Election and term of office; eligibility for office.*

1. Senators shall be chosen at the same time and places as members of the Assembly by the qualified electors of their respective districts, and their term of Office shall be four years from the day next after their election.

2. No person may be elected or appointed as a Senator who has served in that Office, or at the expiration of his current term if he is so serving will have served, 12 years or more, from any district of this State.

[Amended in 1996. Proposed by initiative petition and approved and ratified by the people at the 1994 and 1996 General Elections.]

SECTION 5. *Number of Senators and members of Assembly; apportionment.*
Senators and members of the Assembly shall be duly qualified electors in the

respective counties and districts which they represent, and the number of Senators shall not be less than one-third nor more than one-half of that of the members of the Assembly.

It shall be the mandatory duty of the Legislature at its first session after the taking of the decennial census of the United States in the year 1950, and after each subsequent decennial census, to fix by law the number of Senators and Assemblymen, and apportion them among the several counties of the State, or among legislative districts which may be established by law, according to the number of inhabitants in them, respectively.

[Amended in 1950 and 1970. The first amendment was proposed and passed by the 1947 legislature; agreed to and passed by the 1949 legislature; and approved and ratified by the people at the 1950 general election. See: Statutes of Nevada 1947, p. 881; Statutes of Nevada 1949, p. 685. The second amendment was proposed and passed by the 1967 legislature; agreed to and passed by the 1969 legislature; and approved and ratified by the people at the 1970 general election. See: Statutes of Nevada 1967, p. 1797; Statutes of Nevada 1969, p. 1723.]

SECTION 6. *Power of houses to judge qualifications, elections and returns of members; selection of officers; rules of proceedings; punishment of members.* Each House shall judge of the qualifications, elections and returns of its own members, choose its own officers (except the President of the Senate), determine the rules of its proceedings and may punish its members for disorderly conduct, and with the concurrence of two thirds of all the members elected, expel a member.

SECTION 7. *Punishment of nonmember.* Either House, during the session, may punish, by imprisonment, any person not a member, who shall have been guilty of disrespect to the House by disorderly or contemptuous behavior in its presence; but such imprisonment shall not extend beyond the final adjournment of the session.

SECTION 8. *Senators and members of Assembly ineligible for certain offices.* No Senator or member of Assembly shall, during the term for which he shall have been elected, nor for one year thereafter be appointed to any civil office of profit under this State which shall have been created, or the emoluments of which shall have been increased during such term, except such office as may be filled by elections by the people.

SECTION 9. *Federal officers ineligible for state office; exceptions.* No person holding any lucrative office under the Government of the United States or any other power, shall be eligible to any civil office of Profit under this State; Provided, that Post-Masters whose compensation does not exceed Five Hundred dollars per annum, or commissioners of deeds, shall not be deemed as holding a lucrative office.

SECTION 10. *Embezzler of public money ineligible for office; disqualification for bribery.* Any person who shall be convicted of the embezzlement, or defalcation of the public funds of this State or who may be convicted of having given or offered a bribe to procure his election or appointment to office, or received a bribe to aid in the procurement of office for any other person, shall be disqualified from holding any office of profit or trust in this State; and the Legislature shall, as soon as practicable, provide by law for the punishment of such defalcation, bribery, or embezzlement as a felony.

SECTION 11. *Privilege of members: Freedom from arrest on civil process.* Members of the Legislature shall be privileged from arrest on civil process during the session of the Legislature, and for fifteen days next before the commencement of each session.

SECTION 12. *Vacancy.* In case of the death or resignation of any member of the legislature, either senator or assemblyman, the county commissioners of the county from which such member was elected shall appoint a person of the same political party as the party which elected such senator or assemblyman to fill such vacancy; *provided,* that this section shall apply only in cases where no biennial election or any regular election at which county officers are to [be] elected takes place between the time of such death or resignation and the next succeeding session of the legislature.

[Amended in 1922 and 1944. The first amendment was proposed and passed by the 1919 legislature; agreed to and passed by the 1921 legislature; and approved and ratified by the people at the 1922 general election. See: Statutes of Nevada 1919, p. 478; Statutes of Nevada 1921, p. 412. The second amendment was proposed and passed by the 1941 legislature; agreed to and passed by the 1943 legislature; and approved and ratified by the people at the 1944 general election. See: Statutes of Nevada 1941, p. 563; Statutes of Nevada 1943, p. 311.]

SECTION 13. *Quorum; compelling attendance.* A majority of all the members elected to each House shall constitute a quorum to transact business, but a smaller number may adjourn, from day to day and may compel the attendance of absent members, in such manner, and under such penalties as each house may prescribe[.]

SECTION 14. *Journal.* Each House shall keep a journal of its own proceedings which shall be published and the yeas and nays of the members of either house on any question shall at the desire of any three members present, be entered on the journal.

SECTION 15. *Open sessions and meetings; adjournment for more than 3 days or to another place.* The doors of each House shall be kept open during its session, and neither shall, without the consent of the other, adjourn for more than three days nor to any other place than that in which they may be holding their sessions. The meetings of all legislative committees must be open to the public, except meetings held to consider the character, alleged misconduct, professional competence, or physical or mental health of a person.

[Amended in 1994. Proposed and passed by the 1991 legislature; agreed to and passed by the 1993 legislature; and approved and ratified by the people at the 1994 general election. See: Statutes of Nevada 1991, p. 2573; Statutes of Nevada 1993, p. 2974.]

SECTION 16. *Bills may originate in either house; amendment.* Any bill may originate in either House of the Legislature, and all bills passed by one may be amended in the other.

SECTION 17. *Act to embrace one subject only; title; amendment.* Each law enacted by the Legislature shall embrace but one subject, and matter, properly connected therewith, which subject shall be briefly expressed in the title; and no law shall be revised or amended by reference to its title only; but, in such case, the act as revised or section as amended, shall be re-enacted and published at length.

SECTION 18. *Reading of bill; voting on final passage; number of members necessary to pass bill or joint resolution; signatures; referral of certain measures to voters; consent calendar.*

1. Every bill, except a bill placed on a consent calendar adopted as provided in Subsection 4, must be read by sections on three several days, in each House, unless in case of emergency, two thirds of the House where such bill is pending shall deem it expedient to dispense with this rule. The reading of a bill by sections, on its final passage, shall in no case be dispensed with, and the vote on the final passage of every bill or joint resolution shall be taken by yeas and nays to be entered on the journals of each House. Except as otherwise provided in Subsection 2, a majority of all the members elected to each House is necessary to pass every bill or joint resolution, and all bills or joint resolutions so passed, shall be signed by the presiding officers of the respective Houses and by the Secretary of the Senate and Clerk of the Assembly.

2. Except as otherwise provided in Subsection 3, an affirmative vote of not fewer than two-thirds of the members elected to each House is necessary to pass a bill or joint resolution which creates, generates, or increases any public revenue in any form, including but not limited to taxes, fees, assessments and rates, or changes in the computation bases for taxes, fees, assessments and rates.

3. A majority of all of the members elected to each House may refer any measure which creates, generates, or increases any revenue in any form

to the people of the State at the next general election, and shall become effective and enforced only if it has been approved by a majority of the votes cast on the measure at such election.

4. Each House may provide by rule for the creation of a consent calendar and establish the procedure for the passage of uncontested bills.

[Amended in 1976 and 1996. The first amendment was proposed and passed by the 1973 Legislature; agreed to and passed by the 1975 Legislature; and approved and ratified by the people at the 1976 General Election. See: Statutes of Nevada 1973, p. 1946; Statutes of Nevada 1975, p. 1900. The second amendment was proposed by initiative petition and approved and ratified by the people at the 1994 and 1996 General Elections.]

SECTION 19. *Manner of drawing money from treasury.* No money shall be drawn from the treasury but in consequence of appropriations made by law.

[Amended in 1954. Proposed and passed by the 1951 legislature; agreed to and passed by the 1953 legislature; and approved and ratified by the people at the 1954 general election. See: Statutes of Nevada 1951, p. 584; Statutes of Nevada 1953, p. 717.]

SECTION 20. *Certain local and special laws prohibited.* The legislature shall not pass local or special laws in any of the following enumerated cases—that is to say:

Regulating the jurisdiction and duties of justices of the peace and of constables, and fixing their compensation;

For the punishment of crimes and misdemeanors;

Regulating the practice of courts of justice;

Providing for changing the venue in civil and criminal cases;

Granting divorces;

Changing the names of persons;

Vacating roads, town plots, streets, alleys, and public squares;

Summoning and impaneling grand and petit juries, and providing for their compensation;

Regulating county and township business;

Regulating the election of county and township officers;

For the assessment and collection of taxes for state, county, and township purposes;

Providing for opening and conducting elections of state, county, or township officers, and designating the places of voting;

Providing for the sale of real estate belonging to minors or other persons laboring under legal disabilities;

Giving effect to invalid deeds, wills, or other instruments;

Refunding money paid into the state treasury, or into the treasury of any county;

Releasing the indebtedness, liability, or obligation of any corporation, association, or person to the state, or to any county, town, or city of this state; but nothing in this section shall be construed to deny or restrict the power of the legislature to establish and regulate the compensation and fees of county officers, to authorize and empower the boards of county commissioners of the various counties of the state to establish and regulate the compensation and fees of township officers in their respective counties, to establish and regulate the rates of freight, passage, toll, and charges of railroads, tollroads, ditch, flume, and tunnel companies incorporated under the laws of this state or doing business therein.

[Amended in 1889, 1922 and 1926. The first amendment was proposed and passed by the 1885 Legislature; agreed to and passed by the 1887 Legislature; and approved and ratified by the people at a special election held February 11, 1889. See: Statutes of Nevada 1885, p. 152; Statutes of Nevada 1887, p. 166. The second amendment was proposed and passed by the 1919 Legislature; agreed to and passed by the 1921 Legislature; and approved and ratified by the people at the 1922 General Election. See: Statutes of Nevada 1919, p. 486; Statutes of Nevada 1921, p. 410. The third amendment was proposed and passed by the 1923 Legislature; agreed to and passed by the 1925 Legislature; and approved and ratified by the people at the 1926 General Election. See: Statutes of Nevada 1923, p. 411; Statutes of Nevada 1925, p. 357.]

SECTION 21. *General laws to have uniform application.* In all cases enumerated in the preceding section, and in all other cases where a general law can be made applicable, all laws shall be general and of uniform operation throughout the State.

SECTION 22. *Suit against state.* Provision may be made by general law for bringing suit against the State as to all liabilities originating after the adoption of this Constitution[.]

SECTION 23. *Enacting clause; law to be enacted by bill.* The enacting clause of every law shall be as follows: "The people of the State of Nevada represented in Senate and Assembly, do enact as follows," and no law shall be enacted except by bill.

SECTION 24. *Lotteries.*
1. Except as otherwise provided in Subsection 2, no lottery may be authorized by this State, nor may lottery tickets be sold.
2. The State and the political subdivisions thereof shall not operate a lottery. The Legislature may authorize persons engaged in charitable

activities or activities not for profit to operate a lottery in the form of a raffle or drawing on their own behalf. All proceeds of the lottery, less expenses directly related to the operation of the lottery, must be used only to benefit charitable or nonprofit activities in this State. A charitable or nonprofit organization shall not employ or otherwise engage any person to organize or operate its lottery for compensation. The Legislature may provide by law for the regulation of such lotteries.

[Amended in 1990. Proposed and passed by the 1987 legislature; agreed to and passed by the 1989 legislature; and approved and ratified by the people at the 1990 general election. See: Statutes of Nevada 1987, p. 2468; Statutes of Nevada 1989, p. 2249.]

SECTION 25. *Uniform county and township government.* The Legislature shall establish a system of County and Township Government which shall be uniform throughout the State.

SECTION 26. *Boards of county commissioners: Election and duties.* The Legislature shall provide by law, for the election of a Board of County Commissioners in each County, and such County Commissioners shall jointly and individually perform such duties as may be prescribed by law.

SECTION 27. *Disqualification of jurors; elections.* Laws shall be made to exclude from serving on juries, all persons not qualified electors of this State, and all persons who shall have been convicted of bribery, perjury, foregery [forgery,] larceny or other high crimes, unless restored to civil rights; and laws shall be passed regulating elections, and prohibiting under adequate penalties, all undue influence thereon from power, bribery, tumult, or other improper practice.

SECTION 28. *Compensation of legislative officers and employees; increase or decrease of compensation.* No money shall be drawn from the State Treasury as salary or compensation to any officer or employee of the Legislature, or either branch thereof, except in cases where such salary or compensation has been fixed by a law in force prior to the election or appointment of such officer or employee; and the salary or compensation so fixed, shall neither be increased nor diminished so as to apply to any officer or employee of the Legislature, or either branch thereof at such Session; Provided, that this restriction shall not apply to the first session of the Legislature.

SECTION 29. *Duration of regular and special sessions.* [Repealed in 1958.]

[Section 29 of Article 4 of the original constitution was repealed by vote of the people at the 1958 general election. See: Statutes of Nevada 1955, p. 945; Statutes of Nevada 1957, p. 793. The original section read: "The first regular session of the Legislature under this Constitution may extend to Ninety days, but no subsequent regular session shall exceed sixty days, nor any special session convened by the Governor exceed twenty days."]

SECTION 30. *Homesteads: Exemption from forced sale; joint consent required for alienation; recording of declaration.* A homestead as provided by law, shall be exempt from forced sale under any process of law, and shall not be alienated without the joint consent of husband and wife when that relation exists; but no property shall be exempt from sale for taxes or for the payment of obligations contracted for the purchase of said premises, or for the erection of improvements thereon; Provided, the provisions of this Section shall not apply to any process of law obtained by virtue of a lien given by the consent of both husband and wife, and laws shall be enacted providing for the recording of such homestead within the County in which the same shall be situated[.]

SECTION 31. *Property of married persons.* All property, both real and personal, of a married person owned or claimed by such person before marriage, and that acquired afterward by gift, devise or descent, shall be the separate property of such person. The legislature shall more clearly define the rights of married persons in relation to their separate property and other property.
[Amended in 1978. Proposed and passed by the 1975 legislature; agreed to and passed by the 1977 legislature; and approved and ratified by the people at the 1978 general election. See: Statutes of Nevada 1975, p. 1917; Statutes of Nevada 1977, p. 1703.]

SECTION 32. *County officers: Power of legislature; election, duties and compensation; duties of county clerks.* The Legislature shall have power to increase, diminish, consolidate or abolish the following county officers: County Clerks, County Recorders, Auditors, Sheriffs, District Attorneys and Public Administrators. The Legislature shall provide for their election by the people, and fix by law their duties and compensation. County Clerks shall be ex-officio Clerks of the Courts of Record and of the Boards of County Commissioners in and for their respective counties.
[Amended in 1889 and 1972. The first amendment was proposed and passed by the 1887 legislature; agreed to and passed by the 1889 legislature; and approved and ratified by the people at a special election held February 11, 1889. See: Statutes of Nevada 1887, p. 161; Statutes of Nevada 1889, p. 151. The second amendment was proposed and passed by the 1969 legislature; agreed to and passed by the 1971 legislature; and approved and ratified by the people at the 1972 general election. See: Statutes of Nevada 1969, p. 1723; Statutes of Nevada 1971, p. 2232.]

SECTION 33. *Compensation of members of Legislature; payment for postage, stationery and other expenses; additional allowances for officers.* The members of the Legislature shall receive for their services a compensation to be fixed by law and paid out of the public treasury, for not to exceed 60 days during any regular session of the Legislature and not to exceed 20 days during any special session; but no increase of such compensation shall take effect during the term for which the members of either house shall have been elected;

Provided, that an appropriation may be made for the payment of such actual expenses as members of the Legislature may incur for postage, express charges, newspapers and stationery not exceeding the sum of Sixty dollars for any general or special session to each member; and Furthermore Provided, that the Speaker of the Assembly, and Lieutenant Governor, as President of the Senate, shall each, during the time of their actual attendance as such presiding officers receive an additional allowance of two dollars per diem.

[Amended in 1958 and 2012. The first amendment was proposed and passed by the 1955 Legislature; agreed to and passed by the 1957 Legislature; and approved and ratified by the people at the 1958 General Election. See: Statutes of Nevada 1955, p. 946; Statutes of Nevada 1957, p. 794. The second amendment was proposed and passed by the 2009 Legislature; agreed to and passed by the 2011 Legislature; and approved and ratified by the people at the 2012 General Election. See: Statutes of Nevada 2009, p. 3285; Statutes of Nevada 2011, p. 3856.]

SECTION 34. *Election of United States Senators.* [Repealed in 2004.]
[Section 34 of the original constitution was repealed by vote of the people at the 2004 General Election. See: Statutes of Nevada 2001, p. 3470; Statutes of Nevada 2003, p. 3727. The original section read: "In all elections for United States Senators, such elections shall be held in joint convention of both Houses of the Legislature. It shall be the duty of the Legislature which convenes next preceding the expiration of the term of such Senator, to elect his successor. If a vacancy in such Senatorial representation from any cause occur, it shall be the duty of the Legislature then in Session or at the succeeding Session thereof, to supply such vacancy[.] If the Legislature shall at any time as herein provided, fail to unite in a joint convention within twenty days after the commencement of the Session of the Legislature for the election [of] such Senator it shall be the duty of the Governor, by proclamation to convene the two Houses of the Legislature in joint convention, within not less than five days nor exceeding ten days from the publication of his proclamation, and the joint convention when so assembled shall proceed to elect the Senator as herein provided."]

SECTION 35. *Bills to be presented to governor; approval; disapproval and reconsideration by legislature; failure of governor to return bill.* Every bill which may have passed the Legislature, shall, before it becomes a law be presented to the Governor. If he approve it, he shall sign it, but if not he shall return it with his objections, to the House in which it originated, which House shall cause such objections to be entered upon its journal, and proceed to reconsider it; If after such reconsideration it again pass both Houses by yeas and nays, by a vote of two thirds of the members elected to each House it shall become a law notwithstanding the Governors objections. If any bill shall not be returned within five days after it shall have been presented to him (Sunday excepted) exclusive of the day on which he received it, the same shall be a law, in like manner as if he had signed it, unless the Legislature by its final adjournment, prevent such return, in which case it shall be a law, unless the

Governor within ten days next after the adjournment (Sundays excepted) shall file such bill with his objections thereto, in the office of the Secretary of State, who shall lay the same before the Legislature at its next Session, in like manner as if it had been returned by the Governor, and if the same shall receive the vote of two-thirds of the members elected to each branch of the Legislature, upon a vote taken by yeas and nays to be entered upon the journals of each house, it shall become a law.

[SECTION 36.] *Abolishment of county; approval of voters in county.* The legislature shall not abolish any county unless the qualified voters of the county affected shall at a general or special election first approve such proposed abolishment by a majority of all the voters voting at such election. The legislature shall provide by law the method of initiating and conducting such election.

[Added in 1940. Proposed and passed by the 1937 legislature; agreed to and passed by the 1939 legislature; and approved and ratified by the people at the 1940 general election. See: Statutes of Nevada 1937, p. 564; Statutes of Nevada 1939, p. 360.]

SECTION 37. *Continuity of government in case of enemy attack; succession to public offices; legislative quorum requirements; relocation of seat of government.* The legislature, in order to insure continuity of state and local governmental operations in periods of emergency resulting from disasters caused by enemy attack, shall have the power and the immediate duty to provide for immediate and temporary succession to the powers and duties of public offices, of whatever nature and whether filled by election or appointment, the incumbents of which may become unavailable for carrying on the powers and duties of such offices, and to adopt such other measures as may be necessary and proper for insuring the continuity of governmental operations, including changes in quorum requirements in the legislature and the relocation of the seat of government. In the exercise of the powers hereby conferred, the legislature shall conform to the requirements of this constitution except to the extent that in the judgment of the legislature so to do would be impracticable or would admit of undue delay.

[Added in 1964. Proposed and passed by the 1961 legislature; agreed to and passed by the 1963 legislature; and approved and ratified by the people at the 1964 general election. See: Statutes of Nevada 1961, p. 831; Statutes of Nevada 1963, p. 1416.]

SECTION 37[A]. *Consolidation of city and county containing seat of government into one municipal government; separate taxing districts.* Notwithstanding the general provisions of Sections 20, 25, 26, and 36 of this article, the legislature may by law consolidate into one municipal government, with one set of officers, the city designated as the seat of government of this state and the county in which such city is situated. Such consolidated municipality shall be considered as a county for the purpose of representation in the legislature, shall have all the powers conferred upon counties by this constitution or by general law, and shall have such other powers as may be conferred by its charter. Notwithstanding the general provisions of Section 1 of Article 10, the legislature may create two or more separate taxing districts within such consolidated municipality.

[Added in 1968. Proposed and passed by the 1965 legislature; agreed to and passed by the 1967 legislature; and approved and ratified by the people at the 1968 general election. See: Statutes of Nevada 1965, p. 1515; Statutes of Nevada 1967, p. 1797.]

SECTION 38. *Use of plant of genus Cannabis for medical purposes.*

1. The legislature shall provide by law for:
   (a) The use by a patient, upon the advice of his physician, of a plant of the genus Cannabis for the treatment or alleviation of cancer, glaucoma, acquired immunodeficiency syndrome; severe, persistent nausea of cachexia resulting from these or other chronic or debilitating medical conditions; epilepsy and other disorders characterized by seizure; multiple sclerosis and other disorders characterized by muscular spasticity; or other conditions approved pursuant to law for such treatment.
   (b) Restriction of the medical use of the plant by a minor to require diagnosis and written authorization by a physician, parental consent, and parental control of the acquisition and use of the plant.
   (c) Protection of the plant and property related to its use from forfeiture except upon conviction or plea of guilty or nolo contendere for possession or use not authorized by or pursuant to this section.
   (d) A registry of patients, and their attendants, who are authorized to use the plant for a medical purpose, to which law enforcement officers may resort to verify a claim of authorization and which is otherwise confidential.
   (e) Authorization of appropriate methods for supply of the plant to patients authorized to use it.
2. This section does not:
   (a) Authorize the use or possession of the plant for a purpose other than medical or use for a medical purpose in public.
   (b) Require reimbursement by an insurer for medical use of the plant or accommodation of medical use in a place of employment.

[Added in 2000. Proposed by initiative petition and approved and ratified by the people at the 1998 and 2000 general elections.]

ARTICLE 5.
Executive Department

SECTION
1. Supreme executive power vested in governor.
2. Election and term of governor.
3. Eligibility; qualifications; number of terms.
4. Returns of general election transmitted to secretary of state; canvass by supreme court; declaration of election.
5. Governor is commander in chief of state military forces.
6. Transaction of executive business; reports of executive officers.
7. Responsibility for execution of laws.
8. Vacancies filled by governor.
9. Special sessions of Legislature: Authority of Governor; limitations on business and duration; void actions.
10. Governor's message.
11. Adjournment of legislature by governor.
12. Person holding federal office ineligible for office of governor.
13. Pardons, reprieves and commutations of sentence; remission of fines and forfeitures.
14. Remission of fines and forfeitures; commutations and pardons; suspension of sentence; probation. [Effective through November 23, 2020, and after that date unless the provisions of Senate Joint Resolution No. 1 (2017) are agreed to and passed by the 2019 Legislature and approved and ratified by the voters at the 2020 General Election.]
14. State Board of Pardons Commissioners; remission of fines and forfeitures; commutations and pardons; suspension of sentence; probation. [Effective November 24, 2020, if the provisions of Senate Joint Resolution No. 1 (2017) are agreed to and passed by the 2019 Legislature and approved and ratified by the voters at the 2020 General Election.]
15. The Great Seal.
16. Grants and commissions: Signatures and seal.
17. Election, term, qualifications and duties of Lieutenant Governor; President of Senate; President Pro-tempore of Senate to act as Governor in certain circumstances.
18. Vacancy in office of governor; duties to devolve upon lieutenant governor.
19. Other state officers: Election and term of office; eligibility for office.
20. Secretary of State: Duties.
21. Board of state prison commissioners; board of examiners; examination of claims.
22. Duties of certain state officers.

SECTION 1. *Supreme executive power vested in governor.* The supreme executive power of this State, shall be vested in a Chief Magistrate who shall be Governor of the State of Nevada.

SECTION 2. *Election and term of governor.* The Governor shall be elected by the qualified electors at the time and places of voting for members of the Legislature, and shall hold his office for Four Years from the time of his installation, and until his successor shall be qualified.

SECTION 3. *Eligibility; qualifications; number of terms.* No person shall be eligible to the Office of Governor, who is not a qualified elector, and who, at the time of such election, has not attained the age of twenty five years; and who shall not have been a citizen resident of this State for two years next preceding the election; nor shall any person be elected to the Office of Governor more than twice; and no person who has held the Office of Governor, or acted as Governor for more than two years of a term to which some other person was elected Governor shall be elected to the Office of Governor more than once.

[Amended in 1970. Proposed and passed by the 1967 Legislature; agreed to and passed by the 1969 Legislature; and approved and ratified by the people at the 1970 General Election. See: Statutes of Nevada 1967, p. 1794; Statutes of Nevada 1969, p. 1668.]

SECTION 4. *Returns of general election transmitted to secretary of state; canvass by supreme court; declaration of election.* The returns of every election for United States senator and member of Congress, district and state officers, and for and against any questions submitted to the electors of the State of Nevada, voted for at the general election, shall be sealed up and transmitted to the seat of government, directed to the secretary of state, and the chief justice of the supreme court, and the associate justices, or a majority thereof, shall meet at the office of the secretary of state, on a day to be fixed by law, and open and canvass the election returns for United States senator and member of Congress, district and state officers, and for and against any questions submitted to the electors of the State of Nevada, and forthwith declare the result and publish the names of the persons elected and the results of the vote cast upon any question submitted to the electors of the State of Nevada. The persons having the highest number of votes for the respective offices shall be declared elected, but in case any two or more have an equal and the highest number of votes for the same office, the legislature shall, by joint vote of both houses, elect one of said persons to fill said office.

[Amended in 1940. Proposed and passed by the 1937 legislature; agreed to and passed by the 1939 legislature; and approved and ratified by the people at the 1940 general election. See: Statutes of Nevada 1937, p. 553; Statutes of Nevada 1939, p. 361.]

SECTION 5. *Governor is commander in chief of state military forces.* The Governor shall be Commander in Chief of the Military forces of this State except when they shall be called into the service of the United States.

SECTION 6. *Transaction of executive business; reports of executive officers.* He shall transact all executive business with the Officers of the Government Civil and Military; and may require information in writing, from the Officers of the Executive Department, upon any subject relating to the duties of their respective Offices.

SECTION 7. *Responsibility for execution of laws.* He shall see that the laws are faithfully executed.

SECTION 8. *Vacancies filled by governor.* When any Office shall, from any cause become vacant and no mode is provided by the Constitution and laws for filling such vacancy, the Governor shall have the power to fill such vacancy by granting a commission which shall expire at the next election and qualification of the person elected to such Office.

SECTION 9. *Special sessions of Legislature: Authority of Governor; limitations on business and duration; void actions.*

1. Except as otherwise provided in Section 2A of Article 4 of this Constitution, the Governor may, on extraordinary occasions, convene the Legislature by Proclamation and shall state to both houses, when organized, the business for which they have been specially convened.

2. At a special session convened pursuant to this section, the Legislature shall not introduce, consider or pass any bills except those related to the business for which the Legislature has been specially convened and those necessary to provide for the expenses of the session.

3. Except as otherwise provided in this subsection, the Legislature shall adjourn sine die a special session convened pursuant to this section not later than midnight Pacific time at the end of the 20th consecutive calendar day of that session, inclusive of the day on which that session commences. Any legislative action taken after midnight Pacific time at the end of the 20th consecutive calendar day of that session is void. This subsection does not apply to a special session that is convened to conduct proceedings for:

   (a) Impeachment or removal from office of the Governor and other state and judicial officers pursuant to Article 7 of this Constitution; or

   (b) Expulsion from office of a member of the Legislature pursuant to Section 6 of Article 4 of this Constitution.

4. For the purposes of this section, "midnight Pacific time" must be determined based on the actual measure of time that, on the final calendar day of the session, is being used and observed by the general population as the uniform time for the portion of Nevada which lies within the Pacific time zone, or any legal successor to the Pacific time zone, and which includes the seat of government of this State as designated by Section 1 of Article 15 of this Constitution. The Legislature and its members, officers and employees shall not employ any device, pretense or fiction that adjusts, evades or ignores this measure of time for the purpose of extending the duration of the session.

[Amended in 2012. Proposed and passed by the 2009 Legislature; agreed to and passed by the 2011 Legislature; and approved and ratified by the people at the 2012 General Election. See: Statutes of Nevada 2009, p. 3286; Statutes of Nevada 2011, p. 3857.]

SECTION 10. *Governor's message.* He shall communicate by Message to the Legislature at every regular Session the condition of the State and recommend such measures as he may deem expedient[.]

SECTION 11. *Adjournment of legislature by governor.* In case of a disagreement between the two Houses with respect to the time of adjournment, the Governor shall have power to adjourn the Legislature to such time as he may think proper; Provided, it be not beyond the time fixed for the meeting of the next Legislature.

SECTION 12. *Person holding federal office ineligible for office of governor.* No person shall, while holding any office under the United States Government hold the office of Governor, except as herein expressly provided.

SECTION 13. *Pardons, reprieves and commutations of sentence; remission of fines and forfeitures.* The Governor shall have the power to suspend the collection of fines and forfeitures and grant reprieves for a period not exceeding sixty days dating from the time of conviction, for all offenses, except in cases of impeachment. Upon conviction for treason he shall have power to suspend the execution of the sentence until the case shall be reported to the Legislature at its next meeting, when the Legislature shall either pardon, direct the execution of the sentence, or grant a further reprieve. And if the Legislature should fail or refuse to make final disposition of such case, the sentence shall be enforced at such time and place as the Governor by his order may direct. The Governor shall communicate to the Legislature, at the beginning of every session, every case of fine or forfeiture remitted, or reprieve, pardon, or commutation granted, stating the name of the convict, the crime of which he was convicted, the Sentence, its date, and the date of the remission, commutation, pardon or reprieve.

SECTION 14. *Remission of fines and forfeitures; commutations and pardons; suspension of sentence; probation. [Effective through November 23, 2020, and after that date unless the provisions of Senate Joint Resolution No. 1 (2017) are agreed to and passed by the 2019 Legislature and approved and ratified by the voters at the 2020 General Election.]*

1. The governor, justices of the supreme court, and attorney general, or a major part of them, of whom the governor shall be one, may, upon such conditions and with such limitations and restrictions as they may think proper, remit fines and forfeitures, commute punishments, except as provided in Subsection 2, and grant pardons, after convictions, in all cases, except treason and impeachments, subject to such regulations as may be provided by law relative to the manner of applying for pardons.

2. Except as may be provided by law, a sentence of death or a sentence of life imprisonment without possibility of parole may not be commuted to a sentence which would allow parole.

3. The Legislature is authorized to pass laws conferring upon the district courts authority to suspend the execution of sentences, fix the conditions for, and to grant probation, and within the minimum and maximum periods authorized by law, fix the sentence to be served by the person convicted of crime in said courts.

[Amended in 1950 and 1982. The first amendment was proposed and passed by the 1947 legislature; agreed to and passed by the 1949 legislature; and approved and ratified by the people at the 1950 general election. See: Statutes of Nevada 1947, p. 875; Statutes of Nevada 1949, p. 684. The second amendment was proposed and passed by the 1979 legislature; agreed to and passed by the 1981 legislature; and approved and ratified by the people at the 1982 general election. See: Statutes of Nevada 1979, p. 2005; Statutes of Nevada 1981, p. 2097.]

SECTION 14. *State Board of Pardons Commissioners; remission of fines and forfeitures; commutations and pardons; suspension of sentence; probation. [Effective November 24, 2020, if the provisions of Senate Joint Resolution No. 1 (2017) are agreed to and passed by the 2019 Legislature and approved and ratified by the voters at the 2020 General Election.]*

1. The governor, justices of the supreme court, and attorney general shall constitute the State Board of Pardons Commissioners.

2. The State Board of Pardons Commissioners may, upon such conditions and with such limitations and restrictions as they may think proper, remit fines and forfeitures, commute punishments, except as provided in Subsection 3, and grant pardons, after convictions, in all cases, except treason and impeachments, subject to such regulations as may be provided by law relative to the manner of applying for pardons.

3. Except as may be provided by law, a sentence of death or a sentence of life imprisonment without possibility of parole may not be commuted to a sentence which would allow parole.

4. The State Board of Pardons Commissioners shall meet at least quarterly.

5. Any member of the State Board of Pardons Commissioners may submit matters for consideration by the State Board of Pardons Commissioners.

6. A majority of the members of the State Board of Pardons Commissioners is sufficient for any action taken by the State Board of Pardons Commissioners.

7. The Legislature is authorized to pass laws conferring upon the district courts authority to suspend the execution of sentences, fix the conditions for, and to grant probation, and within the minimum and maximum periods authorized by law, fix the sentence to be served by the person convicted of crime in said courts.

[Amended in 1950 and 1982. The first amendment was proposed and passed by the 1947 legislature; agreed to and passed by the 1949 legislature; and approved and ratified by the people at the 1950 general election. See: Statutes of Nevada 1947, p. 875; Statutes of Nevada 1949, p. 684. The second amendment was proposed and passed by the 1979 legislature; agreed to and passed by the 1981 legislature; and approved and ratified by the people at the 1982 general election. See: Statutes of Nevada 1979, p. 2005; Statutes of Nevada 1981, p. 2097.]—(Proposed amendment passed by the 2017 Legislature; effective November 24, 2020, if agreed to and passed by the 2019 Legislature and approved and ratified by the voters at the 2020 General Election. See: Statutes of Nevada 2017, p. 4588.)

SECTION 15. *The Great Seal.* There shall be a Seal of this State, which shall be kept by the Governor and used by him Officially, and shall be called "The Great Seal of the State of Nevada."

SECTION 16. *Grants and commissions: Signatures and seal.* All grants and commissions shall be in the name and by the authority of the State of Nevada, sealed with the Great Seal of the State, signed by the Governor and counter-signed by the Secretary of State.

SECTION 17. *Election, term, qualifications and duties of Lieutenant Governor; President of Senate; President Pro-tempore of Senate to act as Governor in certain circumstances.* A Lieutenant Governor shall be elected at the same time and places and in the same manner as the Governor and his term of Office, and his eligibility, shall also be the same. He shall be President of the Senate, but shall only have a casting vote therein. If during a Vacancy of the office of Governor, the Lieutenant Governor shall be impeached, displaced, resign, die, or become incapable of performing the duties of the office, or be absent from the State, the President *pro-tempore* of the Senate shall act as Governor until the vacancy be filled or the disability cease.

SECTION 18. *Vacancy in office of governor; duties to devolve upon lieutenant governor.* In case of the impeachment of the Governor, or his removal from Office, death, inability to discharge the duties of the said Office, resignation or absence from the State, the powers and duties of the Office shall devolve upon the Lieutenant Governor for the residue of the term, or until the disability shall cease. But when the Governor shall with the consent of the Legislature be out of the State, in time of War, and at the head of any military force thereof, he shall continue Commander in Chief of the military forces of the State.

SECTION 19. *Other state officers: Election and term of office; eligibility for office.*

1. A Secretary of State, a Treasurer, a Controller, and an Attorney General, shall be elected at the same time and places, and in the same manner as the Governor. The term of office of each shall be the same as is prescribed for the Governor.

2. Any elector shall be eligible to any of these offices, but no person may be elected to any of them more than twice, or more than once if he has previously held the office by election or appointment.

[Amended in 1954 and 1996. The first amendment was proposed and passed by the 1951 Legislature; agreed to and passed by the 1953 Legislature; and approved and ratified by the people at the 1954 General Election. See: Statutes of Nevada 1951, p. 581; Statutes of Nevada 1953, p. 715. The second amendment was proposed by initiative petition and approved and ratified by the people at the 1994 and 1996 General Elections.]

SECTION 20. *Secretary of State: Duties.* The Secretary of State shall keep a true record of the Official Acts of the Legislative and Executive Departments of the Government, and shall when required, lay the same and all matters relative thereto, before either branch of the Legislature.

SECTION 21. *Board of state prison commissioners; board of examiners; examination of claims.* The Governor, Secretary of State and Attorney General shall constitute a Board of State Prison Commissioners, which Board shall have such supervision of all matters connected with the State Prison as may be provided by law. They shall also constitute a Board of Examiners, with power to examine all claims against the State (except salaries or compensation of Officers fixed by law) and perform such other duties as may be prescribed by law, and no claim against the State (except salaries or compensation of Officers fixed by law) shall be passed upon by the Legislature without having been considered and acted upon by said "Board of Examiners."

SECTION 22. *Duties of certain state officers.* The Secretary of State, State Treasurer, State Controller, Attorney General, and Superintendent of Public Instruction shall perform such other duties as may be prescribed by law.

[Amended in 1954. Proposed and passed by the 1951 legislature; agreed to and passed by the 1953 legislature; and approved and ratified by the people at the 1954 general election. See: Statutes of Nevada 1951, p. 581; Statutes of Nevada 1953, p. 716.]

ARTICLE 6.
Judicial Department

SECTION   1. Judicial power vested in court system.
2. Supreme court: Composition; staggered terms of justices; holding of court by panels of justices and full court.
3. Justices of Supreme Court: Election; terms; Chief Justice.
3A. Court of appeals: Composition; panel of judges; appointment, election and terms of judges; chief judge; service of judges as supplemental district judges.
4. Jurisdiction of Supreme Court and court of appeals; appointment of judge to sit for disabled or disqualified justice or judge.
5. Judicial districts; election and terms of district judges.
6. District Courts: Jurisdiction; referees; family court.
7. Terms of courts.
8. Number, qualifications, terms of office and jurisdiction of justices of the peace; appeals; courts of record.
9. Municipal courts.
10. Fees or perquisites of judicial officers.
11. Justices and judges ineligible for other offices.
12. Judge not to charge jury respecting matters of fact; statement of testimony and declaration of law.
13. Style of process.
14. One form of civil action.
15. Compensation of justices and judges.
16. Special fee in civil action for compensation of judges.
17. Absence of judicial officer from state; vacation of office.
18. Territorial judicial officers not superseded until election and qualification of successors.
19. Administration of court system by chief justice.
20. Filling of vacancies occurring before expiration of term of office in Supreme Court or court of appeals or among district judges; Commission on Judicial Selection.
21. Commission on Judicial Discipline; Code of Judicial Conduct.

SECTION 1. *Judicial power vested in court system.* The judicial power of this State is vested in a court system, comprising a Supreme Court, a court of appeals, district courts and justices of the peace. The Legislature may also establish, as part of the system, courts for municipal purposes only in incorporated cities and towns.

[Amended in 1976 and 2014. The first amendment was proposed and passed by the 1973 Legislature; agreed to and passed by the 1975 Legislature; and approved and ratified by the people at the 1976 General Election. See: Statutes of Nevada 1973, p. 1960; Statutes of Nevada 1975, p. 1934. The second amendment was proposed and passed by the 2011 Legislature; agreed to and passed by the 2013 Legislature; and approved and ratified by the people at the 2014 General Election. See: Statutes of Nevada 2011, p. 3836; Statutes of Nevada 2013, p. 3968.]

SECTION 2. *Supreme court: Composition; staggered terms of justices; holding of court by panels of justices and full court.*

1. The Supreme Court consists of the Chief Justice and two or more associate justices, as may be provided by law. In increasing or diminishing the number of associate justices, the Legislature shall provide for the arrangement of their terms so that an equal number of terms, as nearly as may be, expire every 2 years.

2. The Legislature may provide by law:

    (a) If the Court consists of more than five justices, for the hearing and decision of cases by panels of no fewer than three justices, the resolution by the full Court of any conflicts between decisions so rendered, and the kinds of cases which must be heard by the full Court.

    (b) For the places of holding court by panels of justices if established, and by the full Court.

[Amended in 1976. Proposed and passed by the 1973 Legislature; agreed to and passed by the 1975 Legislature; and approved and ratified by the people at the 1976 General Election. See: Statutes of Nevada 1973, p. 1952; Statutes of Nevada 1975, p. 1980.]

SECTION 3. *Justices of Supreme Court: Election; terms; Chief Justice.* The justices of the Supreme Court, shall be elected by the qualified electors of the State at the general election, and shall hold office for the term of six years from and including the first Monday of January next succeeding their election; provided, that there shall be elected, at the first election under this Constitution, three justices of the Supreme Court who shall hold office from and including the first Monday of December A.D., eighteen hundred and sixty four, and continue in office thereafter, two, four and six years respectively, from and including the first Monday of January next suceeding [succeeding] their election. They shall meet as soon as practicable after their election and qualification, and at their first meeting shall determine by lot, the term of office each shall fill, and the justice drawing the shortest term shall be Chief Justice, and after the expiration of his term, the one having the next shortest term shall be Chief Justice, after which the senior justice in commission shall be Chief Justice; and in case the commission of any two or more of said justices shall bear the same date, they shall determine by lot, who shall be Chief Justice.

SECTION 3A. *Court of appeals: Composition; panel of judges; appointment, election and terms of judges; chief judge; service of judges as supplemental district judges.*

1. The court of appeals consists of three judges or such greater number as the Legislature may provide by law. If the number of judges is so increased, the Supreme Court must provide by rule for the assignment of each appeal to a panel of three judges for decision.

2. After the initial terms, each judge of the court of appeals must be elected by the qualified electors of this State at the general election for a term of 6 years beginning on the first Monday of January next after the election. The initial three judges of the court of appeals must be appointed by the Governor from among three nominees selected for each individual seat by the permanent Commission on Judicial Selection described in Subsection 3 of Section 20 of this Article. After the expiration of 30 days from the date on which the permanent Commission on Judicial Selection has delivered to the Governor its list of nominees for the initial judges, if the Governor has not made the appointments required by this Section, the Governor shall make no other appointment to any public office until the Governor has appointed a judge from the list submitted. The term of the initial judges is 2 years beginning on the first Monday of January next after the effective date of this Section, and an initial judge may succeed himself. If there is an increase in the number of judges, each additional judge must be elected by the qualified electors of this State at the first general election following the increase for a term of 6 years beginning on the first Monday of January next after the election.

3. The Chief Justice of the Supreme Court shall appoint one of the judges of the court of appeals to be chief judge. The chief judge serves a term of 4 years, except that the term of the initial chief judge is 2 years. The chief judge may succeed himself. The chief judge may resign the position of chief judge without resigning from the court of appeals.

4. The Supreme Court shall provide by rule for the assignment of one or more judges of the court of appeals to devote a part of their time to serve as supplemental district judges, where needed.

[Added in 2014. Proposed and passed by the 2011 Legislature; agreed to and passed by the 2013 Legislature; and approved and ratified by the people at the 2014 General Election. See: Statutes of Nevada 2011, p. 3835; Statutes of Nevada 2013, p. 3968.]

SECTION 4. *Jurisdiction of Supreme Court and court of appeals; appointment of judge to sit for disabled or disqualified justice or judge.*

1. The Supreme Court and the court of appeals have appellate jurisdiction in all civil cases arising in district courts, and also on questions of law alone in all criminal cases in which the offense charged is within the original jurisdiction of the district courts. The Supreme Court shall fix by rule the jurisdiction of the court of appeals and shall provide for the review, where appropriate, of appeals decided by the court of appeals. The Supreme Court and the court of appeals have power to issue writs of *mandamus, certiorari*, prohibition, *quo warranto* and *habeas corpus* and also all writs necessary or proper to the complete exercise of their jurisdiction. Each justice of the Supreme Court and judge of the court of appeals may issue writs of *habeas corpus* to any part of the State, upon petition by, or on behalf of, any person held in actual custody in this State and may make such writs returnable before the issuing justice or judge or the court of which the justice or judge is a member, or before any district court in the State or any judge of a district court.

2. In case of the disability or disqualification, for any cause, of a justice of the Supreme Court, the Governor may designate a judge of the court of appeals or a district judge to sit in the place of the disqualified or disabled justice. The judge designated by the Governor is entitled to receive his actual expense of travel and otherwise while sitting in the Supreme Court.

3. In the case of the disability or disqualification, for any cause, of a judge of the court of appeals, the Governor may designate a district judge to sit in the place of the disabled or disqualified judge. The judge whom the Governor designates is entitled to receive his actual expense of travel and otherwise while sitting in the court of appeals.

[Amended in 1920, 1976, 1978 and 2014. The first amendment was proposed and passed by the 1917 Legislature; agreed to and passed by the 1919 Legislature; and approved and ratified by the people at the 1920 General Election. See: Statutes of Nevada 1917, p. 491; Statutes of Nevada 1919, p. 485. The second amendment was proposed and passed by the 1973 Legislature; agreed to and passed by the 1975 Legislature; and approved and ratified by the people at the 1976 General Election. See: Statutes of Nevada 1973, p. 1953; Statutes of Nevada 1975, p. 1981. The third amendment was proposed and passed by the 1975 Legislature; agreed to and passed by the 1977 Legislature; and approved and ratified by the people at the 1978 General Election. See: Statutes of Nevada 1975, p. 1951; Statutes of Nevada 1977, p. 1690. The fourth amendment was proposed and passed by the 2011 Legislature; agreed to and passed by the 2013 Legislature; and approved

and ratified by the people at the 2014 General Election. See: Statutes of Nevada 2011,
p. 3835; Statutes of Nevada 2013, p. 3968.]

SECTION 5. *Judicial districts; election and terms of district judges.* The State
is hereby divided into nine judicial districts of which the County of Storey
shall constitute the First; The County of Ormsby the Second; the County
of Lyon the Third; The County of Washoe the Fourth; The Counties of Nye
and Churchill the Fifth; The County of Humboldt the Sixth; The County of
Lander the Seventh; The County of Douglas the Eighth; and the County of
Esmeralda the Ninth. The County of Roop shall be attached to the County
of Washoe for judicial purposes until otherwise provided by law. The Legislature may, however, provide by law for an alteration in the boundaries or
divisions of the districts herein prescribed, and also for increasing or diminishing the number of the judicial districts and judges therein. But no such
change shall take effect, except in case of a vacancy, or the expiration of the
term of an incumbent of the office. At the first general election under this
Constitution there shall be elected in each of the respective districts (except
as in this Section hereafter otherwise provided) one district judge, who shall
hold office from and including the first Monday of December A.D., eighteen
hundred and sixty four and until the first Monday of January in the year
eighteen hundred and sixty seven. After the said first election, there shall be
elected at the general election which immediately precedes the expiration of
the term of his predecessor, one district judge in each of the respective judicial
districts (except in the First District as in this Section hereinafter provided.)
The district judges shall be elected by the qualified electors of their respective districts, and shall hold office for the term of 6 years (excepting those
elected at said first election) from and including the first Monday of January,
next succeeding their election and qualification; provided, that the First Judicial District shall be entitled to, and shall have three district judges, who shall
possess co-extensive and concurrent jurisdiction, and who shall be elected at
the same times, in the same manner, and shall hold office for the like terms as
herein prescribed, in relation to the judges in other judicial districts, any one
of said judges may preside on the empanneling [empaneling] of grand juries
and the presentment and trial on indictments, under such rules and regulations as may be prescribed by law.
[Amended in 1976. Proposed and passed by the 1973 legislature; agreed to and passed by
the 1975 legislature; and approved and ratified by the people at the 1976 general election. See: Statutes of Nevada 1973, p. 1955; Statutes of Nevada 1975, p. 1932.]

SECTION 6. *District Courts: Jurisdiction; referees; family court.*

1. The District Courts in the several Judicial Districts of this State have
   original jurisdiction in all cases excluded by law from the original jurisdiction of justices' courts. They also have final appellate jurisdiction in

cases arising in Justices Courts and such other inferior tribunals as may be established by law. The District Courts and the Judges thereof have power to issue writs of Mandamus, Prohibition, Injunction, Quo-Warranto, Certiorari, and all other writs proper and necessary to the complete exercise of their jurisdiction. The District Courts and the Judges thereof shall also have power to issue writs of Habeas Corpus on petition by, or on behalf of any person who is held in actual custody in their respective districts, or who has suffered a criminal conviction in their respective districts and has not completed the sentence imposed pursuant to the judgment of conviction.

2. The legislature may provide by law for:

    (a) Referees in district courts.

    (b) The establishment of a family court as a division of any district court and may prescribe its jurisdiction.

[Amended in 1978, 1986, 1990 and 1992. The first amendment was proposed and passed by the 1975 legislature; agreed to and passed by the 1977 legislature; and approved and ratified by the people at the 1978 general election. See: Statutes of Nevada 1975, p. 1951; Statutes of Nevada 1977, p. 1690. The second amendment was proposed and passed by the 1983 legislature; agreed to and passed by the 1985 legislature; and approved and ratified by the people at the 1986 general election. See: Statutes of Nevada 1983, p. 2188; Statutes of Nevada 1985, p. 2332. The third amendment was proposed and passed by the 1987 legislature; agreed to and passed by the 1989 legislature; and approved and ratified by the people at the 1990 general election. See: Statutes of Nevada 1987, p. 2444; Statutes of Nevada 1989, p. 2222. The fourth amendment was proposed and passed by the 1989 legislature; agreed to and passed by the 1991 legislature; and approved and ratified by the people at the 1992 general election. See: Statutes of Nevada 1989, p. 2269; Statutes of Nevada 1991, p. 2494.]

SECTION 7. *Terms of courts.* The times of holding the Supreme Court, the court of appeals and the district courts must be as fixed by law. The terms of the Supreme Court must be held at the seat of government unless the Legislature otherwise provides by law, except that the Supreme Court may hear oral argument at other places in the State. The terms of the court of appeals must be held at the place provided by law. The terms of the district courts must be held at the county seats of their respective counties unless the Legislature otherwise provides by law.

[Amended twice in 1976 and in 1998 and 2014. The first and second amendments were proposed and passed by the 1973 Legislature; agreed to and passed by the 1975 Legislature; and approved and ratified by the people at the 1976 General Election. See: Statutes of Nevada 1973, pp. 1940 and 1953; Statutes of Nevada 1975, pp. 1870 and 1981. The first and second amendments were combined pursuant to Nev. Article 16, § 1. The third amendment was proposed and passed by the 1995 Legislature; agreed to and passed by the 1997 Legislature; and approved and ratified by the people at the 1998 General Election. See: Statutes of Nevada 1995, p. 2964; Statutes of Nevada 1997, p. 3598. The fourth amendment was proposed and passed by the 2011 Legislature; agreed to and passed by the 2013 Legislature; and approved and ratified by the people at the 2014 General Election. See: Statutes of Nevada 2011, p. 3835; Statutes of Nevada 2013, p. 3968.]

SECTION 8. *Number, qualifications, terms of office and jurisdiction of justices of the peace; appeals; courts of record.*

1. The Legislature shall determine the number of justices of the peace to be elected in each city and township of the State and shall fix by law their qualifications, their terms of office and the limits of their civil and criminal jurisdiction, according to the amount in controversy, the nature of the case, the penalty provided or any combination of these.

2. The provisions of this section affecting the number, qualifications, terms of office and jurisdiction of justices of the peace become effective on the first Monday of January, 1979.

3. The Legislature shall also prescribe by law the manner, and determine the cases, in which appeals may be taken from justices and other courts. The Supreme Court, the court of appeals, the district courts and such other courts as the Legislature designates are courts of record.

[Amended in 1978 and 2014. The first amendment was proposed and passed by the 1975 Legislature; agreed to and passed by the 1977 Legislature; and approved and ratified by the people at the 1978 General Election. See: Statutes of Nevada 1975, p. 1952; Statutes of Nevada 1977, p. 1691. The second amendment was proposed and passed by the 2011 Legislature; agreed to and passed by the 2013 Legislature; and approved and ratified by the people at the 2014 General Election. See: Statutes of Nevada 2011, p. 3835; Statutes of Nevada 2013, p. 3968.]

SECTION 9. *Municipal courts.* Provision shall be made by law prescribing the powers[,] duties and responsibilities of any Municipal Court that may be established in pursuance of Section 1, of this Article; and also fixing by law the jurisdiction of said Court so as not to conflict with that of the several courts of Record.

SECTION 10. *Fees or perquisites of judicial officers.* No Judicial Officer, except Justices of the Peace and City Recorders shall receive to his own use any fees or perquisites of Office[.]

SECTION 11. *Justices and judges ineligible for other offices.* The justices of the Supreme Court, the judges of the court of appeals and the district judges are ineligible to any office, other than a judicial office, during the term for which they have been elected or appointed. All elections or appointments of any such judges by the people, Legislature or otherwise during said period to any office other than judicial are void.

[Amended in 1950 and 2014. The first amendment was proposed and passed by the 1947 Legislature; agreed to and passed by the 1949 Legislature; and approved and ratified by the people at the 1950 General Election. See: Statutes of Nevada 1947, p. 878; Statutes of Nevada 1949, p. 684. The second amendment was proposed and passed by the 2011 Legislature; agreed to and passed by the 2013 Legislature; and approved and ratified by the people at the 2014 General Election. See: Statutes of Nevada 2011, p. 3835; Statutes of Nevada 2013, p. 3968.]

SECTION 12. *Judge not to charge jury respecting matters of fact; statement of testimony and declaration of law.* Judges shall not charge juries in respect to matters of fact, but may state the testimony and declare the law.

SECTION 13. *Style of process.* The style of all process shall be "The State of Nevada" and all prosecutions shall be conducted in the name and by the authority of the same.

SECTION 14. *One form of civil action.* There shall be but one form of civil action, and law and equity may be administered in the same action.

SECTION 15. *Compensation of justices and judges.* The justices of the Supreme Court, the judges of the court of appeals and the district judges are each entitled to receive for their services a compensation to be fixed by law and paid in the manner provided by law, which must not be increased or diminished during the term for which they have been elected, unless a vacancy occurs, in which case the successor of the former incumbent is entitled to receive only such salary as may be provided by law at the time of his election or appointment. A provision must be made by law for setting apart from each year's revenue a sufficient amount of money to pay such compensation.

[Amended in 1968 and 2014. The first amendment was proposed and passed by the 1965 Legislature; agreed to and passed by the 1967 Legislature; and approved and ratified by the people at the 1968 General Election. See: Statutes of Nevada 1965, p. 1487; Statutes of Nevada 1967, p. 1787. The second amendment was proposed and passed by the 2011 Legislature; agreed to and passed by the 2013 Legislature; and approved and ratified by the people at the 2014 General Election. See: Statutes of Nevada 2011, p. 3835; Statutes of Nevada 2013, p. 3968.]

SECTION 16. *Special fee in civil action for compensation of judges.* The Legislature at its first Session, and from time to time thereafter shall provide by law, that upon the institution of each civil action, and other proceedings, and also upon the perfecting of an appeal in any civil action or proceeding, in the several Courts of Record in this State, a special Court fee, or tax shall be advanced to the Clerks of said Courts, respectively by the party or parties bringing such action or proceeding, or taking such appeal and the money so paid in shall be accounted for by such Clerks, and applied towards the payment of the compensation of the Judges of said Courts, as shall be directed by law.

SECTION 17. *Absence of judicial officer from state; vacation of office.* The Legislature shall have no power to grant leave of absence to a Judicial Officer, and any such Officer who shall absent himself from the State for more than Ninety consecutive days, shall be deemed to have vacated his Office[.]

SECTION 18. *Territorial judicial officers not superseded until election and qualification of successors.* No Judicial Officer shall be superceeded [superseded] nor shall the Organization of the several Courts of the Territory of Nevada be changed until the election and qualification of the several Officers provided for in this article[.]

SECTION 19. *Administration of court system by chief justice.*
1. The chief justice is the administrative head of the court system. Subject to such rules as the supreme court may adopt, the chief justice may:
    (a) Apportion the work of the supreme court among justices.
    (b) Assign district judges to assist in other judicial districts or to specialized functions which may be established by law.
    (c) Recall to active service any retired justice or judge of the court system who consents to such recall and who has not been removed or retired for cause or defeated for retention in office, and may assign him to appropriate temporary duty within the court system.
2. In the absence or temporary disability of the chief justice, the associate justice senior in commission shall act as chief justice.
3. This section becomes effective July 1, 1977.
[Added in 1976. Proposed and passed by the 1973 legislature; agreed to and passed by the 1975 legislature; and approved and ratified by the people at the 1976 general election. See: Statutes of Nevada 1973, p. 1960; Statutes of Nevada 1975, p. 1934.]

SECTION 20. *Filling of vacancies occurring before expiration of term of office in Supreme Court or court of appeals or among district judges; Commission on Judicial Selection.*
1. When a vacancy occurs before the expiration of any term of office in the Supreme Court or the court of appeals or among the district judges, the Governor shall appoint a justice or judge from among three nominees selected for such individual vacancy by the Commission on Judicial Selection.
2. The term of office of any justice or judge so appointed expires on the first Monday of January following the next general election.
3. Each nomination for the Supreme Court or the court of appeals must be made by the permanent Commission, composed of:
    (a) The Chief Justice or an associate justice designated by him;
    (b) Three members of the State Bar of Nevada, a public corporation created by statute, appointed by its Board of Governors; and

> (c) Three persons, not members of the legal profession, appointed by the Governor.

4. Each nomination for the district court must be made by a temporary commission composed of:
   - (a) The permanent Commission;
   - (b) A member of the State Bar of Nevada resident in the judicial district in which the vacancy occurs, appointed by the Board of Governors of the State Bar of Nevada; and
   - (c) A resident of such judicial district, not a member of the legal profession, appointed by the Governor.

5. If at any time the State Bar of Nevada ceases to exist as a public corporation or ceases to include all attorneys admitted to practice before the courts of this State, the Legislature shall provide by law, or if it fails to do so the Supreme Court shall provide by rule, for the appointment of attorneys at law to the positions designated in this Section to be occupied by members of the State Bar of Nevada.

6. The term of office of each appointive member of the permanent Commission, except the first members, is 4 years. Each appointing authority shall appoint one of the members first appointed for a term of 2 years. If a vacancy occurs, the appointing authority shall fill the vacancy for the unexpired term. The additional members of a temporary commission must be appointed when a vacancy occurs, and their terms expire when the nominations for such vacancy have been transmitted to the Governor.

7. An appointing authority shall not appoint to the permanent Commission more than:
   - (a) One resident of any county.
   - (b) Two members of the same political party.

No member of the permanent Commission may be a member of the Commission on Judicial Discipline.

8. After the expiration of 30 days from the date on which the Commission on Judicial Selection has delivered to him its list of nominees for any vacancy, if the Governor has not made the appointment required by this Section, he shall make no other appointment to any public office until he has appointed a justice or judge from the list submitted.

[Added in 1976 and amended in 2014. The addition was proposed and passed by the 1973 Legislature; agreed to and passed by the 1975 Legislature; and approved and ratified by the people at the 1976 General Election. See: Statutes of Nevada 1973, p. 1954; Statutes of Nevada 1975, p. 1872. The first amendment was proposed and passed by the 2011 Legislature; agreed to and passed by the 2013 Legislature; and approved and ratified by the people at the 2014 General Election. See: Statutes of Nevada 2011, p. 3835; Statutes of Nevada 2013, p. 3968.]

SECTION 21. *Commission on Judicial Discipline; Code of Judicial Conduct.*

1. A justice of the Supreme Court, a judge of the court of appeals, a district judge, a justice of the peace or a municipal judge may, in addition to the provision of Article 7 for impeachment, be censured, retired, removed or otherwise disciplined by the Commission on Judicial Discipline. Pursuant to rules governing appeals adopted by the Supreme Court, a justice or judge may appeal from the action of the Commission to the Supreme Court, which may reverse such action or take any alternative action provided in this subsection.

2. The Commission is composed of:
   (a) Two justices or judges appointed by the Supreme Court;
   (b) Two members of the State Bar of Nevada, a public corporation created by statute, appointed by its Board of Governors; and
   (c) Three persons, not members of the legal profession, appointed by the Governor.

The Commission shall elect a Chairman from among its three lay members.

3. If at any time the State Bar of Nevada ceases to exist as a public corporation or ceases to include all attorneys admitted to practice before the courts of this State, the Legislature shall provide by law, or if it fails to do so the Supreme Court shall provide by rule, for the appointment of attorneys at law to the positions designated in this Section to be occupied by members of the State Bar of Nevada.

4. The term of office of each appointive member of the Commission, exceptthe first members, is 4 years. Each appointing authority shall appoint one of the members first appointed for a term of 2 years. If a vacancy occurs, the appointing authority shall fill the vacancy for the unexpired term. An appointing authority shall not appoint more than one resident of any county. The Governor shall not appoint more than two members of the same political party. No member may be a member of a commission on judicial selection.

5. The Legislature shall establish:
   (a) In addition to censure, retirement and removal, the other forms of disciplinary action that the Commission may impose;
   (b) The grounds for censure and other disciplinary action that the Commission may impose, including, but not limited to, violations of the provisions of the Code of Judicial Conduct;
   (c) The standards for the investigation of matters relating to the fitness of a justice or judge; and
   (d) The confidentiality or nonconfidentiality, as appropriate, of proceedings before the Commission, except that, in any event, a

decision to censure, retire or remove a justice or judge must be made public.

6. The Supreme Court shall adopt a Code of Judicial Conduct.

7. The Commission shall adopt rules of procedure for the conduct of its hearings and any other procedural rules it deems necessary to carry out its duties.

8. No justice or judge may by virtue of this Section be:

   (a) Removed except for willful misconduct, willful or persistent failure to perform the duties of his office or habitual intemperance; or

   (b) Retired except for advanced age which interferes with the proper performance of his judicial duties, or for mental or physical disability which prevents the proper performance of his judicial duties and which is likely to be permanent in nature.

9 Any matter relating to the fitness of a justice or judge may be brought to the attention of the Commission by any person or on the motion of the Commission. The Commission shall, after preliminary investigation, dismiss the matter or order a hearing to be held before it. If a hearing is ordered, a statement of the matter must be served upon the justice or judge against whom the proceeding is brought. The Commission in its discretion may suspend a justice or judge from the exercise of his office pending the determination of the proceedings before the Commission. Any justice or judge whose removal is sought is liable to indictment and punishment according to law. A justice or judge retired for disability in accordance with this Section is entitled thereafter to receive such compensation as the Legislature may provide.

10. If a proceeding is brought against a justice of the Supreme Court, no justice of the Supreme Court may sit on the Commission for that proceeding. If a proceeding is brought against a judge of the court of appeals, no judge of the court of appeals may sit on the Commission for that proceeding. If a proceeding is brought against a district judge, no district judge from the same judicial district may sit on the Commission for that proceeding. If a proceeding is brought against a justice of the peace, no justice of the peace from the same township may sit on the Commission for that proceeding. If a proceeding is brought against a municipal judge, no municipal judge from the same city may sit on the Commission for that proceeding. If an appeal is taken from an action of the Commission to the Supreme Court, any justice who sat on the Commission for that proceeding is disqualified from participating in the consideration or decision of the appeal. When any member of

the Commission is disqualified by this subsection, the Supreme Court shall appoint a substitute from among the eligible judges.

11. The Commission may:

    (a) Designate for each hearing an attorney or attorneys at law to act as counsel to conduct the proceeding;

    (b) Summon witnesses to appear and testify under oath and compel the production of books, papers, documents and records;

    (c) Grant immunity from prosecution or punishment when the Commission deems it necessary and proper in order to compel the giving of testimony under oath and the production of books, papers, documents and records; and

    (d) Exercise such further powers as the Legislature may from time to time confer upon it.

[Added in 1976 and amended in 1994, 1998 and 2014. The addition was proposed and passed by the 1973 Legislature; agreed to and passed by the 1975 Legislature; and approved and ratified by the people at the 1976 General Election. See: Statutes of Nevada 1973, p. 1956; Statutes of Nevada 1975, p. 1932. The first amendment was proposed and passed by the 1991 Legislature; agreed to and passed by the 1993 Legislature; and approved and ratified by the people at the 1994 General Election. See: Statutes of Nevada 1991, p. 2590; Statutes of Nevada 1993, p. 2969. The second amendment was proposed and passed by the 1995 Legislature; agreed to and passed by the 1997 Legislature; and approved and ratified by the people at the 1998 General Election. See: Statutes of Nevada 1995, p. 3020; Statutes of Nevada 1997, p. 3596. The third amendment was proposed and passed by the 2011 Legislature; agreed to and passed by the 2013 Legislature; and approved and ratified by the people at the 2014 General Election. See: Statutes of Nevada 2011, p. 3835; Statutes of Nevada 2013, p. 3968.]

ARTICLE 7.
Impeachment and Removal from Office

SECTION   1. Impeachment: Trial; conviction.
    2. Officers subject to impeachment.
    3. Removal of justices of Supreme Court, judges of court of appeals and judges of district courts.
    4. Removal of other civil officers.

SECTION 1. *Impeachment: Trial; conviction.* The Assembly shall have the sole power of impeaching. The concurrence of a majority of all the members elected, shall be necessary to an impeachment. All impeachments shall be tried by the Senate, and when sitting for that purpose, the Senators shall be upon Oath or Affirmation, to do justice according to Law and Evidence. The Chief Justice of the Supreme court, shall preside over the Senate while sitting to try the Governor or Lieutenant Governor upon impeachment. No person shall be convicted without the concurrence of two thirds of the Senators elected.

SECTION 2. *Officers subject to impeachment.* The Governor and other state and judicial officers, except justices of the peace shall be liable to impeachment for misdemeanor or malfeasance in office; but judgment in such case shall not extend further than removal from office and disqualification to hold any office of honor, profit, or trust under this State. The party whether convicted or acquitted, shall, nevertheless, be liable to indictment, trial, judgment and punishment according to law.

SECTION 3. *Removal of justices of Supreme Court, judges of court of appeals and judges of district courts.* For any reasonable cause to be entered on the journals of each House, which may or may not be sufficient grounds for impeachment, the justices of the Supreme Court, the judges of the court of appeals and the judges of the district courts must be removed from office on the vote of two thirds of the members elected to each branch of the Legislature. The justice or judge complained of must be served with a copy of the complaint against him, and have an opportunity of being heard in person or by counsel in his defense. No member of either branch of the Legislature is eligible to fill the vacancy occasioned by such removal.

[Added in 2014. Proposed and passed by the 2011 Legislature; agreed to and passed by the 2013 Legislature, and approved and ratified by the people at the 2014 General Election. See: Statutes of Nevada 2011, p. 3835; Statutes of Nevada 2013, p. 3968.]

SECTION 4. *Removal of other civil officers.* Provision shall be made by law for the removal from Office of any Civil Officer other than those in this Article previously specified, for Malfeasance, or Nonfeasance in the Performance of his duties.

ARTICLE 8.
Municipal and Other Corporations

SECTION   1. Corporations formed under general laws; municipal corporations formed under special acts.

2. Corporate property subject to taxation; exemptions.
3. Individual liability of corporators.
4. Regulation of corporations incorporated under territorial law.
5. Corporations may sue and be sued.
6. Circulation of certain bank notes or paper as money prohibited.
7. Eminent domain by corporations.
8. Municipal corporations formed under general laws.
9. Gifts or loans of public money to certain corporations prohibited.

10. Loans of public money to or ownership of stock in certain corporations by county or municipal corporation prohibited.

SECTION 1. *Corporations formed under general laws; municipal corporations formed under special acts.* The Legislature shall pass no Special Act in any manner relating to corporate powers except for Municipal purposes; but corporations may be formed under general laws; and all such laws may from time to time, be altered or repealed.

SECTION 2. *Corporate property subject to taxation; exemptions.* All real property, and possessory rights to the same, as well as personal property in this State, belonging to corporations now existing or hereafter created shall be subject to taxation, the same as property of individuals; Provided, that the property of corporations formed for Municipal, Charitable, Religious, or Educational purposes may be exempted by law.

SECTION 3. *Individual liability of corporators.* Dues from corporations shall be secured by such means as may be prescribed by law; Provided, that corporators in corporations formed under the laws of this State shall not be individually liable for the debts or liabilities of such corporation.

SECTION 4. *Regulation of corporations incorporated under territorial law.* Corporations created by or under the laws of the Territory of Nevada shall be subject to the provisions of such laws until the Legislature shall pass laws regulating the same, in pursuance of the provisions of this Constitution[.]

SECTION 5. *Corporations may sue and be sued.* Corporations may sue and be sued in all courts, in like manner as individuals.

SECTION 6. *Circulation of certain bank notes or paper as money prohibited.* No bank notes or paper of any kind shall ever be permitted to circulate as money in this State, except the Federal currency, and the notes of banks authorized under the laws of Congress.

SECTION 7. *Eminent domain by corporations.* No right of way shall be appropriated to the use of any corporation until full compensation be first made or secured therefor.

SECTION 8. *Municipal corporations formed under general laws.* The legislature shall provide for the organization of cities and towns by general laws and shall restrict their power of taxation, assessment, borrowing money, contracting debts and loaning their credit, except for procuring supplies of water; *provided, however,* that the legislature may, by general laws, in the manner and to the extent therein provided, permit and authorize the electors of any city or town to frame, adopt and amend a charter for its own government, or to amend any existing charter of such city or town.

[Amended in 1924. Proposed and passed by the 1921 legislature; agreed to and passed by the 1923 legislature; and approved and ratified by the people at the 1924 general election. See: Statutes of Nevada 1921, p. 420; Statutes of Nevada 1923, p. 403.]

SECTION 9. *Gifts or loans of public money to certain corporations prohibited.* The State shall not donate or loan money, or its credit, subscribe to or be, interested in the Stock of any company, association, or corporation, except corporations formed for educational or charitable purposes.

SECTION 10. *Loans of public money to or ownership of stock in certain corporations by county or municipal corporation prohibited.* No county, city, town, or other municipal corporation shall become a stockholder in any joint stock company, corporation or association whatever, or loan its credit in aid of any such company, corporation or association, except, rail-road corporations[,] companies or associations.

ARTICLE 9.
Finance and State Debt

SECTION   1. Fiscal year.
         2. Annual tax for state expenses; trust funds for industrial accidents, occupational diseases and public employees' retirement system; administration of public employees' retirement system.
         3. State indebtedness: Limitations and exceptions.
         4. Assumption of debts of county, city or corporation by state.
         5. Proceeds from fees for licensing and registration of motor vehicles and excise taxes on fuel reserved for construction, maintenance and repair of public highways; exception.

SECTION 1. *Fiscal year.* The fiscal year shall commence on the first day of July of each year.

[Amended in 1930. Proposed and passed by the 1927 legislature; agreed to and passed by the 1929 legislature; and approved and ratified by the people at the 1930 general election. See: Statutes of Nevada 1927, p. 346; Statutes of Nevada 1929, p. 429.]

SECTION 2. *Annual tax for state expenses; trust funds for industrial accidents, occupational diseases and public employees' retirement system; administration of public employees' retirement system.*

1. The legislature shall provide by law for an annual tax sufficient to defray the estimated expenses of the state for each fiscal year; and whenever the expenses of any year exceed the income, the legislature shall provide for levying a tax sufficient, with other sources of income,

to pay the deficiency, as well as the estimated expenses of such ensuing year or two years.

2. Any money paid for the purpose of providing compensation for industrial accidents and occupational diseases, and for administrative expenses incidental thereto, and for the purpose of funding and administering a public employees' retirement system, must be segregated in proper accounts in the state treasury, and such money must never be used for any other purposes, and they are hereby declared to be trust funds for the uses and purposes herein specified.

3. Any money paid for the purpose of funding and administering a public employees' retirement system must not be loaned to the state or invested to purchase any obligations of the state.

4. The public employees' retirement system must be governed by a public employees' retirement board. The board shall employ an executive officer who serves at the pleasure of the board. In addition to any other employees authorized by the board, the board shall employ an independent actuary. The board shall adopt actuarial assumptions based upon the recommendations made by the independent actuary it employs.

[Amended in 1956, 1974 and 1996. The first amendment was proposed and passed by the 1953 legislature; agreed to and passed by the 1955 legislature; and approved and ratified by the people at the 1956 general election. See: Statutes of Nevada 1953, p. 729; Statutes of Nevada 1955, p. 927. The second amendment was proposed and passed by the 1971 legislature; agreed to and passed by the 1973 legislature; and approved and ratified by the people at the 1974 general election. See: Statutes of Nevada 1971, p. 2267; Statutes of Nevada 1973, p. 1948. The third amendment was proposed and passed by the 1993 legislature; agreed to and passed by the 1995 legislature; and approved and ratified by the people at the 1996 general election. See: Statutes of Nevada 1993, p. 3064; Statutes of Nevada 1995, p. 2899.]

SECTION 3. *State indebtedness: Limitations and exceptions.* The State may contract public debts; but such debts shall never, in the aggregate, exclusive of interest, exceed the sum of two per cent of the assessed valuation of the State, as shown by the reports of the county assessors to the State Controller, except for the purpose of defraying extraordinary expenses, as hereinafter mentioned. Every such debt shall be authorized by law for some purpose or purposes, to be distinctly specified therein; and every such law shall provide for levying an annual tax sufficient to pay the interest semiannually, and the principal within twenty years from the passage of such law, and shall specially appropriate the proceeds of said taxes to the payment of said principal and interest; and such appropriation shall not be repealed nor the taxes postponed or diminished until the principal and interest of said debts shall have been wholly paid. Every contract of indebtedness entered into or assumed by or on behalf of the State, when all its debts and liabilities amount to said sum before mentioned, shall be void and of no effect, except in cases of money borrowed to repel invasion, suppress insurrection, defend the State in time of war, or, if hostilities be threatened, provide for the public defense.

The State, notwithstanding the foregoing limitations, may, pursuant to authority of the Legislature, make and enter into any and all contracts necessary, expedient or advisable for the protection and preservation of any of its property or natural resources, or for the purposes of obtaining the benefits thereof, however arising and whether arising by or through any undertaking or project of the United States or by or through any treaty or compact between the states, or otherwise. The Legislature may from time to time make such appropriations as may be necessary to carry out the obligations of the State under such contracts, and shall levy such tax as may be necessary to pay the same or carry them into effect.

[Amended in 1916, 1934 and 1989. The first amendment was proposed and passed by the 1913 Legislature; agreed to and passed by the 1915 Legislature; and approved and ratified by the people at the 1916 General Election. See: Statutes of Nevada 1913, p. 585; Statutes of Nevada 1915, p. 516. The second amendment was proposed and passed by the 1931 Legislature; agreed to and passed by the 1933 Legislature; and approved and ratified by the people at the 1934 General Election. See: Journal of the Senate, 35th Session, p. 167, and Journal of the Assembly, 35th Session, p. 319; Statutes of Nevada 1933, p. 357. The third amendment was proposed and passed by the 1987 Legislature; agreed to and passed by the 1989 Legislature; and approved and ratified by the people at a special election held on May 2, 1989. See: Statutes of Nevada 1987, p. 2422; Statutes of Nevada 1989, p. 2230.]

SECTION 4. *Assumption of debts of county, city or corporation by state.* The State shall never assume the debts of any county, town, city or other corporation whatever, unless such debts have been created to repel invasion[,] suppress insurrection or to provide for the public defense.

SECTION 5. *Proceeds from fees for licensing and registration of motor vehicles and excise taxes on fuel reserved for construction, maintenance and repair of public highways; exception.* The proceeds from the imposition of any license or registration fee and other charge with respect to the operation of any motor vehicle upon any public highway in this State and the proceeds from the imposition of any excise tax on gasoline or other motor vehicle fuel shall, except costs of administration, be used exclusively for the construction, maintenance, and repair of the public highways of this State. The provisions of this section do not apply to the proceeds of any tax imposed upon motor vehicles by the Legislature in lieu of an ad valorem property tax.

[Added in 1940 and amended in 1962. The addition was proposed and passed by the 1937 Legislature; agreed to and passed by the 1939 Legislature; and approved and ratified by the people at the 1940 General Election. See: Statutes of Nevada 1937, p. 567; Statutes of Nevada 1939, p. 359. The amendment was proposed and passed by the 1960

Legislature; agreed to and passed by the 1961 Legislature; and approved and ratified by the people at the 1962 General Election. See: Statutes of Nevada 1960, p. 509; Statutes of Nevada 1961, p. 825.]

ARTICLE 10.
Taxation

SECTION 1. *Uniform and equal rate of assessment and taxation; valuation of property; exceptions and exemptions; inheritance and personal income taxes prohibited. [Effective through November 23, 2020, and after that date unless the provisions of Senate Joint Resolution No. 14 (2017) are agreed to and passed by the 2019 Legislature and approved and ratified by the voters at the 2020 General Election.]*

1. Uniform and equal rate of assessment and taxation; valuation of property; exceptions and exemptions; inheritance and personal income taxes prohibited; program for refunds of property taxes to seniors and persons with disabilities. [Effective November 24, 2020, if the provisions of Senate Joint Resolution No. 14 (2017) are agreed to and passed by the 2019 Legislature and approved and ratified by the voters at the 2020 General Election.]

2. Total tax levy for public purposes limited.

[3]. Household goods and furniture of single household exempt from taxation.

3[A]. Food exempt from taxes on retail sales; exceptions.

3B. Durable medical equipment, oxygen delivery equipment and mobility enhancing equipment exempt from taxes on retail sales.
[Effective November 27, 2018, if the proposed addition is approved and ratified by the voters at the 2018 General Election.]

4. Taxation of estates taxed by United States; limitations.

5. Tax on proceeds of minerals; appropriation to counties; apportionment; assessment and taxation of mines.

6. Enactment of exemption from ad valorem tax on property or excise tax on retail sales.

SECTION 1. *Uniform and equal rate of assessment and taxation; valuation of property; exceptions and exemptions; inheritance and personal income taxes prohibited. [Effective through November 23, 2020, and after that date unless the provisions of Senate Joint Resolution No. 14 (2017) are agreed to and passed by the 2019 Legislature and approved and ratified by the voters at the 2020 General Election.]*

1. The Legislature shall provide by law for a uniform and equal rate of assessment and taxation, and shall prescribe such regulations as shall

secure a just valuation for taxation of all property, real, personal and possessory, except mines and mining claims, which shall be assessed and taxed only as provided in Section 5 of this Article.

2. Shares of stock, bonds, mortgages, notes, bank deposits, book accounts and credits, and securities and choses in action of like character are deemed to represent interest in property already assessed and taxed, either in Nevada or elsewhere, and shall be exempt.

3. The Legislature may constitute agricultural and open-space real property having a greater value for another use than that for which it is being used, as a separate class for taxation purposes and may provide a separate uniform plan for appraisal and valuation of such property for assessment purposes. If such plan is provided, the Legislature shall also provide for retroactive assessment for a period of not less than 7 years when agricultural and open-space real property is converted to a higher use conforming to the use for which other nearby property is used.

4. Personal property which is moving in interstate commerce through or over the territory of the State of Nevada, or which was consigned to a warehouse, public or private, within the State of Nevada from outside the State of Nevada for storage in transit to a final destination outside the State of Nevada, whether specified when transportation begins or afterward, shall be deemed to have acquired no situs in Nevada for purposes of taxation and shall be exempt from taxation. Such property shall not be deprived of such exemption because while in the warehouse the property is assembled, bound, joined, processed, disassembled, divided, cut, broken in bulk, relabeled or repackaged.

5. The Legislature may exempt motor vehicles from the provisions of the tax required by this Section, and in lieu thereof, if such exemption is granted, shall provide for a uniform and equal rate of assessment and taxation of motor vehicles, which rate shall not exceed five cents on one dollar of assessed valuation.

6. The Legislature shall provide by law for a progressive reduction in the tax upon business inventories by 20 percent in each year following the adoption of this provision, and after the expiration of the 4th year such inventories are exempt from taxation. The Legislature may exempt any other personal property, including livestock.

7. No inheritance tax shall ever be levied.

8. The Legislature may exempt by law property used for municipal, educational, literary, scientific or other charitable purposes, or to encourage the conservation of energy or the substitution of other sources for fossil sources of energy.

9. No income tax shall be levied upon the wages or personal income of natural persons. Notwithstanding the foregoing provision, and except as otherwise provided in Subsection 1 of this Section, taxes may be levied upon the income or revenue of any business in whatever form it may be conducted for profit in the State.

10. The Legislature may provide by law for an abatement of the tax upon or an exemption of part of the assessed value of a single-family residence occupied by the owner to the extent necessary to avoid severe economic hardship to the owner of the residence.

[Amended in 1902, 1906, 1942, 1960, 1962, 1974, 1978, 1982, 1986, 1989, 1990 and 2002. The first amendment was proposed and passed by the 1899 Legislature; agreed to and passed by the 1901 Legislature; and approved and ratified by the people at the 1902 General Election. See: Statutes of Nevada 1899, p. 139; Statutes of Nevada 1901, p. 136. The second amendment was proposed and passed by the 1903 Legislature; agreed to and passed by the 1905 Legislature; and approved and ratified by the people at the 1906 General Election. See: Statutes of Nevada 1903, p. 240; Statutes of Nevada 1905, p. 277. The third amendment was proposed and passed by the 1939 Legislature; agreed to and passed by the 1941 Legislature; and approved and ratified by the people at the 1942 General Election. See: Statutes of Nevada 1939, p. 360; Statutes of Nevada 1941, p. 559. The fourth amendment was proposed and passed by the 1957 Legislature; agreed to and passed by the 1959 Legislature; and approved and ratified by the people at the 1960 General Election. See: Statutes of Nevada 1957, p. 805; Statutes of Nevada 1959, p. 939. The fifth amendment was proposed and passed by the 1960 Legislature; agreed to and passed by the 1961 Legislature; and approved and ratified by the people at the 1962 General Election. See: Statutes of Nevada 1960, p. 509; Statutes of Nevada 1961, p. 825. The sixth amendment was proposed and passed by the 1971 Legislature; agreed to and passed by the 1973 Legislature; and approved and ratified by the people at the 1974 General Election. See: Statutes of Nevada 1971, p. 2299; Statutes of Nevada 1973, p. 1938. The seventh amendment was proposed and passed by the 1975 Legislature; agreed to and passed by the 1977 Legislature; and approved and ratified by the people at the 1978 General Election. See: Statutes of Nevada 1975, p. 1925; Statutes of Nevada 1977, p. 1727. The eighth amendment was proposed and passed by the 1979 Legislature; agreed to and passed by the 1981 Legislature; and approved and ratified by the people at the 1982 General Election. See: Statutes of Nevada 1979, p. 1983, Statutes of Nevada 1981, p. 2070. The ninth and tenth amendments were proposed and passed by the 1983 Legislature; agreed to and passed by the 1985 Legislature; and approved and ratified by the people at the 1986 General Election. See: Statutes of Nevada 1983; pp. 2141 and 2225; Statutes of Nevada 1985, pp. 2331 and 2401. The amendments were combined pursuant to Nev. Article 16, § 1. The eleventh amendment was proposed and passed by the 1987 Legislature; agreed to and passed by the 1989 Legislature; and approved and ratified by the people at a special election held on May 2, 1989. See: Statutes of Nevada 1987, p. 2442; Statutes of Nevada 1989, p. 2228. The twelfth amendment was proposed by initiative petition and approved and ratified by the people at the General Elections of 1988 and 1990. The thirteenth amendment was proposed and passed by the 1999 Legislature; agreed to and passed by the 2001 Legislature; and approved and ratified by the people at the 2002 General Election. See: Statutes of Nevada 1999, p. 3968; Statutes of Nevada 2001, p. 3462. The fourteenth amendment was proposed and passed by the 2011 Legislature; agreed to and passed by the 2013 Legislature; and not approved and ratified by the people at the 2014 General Election. See: Statutes of Nevada 2011, p. 3871; Statutes of Nevada 2013, p. 3958.]

SECTION 1. *Uniform and equal rate of assessment and taxation; valuation of property; exceptions and exemptions; inheritance and personal income taxes prohibited; program for refunds of property taxes to seniors and persons with disabilities. [Effective November 24, 2020, if the provisions of Senate Joint Resolution No. 14 (2017) are agreed to and passed by the 2019 Legislature and approved and ratified by the voters at the 2020 General Election.]*

1. The Legislature shall provide by law for a uniform and equal rate of assessment and taxation, and shall prescribe such regulations as shall secure a just valuation for taxation of all property, real, personal and possessory, except mines and mining claims, which shall be assessed and taxed only as provided in Section 5 of this Article.

2. Shares of stock, bonds, mortgages, notes, bank deposits, book accounts and credits, and securities and choses in action of like character are deemed to represent interest in property already assessed and taxed, either in Nevada or elsewhere, and shall be exempt.

3. The Legislature may constitute agricultural and open-space real property having a greater value for another use than that for which it is being used, as a separate class for taxation purposes and may provide a separate uniform plan for appraisal and valuation of such property for assessment purposes. If such plan is provided, the Legislature shall also provide for retroactive assessment for a period of not less than 7 years when agricultural and open-space real property is converted to a higher use conforming to the use for which other nearby property is used.

4. Personal property which is moving in interstate commerce through or over the territory of the State of Nevada, or which was consigned to a warehouse, public or private, within the State of Nevada from outside the State of Nevada for storage in transit to a final destination outside the State of Nevada, whether specified when transportation begins or afterward, shall be deemed to have acquired no situs in Nevada for purposes of taxation and shall be exempt from taxation. Such property shall not be deprived of such exemption because while in the warehouse the property is assembled, bound, joined, processed, disassembled, divided, cut, broken in bulk, relabeled or repackaged.

5. The Legislature may exempt motor vehicles from the provisions of the tax required by this Section, and in lieu thereof, if such exemption is granted, shall provide for a uniform and equal rate of assessment and taxation of motor vehicles, which rate shall not exceed five cents on one dollar of assessed valuation.

6. The Legislature shall provide by law for a progressive reduction in the tax upon business inventories by 20 percent in each year following the adoption of this provision, and after the expiration of the 4th year such inventories are exempt from taxation. The Legislature may exempt any other personal property, including livestock.

7. No inheritance tax shall ever be levied.

8. The Legislature may exempt by law property used for municipal, educational, literary, scientific or other charitable purposes, or to encourage the conservation of energy or the substitution of other sources for fossil sources of energy.

9. No income tax shall be levied upon the wages or personal income of natural persons. Notwithstanding the foregoing provision, and except as otherwise provided in Subsection 1 of this Section, taxes may be levied upon the income or revenue of any business in whatever form it may be conducted for profit in the State.

10. The Legislature may provide by law for an abatement of the tax upon or an exemption of part of the assessed value of a single-family residence occupied by the owner to the extent necessary to avoid severe economic hardship to the owner of the residence.

11. For the purposes of assessment and taxation of property:

    (a) Except as otherwise provided in this paragraph, for the first fiscal year after the sale or transfer of real property, the real property sold or transferred shall not be eligible for any adjustment provided by the Legislature by law based on the age of improvements to the real property, any abatement of the tax upon the real property provided by the Legislature by law pursuant to Subsection 8 or any abatement or exemption provided by the Legislature by law pursuant to Subsection 10. The provisions of this paragraph do not apply to real property for which the Legislature has provided by law for an exemption of the tax on property.

    (b) For any fiscal year following the first fiscal year after the sale or transfer of real property to which the provisions of paragraph (a) apply, any adjustment provided by the Legislature by law based on the age of improvements to the real property must be determined as if the improvements were new improvements on the date of the sale or transfer.

The Legislature shall provide by law for definitions of the terms "sale" and "transfer" as necessary to carry out the provisions of this subsection.

12. The Legislature shall provide by law for a program to provide for the payment of refunds of the taxes imposed on the primary residence of a person domiciled in this State who is 62 years of age or older or

a person with a disability. If such a person rents his or her primary residence, the amount of the refund for which the person is eligible must not exceed the portion of the rent which is deemed to constitute accrued property tax. The Legislature shall establish by law:

(a) The criteria which a person must satisfy to be eligible for such a refund; and

(b) The amount of the refund to be paid to a person eligible for such a refund, which may consist of a graduated refund based on the household income of such a person.

[Amended in 1902, 1906, 1942, 1960, 1962, 1974, 1978, 1982, 1986, 1989, 1990 and 2002. The first amendment was proposed and passed by the 1899 Legislature; agreed to and passed by the 1901 Legislature; and approved and ratified by the people at the 1902 General Election. See: Statutes of Nevada 1899, p. 139; Statutes of Nevada 1901, p. 136. The second amendment was proposed and passed by the 1903 Legislature; agreed to and passed by the 1905 Legislature; and approved and ratified by the people at the 1906 General Election. See: Statutes of Nevada 1903, p. 240; Statutes of Nevada 1905, p. 277. The third amendment was proposed and passed by the 1939 Legislature; agreed to and passed by the 1941 Legislature; and approved and ratified by the people at the 1942 General Election. See: Statutes of Nevada 1939, p. 360; Statutes of Nevada 1941, p. 559. The fourth amendment was proposed and passed by the 1957 Legislature; agreed to and passed by the 1959 Legislature; and approved and ratified by the people at the 1960 General Election. See: Statutes of Nevada 1957, p. 805; Statutes of Nevada 1959, p. 939. The fifth amendment was proposed and passed by the 1960 Legislature; agreed to and passed by the 1961 Legislature; and approved and ratified by the people at the 1962 General Election. See: Statutes of Nevada 1960, p. 509; Statutes of Nevada 1961, p. 825. The sixth amendment was proposed and passed by the 1971 Legislature; agreed to and passed by the 1973 Legislature; and approved and ratified by the people at the 1974 General Election. See: Statutes of Nevada 1971, p. 2299; Statutes of Nevada 1973, p. 1938. The seventh amendment was proposed and passed by the 1975 Legislature; agreed to and passed by the 1977 Legislature; and approved and ratified by the people at the 1978 General Election. See: Statutes of Nevada 1975, p. 1925; Statutes of Nevada 1977, p. 1727. The eighth amendment was proposed and passed by the 1979 Legislature; agreed to and passed by the 1981 Legislature; and approved and ratified by the people at the 1982 General Election. See: Statutes of Nevada 1979, p. 1983, Statutes of Nevada 1981, p. 2070. The ninth and tenth amendments were proposed and passed by the 1983 Legislature; agreed to and passed by the 1985 Legislature; and approved and ratified by the people at the 1986 General Election. See: Statutes of Nevada 1983; pp. 2141 and 2225; Statutes of Nevada 1985, pp. 2331 and 2401. The amendments were combined pursuant to Nev. Article 16, § 1. The eleventh amendment was proposed and passed by the 1987 Legislature; agreed to and passed by the 1989 Legislature; and approved and ratified by the people at a special election held on May 2, 1989. See: Statutes of Nevada 1987, p. 2442; Statutes of Nevada 1989, p. 2228. The twelfth amendment was proposed by initiative petition and approved and ratified by the people at the General Elections of 1988 and 1990. The thirteenth amendment was proposed and passed by the 1999 Legislature; agreed to and passed by the 2001 Legislature; and approved and ratified by the people at the 2002 General Election. See: Statutes of Nevada 1999, p. 3968; Statutes of Nevada 2001, p. 3462. The fourteenth amendment was proposed and passed by the 2011 Legislature; agreed to and passed by the 2013 Legislature; and not approved and ratified by the people at the 2014 General Election. See: Statutes of Nevada 2011, p. 3871; Statutes of Nevada 2013, p. 3958.]—(Proposed amendment passed by the 2017 Legislature; effective November 24, 2020, if agreed to and passed by the 2019 Legislature and approved and ratified by the voters at the 2020 General Election. See: Statutes of Nevada 2017, p. 4596.)

SECTION 2. *Total tax levy for public purposes limited.* The total tax levy for all public purposes including levies for bonds, within the state, or any subdivision thereof, shall not exceed five cents on one dollar of assessed valuation.

[Added in 1936. Proposed and passed by the 1933 legislature; agreed to and passed by the 1935 legislature; and approved and ratified by the people at the 1936 general election. See: Statutes of Nevada 1933, p. 369; Statutes of Nevada 1935, p. 428.]

SECTION [3]. *Household goods and furniture of single household exempt from taxation.* All household goods and furniture used by a single household and owned by a member of that household are exempt from taxation.

[Added in 1982. Proposed by initiative petition and approved by the people at the 1980 and 1982 general elections.]

SECTION 3[A]. *Food exempt from taxes on retail sales; exceptions.* The legislature shall provide by law for:

1. The exemption of food for human consumption from any tax upon the sale, storage, use or consumption of tangible personal property; and
2. These commodities to be excluded from any such exemption:
    (a) Prepared food intended for immediate consumption.
    (b) Alcoholic beverages.

[Added in 1984. Proposed and passed by the 1981 legislature; agreed to and passed by the 1983 legislature; and approved and ratified by the people at the 1984 general election. See: Statutes of Nevada 1981, p. 2093; Statutes of Nevada 1983, p. 2113.]

SECTION 3B. *Durable medical equipment, oxygen delivery equipment and mobility enhancing equipment exempt from taxes on retail sales. [Effective November 27, 2018, if the proposed addition is approved and ratified by the voters at the 2018 General Election.]* The legislature shall provide by law for the exemption of durable medical equipment, oxygen delivery equipment and mobility enhancing equipment prescribed for human use by a licensed provider of health care acting within his or her scope of practice from any tax upon the sale, storage, use or consumption of tangible personal property.

(Addition proposed by initiative petition and approved and ratified by the voters at the 2016 General Election; effective November 27, 2018, if approved and ratified by the voters at the 2018 General Election.)

SECTION 4. *Taxation of estates taxed by United States; limitations.* The legislature may provide by law for the taxation of estates taxed by the United States, but only to the extent of any credit allowed by federal law for the payment of the state tax and only for the purpose of education, to be divided between the common schools and the state university for their support and maintenance. The combined amount of these federal and state taxes may not exceed the estate tax which would be imposed by federal law alone. If another state of the United States imposes and collects death taxes against an estate which is taxable by the State of Nevada under this section, the amount of estate tax to be collected by the State of Nevada must be reduced by the amount of the death taxes collected by the other state. Any lien for the estate tax attaches no sooner than the time when the tax is due and payable, and no restriction on possession or use of a decedent's property may be imposed by law before the time when the tax is due and payable in full under federal law. The State of Nevada shall:

1. Accept the determination by the United States of the amount of the taxable estate without further audit.
2. Accept payment of the tax in installments proportionate to any which may be permitted under federal law.
3. Impose no penalty for such a deferred payment.
4. Not charge interest on a deferred or belated payment at any rate higher than may be provided in similar circumstances by federal law.

[Added in 1986. Proposed and passed by the 1983 legislature; agreed to and passed by the 1985 legislature; and approved and ratified by the people at the 1986 general election. See: Statutes of Nevada 1983, p. 2224; Statutes of Nevada 1985, p. 2400.]

SECTION 5. *Tax on proceeds of minerals, appropriation to counties; apportionment; assessment and taxation of mines.*

1. The legislature shall provide by law for a tax upon the net proceeds of all minerals, including oil, gas and other hydrocarbons, extracted in this state, at a rate not to exceed 5 percent of the net proceeds. No other tax may be imposed upon a mineral or its proceeds until the identity of the proceeds as such is lost.
2. The legislature shall appropriate to each county that sum which would be produced by levying a tax upon the entire amount of the net proceeds taxed in each taxing district in the county at the rate levied in that district upon the assessed valuation of real property. The total amount so appropriated to each county must be apportioned among the respective governmental units and districts within it, including the county itself and the school district, in the same proportion as they share in the total taxes collected on property according to value.
3. Each patented mine or mining claim must be assessed and taxed as other real property is assessed and taxed, except that no value may be attributed to any mineral known or believed to underlie it, and no value may be attributed to the surface of a mine or claim if one hundred

dollars' worth of labor has been actually performed on the mine or
claim during the year preceding the assessment.

[Added in 1989. Proposed and passed by the 1987 legislature; agreed to and passed by
the 1989 legislature; and approved and ratified by the people at a special election held on
May 2, 1989. See: Statutes of Nevada 1987, p. 2443; Statutes of Nevada 1989, p. 2229.
Proposed repeal passed by the 2011 Legislature; agreed to and passed by the 2013 Leg-
islature; and not approved and ratified by the people at the 2014 General Election. See:
Statutes of Nevada 2011, p. 3872; Statutes of Nevada 2013, p. 3959.]

SECTION 6. *Enactment of exemption from ad valorem tax on property or excise
tax on retail sales.*

1. The Legislature shall not enact an exemption from any ad valorem tax
   on property or excise tax on the sale, storage, use or consumption of
   tangible personal property sold at retail unless the Legislature finds
   that the exemption:
   (a) Will achieve a bona fide social or economic purpose and the ben-
       efits of the exemption are expected to exceed any adverse effect
       of the exemption on the provision of services to the public by the
       State or a local government that would otherwise receive revenue
       from the tax from which the exemption would be granted; and
   (b) Will not impair adversely the ability of the State or a local gov-
       ernment to pay, when due, all interest and principal on any out-
       standing bonds or any other obligations for which revenue from
       the tax from which the exemption would be granted was pledged.
2. In enacting an exemption from any ad valorem tax on property or
   excise tax on the sale, storage, use or consumption of tangible personal
   property sold at retail, the Legislature shall:
   (a) Ensure that the requirements for claiming the exemption are as
       similar as practicable for similar classes of taxpayers; and
   (b) Provide a specific date on which the exemption will cease to be
       effective.

[Added in 2008. Proposed and passed by the 2005 Legislature; agreed to and passed by
the 2007 Legislature; and approved and ratified by the people at the 2008 General Election. See: Statutes of Nevada 2005, p. 3048; Statutes of Nevada 2007, p. 3585.]

ARTICLE 11.
Education

SECTION   1. Legislature to encourage education; appointment, term and duties of
               superintendent of public instruction.
           2. Uniform system of common schools.
           3. Pledge of certain property and money, escheated estates and fines col-
               lected under penal laws for educational purposes; apportionment and
               use of interest.

4. Establishment of state university; control by board of regents. [Effective through November 23, 2020, and after that date unless the provisions of Assembly Joint Resolution No. 5 (2017) are agreed to and passed by the 2019 Legislature and approved and ratified by the voters at the 2020 General Election.]

4. Establishment of State University; Legislature to provide by law for governance, control and management of State University and protection of academic freedom. [Effective November 24, 2020, if the provisions of Assembly Joint Resolution No. 5 (2017) are agreed to and passed by the 2019 Legislature and approved and ratified by the voters at the 2020 General Election.]

5. Establishment of normal schools and grades of schools; oath of teachers and professors.

6. Support of university and common schools by direct legislative appropriation; priority of appropriations.

7. Board of Regents: Election and duties. [Effective through November 23, 2020, and after that date unless the provisions of Assembly Joint Resolution No. 5 (2017) are agreed to and passed by the 2019 Legislature and approved and ratified by the voters at the 2020 General Election.]

7. Board of Regents: Election and duties. Repealed. (See File No. 34, Statutes of Nevada 2017, at page 4584.) [Effective November 24, 2020, if the provisions of Assembly Joint Resolution No. 5 (2017) are agreed to and passed by the 2019 Legislature and approved and ratified by the voters at the 2020 General Election.]

8. Immediate organization and maintenance of state university. [Effective through November 23, 2020, and after that date unless the provisions of Assembly Joint Resolution No. 5 (2017) are agreed to and passed by the 2019 Legislature and approved and ratified by the voters at the 2020 General Election.]

8. Use of proceeds from public lands donated by Act of Congress for benefit of certain departments of State University. [Effective November 24, 2020, if the provisions of Assembly Joint Resolution No. 5 (2017) are agreed to and passed by the 2019 Legislature and approved and ratified by the voters at the 2020 General Election.]

9. Sectarian instruction prohibited in common schools and university.

10. No public money to be used for sectarian purposes.

SECTION 1. *Legislature to encourage education; appointment, term and duties of superintendent of public instruction.* The legislature shall encourage by all suitable means the promotion of intellectual, literary, scientific, mining, mechanical, agricultural, and moral improvements, and also provide for a superintendent of public instruction and by law prescribe the manner of appointment, term of office and the duties thereof.

[Amended in 1956. Proposed and passed by the 1953 legislature; agreed to and passed by the 1955 legislature; approved and ratified by the people at the 1956 general election. See: Statutes of Nevada 1953, p. 716; Statutes of Nevada 1955, p. 926.]

SECTION 2. *Uniform system of common schools.* The legislature shall provide for a uniform system of common schools, by which a school shall be established and maintained in each school district at least six months in every year, and any school district which shall allow instruction of a sectarian character therein may be deprived of its proportion of the interest of the public school fund during such neglect or infraction, and the legislature may pass such laws as will tend to secure a general attendance of the children in each school district upon said public schools.

[Amended in 1938. Proposed and passed by the 1935 legislature; agreed to and passed by the 1937 legislature; and approved and ratified by the people at the 1938 general election. See: Statutes of Nevada 1935, p. 440; Statutes of Nevada 1937, p. 550.]

SECTION 3. *Pledge of certain property and money, escheated estates and fines collected under penal laws for educational purposes; apportionment and use of interest.* All lands granted by Congress to this state for educational purposes, all estates that escheat to the state, all property given or bequeathed to the state for educational purposes, and the proceeds derived from these sources, together with that percentage of the proceeds from the sale of federal lands which has been granted by Congress to this state without restriction or for educational purposes and all fines collected under the penal laws of the state are hereby pledged for educational purposes and the money therefrom must not be transferred to other funds for other uses. The interest only earned on the money derived from these sources must be apportioned by the legislature among the several counties for educational purposes, and, if necessary, a portion of that interest may be appropriated for the support of the state university, but any of that interest which is unexpended at the end of any year must be added to the principal sum pledged for educational purposes.

[Amended in 1886, 1889, 1912, 1916, 1980, and 1988. The first amendment was approved and ratified by the people at the 1886 general election, but no entry of the proposed amendment had been made upon the journal of either house of the legislature, and such omission was fatal to the adoption of the amendment. See: State ex rel. Stevenson v. Tufly, 19 Nev. 391 (1887). The second amendment was proposed and passed by the 1885 legislature; agreed to and passed by the 1887 legislature; and approved and ratified by the people at a special election held February 11, 1889. See: Statutes of Nevada 1885, p. 160; Statutes of Nevada 1887, p. 168. The third amendment was proposed and passed by the 1909 legislature; agreed to and passed by the 1911 legislature; and approved and ratified by the people at the 1912 general election. See: Statutes of Nevada 1909, p. 340; Statutes of Nevada 1911, p. 453. The fourth amendment was proposed and passed by the

1913 legislature; agreed to and passed by the 1915 legislature; and approved and ratified by the people at the 1916 general election. See: Statutes of Nevada 1913, p. 591; Statutes of Nevada 1915, p. 513. The fifth amendment was proposed and passed by the 1977 legislature; agreed to and passed by the 1979 legislature; and approved and ratified by the people at the 1980 general election. See: Statutes of Nevada 1977, p. 1716; Statutes of Nevada 1979, p. 1953. The sixth amendment was proposed and passed by the 1985 legislature; agreed to and passed by the 1987 legislature; and approved and ratified by the people at the 1988 general election. See: Statutes of Nevada 1985, p. 2361; Statutes of Nevada 1987, p. 2355.]

SECTION 4. *Establishment of state university; control by board of regents. [Effective through November 23, 2020, and after that date unless the provisions of Assembly Joint Resolution No. 5 (2017) are agreed to and passed by the 2019 Legislature and approved and ratified by the voters at the 2020 General Election.]* The Legislature shall provide for the establishment of a State University which shall embrace departments for Agriculture, Mechanic Arts, and Mining to be controlled by a Board of Regents whose duties shall be prescribed by Law.

SECTION 4. *Establishment of State University; Legislature to provide by law for governance, control and management of State University and protection of academic freedom. [Effective November 24, 2020, if the provisions of Assembly Joint Resolution No. 5 (2017) are agreed to and passed by the 2019 Legislature and approved and ratified by the voters at the 2020 General Election.]*

1. The Legislature shall provide for the establishment of a State University which shall embrace departments for Agriculture, Mechanic Arts, and Mining, and other departments deemed appropriate for the State University.
2. The Legislature shall provide by law for:
   (a) The governance, control and management of the State University.
   (b) The reasonable protection of individual academic freedom for persons who are enrolled in or who are employees or contractors of the State University and other public institutions of higher education in this State in order to facilitate the policies of Section 1 of this Article to encourage by all suitable means the promotion of intellectual, literary, scientific, mining, mechanical, agricultural, ethical and other educational improvements.

(Proposed amendment passed by the 2017 Legislature; effective November 24, 2020, if agreed to and passed by the 2019 Legislature and approved and ratified by the voters at the 2020 General Election. See: Statutes of Nevada 2017, p. 4583.)

SECTION 5. *Establishment of normal schools and grades of schools; oath of teachers and professors.* The Legislature shall have power to establis [establish] Normal schools, and such different grades of schools, from the primary department to the University, as in their discretion they may deem necessary, and all Professors in said University, or Teachers in said Schools of whatever grade, shall be required to take and subscribe to the oath as prescribed in Article 15 of this Constitution. No Professor or Teacher who fails to comply with the provisions of any law framed in accordance with the provisions of this Section, shall be entitled to receive any portion of the public monies set apart for school purposes.

SECTION 6. *Support of university and common schools by direct legislative appropriation; priority of appropriations.*

1. In addition to other means provided for the support and maintenance of said university and common schools, the legislature shall provide for their support and maintenance by direct legislative appropriation from the general fund, upon the presentation of budgets in the manner required by law.

2. During a regular session of the Legislature, before any other appropriation is enacted to fund a portion of the state budget for the next ensuing biennium, the Legislature shall enact one or more appropriations to provide the money the Legislature deems to be sufficient, when combined with the local money reasonably available for this purpose, to fund the operation of the public schools in the State for kindergarten through grade 12 for the next ensuing biennium for the population reasonably estimated for that biennium.

3. During a special session of the Legislature that is held between the end of a regular session in which the Legislature has not enacted the appropriation or appropriations required by Subsection 2 to fund education for the next ensuing biennium and the first day of that next ensuing biennium, before any other appropriation is enacted other than appropriations required to pay the cost of that special session, the Legislature shall enact one or more appropriations to provide the money the Legislature deems to be sufficient, when combined with the local money reasonably available for this purpose, to fund the operation of the public schools in the State for kindergarten through grade 12 for the next ensuing biennium for the population reasonably estimated for that biennium.

4. During a special session of the Legislature that is held in a biennium for which the Legislature has not enacted the appropriation or appropriations required by Subsection 2 to fund education for the biennium in which the special session is being held, before any other appropriation is enacted other than appropriations required to pay the cost of that special session, the Legislature shall enact one or more appropriations to provide the money the Legislature deems to be sufficient, when

combined with the local money reasonably available for this purpose, to fund the operation of the public schools in the State for kindergarten through grade 12 for the population reasonably estimated for the biennium in which the special session is held.

5. Any appropriation of money enacted in violation of Subsection 2, 3 or 4 is void.

6. As used in this section, "biennium" means a period of two fiscal years beginning on July 1 of an odd-numbered year and ending on June 30 of the next ensuing odd-numbered year.

[Amended in 1889, 1938, 1954 and 2006. The first amendment was proposed and passed by the 1885 legislature; agreed to and passed by the 1887 legislature; and approved and ratified by the people at a special election held February 11, 1889. See: Statutes of Nevada 1885, p. 161; Statutes of Nevada 1887, p. 169. The second amendment was proposed and passed by the 1935 legislature; agreed to and passed by the 1937 legislature; and approved and ratified by the people at the 1938 general election. See: Statutes of Nevada 1935, p. 440; Statutes of Nevada 1937, p. 550. The third amendment was proposed and passed by the 1951 legislature; agreed to and passed by the 1953 legislature; and approved and ratified by the people at the 1954 general election. See: Statutes of Nevada 1951, p. 591; Statutes of Nevada 1953, p. 716. The fourth amendment was proposed by initiative petition and approved and ratified by the people at the 2004 and 2006 General Elections.]

SECTION 7. *Board of Regents: Election and duties. [Effective through November 23, 2020, and after that date unless the provisions of Assembly Joint Resolution No. 5 (2017) are agreed to and passed by the 2019 Legislature and approved and ratified by the voters at the 2020 General Election.]* The Governor, Secretary of State, and Superintendent of Public Instruction, shall for the first four years and until their successors are elected and qualified constitute a Board of Regents to control and manage the affairs of the University and the funds of the same under such regulations as may be provided by law. But the Legislature shall at its regular session next preceding the expiration of the term of office of said Board of Regents provide for the election of a new Board of Regents and define their duties.

SECTION 7. *Board of Regents: Election and duties. Repealed. (See File No. 34, Statutes of Nevada 2017, at page 4584.) [Effective November 24, 2020, if the provisions of Assembly Joint Resolution No. 5 (2017) are agreed to and passed by the 2019 Legislature and approved and ratified by the voters at the 2020 General Election.]*

(Proposed repeal passed by the 2017 Legislature; effective November 24, 2020, if agreed to and passed by the 2019 Legislature and approved and ratified by the voters at the 2020 General Election. See: Statutes of Nevada 2017, p. 4584.)

SECTION 8. *Immediate organization and maintenance of state university. [Effective through November 23, 2020, and after that date unless the provisions of*

Assembly Joint Resolution No. 5 (2017) are agreed to and passed by the 2019 Legislature and approved and ratified by the voters at the 2020 General Election.] The Board of Regents shall, from the interest accruing from the first funds which come under their control, immediately organize and maintain the said Mining department in such manner as to make it most effective and useful, Provided, that all the proceeds of the public lands donated by Act of Congress approved July second AD. Eighteen hundred and sixty Two, for a college for the benefit of Agriculture[,] the Mechanics Arts, and including Military tactics shall be invested by the said Board of Regents in a separate fund to be appropriated exclusively for the benefit of the first named departments to the University as set forth in Section 4 above; And the Legislature shall provide that if through neglect or any other contingency, any portion of the fund so set apart, shall be lost or misappropriated, the State of Nevada shall replace said amount so lost or misappropriated in said fund so that the principal of said fund shall remain forever undiminished[.]

SECTION 8. *Use of proceeds from public lands donated by Act of Congress for benefit of certain departments of State University. [Effective November 24, 2020, if the provisions of Assembly Joint Resolution No. 5 (2017) are agreed to and passed by the 2019 Legislature and approved and ratified by the voters at the 2020 General Election.]* The proceeds of the public lands donated by Act of Congress approved July 2, 1862, ch. 130, 12 Stat. 503, and thereafter amended by Act of Congress, for a college for the benefit of Agriculture and Mechanic Arts, including Military tactics, shall be invested by the State of Nevada in the manner required by law in a separate fund to be appropriated exclusively for the benefit of the first named departments to the State University as set forth in Section 4 of this Article. And the Legislature shall provide that if through neglect or any other contingency, any portion of the fund so set apart is lost or misappropriated, the State of Nevada shall replace said amount so lost or misappropriated in said fund so that the principal of said fund shall remain forever undiminished.

(Proposed amendment passed by the 2017 Legislature; effective November 24, 2020, if agreed to and passed by the 2019 Legislature and approved and ratified by the voters at the 2020 General Election. See: Statutes of Nevada 2017, p. 4583.)

SECTION 9. *Sectarian instruction prohibited in common schools and university.* No sectarian instruction shall be imparted or tolerated in any school or University that may be established under this Constitution.

SECTION 10. *No public money to be used for sectarian purposes.* No public funds of any kind or character whatever, State, County or Municipal, shall be used for sectarian purpose.

[Added in 1880. Proposed and passed by the 1877 legislature; agreed to and passed by the 1879 legislature; and approved and ratified by the people at the 1880 general election. See: Statutes of Nevada 1877, p. 221; Statutes of Nevada 1879, p. 149.]

ARTICLE 12.
Militia

SECTION   1. Legislature to provide for militia.
          2. Power of governor to call out militia.

SECTION. 1. *Legislature to provide for militia.* The Legislature shall provide by law for organizing and disciplining the Militia of this State, for the effectual encouragement of Volunteer Corps and the safe keeping of the public Arms.

SECTION 2. *Power of governor to call out militia.* The Governor shall have power to call out the Militia to execute the laws of the State or to suppress insurrection or repel invasion.

ARTICLE 13.
Public Institutions

SECTION   1. Institutions for insane, blind, deaf and dumb to be fostered and supported by state.
          2. State prison: Establishment and maintenance; juvenile offenders.
          3. County public welfare. [Repealed in 1937.]

SECTION 1. *Institutions for insane, blind, deaf and dumb to be fostered and supported by state.* Institutions for the benefit of the Insane, Blind and Deaf and Dumb, and such other benevolent institutions as the public good may require, shall be fostered and supported by the State, subject to such regulations as may be prescribed by law.

SECTION 2. *State prison: Establishment and maintenance; juvenile offenders.* A State Prison shall be established and maintained in such manner as may be prescribed by law, and provision may be made by law for the establishment and maintainance [maintenance] of a House of Refuge for Juvenile Offenders.

SECTION 3. *County public welfare.* [Repealed in 1937.]
[Section 3 of the original constitution was repealed by vote of the people at a special election held March 17, 1937. See: Statutes of Nevada 1935, p. 439; Statutes of Nevada 1937, pp. 19, 50. The original section read: "The respective counties of the State shall provide as may be prescribed by law, for those inhabitants who, by reason of age and infirmity or misfortunes, may have claim upon the sympathy and aid of Society."]

ARTICLE 14.
Boundary

SECTION 1. *Boundary of the State of Nevada.* The boundary of the State of Nevada is as follows:

Commencing at a point formed by the intersection of the forty-third degree of longitude West from Washington with the forty-second degree of North latitude; thence due East along the forty-second degree of North latitude to its intersection with the thirty-seventh degree of longitude West from Washington; thence South on the thirty-seventh degree of longitude West from Washington to its intersection with the middle line of the Colorado River of the West; thence down the middle line of the Colorado River of the West to its intersection with the Eastern boundary of the State of California; thence in a North Westerly direction along the Eastern boundary line of the State of California to the forty-third degree of Longitude West from Washington; Thence North along the forty-third degree of West Longitude, and the Eastern boundary line of the State of California to the place of beginning. All territory lying West of and adjoining the boundary line herein prescribed, which the State of California may relinquish to the Territory or State of Nevada, shall thereupon be embraced within and constitute a part of this State.

[Amended in 1982. Proposed and passed by the 1979 legislature; agreed to and passed by the 1981 legislature; and approved and ratified by the people at the 1982 general election. See: Statutes of Nevada 1979, p. 1978; Statutes of Nevada 1981, p. 2140.]

ARTICLE 15.
Miscellaneous Provisions

SECTION   1. Carson City seat of government.
2. Oath of office.
3. Eligibility for public office.
4. Perpetuities; eleemosynary purposes.
5. Time of general election.
6. Number of members of legislature limited.
7. County offices at county seats.
8. Publication of general statutes; publication and effective date of decisions of Supreme Court and court of appeals.
9. Increase or decrease of compensation of officers whose compensation fixed by constitution.
10. Election or appointment of officers.
11. Term of office when not fixed by Constitution; limitation; municipal officers and employees.

12. Certain state officers to keep offices at Carson City.
13. Census by legislature and Congress: Basis of representation in houses of legislature.
14. Election by plurality.
15. Merit system governing employment in executive branch of state government.
16. Payment of minimum compensation to employees. [Effective through November 23, 2020, and after that date unless the provisions of Senate Joint Resolution No. 6 (2017) are agreed to and passed by the 2019 Legislature and approved and ratified by the voters at the 2020 General Election.]
16. Payment of minimum compensation to employees; incremental annual increase. [Effective November 24, 2020, if the provisions of Senate Joint Resolution No. 6 (2017) are agreed to and passed by the 2019 Legislature and approved and ratified by the voters at the 2020 General Election.]
17. Emergency Medical Services: Hospital or independent facility for emergency medical care prohibited from denying treatment regardless of whether person has health insurance; establishment of reasonable cost for services; Legislature may set different rate if commission established to ensure services provided at reasonable cost. [Effective November 24, 2020, if the provisions of Assembly Joint Resolution No. 14 (2017) are agreed to and passed by the 2019 Legislature and approved and ratified by the voters at the 2020 General Election.]

SECTION 1. *Carson City seat of government.* The seat of Government shall be at Carson City, but no appropriation for the erection or purchase of Capitol buildings shall be made during the next three Years[.]

SECTION 2. *Oath of office.* Members of the legislature, and all officers, executive, judicial and ministerial, shall, before they enter upon the duties of their respective offices, take and subscribe to the following oath:

I,................, do solemnly [solemnly] swear (or affirm) that I will support, protect and defend the constitution and government of the United States, and the constitution and government of the State of Nevada, against all enemies, whether domestic or foreign, and that I will bear true faith, allegiance and loyalty to the same, any ordinance, resolution or law of any state notwithstanding, and that I will well and faithfully perform all the duties of the office of................, on which I am about to enter; (if an oath) so help me God; (if an affirmation) under the pains and penalties of perjury.

[Amended in 1914. Proposed and passed by the 1911 legislature; agreed to and passed by the 1913 legislature; and approved and ratified by the people at the 1914 general election. See: Statutes of Nevada 1911, p. 458; Journal of the Assembly, 26th Session, p. 20 and Journal of the Senate, 26th Session, p. 37.]

SECTION 3. *Eligibility for public office.*

1. No person shall be eligible to any office who is not a qualified elector under this Constitution.

2. No person may be elected to any state office or local governing body who has served in that office, or at the expiration of his current term if he is so serving will have served, 12 years or more, unless the permissible number of terms or duration of service is otherwise specified in this Constitution.

[Amended in 1889, 1912, 1978 and 1996. The first amendment was proposed and passed by the 1887 Legislature; agreed to and passed by the 1889 Legislature; and approved and ratified by the people at a Special Election held February 11, 1889. See: Statutes of Nevada 1887, p. 162; Statutes of Nevada 1889, p. 151. The second amendment was proposed and passed by the 1909 Legislature; agreed to and passed by the 1911 Legislature; and approved and ratified by the people at the 1912 General Election. See: Statutes of Nevada 1909, p. 349; Statutes of Nevada 1911, p. 454. The third amendment was proposed and passed by the 1975 Legislature; agreed to and passed by the 1977 Legislature; and approved and ratified by the people at the 1978 General Election. See: Statutes of Nevada 1975, p. 1902; Statutes of Nevada 1977, p. 1687. The fourth amendment was proposed by initiative petition and approved and ratified by the people at the 1994 and 1996 General Elections.]

SECTION 4. *Perpetuities; eleemosynary purposes.* No perpetuities shall be allowed except for eleemosynary purposes.

SECTION 5. *Time of general election.* The general election shall be held on the Tuesday next after the first Monday of November.

SECTION 6. *Number of members of legislature limited.* The aggregate number of members of both branches of the Legislature shall never exceed Seventy five.

SECTION 7. *County offices at county seats.* All county Officers shall hold their Offices at the County seat of their respective Counties.

SECTION 8. *Publication of general statutes; publication and effective date of decisions of Supreme Court and court of appeals.* The Legislature shall provide for the speedy publication of all statute laws of a general nature and such decisions of the Supreme Court and the court of appeals as it may deem expedient. All laws and judicial decisions must be free for publication by any person. No judgment of the Supreme Court or the court of appeals shall take effect and be operative until the opinion of the court in such case is filed with the clerk of said court.

[Added in 2014. Proposed and passed by the 2011 Legislature; agreed to and passed by the 2013 Legislature; and approved and ratified by the people at the 2014 General Election. See: Statutes of Nevada 2011, p. 3835; Statutes of Nevada 2013, p. 3968.]

SECTION 9. *Increase or decrease of compensation of officers whose compensation fixed by constitution.* The Legislature may, at any time, provide by law for increasing or diminishing the salaries or compensation of any of the Officers, whose salaries or compensation is fixed in this Constitution; Provided, no such change of Salary or compensation shall apply to any Officer during the term for which he may have been elected.

SECTION 10. *Election or appointment of officers.* All officers whose election or appointment is not otherwise provided for, shall be chosen or appointed as may be prescribed by law.

SECTION 11. *Term of office when not fixed by Constitution; limitation; municipal officers and employees.* The tenure of any office not herein provided for may be declared by law, or, when not so declared, such office shall be held during the pleasure of the authority making the appointment, but the Legislature shall not create any office the tenure of which shall be longer than four (4) years, except as herein otherwise provided in this Constitution. In the case of any officer or employee of any municipality governed under a legally adopted charter, the provisions of such charter with reference to the tenure of office or the dismissal from office of any such officer or employee shall control.
[Amended in 1946. Proposed and passed by the 1943 Legislature; agreed to and passed by the 1945 Legislature; and approved and ratified by the people at the 1946 General Election. See: Statutes of Nevada 1943, p. 325; Statutes of Nevada 1945, p. 505.]

SECTION 12. *Certain state officers to keep offices at Carson City.* The Governor, Secretary of State, State Treasurer, State Controller, and Clerk of the Supreme Court, shall keep their respective offices at the seat of Government.

SECTION 13. *Census by legislature and Congress: Basis of representation in houses of legislature.* The enumeration of the inhabitants of this State shall be taken under the direction of the Legislature if deemed necessary in AD Eighteen hundred and Sixty five, AD Eighteen hundred and Sixty seven, AD Eighteen hundred and Seventy five, and every ten years thereafter; and these enumerations, together with the census that may be taken under the direction of the Congress of the United States in A.D. Eighteen hundred and Seventy, and every subsequent ten years shall serve as the basis of representation in both houses of the Legislature.

SECTION 14. *Election by plurality.* A plurality of votes given at an election by the people, shall constitute a choice, where not otherwise provided by this Constitution[.]

SECTION 15. *Merit system governing employment in executive branch of state government.* The legislature shall provide by law for a state merit system governing the employment of employees in the executive branch of state government.

[Added in 1970. Proposed and passed by the 1967 legislature; agreed to and passed by the 1969 legislature; and approved and ratified by the people at the 1970 general election. See: Statutes of Nevada 1967, p. 1829; Statutes of Nevada 1969, p. 1720.]

SECTION 16. *Payment of minimum compensation to employees.* [*Effective through November 23, 2020, and after that date unless the provisions of Senate Joint Resolution No. 6 (2017) are agreed to and passed by the 2019 Legislature and approved and ratified by the voters at the 2020 General Election.*]

A. Each employer shall pay a wage to each employee of not less than the hourly rates set forth in this section. The rate shall be five dollars and fifteen cents ($5.15) per hour worked, if the employer provides health benefits as described herein, or six dollars and fifteen cents ($6.15) per hour if the employer does not provide such benefits. Offering health benefits within the meaning of this section shall consist of making health insurance available to the employee for the employee and the employee's dependents at a total cost to the employee for premiums of not more than 10 percent of the employee's gross taxable income from the employer. These rates of wages shall be adjusted by the amount of increases in the federal minimum wage over $5.15 per hour, or, if greater, by the cumulative increase in the cost of living. The cost of living increase shall be measured by the percentage increase as of December 31 in any year over the level as of December 31, 2004 of the Consumer Price Index (All Urban Consumers, U.S. City Average) as published by the Bureau of Labor Statistics, U.S. Department of Labor or the successor index or federal agency. No CPI adjustment for any one-year period may be greater than 3%. The Governor or the State agency designated by the Governor shall publish a bulletin by April 1 of each year announcing the adjusted rates, which shall take effect the following July 1. Such bulletin will be made available to all employers and to any other person who has filed with the Governor or the designated agency a request to receive such notice but lack of notice shall not excuse noncompliance with this section. An employer shall provide written notification of the rate adjustments to each of its employees and make the necessary payroll adjustments by July 1 following the publication of the bulletin. Tips or gratuities received by employees shall not be credited as being any part of or offset against the wage rates required by this section.

B. The provisions of this section may not be waived by agreement between an individual employee and an employer. All of the provisions of this section, or any part hereof, may be waived in a bona fide collective bargaining agreement, but only if the waiver is explicitly set forth in such agreement in clear and unambiguous terms. Unilateral implementation of terms and conditions of employment by either party to a collective bargaining relationship shall not constitute, or be permitted, as a waiver of all or any part of the provisions of this section. An employer shall not discharge, reduce the compensation of or otherwise discriminate against any employee for using any civil remedies to enforce this section or otherwise asserting his or her rights under this section. An employee claiming violation of this section may bring an action against his or her employer in the courts of this State to enforce the provisions of this section and shall be entitled to all remedies available under the law or in equity appropriate to remedy any violation of this section, including but not limited to back pay, damages, reinstatement or injunctive relief. An employee who prevails in any action to enforce this section shall be awarded his or her reasonable attorney's fees and costs.

C. As used in this section, "employee" means any person who is employed by an employer as defined herein but does not include an employee who is under eighteen (18) years of age, employed by a nonprofit organization for after school or summer employment or as a trainee for a period not longer than ninety (90) days. "Employer" means any individual, proprietorship, partnership, joint venture, corporation, limited liability company, trust, association, or other entity that may employ individuals or enter into contracts of employment.

D. If any provision of this section is declared illegal, invalid or inoperative, in whole or in part, by the final decision of any court of competent jurisdiction, the remaining provisions and all portions not declared illegal, invalid or inoperative shall remain in full force or effect, and no such determination shall invalidate the remaining sections or portions of the sections of this section.

[Added in 2006. Proposed by initiative petition and approved and ratified by the people at the 2004 and 2006 General Elections.]

SECTION 16. *Payment of minimum compensation to employees; incremental annual increase.* [*Effective November 24, 2020, if the provisions of Senate Joint Resolution No. 6 (2017) are agreed to and passed by the 2019 Legislature and approved and ratified by the voters at the 2020 General Election.*]

1. Except as otherwise provided in this section, each employer shall pay a

wage to each employee of not less than the hourly rate set forth in this subsection. Beginning on January 1, 2021, the rate must be nine dollars and forty cents ($9.40) per hour worked. Beginning on January 1, 2022, this rate must be increased on January 1 of each year by one dollar and fifteen cents ($1.15) per hour worked until the rate is fourteen dollars ($14.00) per hour worked.

2. If, at any time, the federal minimum wage is higher than the rate set forth in Subsection 1, each employer must pay a wage to each employee of not less than the hourly rate set forth in the federal minimum wage.

3. The Legislature may establish by law a minimum wage that an employer must pay to each employee that is higher than the hourly rate set forth in Subsection 1 or 2.

4. Tips or gratuities received by employees shall not be credited as being any part of or offset against the minimum wage rate required by this section.

5. Except as otherwise provided in this subsection, the provisions of this section may not be waived by agreement between any employee and his or her employer. All of the provisions of this section, or any part hereof, may be waived in a bona fide collective bargaining agreement, but only if the waiver is explicitly set forth in such agreement in clear and unambiguous terms. Unilateral implementation of terms and conditions of employment by either party to a collective bargaining relationship shall not constitute, or be permitted, as a waiver of all or any part of the provisions of this section.

6. An employer shall not discharge, reduce the compensation of or otherwise discriminate against any employee for using any civil remedies to enforce this section or otherwise asserting his or her rights under this section in any manner. An employee claiming a violation of this section is entitled to bring an action against his or her employer in the courts of this State, either in his or her individual capacity or as a representative of a class of similarly situated individuals, to enforce the provisions of this section and shall be entitled to all remedies available under the law or in equity appropriate to remedy any violation of this section. An employee who prevails in any action to enforce this section must be awarded damages in an amount equal to three times the amount which the employee would have been paid if his or her employer had complied with the provisions of this section and his or her reasonable attorney's fees and costs.

7. As used in this section, "employee" means any person who is employed by an employer as defined herein but does not include an employee

who is under eighteen (18) years of age, employed by a nonprofit organization for after school or summer employment or as a trainee for a period not longer than ninety (90) days. "Employer" means any individual, proprietorship, partnership, joint venture, corporation, limited liability company, trust, association, or other entity that may employ individuals or enter into contracts of employment.

8. If any provision of this section is declared illegal, invalid or inoperative, in whole or in part, by the final decision of any court of competent jurisdiction, the remaining provisions and all portions not declared illegal, invalid or inoperative shall remain in full force or effect, and no such determination shall invalidate the remaining sections or portions of the sections of this section.

[Added in 2006. Proposed by initiative petition and approved and ratified by the people at the 2004 and 2006 General Elections.]—(Proposed amendment passed by the 2017 Legislature; effective November 24, 2020, if agreed to and passed by the 2019 Legislature and approved and ratified by the voters at the 2020 General Election. See: Statutes of Nevada 2017, p. 4594.)

SECTION 17. *Emergency Medical Services: Hospital or independent facility for emergency medical care prohibited from denying treatment regardless of whether person has health insurance; establishment of reasonable cost for services; Legislature may set different rate if commission established to ensure services provided at reasonable cost.* [Effective November 24, 2020, if the provisions of Assembly Joint *Resolution No. 14 (2017) are agreed to and passed by the 2019 Legislature and approved and ratified by the voters at the 2020 General Election.*]

1. No hospital or independent facility for emergency medical care shall deny treatment or services to a person who arrives at the hospital or facility seeking medically necessary emergency services, regardless of whether the person has health insurance and regardless of the ability of the person to pay for such services.

2. All persons in this State have a right to receive medically necessary emergency services at a reasonable cost, and except as otherwise provided in Subsection 3, no hospital or independent facility for emergency medical care shall charge for any treatment, service or medication or other product provided to a person who arrives at the hospital or facility seeking medically necessary emergency services, whether or not the person has insurance, an amount which is:

   (a) Greater than 150 percent of the lowest rate which the hospital or facility has agreed to accept from a federal public insurer for the treatment, service or medication or other product; or

   (b) If the Legislature provides by law for a different rate pursuant to Subsection 5, greater than the rate provided by law.

3. If the Legislature has not provided by law for a different rate pursuant to subsection 5, the state agency authorized by law to regulate the hospital or independent facility for emergency medical care may allow the hospital or facility to increase the rate above the rate provided in paragraph (a) of Subsection 2 only if the hospital or facility proves that the increase is absolutely necessary to avoid a rate that is confiscatory under the Constitution of the United States. If the state agency allows such an increase, the amount of the increase must not exceed the amount that the hospital or facility proves is absolutely necessary to avoid an unconstitutional result.

4. The provisions of Subsections 1, 2 and 3:
   (a) Are self-executing.
   (b) May not be waived in any manner or altered or varied by agreement.
   (c) May be enforced by:
       (1) The State of Nevada or a political subdivision of the State of Nevada.
       (2) A civil action brought by a person who is denied any right protected by those provisions.

5. The Legislature:
   (a) Shall provide by law for the administration and enforcement of the provisions of this section.
   (b) May provide by law for a different rate than the rate provided in paragraph (a) of Subsection 2 if the Legislature establishes, by law, a commission to ensure that hospitals and independent facilities for emergency medical care provide medically necessary emergency services at a reasonable cost. If such a commission is established, the Legislature shall provide by law for:
       (1) The appointment of the members of the commission; and
       (2) The powers and duties of the commission consistent with the provisions of this section.

(Proposed new section passed by the 2017 Legislature; effective November 24, 2020, if agreed to and passed by the 2019 Legislature and approved and ratified by the voters at the 2020 General Election. See: Statutes of Nevada 2017, p. 4609.)

ARTICLE 16.
Amendments

SECTION   1. Constitutional amendments: Procedure; concurrent and consecutive amendments.
2. Convention for revision of constitution: Procedure.

SECTION 1. *Constitutional amendments: Procedure; concurrent and consecutive amendments.*

1. Any amendment or amendments to this Constitution may be proposed in the Senate or Assembly; and if the same shall be agreed to by a Majority of all the members elected to each of the two houses, such proposed amendment or amendments shall be entered on their respective journals, with the Yeas and Nays taken thereon, and referred to the Legislature then next to be chosen, and shall be published for three months next preceding the time of making such choice. And if in the Legislature next chosen as aforesaid, such proposed amendment or amendments shall be agreed to by a majority of all the members elected to each house, then it shall be the duty of the Legislature to submit such proposed amendment or amendments to the people, in such manner and at such time as the Legislature shall prescribe; and if the people shall approve and ratify such amendment or amendments by a majority of the electors qualified to vote for members of the Legislature voting thereon, such amendment or amendments shall, unless precluded by Subsection 2 or Section 2 of Article 19 of this constitution, become a part of the Constitution.

2. If, two or more amendments which affect the same section of the constitution are ratified by the people pursuant to this section at the same election:
   (a) If all can be given effect without contradiction in substance, each shall become a part of the constitution.
   (b) If one or more contradict in substance the other or others, that amendment which received the largest favorable vote, and any other ratified amendment or amendments compatible with it, shall become a part of the constitution.

3. If, after the proposal of an amendment, another amendment is ratified pursuant to this section which affects the same section of the constitution but is compatible with the proposed amendment, the next legislature if it agrees to the proposed amendment shall submit such proposal to the people as a further amendment to the amended section. If, after the proposal of an amendment, another amendment is ratified pursuant to this section which contradicts in substance the proposed amendment, such proposed amendment shall not be submitted to the people.

[Amended in 1972 and 1998. The first amendment was proposed and passed by the 1969 legislature; agreed to and passed by the 1971 legislature; and approved and ratified by the people at the 1972 general election. See: Statutes of Nevada 1969, p. 1728; Statutes of Nevada 1971, p. 2265. The second amendment was proposed and passed by the 1995 legislature; agreed to and passed by the 1997 legislature; and approved and ratified by the people at the 1998 general election. See: Statutes of Nevada 1995, p. 2949; Statutes

of Nevada 1997, p. 3592. A previous amendment to this section was approved and ratified by the people at the 1886 general election, but no entry of the proposed amendment
had been made upon the journal of either house of the legislature, and such omission
was fatal to the adoption of the amendment. See: State ex rel. Stevenson v. Tufly, 19 Nev.
391 (1887).]

SECTION 2. *Convention for revision of constitution: Procedure.* If at any time
the Legislature by a vote of two thirds of the Members elected to each house,
shall determine that it is necessary to cause a revision of this entire Constitution they shall recommend to the electors at the next election for Members of
the Legislature, to vote for or against a convention, and if it shall appear that
a majority of the electors voting at such election, shall have voted in favor of
calling a Convention, the Legislature shall, at its next session provide by law
for calling a Convention to be holden within six months after the passage
of such law, and such Convention shall consist of a number of Members not
less than that of both branches of the Legislature. In determining what is a
majority of the electors voting at such election, reference shall be had to the
highest number of votes cast at such election for the candidates for any office
or on any question.

[An amendment to this section was approved and ratified by the people at the 1886 general election, but no entry of the proposed amendment had been made upon the journal of either house of the legislature, and such omission was fatal to the adoption of the
amendment. See: State ex rel. Stevenson v. Tufly, 19 Nev. 391 (1887).]

ARTICLE 17.
Schedule

SECTION 1. Saving existing rights and liabilities.
2. Territorial laws to remain in force.
3. Fines, penalties and forfeitures to inure to state.
4. Existing obligations and pending suits.
5. Salaries of state officers for first term of office.
6. Apportionment of Senators and members of Assembly.
7. Assumption of territorial debts and liabilities.
8. Terms of elected state officers.
9. Terms of senators.
10. Terms of Senators and members of Assembly after 1866.
11. Terms of members of Assembly elected at first general election or in 1865.
12. Commencement date of first three legislative sessions; regular sessions of legislature to be held biennially.
13. Continuation of territorial county and township officers; probate judges.
14. Duties of certain territorial officers continued.

15. Terms of supreme court and district courts.
16. Salaries of district judges.
17. Alteration of salary of district judge authorized.
18. Qualification and terms of certain elective state officers.
19. When justices of supreme court and district judges enter upon duties.
20. State officers and district judges to be commissioned by territorial governor; state controller and treasurer to furnish bonds.
21. Support of county and city officers.
22. Vacancies in certain state offices: How filled.
23. Civil and criminal cases pending in probate courts transferred to district courts.
24. Levy of tax limited for 3 years.
25. Roop County attached to Washoe County.
26. Constitutional debates and proceedings: Publication; payment of reporter.

SECTION 1. *Saving existing rights and liabilities.* That no inconvenience may arise by reason of a change from a Territorial to a permanent State Government, it is declared, that all rights, actions, prosecutions, judgements[,] Claims and Contracts, as well of individuals, as of bodies corporate, including counties, towns and cities, shall continue as if no change had taken place; and all process which may issue under the Authority of the Territory of Nevada, previous to its admission into the Union as one of the United States, shall be as valid as if issued in the name of the State of Nevada.

SECTION 2. *Territorial laws to remain in force.* All laws of the Territory of Nevada in force at the time of the admission of this State, not repugnant to this Constitution, shall remain in force until they expire by their own limitations or be altered or repealed by the Legislature.

SECTION 3. *Fines, penalties and forfeitures to inure to state.* All fines, penalties and forfeitures accruing to the Territory of Nevada or to the people of the United States in the Territory of Nevada, shall inure to the State of Nevada.

SECTION 4. *Existing obligations and pending suits.* All recognizances heretofore taken, or which may be taken before the change from a Territorial, to a State Government, shall remain valid, and shall pass to, and may be prosecuted in the name of the State, and all bonds, executed to the Governor of the Territory or to any other Officer or Court in his or their official capacity, or to the people of the United States in the Territory of Nevada, shall pass to the Governor, or other officer or court, and his or their successors in office for the uses therein respectively expressed, and may be sued on, and recovery had accordingly; And all property real, personal or mixed, and all judgements, bonds, specialties, choses in Action, claims and debts of whatsoever description, and all records, and public Archives of the Territory of Nevada, shall issue to and vest in the State of Nevada, and may be sued for and recovered in the same manner and to the same extent by the State of Nevada, as the same could have been by the Territory of Nevada. All criminal prosecutions and penal Actions, which may have arisen, or which may arise before the change from a Territorial to a State Government, and which shall then be pending, shall be prosecuted to judgement and execution in the name of the State. All offenses committed against the laws of the Territory of Nevada, before the change from a Territorial to a State Government, and which shall not be prosecuted before such change, may be prosecuted in the name and by the Authority of the State of Nevada, with like effect as though such change had not taken place; And all penalties incurred, shall remain the same as if this Constitution had not been adopted; All actions at law, and suits in equity, and other legal proceedings, which may be pending in any of the Courts of the Territory of Nevada at the time of the change from a Territorial to a State Government may be continued and transferred to, and determined by, any court of the State, which shall have jurisdiction of the subject matter thereof. All actions at law and suits in Equity, and all other legal proceedings, which may be pending in any of the Courts of the Territory of Nevada at the time of the change from a Territorial to a State Government, shall be continued and transferred to, and may be prosecuted to judgement and execution in any Court of the State which shall have jurisdiction of the subject matter thereof; And all books, papers and records, relating to the same shall be transferred in like manner to such Court.

SECTION 5. *Salaries of state officers for first term of office.* For the first term of office succeeding the formation of a State Government, the Salary of the Governor shall be Four Thousand Dollars per annum; The salary of the Secretary of State shall be Three Thousand, Six hundred Dollars per annum; The salary of the State Controller shall be Three Thousand, Six hundred Dollars per annum; The salary of the State Treasurer shall be Three Thousand Six hundred Dollars per Annum; The salary of the Surveyor General shall be One Thousand Dollars per annum; The salary of the Attorney General shall be Two Thousand Five hundred Dollars per annum; The salary of the Superintendent of Public Instruction shall be Two Thousand Dollars per annum; The salary of each judge of the Supreme Court shall be Seven Thousand Dollars per annum; The salaries of the foregoing officers, shall be paid quarterly, out of the State Treasury. The pay of State Senators and Members of Assembly shall be Eight Dollars per day, for each day of actual service, and forty cents per mile for mileage going to, and returning from, the place of meeting.

No officer mentioned in this Section, shall receive any fee or perquisites, to his own use for the performance of any duty connected with his office, or for the performance of any additional duty imposed upon him by law.

SECTION 6. *Apportionment of Senators and members of Assembly.* Until otherwise provided by Law the apportionment of Senators and Assemblymen in the different counties shall be as follows, to Wit: Storey County four Senators and Twelve Assemblymen, Douglas County One Senator and Two Assemblymen; Esmeralda County, Two Senators and Four Assemblymen; Humboldt County, Two Senators and Three Assemblymen; Lander County Two Senators and Four Assemblymen; Lyon County, One Senator and Three Assemblymen; Lyon and Churchill Counties, One Senator jointly; Churchill County One Assemblyman; Nye County One Senator and one Assemblyman; Ormsby County Two Senators and Three Assemblymen; Washoe and Roop Counties, Two Senators and Three Assemblymen.

SECTION 7. *Assumption of territorial debts and liabilities.* All debts and liabilities of the Territory of Nevada, lawfully incurred and which remain unpaid, at the time of the admission of this State into the Union shall be assumed by and become the debt of the State of Nevada; Provided that the assumption of such indebtedness shall not prevent the State from contracting the additional indebtedness as provided in Section 3 of Article 9 of this Constitution.

SECTION 8. *Terms of elected state officers.* The term of State Officers, except Judicial, elected at the first election under this Constitution shall continue until the Tuesday after the first Monday of January AD. Eighteen hundred and sixty seven, and until the election and qualification of their successors.

SECTION 9. *Terms of senators.* The Senators to be elected at the first election under this Constitution shall draw lots, so that, the term of one half of the number as nearly as may be, shall expire on the day succeeding the general election in A.D. Eighteen Hundred and Sixty Six; and the term of the other half shall expire on the day succeeding the general election in A.D. Eighteen hundred and sixty eight, Provided, that in drawing lots for all Senatorial terms, the Senatorial representation shall be allotted, so that in the Counties having two or more Senators, the terms thereof shall be divided as nearly as may be between the long and short terms.

SECTION 10. *Terms of Senators and members of Assembly after 1866.* At the general election in A.D. Eighteen hundred and Sixty Six; and thereafter, the term of Senators shall be for Four Years from the day succeeding such general election, and members of Assembly for Two Years from the day succeeding such general election, and the terms of Senators shall be allotted by the

Legislature in long and short terms as hereinbefore provided; so that one half the number as nearly as may be, shall be elected every Two Years.

SECTION 11. *Terms of members of Assembly elected at first general election or in 1865.* The term of the members of the Assembly elected at the first general election under this Constitution shall expire on the day succeeding the general election in AD. Eighteen hundred and Sixty Five; and the terms of those elected at the general election in AD. Eighteen hundred and Sixty Five, shall expire on the day succeeding the general election in A.D. Eighteen hundred and Sixty six.

SECTION 12. *Commencement date of first three legislative sessions; regular sessions of legislature to be held biennially.* The first regular session of the Legislature shall commence on the second Monday of December A.D. Eighteen hundred and Sixty Four, and the second regular session of the same shall commence on the first Monday of January A.D. Eighteen hundred and Sixty Six; and the third regular session of the Legislature shall be the first of the biennial sessions, and shall commence on the first Monday of January A.D. Eighteen hundred and Sixty Seven; and the regular sessions of the Legislature shall be held thereafter biennially.

[See Article 4, Section 2, as amended in 1889. Amended in 1998. Proposed and passed by the 1995 legislature; agreed to and passed by the 1997 legislature; and approved and ratified by the people at the 1998 general election. See: Statutes of Nevada 1995, p. 2972; Statutes of Nevada 1997, p. 3726.]

SECTION 13. *Continuation of territorial county and township officers; probate judges.* All county officers under the laws of the Territory of Nevada at the time when the Constitution shall take effect, whose offices are not inconsistent with the provisions of this Constitution, shall continue in office until the first Monday of January A.D. Eighteen hundred and Sixty Seven, and until their successors are elected and qualified; and all township officers shall continue in office until the expiration of their terms of office, and until their successors are elected and qualified; Provided, that the Probate Judges of the several counties respectively, shall continue in office until the election and qualification of the District Judges of the several counties or Judicial Districts; And Provided further, that the term of office of the present county officers of Lander County, shall expire on the first Monday of January AD Eighteen hundred and Sixty Five, except the Probate Judge of said County whose term of office shall expire upon the first Monday of December A.D. Eighteen hundred and Sixty Four, and there shall be an election for County Officers of Lander County at the general election in November A.D. Eighteen hundred and Sixty Four, and the officers then elected, shall hold office from the first Monday of January AD. Eighteen hundred and Sixty five until the first Monday of January AD. Eighteen hundred and sixty seven, and until their successors are elected and qualified.

SECTION 14. *Duties of certain territorial officers continued.* The Governor, Secretary, Treasurer and Superintendent of Public Instruction of the Territory of Nevada shall each continue to discharge the duties of their respective offices after the admission of this State into the Union, and until the time designated for the qualification of the above named officers to be elected under the State Government, and the Territorial Auditor shall continue to discharge the duties of his said office until the time appointed for the qualification of the State Controller; Provided, that the said officers shall each receive the salaries, and be subject to the restrictions and conditions provided in this Constitution; And Provided further, that none of them shall receive to his own use any fees or perquisites for the performance of any duty connected with his office.

SECTION 15. *Terms of supreme court and district courts.* The terms of the Supreme Court shall, until provision be made by law, be held at such times as the Judges of the said Court or a majority of them may appoint. The first terms of the several District Courts (except as hereinafter mentioned) shall commence on the first Monday of December A.D. Eighteen Hundred and Sixty Four. The first term of the District Court in the Fifth Judicial District, shall commence on the first Monday of December A.D. Eighteen Hundred and Sixty Four in the County of Nye; and shall commence on the first Monday of January A.D. Eighteen Hundred and Sixty Five in the County of Churchill. The terms of the Fourth Judicial District Court shall until otherwise provided by law be held at the County Seat of Washoe County, and the first term thereof commence on the first Monday of December, AD. Eighteen Hundred and Sixty Four.

SECTION 16. *Salaries of district judges.* The Judges of the several District Courts of this State shall be paid as hereinbefore provided Salaries at the following rates per Annum: First Judicial District (Each Judge) Six Thousand Dollars; Second Judicial District Four Thousand Dollars; Third Judicial District, Five Thousand Dollars; Fourth Judicial District Five Thousand Dollars; Fifth Judicial District Thirty Six Hundred Dollars; Sixth Judicial District Four Thousand Dollars; Seventh Judicial District Six Thousand Dollars; Eighth Judicial District Thirty Six Hundred Dollars; Ninth Judicial District Five Thousand Dollars.

SECTION 17. *Alteration of salary of district judge authorized.* The salary of any Judge in said Judicial Districts may by law be altered or changed, subject to the provisions contained in this Constitution.

268   APPENDIX

SECTION 18. *Qualification and terms of certain elective state officers.* The Governor, Lieutenant Governor, Secretary of State, State Treasurer, State Controller, Attorney General, Surveyor General, Clerk of the Supreme Court and Superintendent of Public Instruction, to be elected at the first election under this Constitution shall each qualify and enter upon the duties of their respective offices on the first Monday of December succeeding their election and shall continue in office until the first Tuesday after the first Monday of January AD. Eighteen hundred and Sixty Seven, and until the election and qualification of their successors respectively.

SECTION 19. *When justices of supreme court and district judges enter upon duties.* The Judges of the Supreme Court and District Judges to be elected at the first election under this Constitution shall qualify and enter upon the duties of their respective offices on the first Monday of December succeeding their election.

SECTION 20. *State officers and district judges to be commissioned by territorial governor; state controller and treasurer to furnish bonds.* All officers of State, and District Judges first elected under this Constitution shall be commissioned by the Governor of this Territory, which commission shall be countersigned by the Secretary of the same, and shall qualify before entering upon the discharge of their duties, before any officer authorized to administer oaths under the Laws of this Territory; and also the State Controller and State Treasurer shall each respectively, before they qualify, and enter upon the discharge of their duties, execute and deliver to the Secretary of the Territory of Nevada an Official Bond, made payable to the People of the State of Nevada in the sum of Thirty Thousand Dollars, to be approved by the Governor of the Territory of Nevada; and shall also execute and deliver to the Secretary of State such other or further official Bond or Bonds as may be required by law.

SECTION 21. *Support of county and city officers.* Each County, Town, City, and Incorporated Village shall make provision for the support of its own officers, subject to such regulations as may be prescribed by law.

SECTION 22. *Vacancies in certain state offices: How filled.* In case the office of any State officer, except a judicial officer, shall become vacant before the expiration of the regular term for which he was elected, the vacancy may be filled by appointment by the Governor until it shall be supplied at the next general election, when it shall be filled by election for the residue of the unexpired term.

[Amended in 1976. Proposed and passed by the 1973 legislature; agreed to and passed by the 1975 legislature; and approved and ratified by the people at the 1976 general election. See: Statutes of Nevada 1973, p. 1955; Statutes of Nevada 1975, p. 1873.]

SECTION 23. *Civil and criminal cases pending in probate courts transferred to district courts.* All cases both civil and criminal, which may be pending and undetermined in the Probate Courts of the several counties at the time when under the provisions of this Constitution, said Probate Courts are to be abolished, shall be transferred to and determined by the District Courts of such counties respectively.

SECTION 24. *Levy of tax limited for 3 years.* For the first Three Years after the adoption of this Constitution the Legislature shall not levy a tax for State purposes, exceeding one per cent per annum on the taxable property in the State, Provided, the Legislature may levy a special tax not exceeding one fourth of one per cent per annum, which shall be appropriated to the payment of the indebtedness of the Territory of Nevada, assumed by the State of Nevada, and for that purpose only, until all of said indebtedness is paid.

SECTION 25. *Roop County attached to Washoe County.* The County of Roop shall be attached to the County of Washoe for Judicial[,] Legislative, Revenue and County purposes, until otherwise provided by law.

SECTION 26. *Constitutional debates and proceedings: Publication; payment of reporter.* At the first regular session of the Legislature to convene under the requirements of this Constitution, provisions shall be made by law for paying for the publication of Six Hundred copies of the Debates and proceedings of this Convention in Book form, to be disposed of as the Legislature may direct; and the Hon. J Neely Johnson President of this Convention, shall contract for, and A. J Marsh, official reporter of this convention under the direction of the President, shall supervise the publication of such debates and proceedings. Provision shall be made by law, at such first session of the Legislature for the compensation of the official reporter of this convention, and he shall be paid in coin or its equivalent. He shall receive for his services in reporting the debates and proceedings, Fifteen Dollars per day during the session of the Convention, and Seven and one half dollars additional for each evening session, and thirty cents per folio of one hundred words for preparing the same for publication, and for supervising and indexing such publication the sum of Fifteen Dollars per day during the time actually engaged in such service.

ARTICLE XVIII.
[*Right of Suffrage*]

Rights of suffrage and officeholding. [Repealed in 1992.]
[Added in 1880. Article XVIII was proposed and passed by the 1877 legislature; agreed to and passed by the 1879 legislature; and approved and ratified by the people at the 1880

general election. See: Statutes of Nevada 1877, p. 213; Statutes of Nevada 1879, p. 149. Article XVIII was repealed by vote of the people at the 1992 general election. See: Statutes of Nevada 1989, p. 2295; Statutes of Nevada 1991, p. 2498. The original section read: "The rights of suffrage and officeholding shall not be withheld from any male citizen of the United States by reason of his color or previous condition of servitude."]

ARTICLE 19.
Initiative and Referendum

Section 1. Referendum for approval or disapproval of statute or resolution enacted by legislature.

2. Initiative petition for enactment or amendment of statute or amendment of Constitution; concurrent and consecutive amendments.

3. Referendum and initiative petitions: Contents and form; signatures; enacting clause; manner of verification of signatures.

4. Powers of initiative and referendum of registered voters of counties and municipalities.

5. Provisions of article self-executing; legislative procedures.

6. Limitation on initiative making appropriation or requiring expenditure of money.

SECTION 1. *Referendum for approval or disapproval of statute or resolution enacted by legislature.*

1. A person who intends to circulate a petition that a statute or resolution or part thereof enacted by the legislature be submitted to a vote of the people, before circulating the petition for signatures, shall file a copy thereof with the secretary of state. He shall file the copy not earlier than August 1 of the year before the year in which the election will be held.

2. Whenever a number of registered voters of this state equal to 10 percent or more of the number of voters who voted at the last preceding general election shall express their wish by filing with the secretary of state, not less than 120 days before the next general election, a petition in the form provided for in Section 3 of this Article that any statute or resolution or any part thereof enacted by the legislature be submitted to a vote of the people, the officers charged with the duties of announcing and proclaiming elections and of certifying nominations or questions to be voted upon shall submit the question of approval or disapproval of such statute or resolution or any part thereof to a vote of the voters at the next succeeding election at which such question may be voted upon by the registered voters of the entire State. The circulation of the petition shall cease on the day the petition is filed with the secretary of state or such other date as may be prescribed for the

verification of the number of signatures affixed to the petition, whichever is earliest.

3. If a majority of the voters voting upon the proposal submitted at such
   election votes approval of such statute or resolution or any part thereof,
   such statute or resolution or any part thereof shall stand as the law of
   the state and shall not be amended, annulled, repealed, set aside, suspended or in any way made inoperative except by the direct vote of the
   people. If a majority of such voters votes disapproval of such statute or
   resolution or any part thereof, such statute or resolution or any part
   thereof shall be void and of no effect.

[Added in 1904, amended in 1962 and 1988. The addition was proposed and passed by
the 1901 Legislature; agreed to and passed by the 1903 Legislature; and approved and
ratified by the people at the 1904 General Election. See: Statutes of Nevada 1901, p. 139;
Journal of the Senate, 21st Session, p. 88 and Journal of the Assembly, 21st Session,
p. 191. The first amendment was proposed and passed by the 1960 Legislature; agreed to
and passed by the 1961 Legislature; and approved and ratified by the people at the 1962
General Election. See: Statutes of Nevada 1960, p. 512; Statutes of Nevada 1961, p. 813.
The second amendment was proposed and passed by the 1985 Legislature; agreed to and
passed by the 1987 Legislature; and approved and ratified by the people at the 1988 General Election. See: Statutes of Nevada 1985, p. 2363; Statutes of Nevada 1987, p. 2347.]

SECTION 2. *Initiative petition for enactment or amendment of statute or
amendment of Constitution; concurrent and consecutive amendments.*

1. Notwithstanding the provisions of Section 1 of Article 4 of this Constitution, but subject to the limitations of Section 6 of this Article, the
   people reserve to themselves the power to propose, by initiative petition, statutes and amendments to statutes and amendments to this
   Constitution, and to enact or reject them at the polls.

2. An initiative petition shall be in the form required by Section 3 of this
   Article and shall be proposed by a number of registered voters equal to
   10 percent or more of the number of voters who voted at the last preceding general election in not less than 75 percent of the counties in the
   State, but the total number of registered voters signing the initiative
   petition shall be equal to 10 percent or more of the voters who voted in
   the entire State at the last preceding general election.

3. If the initiative petition proposes a statute or an amendment to a statute, the person who intends to circulate it shall file a copy with the
   Secretary of State before beginning circulation and not earlier than January 1 of the year preceding the year in which a regular session of the
   Legislature is held. After its circulation, it shall be filed with the Secretary of State not less than 30 days prior to any regular session of the
   Legislature. The circulation of the petition shall cease on the day the
   petition is filed with the Secretary of State or such other date as may

be prescribed for the verification of the number of signatures affixed to the petition, whichever is earliest. The Secretary of State shall transmit such petition to the Legislature as soon as the Legislature convenes and organizes. The petition shall take precedence over all other measures except appropriation bills, and the statute or amendment to a statute proposed thereby shall be enacted or rejected by the Legislature without change or amendment within 40 days. If the proposed statute or amendment to a statute is enacted by the Legislature and approved by the Governor in the same manner as other statutes are enacted, such statute or amendment to a statute shall become law, but shall be subject to referendum petition as provided in Section 1 of this Article. If the statute or amendment to a statute is rejected by the Legislature, or if no action is taken thereon within 40 days, the Secretary of State shall submit the question of approval or disapproval of such statute or amendment to a statute to a vote of the voters at the next succeeding general election. If a majority of the voters voting on such question at such election votes approval of such statute or amendment to a statute, it shall become law and take effect upon completion of the canvass of votes by the Supreme Court. An initiative measure so approved by the voters shall not be amended, annulled, repealed, set aside or suspended by the Legislature within 3 years from the date it takes effect. If a majority of such voters votes disapproval of such statute or amendment to a statute, no further action shall be taken on such petition. If the Legislature rejects such proposed statute or amendment, the Governor may recommend to the Legislature and the Legislature may propose a different measure on the same subject, in which event, after such different measure has been approved by the Governor, the question of approval or disapproval of each measure shall be submitted by the Secretary of State to a vote of the voters at the next succeeding general election. If the conflicting provisions submitted to the voters are both approved by a majority of the voters voting on such measures, the measure which receives the largest number of affirmative votes shall thereupon become law. If at the session of the Legislature to which an initiative petition proposing an amendment to a statute is presented which the Legislature rejects or upon which it takes no action, the Legislature amends the statute which the petition proposes to amend in a respect which does not conflict in substance with the proposed amendment, the Secretary of State in submitting the statute to the voters for approval or disapproval of the proposed amendment shall include the amendment made by the Legislature.

4. If the initiative petition proposes an amendment to the Constitution,

the person who intends to circulate it shall file a copy with the Secretary of State before beginning circulation and not earlier than September 1 of the year before the year in which the election is to be held. After its circulation it shall be filed with the Secretary of State not less than 90 days before any regular general election at which the question of approval or disapproval of such amendment may be voted upon by the voters of the entire State. The circulation of the petition shall cease on the day the petition is filed with the Secretary of State or such other date as may be prescribed for the verification of the number of signatures affixed to the petition, whichever is earliest. The Secretary of State shall cause to be published in a newspaper of general circulation, on three separate occasions, in each county in the State, together with any explanatory matter which shall be placed upon the ballot, the entire text of the proposed amendment. If a majority of the voters voting on such question at such election votes disapproval of such amendment, no further action shall be taken on the petition. If a majority of such voters votes approval of such amendment, the Secretary of State shall publish and resubmit the question of approval or disapproval to a vote of the voters at the next succeeding general election in the same manner as such question was originally submitted. If a majority of such voters votes disapproval of such amendment, no further action shall be taken on such petition. If a majority of such voters votes approval of such amendment, it shall, unless precluded by Subsection 5 or 6, become a part of this Constitution upon completion of the canvass of votes by the Supreme Court.

5. If two or more measures which affect the same section of a statute or of the Constitution are finally approved pursuant to this Section, or an amendment to the Constitution is finally so approved and an amendment proposed by the Legislature is ratified which affect the same section, by the voters at the same election:

   (a) If all can be given effect without contradiction in substance, each shall be given effect.

   (b) If one or more contradict in substance the other or others, the measure which received the largest favorable vote, and any other approved measure compatible with it, shall be given effect. If the one or more measures that contradict in substance the other or others receive the same number of favorable votes, none of the measures that contradict another shall be given effect.

6. If, at the same election as the first approval of a constitutional amendment pursuant to this Section, another amendment is finally approved pursuant to this Section, or an amendment proposed by the Legislature

is ratified, which affects the same section of the Constitution but is compatible with the amendment given first approval, the Secretary of State shall publish and resubmit at the next general election the amendment given first approval as a further amendment to the section as amended by the amendment given final approval or ratified. If the amendment finally approved or ratified contradicts in substance the amendment given first approval, the Secretary of State shall not submit the amendment given first approval to the voters again.

[Added in 1912, amended in 1958, 1962, twice in 1972 and in 1988 and 1998. The addition was proposed and passed by the 1909 legislature; agreed to and passed by the 1911 legislature; and approved and ratified by the people at the 1912 general election. See: Statutes of Nevada 1909, p. 347; Statutes of Nevada 1911, p. 446. The first amendment was proposed by initiative petition and approved and ratified by the people at the general election of 1958. The second amendment was proposed and passed by the 1960 legislature; agreed to and passed by the 1961 legislature; and approved and ratified by the people at the 1962 general election. See: Statutes of Nevada 1960, p. 512; Statutes of Nevada 1961, p. 813. The third and fourth amendments were proposed and passed by the 1969 legislature; agreed to and passed by the 1971 legislature; and approved and ratified by the people at the 1972 general election. See: Statutes of Nevada 1969, pp. 1680, 1719; Statutes of Nevada 1971, pp. 2230, 2260. The fifth amendment was proposed and passed by the 1985 legislature; agreed to and passed by the 1987 legislature; and approved and ratified by the people at the 1988 general election. See: Statutes of Nevada 1985, p. 2364; Statutes of Nevada 1987, p. 2348. The sixth amendment was proposed and passed by the 1995 legislature; agreed to and passed by the 1997 legislature; and approved and ratified by the people at the 1998 general election. See: Statutes of Nevada 1995, p. 2949; Statutes of Nevada 1997, p. 3593.]

SECTION 3. *Referendum and initiative petitions: Contents and form; signatures; enacting clause; manner of verification of signatures.*

1. Each referendum petition and initiative petition shall include the full text of the measure proposed. Each signer shall affix thereto his or her signature, residence address and the name of the county in which he or she is a registered voter. The petition may consist of more than one document, but each document shall have affixed thereto an affidavit made by one of the signers of such document to the effect that all of the signatures are genuine and that each individual who signed such document was at the time of signing a registered voter in the county of his or her residence. The affidavit shall be executed before a person authorized by law to administer oaths in the State of Nevada. The enacting clause of all statutes or amendments proposed by initiative petition shall be: "The People of the State of Nevada do enact as follows:"

2. The Legislature may authorize the Secretary of State and the other public officers to use generally accepted statistical procedures in

conducting a preliminary verification of the number of signatures submitted in connection with a referendum petition or an initiative petition, and for this purpose to require petitions to be filed no more than 65 days earlier than is otherwise required by this Article.

[Added in 1912, amended in 1958, 1962, and 1988. The addition was proposed and passed by the 1909 legislature; agreed to and passed by the 1911 legislature; and approved and ratified by the people at the 1912 general election. See: Statutes of Nevada 1909, p. 347; Statutes of Nevada 1911, p. 446. The first amendment was proposed by initiative petition and approved and ratified by the people at the general election of 1958. The second amendment was proposed and passed by the 1960 legislature; agreed to and passed by the 1961 legislature; and approved and ratified by the people at the 1962 general election. See: Statutes of Nevada 1960, p. 512; Statutes of Nevada 1961, p. 813. The third amendment was proposed and passed by the 1985 legislature; agreed to and passed by the 1987 legislature; and approved and ratified by the people at the 1988 general election. See: Statutes of Nevada 1985, p. 2365; Statutes of Nevada 1987, p. 2349.]

SECTION 4. *Powers of initiative and referendum of registered voters of counties and municipalities.* The initiative and referendum powers provided for in this article are further reserved to the registered voters of each county and each municipality as to all local, special and municipal legislation of every kind in or for such county or municipality. In counties and municipalities initiative petitions may be instituted by a number of registered voters equal to 15 percent or more of the voters who voted at the last preceding general county or municipal election. Referendum petitions may be instituted by 10 percent or more of such voters.

[Added in 1962. Proposed and passed by the 1960 legislature; agreed to and passed by the 1961 legislature; and approved and ratified by the people at the 1962 general election. See: Statutes of Nevada 1960, p. 512; Statutes of Nevada 1961, p. 813.]

SECTION 5. *Provisions of article self-executing; legislative procedures.* The provisions of this article are self-executing but the legislature may provide by law for procedures to facilitate the operation thereof.

[Added in 1962. Proposed and passed by the 1960 legislature; agreed to and passed by the 1961 legislature; and approved and ratified by the people at the 1962 general election. See: Statutes of Nevada 1960, p. 512; Statutes of Nevada 1961, p. 813.]

SECTION 6. *Limitation on initiative making appropriation or requiring expenditure of money.* This Article does not permit the proposal of any statute or statutory amendment which makes an appropriation or otherwise requires the expenditure of money, unless such statute or amendment also imposes a sufficient tax, not prohibited by the Constitution, or otherwise constitutionally provides for raising the necessary revenue.

[Added in 1972. Proposed and passed by the 1969 Legislature; agreed to and passed by the 1971 Legislature; and approved and ratified by the people at the 1972 General Election. See: Statutes of Nevada 1969, p. 1720; Statutes of Nevada 1971, p. 2262.]

[CONGRESSIONAL TERM LIMITS ACT OF 1996.]

[Added in 1998. Proposed by initiative petition and approved and ratified by the people at the 1996 and 1998 general elections.]

SECTION A. BALLOT TITLE

The congressional term limits act of 1996. This amendment to the constitution of nevada informs citizens on the voting record of incumbent state and federal legislators and on a federal constitutional amendment limiting the members of the united states house of representatives to three terms and members of the united states senate to two terms. This amendment also informs the voters about the position of non-incumbent candidates toward the same congressional term limits. This amendment instructs state legislators to apply to the congress to convene an Article 5 convention upon the applications of two-thirds of the states (34) for the purpose of proposing an amendment to the united states constitution to limit congressional terms to three terms in the united states house of representatives and two terms in the united states senate. This amendment instructs members of congress from nevada to work to propose a congressional term limits amendment to the constitution. A term limits amendment proposed either by congress or by an Article 5 convention would become part of the united states constitution upon ratification by three-fourths of the states (38).

SECTION B. PREAMBLE

The People of the State of Nevada want to amend the United States Constitution to establish Term Limits on Congress that will ensure representation in Congress by true citizen lawmakers. The President of the United States is limited by the XXII Amendment to two terms in office. Governors in forty (40) states are limited to two terms or less. Voters have established term limits for over 2,000 state legislators as well as over 17,000 local officials across the country. Nevada voters have supported such limits.

Nevertheless Congress has ignored our desire for Term Limits not only by proposing excessively long terms for its own members but also by utterly refusing to pass an amendment for genuine Congressional term limits. Congress has a clear conflict of interest in proposing a term limits amendment to the United States Constitution. A majority of both Republicans and Democrats in the 104th Congress voted against a constitutional amendment containing the term limits passed by a wide margin of Nevada voters.

The People, not Congress, should set Term Limits. We hereby establish as the official position of the Citizens and State of Nevada that our elected officials should enact by Constitutional Amendment congressional Term Limits of three (3) terms in the United States House of Representatives, and of two (2) terms in the United States Senate.

The career politicians dominating Congress have a conflict of interest that prevents Congress from being what the Founders intended, the branch of government closest to the people. The politicians have refused to heed the will of the people for term limits; they have voted to dramatically raise their own pay; they have provided lavish million dollar pensions for themselves; and they have granted themselves numerous other privileges at the expense of the people. Most importantly, members of Congress have enriched themselves while running up huge deficits to support their spending. They have put the government nearly $5,000,000,000,000.00 (five trillion dollars) in debt, gravely threatening the future of our children and grandchildren.

The corruption and appearance of corruption brought about by political careerism is destructive to the proper functioning of the first branch of our representative government. Congress has grown increasingly distant from the People of the States. The People have the sovereign right and a compelling interest in creating a citizen Congress that will more effective protect our freedom and prosperity. This interest and right may not effectively be served in any way other than that proposed by this initiative.

We hereby state our intentions on behalf of the People of Nevada, that this Amendment lead to the adoption of the following Constitutional Amendment:

CONGRESSIONAL TERM LIMITS AMENDMENT

SECTION 1. No person shall serve in the office of the United States Representative for more than three terms, but upon ratification of this amendment no person who has held the office of United States Representative or who then holds the office shall serve for more than two additional terms.

SECTION 2. No person shall serve in the office of United States Senator for more than two terms, but upon ratification of this amendment no person who has held the office of United States Senator or who then holds the office shall serve for more than one additional term.

SECTION 3. This article shall have no time limit within which it must be ratified by the legislatures of three-fourths of the several States.

Therefore, We, the People of the State of Nevada, have chosen to amend the state constitution to inform voters regarding incumbent and non-incumbent

federal and state legislative candidates' support for the above proposed CON-
GRESSIONAL TERM LIMITS AMENDMENT.

SECTION C. VOTER INSTRUCTION ON TERM LIMITS FOR MEMBERS OF CONGRESS

1. We, the Voters of Nevada, hereby instruct each member of our congressional delegation to use all of his or her delegated powers to pass the
   Congressional Term Limits Amendment set forth above.
2. All primary and general election ballots shall have printed the information "DISREGARDED VOTERS' INSTRUCTION ON TERM LIMITS" adjacent
   to the name of any United States Senator or Representative who:
   a. fails to vote in favor of the proposed Congressional Term Limits
      Amendment set forth above when brought to a vote or;
   b. fails to second the proposed Congressional Term Limits Amend-
      ment set forth above if it lacks for a second before any proceeding
      of the legislative body or;
   c. fails to propose or otherwise bring to a vote of the full legislative
      body the proposed Congressional Term Limits Amendment set
      forth above if it otherwise lacks a legislator who so proposes or
      brings to a vote of the full legislative body the proposed Congres-
      sional Term Limits Amendment set forth above or;
   d. fails to vote in favor of all votes bringing the proposed Congressio-
      nal Term Limits Amendment set forth above before any commit-
      tee or subcommittee of the respective house upon which he or she
      serves or;
   e. fails to reject any attempt to delay, table or otherwise prevent a
      vote by the full legislative body of the proposed Congressional
      Term Limits Amendment set forth above or;
   f. fails to vote against any proposed constitutional amendment that
      would establish longer term limits than those in the proposed
      Congressional Term Limits Amendment set forth above regard-
      less of any other actions in support of the proposed Congressional
      Term Limits Amendment set forth above or;
   g. sponsors or cosponsors any proposed constitutional amendment or
      law that would establish longer term limits than those in the pro-
      posed Congressional Term Limits Amendment set forth above, or;
   h. fails to ensure that all votes on Congressional Term Limits are
      recorded and made available to the public.
3. The information "DISREGARDED VOTERS' INSTRUCTION ON TERM
   LIMITS" shall not appear adjacent to the name of any incumbent

candidates for Congress if the Congressional Term Limits Amendment set forth above is before the states for ratification or has become part of the United States Constitution.

SECTION D. VOTER INSTRUCTION ON TERM LIMIT PLEDGE FOR NON-INCUMBENTS

1. Non-incumbent candidates for United States Senator and Representative, and the Nevada Legislature shall be given an opportunity to take a "Term Limits" pledge regarding term Limits each time he or she files to run for such office. Any such candidate who declines to take the "Term Limits" pledge shall have the information "DECLINED TO PLEDGE TO SUPPORT TERM LIMITS" printed adjacent to his or her name on every primary and general election ballot.

2. The "Term Limits" pledge shall be offered to non-incumbent candidates for United States Senator and Representative, and the Nevada Legislature until a Constitutional Amendment which limits the number of terms of United States Senators to no more than two and United States Representatives to no more than three shall have become part of our United States Constitution.

3. The "Term Limits" pledge that each non-incumbent candidate, set forth above, shall be offered is as follows:

I support term limits and pledge to use all my legislative powers to enact the proposed Constitutional Amendment set forth in the Term Limits Act of 1996. If elected, I pledge to vote in such a way that the designation "DISRE-GARDED VOTER INSTRUCTION ON TERM LIMITS" will not appear adjacent to my name.

_____

Signature of Candidate

SECTION E. VOTER INSTRUCTION ON TERM LIMITS FOR STATE LEGISLATORS

1. We, the Voters of Nevada, hereby instruct each member of the Nevada Legislature to use all of his or her delegated powers to pass the Article 5 application to Congress set forth herein, and to ratify, if proposed, the Congressional Term Limits Amendment set forth above.

2. Application:
   We, the People and Legislature of the State of Nevada, due to our desire to establish term limits on Congress, hereby make application to

Congress, pursuant to our power under Article 5, to call a convention for proposing amendments to the Constitution.

3. All primary and general election ballots shall have the information "DISREGARDED VOTERS' INSTRUCTION ON TERM LIMITS" printed adjacent to the name of any respective member of the Nevada Legislature who:

  a. fails to vote in favor of the application set forth above when brought to a vote or;

  b. fails to second the application set forth above if it lacks for a second or;

  c. fails to vote in favor of all votes bringing the application set forth above before any committee or subcommittee upon which he or she serves;

  d. fails to propose or otherwise bring to a vote of the full legislative body the application set forth above if it otherwise lacks a legislator who so proposes or brings to a vote of the full legislative body the application set forth above or;

  e. fails to vote against any attempt to delay, table or otherwise prevent a vote by the full legislative body of the application set forth above or;

  f. fails in any way to ensure that all votes on the application set forth above are recorded and made available to the public or;

  g. fails to vote against any change, addition or modification to the application set forth above or;

  h. fails to vote in favor of the amendment set forth above if it is sent to the states for ratification or;

  i. fails to vote against any term limits amendment, with longer terms if such an amendment is sent to the states for ratification.

4. The information "DISREGARDED VOTERS' INSTRUCTION ON TERM LIMITS" shall not appear adjacent to the names of candidates for the Nevada Legislature as required by any of Subsections 3 (a) through 3 (g) if the State of Nevada has made an application to Congress for a convention for proposing amendments to the Constitution pursuant to this act and such application has not been withdrawn or, the Congressional Term Limits Amendment set forth in this act has been submitted to the states for ratification.

5. The information "DISREGARDED VOTERS' INSTRUCTION ON TERM LIMITS" shall not appear adjacent to the names of candidates for the Nevada Legislature as required by any of Subsections 3 (h) through 3 (i) if the State of Nevada has ratified the proposed Congressional Term Limits Amendment set forth in this act.

6. The information "DISREGARDED VOTERS' INSTRUCTION ON TERM LIMITS" shall not appear adjacent to the names of candidates for the Nevada Legislature as required by any of Subsections 3 (a) through 3 (i) if the proposed Congressional Term Limits Amendment set forth above has become part of the United States Constitution.

SECTION F. DESIGNATION

1. The Secretary of State shall be responsible to make an accurate determination as to whether a candidate for the federal or state legislature shall have placed adjacent to his or her name on the election ballot the information "DISREGARDED VOTERS' INSTRUCTION ON TERM LIMITS" or "DECLINED TO PLEDGE TO SUPPORT TERM LIMITS."

2. The Secretary of State shall consider timely submitted public comments prior to making the determination required in Subsection (1) of this section and may rely on such comments and any information submitted by the candidates in making the determination required in Subsection (1).

3. The Secretary of State, in accordance with Subsection (1) of this section shall determine and declare what information, if any, shall appear adjacent to the names of each incumbent federal legislator if he or she was to be a candidate in the next election. In the case of United States Representatives and United States Senators, this determination and declaration shall be made in a fashion necessary to ensure the orderly printing of primary and general election ballots with allowance made for all legal action provided in Section (5) and (6) below, and shall be based upon each member of Congress's action during their current term of office and any action taken in any concluded term, if such action was taken after the determination and declaration was made by the Secretary of State in a previous election. In the case of incumbent state legislators, this determination and declaration shall be made not later than (30) days after the end of the regular session following each general election, and shall be based upon legislative action in the previous regular session and any action taken in any concluded term, if such action was taken after the determination and declaration was made by the Secretary of State in a previous election.

4. The Secretary of State shall determine and declare what information, if any, will appear adjacent to the names of non-incumbent candidates for the state and federal legislatures, not later than five (5) business days after the deadline for filing for the office.

5. If the Secretary of State makes the determination that the information

"DISREGARDED VOTERS' INSTRUCTION ON TERM LIMITS" or
"DECLINED TO PLEDGE TO SUPPORT TERM LIMITS" shall not be placed
on the ballot adjacent to the name of a candidate for the federal or state
legislature, any elector may appeal such decision within five (5) business days to the Nevada Supreme Court as an original action or shall
waive any right to appeal such decision; in which case the burden of
proof shall be upon the Secretary of State to demonstrate by clear and
convincing evidence that the candidate has met the requirements set
forth in this Act and therefore should not have the information "DIS-
REGARDED VOTERS' INSTRUCTION ON TERM LIMITS" or "DECLINED
TO PLEDGE TO SUPPORT TERM LIMITS" printed on the ballot adjacent
to the candidate's name.

6. If the Secretary of State determines that the information "DISRE-
GARDED VOTERS' INSTRUCTION ON TERM LIMITS" or "DECLINED TO
PLEDGE TO SUPPORT TERM LIMITS" shall be placed on the ballot adjacent to a candidate's name, the candidate may appeal such decision
within (5) business days to the Nevada Supreme Court as an original action or shall waive any right to appeal such decision; in which
case the burden of proof shall be upon the candidate to demonstrate by
clear and convincing evidence that he or she should not have the information "DISREGARDED VOTERS' INSTRUCTION ON TERM LIMITS" or
"DECLINED TO PLEDGE TO SUPPORT TERM LIMITS" printed on the
ballot adjacent to the candidate's name.

7. The Supreme Court shall hear the appeal provided for in Subsection (5)
and issue a decision within 60 days. The Supreme Court shall hear the
appeal provided for in Subsection (6) and issue a decision not later than
61 days before the date of the election.

SECTION G. AUTOMATIC REPEAL

At such time as the Congressional Term Limits Amendment set forth above
has become part of the U.S. Constitution, Sections A through Section I of this
Article automatically shall be repealed.

SECTION H. JURISDICTION

Any legal challenge to this amendment shall be filed as an original action
before the Supreme Court of this state.

SECTION I. SEVERABILITY

If any portion, clause, or phrase of this initiative is, for any reason, held
to be invalid or unconstitutional by a court of competent jurisdiction, the

remaining portions, clauses, and phrases shall not be affected, but shall remain in full force and effect.

[ELECTION ORDINANCE.]
Whereas,

The enabling act passed by Congress and approved March Twenty first A.D. Eighteen Hundred and Sixty four, requires that the convention charged with the duty of framing a Constitution for a State Government "shall provide by ordinance for submitting said Constitution to the People of the Territory of Nevada, for their ratification or rejection" on a certain day prescribed therein; therefore this Convention organized in pursuance of said enabling act, do establish the following:

ORDINANCE.

SECTION 1. *Proclamation by territorial governor; general election.* The Governor of the Territory of Nevada is hereby authorized to issue his proclamation for the submission of this Constitution to the people of said Territory for their approval or rejection on the day provided for such submission, by Act of Congress; and this Constitution shall be submitted to the qualified electors of said Territory, in the several counties thereof, for their approval or rejection, at the time provided by such Act of Congress, and further, on the first Tuesday after the first Monday of November A.D. Eighteen hundred and Sixty four, there shall be a general election in the several counties of said Territory for the election of State Officers, Supreme and District Judges, members of the Legislature, Representative in Congress and three Presidential Electors.

SECTION 2. *Qualified electors may vote for adoption or rejection of constitution.* All persons qualified by the laws of said Territory to vote for Representatives to the General Assembly on the said Twenty first day of March, including those in the Army of the United States, both within and beyond the boundaries of said Territory, and also all persons who may by the aforesaid laws, be qualified to vote on the first Wednesday of September AD. Eighteen hundred and Sixty four, including those in the aforesaid Army of the United States, within and without the boundaries of said Territory may vote for the adoption or rejection of said Constitution, on the day last above named. In voting upon this Constitution, each elector shall deposite [deposit] in the ballot box a ticket whereon shall be clearly written, or printed "Constitution Yes" or "Constitution No," or other such words that shall clearly indicate the intention of the Elector.

SECTION 3. *Qualified electors for first general election.* All persons qualified by the laws of said Territory to vote on the Tuesday after the first Monday of November AD. Eighteen hundred and Sixty four, including those in the Army of the United States, within and beyond the boundaries of said Territory, may vote on the day last above named, for State Officers, Supreme and District Judges, Members of the Legislature, Representative in Congress, and three Presidential electors, to the electoral college.

SECTION 4. *Elections: Places, judges, inspectors and procedure.* The elections provided in this Ordinance shall be holden at such places as shall be designated by the Boards of Commissioners of the several counties in said Territory. The Judges, and inspectors of said elections, shall be appointed by said Commissioners, and the said elections shall be conducted in conformity with the existing laws of said Territory in relation to holding the General election.

SECTION 5. *Election returns.* The Judges and Inspectors of said elections shall carefully count each ballot immediately after said elections, and forthwith make duplicate returns thereof to the clerks of the said County Commissioners of their respective Counties, and said Clerks, within fifteen days after said elections shall transmit an abstract of the votes including the soldiers vote, as herein provided, given for State Officers, Supreme and District Judges, Representative in Congress and three Presidential Electors, enclosed in an envelope, by the most safe and expeditious conveyance to the Governor of said Territory marked "Election Returns"[.]

SECTION 6. *Canvass of votes; proclamation; issuance of certificates of election.* Upon the receipt of said returns, including those of the soldiers vote, or within Twenty days after the election, if said returns be not sooner received, it shall be the duty of the Board of Canvassers, to consist of the Governor, United States District Attorney and Chief Justice of said Territory or any two of them to canvass the returns in the presence of all who may wish to be present, and if a majority of all the votes given upon this Constitution, shall be in its favor, the said Governor shall immediately publish an abstract of the same, and make proclamation of the fact in some newspaper in said Territory and certify the same to the President of the United States, together with a copy of the Constitution and Ordinance. The said Board of Canvassers, after canvassing the votes of the said November elections shall issue certificates of election, to such persons as were elected State Officers, Judges of the Supreme and District Courts, Representative in Congress and three Presidential Electors. When the President of the United States shall issue his proclamation, declaring this State admitted into the Union, on an equal footing, with the original states; This Constitution shall thenceforth be ordained and established as the Constitution of the State of Nevada.

SECTION 7. *List of electors in Army of the United States.* For the purpose of taking the vote of the Electors of said Territory who may be in the Army of the United States: the Adjutant General of said Territory, shall on or before the fifth day of August next following, make out a list in alphabetical order and deliver the same to the Governor, of the names of all the electors, residents of said Territory, who shall be in the Army of the United States, stating the number of the Regiment, Battalion, Squadron, or Battery, to which he belongs, and also the County or Township, of his residence in said Territory.

SECTION 8. *Transmission of lists of electors in Army of the United States.* The Governor shall classify and arrange the aforesaid returned list, and shall make therefrom separate lists of the electors belonging to each Reigment [Regiment], Battalion, Squadron and Battery from said Territory in the Service of the United States, and shall, on or before the Fifteenth day of August following, transmit by mail or otherwise, to the Commanding Officer of each Regiment, Battalion[,] Squadron and Battery, a list of electors belonging thereto, which said list shall specify the name[,] residence and rank of each elector, and the company to which he belongs, if to any, and also the County and Township to which he belongs, and in which he is entitled to vote.

SECTION 9. *Voting by soldiers: Qualifications.* Between the hours of Nine O'Clock A.M. and Three O'Clock P.M. on each of the election days hereinbefore named, a ballot box or suitable receptacle for votes shall be opened under the immediate charge and direction of three of the highest Officers in command, for the reception of Votes from the electors whose names are upon said list, at each place where a Regiment, Battalion[,] Squadron or Battery of Soldiers from said Territory in the Army of the United States may be on that day; at which time and place, said Electors shall be entitled to vote for all Officers for which by reason of their residence in the several counties in said Territory they are authorized to vote, as fully as they would be entitled to vote in the several Counties or Townships in which they reside, and the votes so given by such electors at such time and place, shall be considered, taken and held to have been given by them in the respective Counties and Townships in which they are resident.

SECTION 10. *Voting by soldiers: Procedure; count of votes.* Each ballot deposited for the adoption or rejection of this Constitution, in the Army of the United States shall have, distinctly written or printed thereon "Constitution Yes", or "Constitution No"; or words of a similar import, and further, for the election of State Officers, Supreme and District Judges, Members of the Legislature, Representative in Congress and three Presidential Electors, the name and Office of the person voted for shall be plainly written or printed on one piece of paper. The name of each elector voting as aforesaid shall be checked upon the said list, at the time of voting by one of the said Officers, having charge of the ballot box. The said Officers having charge of the election shall count the votes and compare them with the checked list, immediately after the closing of the ballot box[.]

SECTION 11. *Voting by soldiers: Transmission of results.* All the ballots cast, together with the said voting list, checked as aforesaid, shall be immediately sealed up, and sent forthwith to the Governor of said Territory at Carson City by mail or otherwise, by the Commanding Officer, who shall make out and certify duplicate returns of Votes given, according to the forms hereinafter prescribed, seal up and immediately transmit the same to the said Governor at Carson City by mail or otherwise, the day following the transmission of the ballots and the voting list herein named, the said Commanding Officer shall also immediately transmit to the several County Clerks in said Territory an abstract of the votes given at the general election in November, for County Officers marked "Election Returns"[.]

SECTION 12. *Voting by soldiers: Form of return.* The form of returns of votes to be made by the Commanding Officer to the Governor and County Clerks of said Territory shall be in substance as follows, Viz:

"Returns of Soldiers, votes in the (here insert the regiment, detachment, battalion, squadron or battery)"— (For first election on the Constitution.) .... I.................... hereby certify, that, on the first Wednesday of September A.D. Eighteen hundred and sixty four the Electors belonging to the (here insert the name of the regiment, detachment, battalion[,] squadron or battery.) cast the following number of votes for and against the Constitution for the State of Nevada, Viz: For "Constitution" (number of votes written in full and in figures.) Against "Constitution" (number of votes written in full and in figures).................... (Second election for State and other Officers).................... I.................... hereby certify that on the first Tuesday after the first Monday in November A.D. Eighteen hundred and Sixty four, the Electors belonging to the (here insert as above) cast the following number of votes for the several officers and persons hereinafter named Viz:.................... For Governor....................names of persons voted for, number of votes for each person voted for written in full and also in figures, against the name of each person. ....

For Lieutenant Governor .... name of Candidates, number of votes cast for each, written out and in figures as above. ....

Continue as above till the list is completed. ....

....................Attest....................

....

....

I, A.B..............................
Commanding Officer of the (here
Insert regiment[,] detachment, battalion, squadron, or battery as the case
may be).

SECTION 13. *Voting by soldiers: Territorial governor to furnish form of return.*
The Governor of this Territory is requested to furnish each Commanding
Officer within and beyond the boundaries of said Territory, proper and suffi-
cient blanks for said returns.

SECTION 14. *Applicability to future votes of soldiers.* The provisions of this
Ordinance in regard to the Soldiers vote shall apply to future elections under
this Constitution, and be in full force until the Legislature shall provide by
law for taking the votes of citizens of said Territory in the Army of the United
States[.]

DONE IN CONVENTION, at Carson City the Twenty Eighth day of July,
in the year of our Lord One Thousand Eight Hundred and Sixty Four and of
the Independence of the United States the Eighty-ninth, and signed by the
Delegates.

[Then follow the names of delegates who signed the constitution.]

Notes

Chapter One. Nevada—Origins and Early History

1. Russell R. Elliott, with the assistance of William D. Rowley, *History of Nevada*, 2d ed., rev. (Lincoln: University of Nebraska Press, 1987), 33. James Hulse, however, suggests that whether Father Garcés crossed southern Nevada is still an open question (James W. Hulse, *The Silver State: Nevada's Heritage Reinterpreted* [Reno: University of Nevada Press, 1991], 34).

2. Hulse, *The Silver State*, 35. 3.

3. Ibid., 37.

4. The party is one of the best known as a result of Washington Irving's 1837 book, *The Adventures of Captain Bonneville, U.S.A., in the Rocky Mountains and the Far West*.

5. Elliott and Rowley, *History of Nevada*, 38, and Hulse, *The Silver State*, 40.

6. Eleanore Bushnell and Don W. Driggs, *The Nevada Constitution: Origin and Growth*, 6th ed. (Reno: University of Nevada Press, 1984), 4.

7. Frankie Sue Del Papa, *Political History of Nevada, 1990* (Carson City: State Printing Office, 1990), 33.

8. Mack and Bancroft, among others, mistakenly list the year of this first post as 1849. See Effie Mona Mack, *Nevada: A History of the State from the Earliest Times Through the Civil War* (Glendale, Calif.: Arthur H. Clark, 1935), 147, and Hubert Howe Bancroft, *History of Nevada, Colorado, and Wyoming, 1540–1888*, vol. 25 of *The Works of Hubert Howe Bancroft* (San Francisco: History Company, 1890), 65–66. However, the more recent work of Russell R. Elliott provides conclusive evidence that the 1850 date is correct. See Russell R. Elliott, "Nevada's First Trading Post: A Study in Historiography," *Nevada Historical Society Quarterly* 8 (spring 1965): 11.

9. "History of the Las Vegas Mission," in *Nevada State Historical Society Papers, 1925–1926*, comp. Andrew Jenson (Reno: Nevada State Historical Society, 1926), 152.

10. Ibid., 153.

11. *Los*, rather than *Las*, was used to prevent confusion with Las Vegas, New Mexico. These episodes and many more are described in Eugene P. Moehring, *Resort City in the Sunbelt: Las Vegas, 1930–1970* (Reno: University of Nevada Press, 1989), 1–3.

12. Myron Angel, ed., *History of Nevada, 1881, with Illustrations* (New York: Arno Press, 1973), 32. Angel's work was originally published in 1881 by Thompson and West of Oakland, California.

13. Bancroft, *History of Nevada, Colorado, and Wyoming*, 74–75.

14. Elliott and Rowley, *History of Nevada*, 54.

15. *Pamphlets on California* 26, no. 28. Quoted in Mack, *Nevada*, 157.

16. Elliott and Rowley, *History of Nevada*, 56.

17. Angel, *History of Nevada*, 41.

18. See, for example, Hulse, *The Silver State*, 60, and Elliott and Rowley, *History of Nevada*, 56. Angel, for instance, notes that Judge W.W. Drummond, who had replaced federal Judge Styles in Carson County, erroneously reported to his superiors that the Mormons had burned the library and records of the United States District Court (*History of Nevada*, 168).

19. Angel, *History of Nevada*, 42.

20. Quoted in Bancroft, *History of Nevada, Colorado, and Wyoming*, 83–84.

21. See Angel, *History of Nevada*, 49–51.

22. Gordon Morris Bakken, *Rocky Mountain Constitution Making, 1850–1912* (Westport, Conn.: Greenwood Press, 1987), 9.

23. Quoted in C.V. Waite, *The Mormon Prophet and His Harem: or, An Authentic History of Brigham Young, His Numerous Wives and Children* (Cambridge, Mass.: Riverside Press, 1866), 33.

24. Bancroft, *History of Nevada, Colorado, and Wyoming*, 88.

25. J.H. Purkitt, "Nevada Territory," *San Francisco Evening Bulletin*, February 15, 1860. Quoted in Mack, *Nevada*, 184.

Chapter Two. Nevada Territory and Statehood

1. Bushnell and Driggs, *The Nevada Constitution*, 13.

2. Address of Governor Nye to the Territorial Legislature, in *Journal of the Council of the First Legislative Assembly of the Territory of Nevada* (San Francisco: Commercial Steam Printing, 1862), 14–27. Quoted in Elliott and Rowley, *History of Nevada*, 72.

3. Richard G. Lillard, *Desert Challenge: An Interpretation of Nevada* (New York: Alfred A. Knopf, 1942), 25.

4. The actual results are in some dispute. Elliott and Rowley, (*History of Nevada*, 77), Angel (*History of Nevada*, 81), Mack (*Nevada*, 249), and Hulse (*The Silver State*, 81) adopt these figures. However, Bancroft (*History of Nevada, Colorado, and Wyoming*, 178) concludes that of a total vote of 8,162, only 5,150 voted for the statehood measure. In any case, support for statehood was overwhelming.

5. Del Papa, *Political History*, 83. However, Mack (*Nevada*, 250) and Elliott and Rowley (*History of Nevada*, 78) claim that all but four came directly from California.

6. Bakken, *Rocky Mountain Constitution Making*, 6.

7. William C. Miller and Eleanore Bushnell, eds., *Reports of the 1863 Constitutional Convention of the Territory of Nevada* (Carson City: Legislative Counsel Bureau, 1972), 273.

8. Mack, *Nevada*, 251.

9. Nevada Constitution (1863), art. X, sec. 1, quoted in Miller and Bushnell, *Reports of the 1863 Constitutional Convention*, 429.

10. See David A. Johnson, *Founding the Far West: California, Oregon, and Nevada, 1840–1890* (Berkeley: University of California Press, 1992), 83–89.

11. Del Papa, *Political History*, 84.

12. Angel, *History of Nevada*, 84.

13. David A. Johnson, "A Case of Mistaken Identity: William M. Stewart and the

Rejection of Nevada's First Constitution," *Nevada Historical Society Quarterly* 22 (fall 1979): 188.

14. Quoted in Bushnell and Driggs, *The Nevada Constitution*, 18.

15. Andrew J. Marsh, *Official Report of the Debates and Proceedings in the Constitutional Convention of the State of Nevada* (San Francisco: Frank Eastman, 1866), 325.

16. Ibid., 224.

17. Del Papa, *Political History*, 86. These limits can be found in the "Ordinance" of the Constitution of the State of Nevada.

18. Although many portions of the book are now outdated, Bushnell and Driggs's work still provides one of the best discussions available of the many disputes dividing the delegates of the 1864 convention, and that section is well worth a read by those interested (*Nevada Constitution*, 26–41).

19. Ibid., 27.

20. Bakken, *Rocky Mountain Constitution Making*, 20.

21. Marsh, *Debates and Proceedings*, 224.

22. Quoted in Lillard, *Desert Challenge*, 73.

23. Marsh, *Debates and Proceedings*, 356. 24.

24. Ibid., 361.

25. Ibid., 335.

26. Johnson, *Founding the Far West*, 222–28.

27. Nevada Constitution (1864), art. X, sec. 1.

28. Johnson, *Founding the Far West*, 223.

29. Marsh, *Debates and Proceedings*, 820, 827.

30. Ibid., xiv, 827. This figure is the one generally accepted and is noted in Elliott and Rowley (*History of Nevada*, 88), Bushnell and Driggs (*The Nevada Constitution*, 42), and Hulse (*The Silver State*, 84). Inexplicably, however, Angel (*History of Nevada*, 86) puts the vote at 11,393 to 2,262, and Gilman M. Ostrander counts the tally as 6,530 to 2,260 (*Nevada: The Great Rotten Borough, 1859–1964* [New York: Alfred A. Knopf, 1966], 39).

31. Del Papa, *Political History*, 90.

32. Johnson, "A Case of Mistaken Identity," 198.

33. Johnson, *Founding the Far West*, 226.

34. *Virginia City Territorial Enterprise*, August 19, 1864. Quoted in Johnson, *Founding the Far West*, 315. William M. Stewart also argued in favor of the constitution on the basis that statehood would bring the territory out of its mining depression. See David A. Johnson, "Industry and the Individual on the Far Western Frontier: A Case Study of Politics and Social Change in Early Nevada," *Pacific Historical Review* 51 (August 1982): 243–64.

35. Marsh, *Debates and Proceedings*, 173.

36. Bancroft, *History of Nevada, Colorado, and Wyoming*, 172.

37. Ostrander, *Great Rotten Borough*, 28.

38. Johnson, *Founding the Far West*, 316.

39. Ibid.

40. Samuel P. Davis, ed., *The History of Nevada*, 2 vols. (Reno: Elms Publishing Co., 1913), 302.

41. Daniel J. Elazar, "The Principles and Traditions Underlying State Constitutions," *Publius: The Journal of Federalism* 12 (winter 1982): 21–22.

42. Christopher W. Hammons, "State Constitutional Reform: Is It Necessary?," *Albany Law Review* 64, no. 4 (2000–2001): 1350. In contrast, the longest state constitution is that of Alabama (310,296 words) and the shortest belongs to Vermont (8,295 words).

Chapter Three. Civil Rights and Liberties in Nevada

1. Jack C. Plano and Milton Greenberg, *The American Political Dictionary*, 3d ed. (Hinsdale, Ill.: Dryden Press, 1972), 63.

2. Ibid.

3. Marsh, *Debates and Proceedings*, 786.

4. Elmer R. Rusco, "The Status of Indians in Nevada Law," in *Native American Politics: Power Relationships in the Western Great Basin Today*, ed. Ruth M. Houghton (Reno: Bureau of Governmental Research, 1973), 59–87.

5. Ibid.

6. Johnson, *Founding the Far West*, 328.

7. See Sue Fawn Chung, "The Chinese Experience in Nevada: Success Despite Discrimination," *Nevada Public Affairs Review* no. 2 (1987): 43–51.

8. Russell M. Magnaghi, "Virginia City's Chinese Community, 1860–1880," *Nevada Historical Society Quarterly* 24 (summer 1981): 153.

9. James Edward Wright, *The Politics of Populism: Dissent in Colorado* (New Haven: Yale University Press, 1974), 26.

10. Moehring, *Resort City in the Sunbelt*, 199.

11. Ed Vogel, "GOP Legislators Look Old, White, Male: No Minorities, Three Women in Republican Caucus," *Las Vegas Review-Journal*, November 26, 2010, b1, 5.

12. M. L. "Tony" Miranda, *A History of Hispanics in Southern Nevada* (Reno: University of Nevada Press, 1997), 80–82.

13. Carey McWilliams, *North from Mexico: The Spanish-Speaking of the United States* (New York: J.B. Lippincott Co., 1968), 168. Quoted in Miranda, *History of Hispanics*, 126.

14. Miranda, *History of Hispanics*, 167–68.

15. Jim Frey, "Preliminary Report: Assessment of the Accessibility of hew Assisted Programs to the Hispanic Population of Clark County, Nevada" (University of Nevada, Las Vegas, report, 1978), 27. Quoted in Miranda, *History of Hispanics*, 190.

16. M. L. "Tony" Miranda, "Some Observations on Hispanics in Nevada in the Eighties," *Nevada Public Affairs Review* 2 (1987): 39.

17. "In Brief," *Las Vegas Review-Journal*, September 15, 2004, sec. D, p. 2.

18. Moehring, *Resort City in the Sunbelt*, 201–2.

19. "Women Making Great Strides in Nevada Business," *Las Vegas Sun*, May 9, 2011, 1, 5.

20. According to the publication *vegasinc*, various studies show not only that gays

and lesbians have an income of about 80 percent more than the average household but that they are also twice as likely to go on trips and vacations as straight people and that they spend nearly twice as much when they do travel. "Gay Dollars: Vegas Style," *vegasinc* 12, no. 7 (2011).

21. 32 U.S. (7 Pet.) 243 (1833).

Chapter Four. Political Parties and Elections

1. The first four of these are noted in Bushnell and Driggs, *The Nevada Constitution*, 66–68. The fifth has come about since the publication of their work. 2.

2. Ibid., 66.

3. Michael McDonald, "2008 General Election Turnout Rates," United States Elections Project, http://elections.gmu.edu/Turnout_2008G.html.

4. *Buckley v. Valeo*, 424 U.S. 1 (1976).

5. *Arvey v. Sheriff;* 93 Nev. 469, 567 P.2d 470 (1977).

6. Steve Kanigher, "Wallets Open, Mouths Shut," *Las Vegas Sun*, December 24, 1995, sec. K, p. 1.

7. 410 U.S. 113 (1973).

8. *U.S. Term Limits v. Thornton*, 514 U.S. 779 (1995).

Chapter Five. Interest Groups and Lobbying

1. Don W. Driggs, "Nevada: Powerful Lobbyists and Conservative Politics," in *Interest Group Politics in the American West*, ed. Ronald J. Hrebenar and Clive S. Thomas (Salt Lake City: University of Utah Press, 1987), 85–92.

2. Jennifer Robison, "Precious Metal: Nevadans Have Long Bet Their Lives and Fortunes on Mining," *Las Vegas Review-Journal*, September 23, 2012, e1.

3. *Reno Gazette-Journal*, July 2, 1993, sec. A, p. 6. Quoted in Don W. Driggs and Leonard E. Goodall, *Nevada Politics and Government: Conservatism in an Open Society* (Lincoln: University of Nebraska Press, 1996), 147.

4. Faun Mortara, "Lobbying in Nevada," in *Sagebrush and Neon: Studies in Nevada Politics*, rev. ed., ed. Eleanore Bushnell (Reno: Bureau of Governmental Research, 1976), 45.

5. Ibid., 44.

6. Driggs, "Powerful Lobbyists," 86.

7. Jane Ann Morrison, "Casinos Gamble on Politicians," *Las Vegas Review-Journal*, May 22, 1993, sec. B, pp. 1, 3.

8. Jon Ralston, *The Anointed One: An Inside Look at Nevada Politics* (Las Vegas: Huntington Press, 2000).

9. Driggs and Goodall, *Nevada Politics*, 147.

10. Albert Deutsch, "The Sorry State of Nevada," *Collier's* 135 (March 18, 1955): 74–85. Quoted in James W. Hulse, *Forty Years in the Wilderness: Impressions of Nevada, 1940–1980* (Reno: University of Nevada Press, 1986), 88.

Chapter Six. The Nevada Legislature

1. It is worth noting that a few explicit exceptions to this rule are provided for in the constitution itself. In Article 5, Section 17, the lieutenant governor (a member of the executive branch) is given the duty of serving as president of the senate with the power of a "casting vote," and the president pro tempore of the senate (a member of the legislative branch) serves as acting governor when the governor and lieutenant governor are both absent from the state or the two offices become vacant in some other way.

2. Marsh, *Debates and Proceedings*, 144.

3. Eleanore Bushnell, "Reapportionment and Responsibility," in *Sagebrush and Neon*, ed. Bushnell, 102–3.

4. 377 U.S. 533 (1964).

5. *Dungan v. Sawyer*, 250 F. Supp. 480 (D. Nev. 1965).

6. Driggs and Goodall, *Nevada Politics*, for data through 1995. Data after 1995 compiled by the author from election returns.

Chapter Seven. The Nevada Executive

1. These summaries can be found in Driggs and Goodall, *Nevada Politics*, 93–94; additional data by the author based on various sources.

2. Ibid, 94–96.

3. Ibid, 105.

4. Marsh, *Debates and Proceedings*, 159.

5. Terry Reynolds, "The Executive Veto in Nevada," 4. Quoted in Bushnell and Driggs, *The Nevada Constitution*, 115–16.

6. Driggs and Goodall, *Nevada Politics*, 92. 7.

7. 82 Nev. 53, 410 P.2d 748 (1966).

Chapter Eight. The Nevada Judiciary

1. Bakken, *Rocky Mountain Constitution Making*, 9.

2. Bancroft, *History of Nevada, Colorado, and Wyoming*, 121.

3. Marsh, *Debates and Proceedings*, 642.

4. Driggs and Goodall, *Nevada Politics*, 124.

5. Bakken, *Rocky Mountain Constitution Making*, 40.

6. Michael W. Bowers, "The Impact of Judicial Selection Methods in Nevada: Some Empirical Observations," *Nevada Public Affairs Review* no. 2 (1990): 5.

Chapter Nine. City and County Governments

1. John F. Dillon, *Commentaries on the Laws of Municipal Corporations*, 5th ed. (Boston: Little, Brown, 1911), 448.

2. *County of Clark v. City of Las Vegas*, 97 Nev. 260, 628 P.2d 1120 (1981).

3. Bushnell and Driggs, *The Nevada Constitution*, 156.

4. Driggs and Goodall, *Nevada Politics*, 175–76.

Chapter Ten. State and Local Finance

1. John Gunther, *Inside U.S.A.* (New York: Harper and Brothers, 1947), 31. Quoted in David R. Berman, "Financing State and Local Government," in *Politics and Public Policy in the Contemporary American West,* ed. Clive S. Thomas (Albuquerque: University of New Mexico Press, 1991), 305.

2. State & Local Government Finance Data Query System. http://slfdqs.taxpolicy center.org/pages.cfm. The Urban Institute-Brookings Institution Tax Policy Center. Data from U.S. Census Bureau, Annual Survey of State and Local Government Finances, Government Finances, Volume 4, and Census of Governments (2015).

3. "America's Richest (And Poorest) States. https://www.huffingtonpost.com/entry /americas-richest-and-poorest-states_us57db167be4b04fa361d99639. Data from U.S. Census Bureau Nationwide Population Survey (2015).

4. Berman, "Financing State and Local Government," 310.

5. *Matthews v. State of Nevada, ex rel. Nevada Tax Commission,* 83 Nev. 269 (1967).

6. Berman, "Financing State and Local Government," 322.

7. Mike O'Callaghan, "Making Budget Ends Meet," *Las Vegas Sun,* February 25, 2001, sec. E, p. 3.

8. Ed Vogel, "Magazine Ranks Nevada Tax System Nation's Worst," *Las Vegas Review-Journal,* February 3, 2003, sec. B, p. 3.

Chapter Eleven. Nevada—Past, Present, and Future

1. Hulse, *Forty Years in the Wilderness.*

2. Quoted in Lillard, *Desert Challenge,* 224.

3. Ostrander, *Great Rotten Borough,* 46.

4. Elliott and Rowley, *History of Nevada,* 153.

5. *State of Nevada v. Daniel E. Eastabrook,* 3 Nev. 173 (1867). The legislature acted even before the decision by the court, in part because it assumed the revenue act would be struck down.

6. House, "Railroad Wrongs in Nevada," *Congressional Record,* 46th Cong., 3d sess., 2, pt. 3, Appendix: 181–90. Quoted in Elliott and Rowley, *History of Nevada,* 158.

7. Quoted in Hulse, *The Silver State,* 130.

8. Elliott and Rowley, *History of Nevada,* 161–64. 9.

9. Ibid., 160.

10. Russell R. Elliott, *Servant of Power: A Political Biography of Senator William M. Stewart* (Reno: University of Nevada Press, 1983), 64.

11. Leonard Arrington, "The New Deal in the West: A Preliminary Statistical Inquiry," *Pacific Historical Review* 38 (August 1969): 311–17.

12. Michael W. Bowers and A. Costandina Titus, "Nevada's Black Book: The Constitutionality of Exclusion Lists in Casino Gaming Regulation," *Whittier Law Review* 9 (1987): 315.

13. U.S. Census Bureau, 2011.

14. Driggs and Goodall, *Nevada Politics,* 169–70.

15. "Casino Study Sparks Debate in Reno," *Las Vegas Review-Journal*, April 4, 2001, sec. D, p. 3.

16. H. Josef Hebert, "Mining Law Forces Cheap Sale of Potentially Rich Land," *Las Vegas Review-Journal*, September 7, 1995, sec. D, p. 9.

17. Molly Ball, "Report Blasts Parole System," *Las Vegas Sun*, December 27, 2005, pp. 12.

Selected Bibliography

Angel, Myron, ed. *History of Nevada, 1881, with Illustrations*. Oakland: Thompson and West, 1881. Reissued, Berkeley: Howell-North, 1958; New York: Arno Press, 1973.

Archer, Michael. *A Man of His Word: The Life and Times of Nevada's Senator William J. Raggio*. Ashland, Ore.: Hellgate Press, 2011.

Bakken, Gordon Morris. *Rocky Mountain Constitution Making, 1850–1912*. Westport, Conn.: Greenwood Press, 1987.

Bancroft, Hubert Howe. *The Works of Hubert Howe Bancroft. Vol. 25, History of Nevada, Colorado, and Wyoming, 1540–1888*. San Francisco: History Company, 1890. Reprinted, in part, as *History of Nevada, 1540–1888*. Reno: University of Nevada Press, 1981.

Bowers, Michael W. *The Nevada State Constitution: A Reference Guide*. 2nd ed. Oxford: Oxford University Press, 2014.

Bubb, Daniel. *Landing in Las Vegas: Commercial Aviation and the Making of a Tourist City*. Reno and Las Vegas: University of Nevada Press, 2012.

Bushnell, Eleanore, ed. *Sagebrush and Neon: Studies in Nevada Politics*. Rev. ed. Reno: Bureau of Governmental Research, 1976.

Bushnell, Eleanore, and Don W. Driggs. *The Nevada Constitution: Origin and Growth*. 6th ed. Reno: University of Nevada Press, 1984.

Cegavske, Barbara K. *Political History of Nevada*. 12th ed. Carson City: State Printing Office, 2016.

Davis, Samuel P., ed. *The History of Nevada*. 2 vols. Reno: Elms Publishing Co., 1913.

Douglass, William A., and Robert A. Nylen, eds. *Letters from the Nevada Frontier: Correspondence of Tasker L. Oddie, 1898–1902*. Reno and Las Vegas: University of Nevada Press, 2004.

Driggs, Don W. *The Constitution of the State of Nevada: A Commentary*. Carson City: State Printing Office, 1961.

Driggs, Don W., and Leonard E. Goodall. *Nevada Politics and Government: Conservatism in an Open Society*. Lincoln: University of Nebraska Press, 1996.

Edwards, Jerome E. "Gambling and Politics in Nevada." In *Politics in the Postwar West*, edited by Richard Lowitt. Norman: University of Oklahoma Press, 1995.

———. *Pat McCarran: Political Boss of Nevada*. Reno: University of Nevada Press, 1982.

Elliott, Gary E. *Senator Alan Bible and the Politics of the New West*. Reno: University of Nevada Press, 1994.

Elliott, Russell R. *Servant of Power: A Political Biography of Senator William M. Stewart*. Reno: University of Nevada Press, 1983.

Elliott, Russell, and Helen J. Poulton. *Writings on Nevada: A Selected Bibliography*. Reno: University of Nevada Press, 1963.

Elliott, Russell, with the assistance of William D. Rowley. *History of Nevada.* 2d ed., rev. Lincoln: University of Nebraska Press, 1987.

Garate, Donald T. *Juan Bautista de Anza: Basque Explorer in the New World, 1693–1740.* Reno and Las Vegas: University of Nevada Press, 2003.

Geran, Trish. *Beyond the Glimmering Lights: The Pride and Perseverance of African Americans in Las Vegas.* Las Vegas: Stephens Press, 2006.

Glass, Mary Ellen. *Nevada's Turbulent '50s: Decade of Political and Economic Change.* Reno: University of Nevada Press, 1981.

———. *Silver and Politics in Nevada, 1892–1902.* Reno: University of Nevada Press, 1969.

Green, Michael S. *Nevada: A History of the Silver State.* Reno and Las Vegas: University of Nevada Press, 2014.

Gold, David M. "Reforming the Civil Jury in the Nineteenth-Century West: Jury Size and Unanimity of Verdicts." *Western Legal History* 15 (summer/fall 2002): 137–64.

Heller, Dean. *Political History of Nevada, 1996.* 10th ed. Carson City: State Printing Office, 1997.

Hardy, David A. *The Nevada Territorial Supreme Court: A Transitional Influence From Frontier Lawlessness to Statehood.* Unpublished Ph.D dissertation. University of Nevada, Reno.

Howard, Anne Bail. *The Long Campaign: A Biography of Anne Martin.* Reno: University of Nevada Press, 1985.

Hrebenar, Ronald J., and Clive S. Thomas, eds. *Interest Group Politics in the American West.* Salt Lake City: University of Utah Press, 1987.

Hulse, James W. *Forty Years in the Wilderness: Impressions of Nevada, 1940–1980.* Reno: University of Nevada Press, 1986.

———. *Nevada's Environmental Legacy: Progress or Plunder?* Reno and Las Vegas: University of Nevada Press, 2009.

———. *The Silver State: Nevada's Heritage Reinterpreted.* Reno: University of Nevada Press, 1991.

Johns, Albert C. *Nevada Politics.* Dubuque, Iowa: Kendall/Hunt Publishing Co., 1973.

Johnson, David A. "A Case of Mistaken Identity: William M. Stewart and the Rejection of Nevada's First Constitution." *Nevada Historical Society Quarterly* 22 (fall 1979): 186–98.

———. *Founding the Far West: California, Oregon, and Nevada, 1840–1890.* Berkeley: University of California Press, 1992.

Jonas, Frank Herman, ed. *Politics in the American West.* Salt Lake City: University of Utah Press, 1969.

Land, Barbara, and Myrick Land. *A Short History of Las Vegas.* 2d ed. Reno and Las Vegas: University of Nevada Press, 2004.

Lillard, Richard G. *Desert Challenge: An Interpretation of Nevada.* New York: Alfred A. Knopf, 1942.

Lyman, Edward Leo. *The Overland Journey from Utah to California: Wagon Travel from the City of Saints to the City of Angels.* Reno and Las Vegas: University of Nevada Press, 2004.

Mack, Effie Mona. *Nevada: A History of the State from the Earliest Times Through the Civil War*. Glendale, Calif.: Arthur H. Clark, 1935.

Mack, Effie Mona, Idel Anderson, and Beulah E. Singleton. *Nevada Government: A Study of the Administration and Politics of State, County, Township, and Cities*. Caldwell, Idaho: Caxton Printers, 1953.

Magnaghi, Russell M. "Virginia City's Chinese Community, 1860–1880." *Nevada Historical Society Quarterly* 24 (summer 1981): 130–57.

Makley, Michael J. *The Infamous King of the Comstock: William Sharon and the Gilded Age in the West*. Reno and Las Vegas: University of Nevada Press, 2006.

———. *John Mackay: Silver King in the Gilded Age*. Reno and Las Vegas: University of Nevada Press, 2011.

Marsh, Andrew J. *Official Report of the Debates and Proceedings in the Constitutional Convention of the State of Nevada*. San Francisco: Frank Eastman, 1866.

Miller, William C., and Eleanore Bushnell, eds. *Reports of the 1863 Constitutional Convention of the Territory of Nevada*. Carson City: Legislative Counsel Bureau, 1972.

Miranda, M. L. *A History of Hispanics in Southern Nevada*. Reno: University of Nevada Press, 1997.

Moehring, Eugene P. *Resort City in the Sunbelt: Las Vegas, 1930–1970*. Reno: University of Nevada Press, 1989.

———. *Reno, Las Vegas, and the Strip: A Tale of Three Cities*. Reno and Las Vegas: University of Nevada Press, 2014.

Moehring, Eugene P., and Michael S. Green. *Las Vegas: A Centennial History*. Reno and Las Vegas: University of Nevada Press, 2005.

Ostrander, Gilman M. *Nevada: The Great Rotten Borough, 1859–1964*. New York: Alfred Knopf, 1966.

Parker, Elliott with Kate Marshall. *Nevada's Great Recession: Looking Back, Moving Forward*. Reno and Las Vegas: University of Nevada Press, 2017.

Ralston, Jon. *The Anointed One: An Inside Look at Nevada Politics*. Las Vegas: Huntington Press, 2000.

Reid, John B., and Ronald M. James, eds. *Uncovering Nevada's Past: A Primary Source History of the Silver State*. Reno and Las Vegas: University of Nevada Press, 2004.

Rothman, Hal K. *The Making of Modern Nevada*. Reno and Las Vegas: University of Nevada Press, 2010.

Rusco, Elmer R. *"Good Time Coming?" Black Nevadans in the Nineteenth Century*. Westport, Conn.: Greenwood Press, 1975.

———. *Minority Groups in Nevada*. Reno: Bureau of Governmental Research, 1966.

Rusco, Elmer, and Sue Fawn Chung, eds. "Ethnicity and Race in Nevada." *Nevada Public Affairs Review* 2 (1987).

Simich, Jerry L., and Thomas C. Wright, eds. *The Peoples of Las Vegas: One City, Many Faces*. Reno and Las Vegas: University of Nevada Press, 2005.

Soden, Dennis L., and Eric Herzik, eds. *Towards 2000: Public Policy in Nevada*. Dubuque, Iowa: Kendall/Hunt Publishing Co., 1997.

Southerland, Cindy. *Mister Speaker to Madam Speaker: A Compilation of Biographies of the Speakers of the Nevada Assembly*. Self-published, 2017.

Thomas, Clive S., ed. *Politics and Public Policy in the Contemporary American West*. Albuquerque: University of New Mexico Press, 1991.

Titus, A. Costandina, ed. *Battle Born: Federal-State Conflict in Nevada During the Twentieth Century*. Dubuque, Iowa: Kendall/Hunt Publishing Co., 1989.

Vernetti, Michael. *Senator Howard Cannon of Nevada: A Biography*. Reno and Las Vegas: University of Nevada Press, 2008.

Zanjani, Sally. *Devils Will Reign: How Nevada Began*. Reno and Las Vegas: University of Nevada Press, 2006.

Index

Page numbers in italics refer to figures and table data.

abortion statutes, 69
"absence from the state," 111
An Act to Organize the Territory of
    Nevada, 19
Adams, Jewett W., *102*
adjutant general, 50, 110
advisory legal opinions, 112
Affordable Care Act, 176
African Americans, 40–44, *45*
airports, 168
Aladdin Casino, 165
alcoholism, 175–76
alcohol prohibition, 161
Alta California, Province of, 99
Amazon, 167
amendments, 67–68, 71–72, 94–95
American Barrick Resources, 174
American River, 4
amicus curiae briefs, 78
Amodei, Mark, 74
Andress-Tobiasson, Melanie, 130
Angle, Sharron, 93
Anointed One, The (Ralston), 81
anti-sodomy law, 51
Anza, Juan Bautista de, 3
appellate court, 121, 124
appellate jurisdiction, 123, 127
Applied Economics, 173
appropriations, 150–54
Arizona, 9, 170, 172
Armijo, Antonio, 4–5
Army Air Corps, 163
Asian Indians, *40*
Asians, 38–39, *40*

Assembly. *See* Nevada State Assembly
Atomic Energy Commission, 163
attorney general, 99, 100–101, *106*, 107,
    112–13
Augustine, Kathy, *103*, *113*

Backus, Gary, 110
balanced budget, 120, 141–42
ballot questions: campaign finance
    and, 65
ballots, official, 114
Balzar, Fred B., *102*, 162
Bancroft, Hubert Howe, 31
Bank Crowd, 75, 76, 156, 157, 174
Bank of California, 156
Banks, James A., 122
banks, taxing of, 148–49
Bannock Indians, 36
Barden, Don, 42
barite, 165
Barrick Gold Corporation, 66
Barron v. Baltimore, 53
bartending, women and, 48–49
Bartleson, John, 5
Basic Magnesium (plant), 163
Bates, Edward, 19
Becker, Nancy, 110
Bell, Frank, *102*
Bellagio Hotel, 168
Bennett-Haron, Karen, *131*
Benton, Thomas Hart, 6
Bernhisel, John M., 9
Berry, Ondra, *113*
Bidwell, John, 5

Bidwell-Bartleson party, 5
"Big Bonanza" gold-and-silver ore lode,
    156
"Big Four," 158
Bilbray, James, 166
bill of rights (state), 34, 52, 53, 54–55, 84
Bill of Rights (U.S.), 53, 54
bills: divorce, 162; nongermane amend-
    ments and, 94–95; origination of,
    94; signing into law, 95–96; super-
    majority requirements, 95; vetoing,
    95–97, 109–10
Biltz, Norman, 76
bimetallism, 159
Binion's Horseshoe Casino, 168
bisexuals, 51, 52
Bizpac (Las Vegas Chamber of
    Commerce–political action
    committee), 65
Black Book, 164
Black Entertainment Network, 42
Blasdel, Henry G., 99, 102
Board of Bank Commissioners, 161
Board of County Commissioners,
    136–37
Board of Education, 139
Board of Examiners, 107, 112, 114
Board of Pardons Commissioners, 107,
    112
Board of Parole Commissioners, 175
Board of Regents, 139
Board of State Prison Commissioners,
    107, 112, 114
Bonanza Firm, 156
Bonanza Kings, 156–57
Bonaventure, Joe, 117–18
bonds, 141, 145, 150–51, 170
Bonneville, Benjamin L. E., 5
Boulder City, 138, 154, 162
Boyle, Emmet D., 102, 103
Bradley, Lewis R., 100, 102
Bringhurst, William, 10
Bryan, Richard, 100, 102, 104
Bryan, William Jennings, 58

Buchanan, James, 14, 17, 19
Buckley, Barbara, 96
budget, state, 108–9, 120, 141–42,
    150–54
Bundy, Cliven, 171
Bunker, Richard, 81
Bureau of Land Management, 171, 172
Bushnell, Eleanore, 7
business, 42-43, 49, 148–49
business buying power, 43, 47–48

Caesars, 52–53
Caesars Entertainment Corporation,
    42, 66
Cafferata, Patricia D., 113
Caliente, 138
California: Compromise of 1850 and, 8;
    control of mineral wealth in Nevada,
    27; gold rush, 7, 8; Nevada's constitu-
    tions and, 22, 26, 32; Nevada settlers
    request to be annexed by, 11, 13;
    Proposition 13, 146
Cal-Neva Lodge, 164
campaign finance, 64–67
Camp Sibert, 163
Cancela, Yvanna, 96
Cannon, Howard, 166, 168
Carlin, 138
Carpenter, John, 74
Carson, Kit, 6
Carson City: government operations
    in, 19–20, 74; legislative building
    in, 150; lobbying in, 78; location of,
    12; Mormon judges in, 18; Ormsby
    County, consolidation with, 135; as
    state capital, 21; supreme court opera-
    tions in, 122; taxes in, 170
Carson County: controversies and
    political strife, 17; controversies in,
    16; creation of, 11–12, 136; maps, 29;
    Mormon-non-Mormon relations in,
    12-15
Carson River, 7
Carson Valley, 9, 11, 13, 14

Carson Valley constitution, 12
Carter, Jimmy, 58
Carville, Edward P., *102*
Casino (film), 165
casinos: African American executives and, 42; hiring of women and, 48–49; income of, 145; offerings, 150; racial discrimination and, 41. *See also* gaming industry; *individual casinos*
"casting vote," 91, 111-2
"central clearance" system, 108
Central Pacific Railroad, 38, 75, 157, 158
certificates of election, 114
Chamber of Commerce, 65, 82, 83
charitable lotteries, 145
Chicanos, 45
chief executive, 99, 104–5, 107
chief justice, 101, 123
chief of state, 107–8
Child, John S., 15, 16, 17, 18
Chinese/Chinese immigrants, 38–39, *40*
Chiquito ("Little") Winnemucca, 36
Chollar Mining Company, 117
Churchill County, 12, *136*
Church of Jesus Christ of Latter-day Saints. *See* Mormons
cigarette taxes, 149, *153*
Circus Circus Casino, 168
CityCenter, 168
city-county relief tax, 146, 169
city governments, 137–38
city managers, 138
civil cases: juries and, 54, 126–27
Civilian Conservation Corps (CCC), 162
civil liberties, 34, 53–55, 134
civil rights: African Americans and, 40–44; Chinese immigrants and, 38–39; defined, 34; Hispanics and, 44–48; historic overview, 34–36; legislation, 41; lgbt individuals and, 51–53; Native Americans and, 36–38; women and, 48–51
Civil Rights Act of 1964 (U.S.), 41
civil service reform, 67

Civil War, 56, 85
Clark County: creation of, *136*; education needs in, 151, 153; Eighth Judicial District, 126; Fairgrounds, 154; "fair share" disputes, 169–70; Family and Youth Services Division, 43; Heritage Museum, 154; Hispanic political power, 46; legislative power, 86; lgbt individuals in, 52; population, 85, 142, 168; School District, 52; water resources in, 172
Clark County Board of Commissioners, 50
Clark County Clean Water Coalition, 169–70
Clark County School District, 139
Clarke, Robert M., 32
Clemens, Orion, 19
Clinton, Hillary, 58
closed primaries, 62
Coffin, Bob, *96*
cohabitation, interracial, prohibition against, 35–36
Colcord, Roswell K., *102*
Collins, John A., 24
Colorado River, 172
commander-in-chief, 110
commerce and industry, *152*
Commerce Tax, *144*, 149, *153*, 176
commercial projects, 167
Commission on Judicial Discipline, 118, 119, 129–31
Commission on Tourism, 112
Common Cause of Nevada, 77, 79
company towns, 160
Compromise of 1850, 8, 99
Comstock Lode, 17–18, 19, 31, 44, 156
Comstock mines, 115
conservation, *152*
constitutional agencies, *154*
constitutional amendments, 67–68, 71–72
constitutional officers, *152*
constitutions: of 1859, 16–17; of 1863,

21–25, 26, 28, 32, 100, 116, 141; of
1864, 25–32, 34, 48, 60, 61, 95, 99,
100, 107, 122, 141. *See also* Nevada
State Constitution; U.S. Constitution
construction industry, 166–67, 168
controller, 99, 100–101, 106, 114
copper mining, 160, 161
Cord, E. L., 76
Cornwall, William A., 12
Cornwall Constitution, 12, 32
Corporate Gaming Act, 164
counties, 135–37
county boards of commissioners, 136–37
county supremacy movement, 171
court of appeals, 124
court of last resort, 121
courts of general jurisdiction, 121
courts of limited jurisdiction, 121
courts of record, 127
Cox, Walter, 77
Coyote Springs Valley, 172
Cradlebaugh, John, 16, 17, 18, 20
Crane, James M., 15, 16, 17
Crawford, Israel, 28
Creighton, Lorenzo, 42
Crime of '73, 159
criminal cases, juries and, 54, 126–27
Crocker, Charles, 158
Cubans, 44, 45–46, 47
Cumming, Alfred, 14, 15, 19
Curry, Abe, 20

Daggett, Rollin, 157–58
Davis, Gary, 130
Davis, Sammy, Jr., 41
dealing, women and, 48, 49
Death Valley, 38
Declaration of Rights, 34, 52, 53, 54–55,
84
defense plants, 163
DeLong, Charles E., 24, 28, 30
Del Papa, Frankie Sue, 65, 73, 81, 113
Del Vecchio, Nicholas, 130
Democratic Party: control of legislature,

92, 93; issues important to, 59; Nevada
governorship and, 103, 106, 107; in
Nevada politics, 56, 57; in the 1930's,
161, 162; since 1980, 57, 165–66
demographics: African American popu-
lation, 40, 43–44; Asian population,
38–39; Clark County growth rate,
142; Hispanic population, 46–47, 48;
Nevada's population growth, 142, 150,
165, 173; racial diversity, 35
Demont, Joseph, 9
Denis, Moises "Mo," 96
Department of Employment Security,
104
Department of Human Resources, 104
Department of Motor Vehicles, 104
Department of Public Safety, 104
Deseret, State of, 8, 9
Desert Inn, 164
Dickerson, Denver S., 102
Dillon, John F., 134–35, 294
Dillon's rule, 134–35
Dini, Joe, 93
direct democracy elections, 67–71, 159,
160
direct primary, 67, 173
Direct Primary Law, 59–60, 62, 160
disabilities, students with, 151
disabled, social services for, 143
discrimination: against African Americans, 40–43; against Chinese immigrants, 38–39; against Hispanics,
45; against lgbt individuals, 51–53;
against Native Americans, 37; in
Nevada's history, 35–36; in voting
rights, 34–35, 48; against women,
48–49
district attorneys, 113
District Court Commission on Law
Libraries, 120
district courts: appellate jurisdiction,
127; as courts of general jurisdiction, 121; judicial districts, 126; jury
trials, 126–27; original jurisdiction,

127; overview of, 125–29; terms and eligibility, 125–26

district governments, 139–40

divorce, 20, 162

D Las Vegas, 42

Dole, Robert, 58, 63

domestic partnerships, 52

domestic violence, 127, 175

Donner Lake, 6

Donner Party, 6

Donner Pass, 6

Doolittle, James R., 24–25

Douglas, Michael, 131

Douglas County, 12, 126, 136

Downtown Grand, 168

Driggs, Don, 7, 75, 76

Duck Valley Reservation, 37

due process clause, 54

Dungan, Flora, 85

Dunne, E. F., 27, 84

Echelon Place, 168

Echeverria, Peter, 96

economic disparities, racial, 42, 43

education: funding, 120, 146, 151, 152, 153, 154; racial disparities in, 42; statistics, 175–76

Elazar, Daniel J., 33

election(s): campaign finance, 64–67; direct democracy elections, 67–71, 160; eligibility to vote, 60–62; gaming industry contributions and, 81; initiatives, 67–68; "none of these candidates" option, 63–64; percent of voters who participate, 61–62; presidential, 57, 58–59, 61, 62–63; primary, 60, 62–64, 65, 160; recalls, 67, 69–71, 101, 131, 160, 173; referendums, 67-69, 160, 173; secretary of state and, 114; state elections of 1864, 32; winners decided by plurality, 62

electors, 86, 100, 128, 159, 165

electrical industry, 160

electric automobile, 167

electronic and social media, 77

Elko, 138

Elko County, 85, 126, 136

Elliott, Russell, 157

Ely, 137, 138, 160

Emancipation Proclamation, 25

eminent domain, 53, 55

Enabling Act, 25–26, 28, 29, 71–72, 171

English language learners, 151, 153

Ensign, John, 166

Equal Franchise Society, 48

Equal Rights Amendment, 50–51

Equal Rights Commission, 41, 52

Ernaut, Pete, 82

Esmeralda County, 12, 21, 26, 126, 136, 146

Eureka County, 126, 136, 146

Excalibur Hotel, 168

excise taxes, 149

executive branch: eligibility requirements, 100; executive power defined, 99; famous firsts, 113; impeachment process, 101, 103; interest group lobbying and, 78 80; party control of, 106; plural executive system, 99–100; terms and term limits, 72-3, 100–101

executive power: defined, 99

ex parte conversations, 130

Fair, James G., 156

fair housing act (Nev.), 42

Fair Housing Act of 1968 (U.S.), 41

"fair share" disputes, 169–70

Fallon, 136, 138, 163

family courts, 120, 126, 127–28

Federal Bureau of Investigation (FBI), 164

Federal Election Campaign Act of 1974, 64

Federal Election Commission, 64

federal estate tax, 143, 145

federal government, attitude of Nevadans toward, 170

federal government, investment in Nevada, 161–62, 163

federal lands, 171
Fernley, 69, *138*
Ferraro, Greg, 82
Fifteenth Amendment (U.S.), 40, 60,
    173
Filipinos, 39, *40*
Fillmore, Millard, 9
finance and administration, *152, 154*
Fine, Fran, 130
First Amendment (U.S.), 65
Fitzgerald's casino, 42
Flamingo Hotel, 42, 164
Flenniken, R.P., *17, 18*
Flood, James C., 156
Florida, 170
Fontainebleau, 168
food exemption from sales tax, 147
Ford, Gerald, 58
Fort Churchill, 36
Fourteenth Amendment (U.S.), 40, 54,
    173
Fourth Amendment, 121
"Frame of Government" constitutions,
    33
Frazier, Maude, *113*
Frémont, Jessie, 6
Frémont, John C., 6–7, 25
Frey, Jim, 45–46
Friedhoff, Frances G., *96*
Frierson, Jason, *96*
frontier, opening of new, 155
fuel taxes, 143, 149, 170
functional home rule, 135, 137–38
fur-trapping, 3–5

gambling: addiction, 175–76; legalized,
    162; prohibition of, 20–21, 161, 163
Gaming Commission, 104
Gaming Control Board, 104, 164
gaming industry: African American
    executives and, 42; federal aid to, 163;
    growth in, 163, 167–68; lgbt individ-
    uals and, 52–53; lobbying and, 76,
80–82, 83; Native American participa-
    tion in, 150, 173–74; organized crime
    and, 81, 163–64, 165; post-Recession,
    167; racial discrimination and, 41;
    recent trends in, 173–74; regulation
    of, 163–64, 170; state governments
    and, 62; taxes, 142, 145–46, 149–50,
    153; women and, 48–49
Garcés, Fr. Francisco, 3
Gass, Octavius Decatur, 10
Gay, Lesbian and Straight Education
    Network, 52
gender identity and expression laws
    addressing, 51, 52
general charters, 137
general elections, 65, 110
Genoa (Nev.), 9, 16, 17, 20
genocide, 36
George, Lloyd, 171
Giancana, Sam, 164
Gibbons, Jim: budget balancing mea-
    sures undertaken by, 169; educa-
    tion, 103; Great Recession, response
    to, 109; initiative legislation signed
    by, 68; lgbt domestic partnerships
    opposed by, 52; political party, 103;
    renomination denied to, *113*; tax
    amendment sponsored by, 95; term
    served by, *102*; troubled tenure of, 90
Gibbons Tax Restraint Initiative, 95,
    120
Gold Canyon, 9
Golden Nugget Casino, 168
Goldfield, 159
gold/gold mining: Comstock Lode,
    17–18, 19, 31, 44, 156; heap leaching,
    76; Hispanics and, 44; ore, discovery
    of, 159; settlement of Nevada and,
    7, 8, 9, 10; since the 1980's, 165, 174;
    Tonopah-Goldfield boom, 159–60; in
    World War I, 161
Gold Hill, 31
Goldman, Paul, 130

gold standard, 159

Goodman, Carolyn, 50

Governing magazine, 147

governor(s): "absence from the state,"
  111; appointments by, 104–5, 107;
  budget proposals and, 108–9, 150;
  calling of special legislative sessions,
  85–86, 89–90; as chief executive,
  104–5, 107; as chief legislator, 108–10;
  as chief of his political party, 110; as
  chief of state, 107–8; as commander-
  in-chief of the Nevada National
  Guard, 110; filling judicial vacancies,
  132–33; Hispanic, 46; impeachment
  and, 101, 103; lawmaking process and
  veto power, 95–97, 109–10, line of
  succession, 104; list of, *102, 106*; pardons and, 107; party affiliations, *102,
  103, 106*; patterns among, 103–4; in
  "plural executive" system, 99; power
  and limits, 105, 107; recall process, 70;
  tax proposals, 120–21; terms and term
  limit, *72, 73,* 100

Gragson, Oran, 41

grazing lands: fair market rents and,
  171

Great Basin, 4, 5–6, 7, 8, 36

Great Depression, 156, 162

Great Recession: education spending
  cuts during, 151; end of, 167; gaming
  and tourism industries impacted by,
  168, 173; governor response to, 109;
  growth slowdown in wake of, 166;
  human services need during, 153;
  property taxes impacted by, 148; social
  problems worsened by, 176; women in
  aftermath of, 49

Great Salt Lake, 4

Great Salt Lake County, 14

Greenspun, Hank, 77

Griswold, Morley, *102*

gross receipts tax, 145, 149

gubernatorial elections, 66

Guinn, Kenny, 81, 82, 95, *102, 103,* 110,
  120

Guinn Center for Policy Priorities, 59

Guy, Dell, *131*

Hafen, Conrad, 130

Halverson, Elizabeth, 130

Hammargren, Lonnie, 111, 112

Harrah's, 52–53

Harris, Becky, *113*

hate crime statute, 51

Haviland, Dawn, 130

Hawthorne Naval Ammunition Depot,
  162

heap leaching, 76

heart transplant, 134

Hecht, Chic, 166

Heller, Dean, 65, 67, 111

Henderson, *138,* 169

higher education, 151, *154,* 173

high school dropouts, 175–76

highways, state spending on, 153

highways: federal assistance for, 161–
  62, 163

Hilton Hotels Corporation, 42

Hispanics, 44–48, *47,* 153

Hoffa, Jimmy, 164

Holmes, Oliver Wendell, 141

"home rule," 135

homosexuals, 51–53

Hoover Dam, 10, 40, 162, 163

Hopkins, Mark, 158

Horne, Lena, 41

Horsford, Steven, *96*

hotel industry, 41

housing market, 166, 167

Hudson's Bay Company, 4

Hughes, Howard, 164

Hulse, Benjamin R., 10

Hulse, James, 155

human resources, 152

human services, *152,* 153, *154*

Humboldt County, 12, 29, *136*

Humboldt River, 4, 7
Humboldt Trail, 5–6
Huntington, Collis P., 158
Hurst, Sadie D., 96
Hutchison, Mark, 112
Hyde, Orson, 12, 13, 14

immigration quotas, 38
impeachment process, 101, 103, 131, 132
income tax, 143, 147
incorporation, 54, 114
Indian Affairs Commission, 37
Indian Claims Commission, 37
Indians. See Asian Indians; Native
    Americans
industrial revolution, 160
infant mortality, 175
infrastructure: general fund appropria-
    tions, 152, 154
inheritance taxes, 143, 145
initiatives, 67–68, 71-2, 160-1, 173
Institute on Taxation and Economic
    Policy, 147
insurance premium tax, 149, 153
interest groups: gaming industry, 80–82,
    83; historical overview of, 75–77;
    lobbying, 77–78; political machines,
    75–76; purpose of, 75; railroads, 157–
    58; winners and losers, 80–83
Interim Finance Committee, 90, 97
intermarriage, prohibition against, 37
Internet: state legislature and, 97
Interstate Commerce Act, 158
Interstate Highway Act of 1956, 163,
    168
intoxication blood levels, 83
Iraq, 165

Japanese, 39
Johnson, David A., 23–24
Johnson, J. Neely, 25, 28
Johnson, Robert, 42
Johnston, Albert Sidney, 14

Jones, Horatio N., 115, 117
Jones, John E., 102
Jones, John P., 158
Jones, Nathaniel V., 10
Jones, Steve (Steven), 118, 130
Joyce, Jim, 81
Joyce, Robin, 81
judges: court of appeals, 124; filling
    vacant seats of, 132–33; recall of, 131;
    reelection of incumbents, 133; re-
    moval, 130; suspension of, 130–31;
    terms, 72, 128; territorial, 115–17
judicial districts, 126
judicial removal, 131–32
judiciary/justice system: African
    Americans and, 43; Commission on
    Judicial Discipline, 118, 119, 129–31;
    district courts, 121, 125–28; family
    courts, 120, 126, 127–28; famous
    firsts, 131; filling judicial vacancies,
    132–33; historic overview, 115–
    21; interest group lobbying and,
    78; judicial removal, 131–32; jus-
    tice courts, 121, 127, 128–29, 133;
    mining-claims cases, 115–17; munici-
    pal courts, 121, 127, 128, 129, 133;
    structure and functions of, 121–24;
    territorial, 20, 30–32, 115–17. See
    also Nevada Supreme Court
juries, 54–55, 126–27
justice courts, 121, 127, 128–29, 133
justices of the peace, 128, 131, 137

Kane, Thomas L., 14
Kefauver, Estes, 163–64
Kelsey, Nancy, 5
Kennedy, Robert F., 164
Kinkead, John H., 102
Kirkland, Cindy, 50
Kirman, Richard, Sr., 102
Knapp, George, 77
Koreans, 39
Krolicki, Brian, 112

labor unions, 81, 82

Lady Luck, 168

laissez-faire, 161

Lake Mead, 172

Lake Tahoe, 38

Lander County, 136

Langan, Frank P., 96

Las Vegas: African American population, 40, 45; City Commission, 48; commercial and population center of Nevada, 168–69; "fair share" dispute over sales taxes, 169; government of, 137; Hispanic community in, 45; as incorporated city, 138; mayor, 138; migration to, 172; Nevada Supreme Court southern panel in, 122; representation, 85

Las Vegas Chamber of Commerce, 65, 82, 83

Las Vegas Chamber of Commerce–political action committee, 65

Las Vegas Mission, 10

Las Vegas Raiders National Football League, 167

Las Vegas Review-Journal, 77, 119

Las Vegas Sun, 77, 120

Las Vegas Valley, 5, 10, 45

Las Vegas Valley Water District, 172

Lau, Cheryl, 113

Laughlin, 168

Laveaga, Pablo, 96

law enforcement: attorney general and, 113

Lawlor Events Center, 145

laws: bills, signing into, 95–96; initiative process and, 67–68; lawmaking in the legislature, 93–97; referendum process and, 69

Laxalt, Paul, 102, 104, 111

lead mining, 10

Legislative Commission, 97

Legislative committees, 94, 94

Legislative Counsel Bureau (lcb), 78, 79, 88, 97–98

Legislative Counsel Bureau (lcb), Fiscal Analysis Division, 98, 108

legislative proposals, 71

legislators, 70–71, 73, 86, 90–91

legislature: African Americans in, 43-4; amending the state constitution, 69–70; apportionment, 84–86, 89; budget proposals and, 108, 150; controller and treasurer, votes concerning, 114; election spending limits imposed by, 64; executive branch impeachments and, 101, 103, 131; famous firsts, 96; governor as chief legislator, 108–10; governor's State of the State address, 108; Hispanics in, 46; interest group lobbying and, 78; judicial removal and, 131–32; lawmaking in, 93–97; mining taxes and, 148–49; modernization of, 97–98; municipal government creation and, 137; organization of, 91, 93; party control of, 92, 93; power over executive branch regulations, 105; qualifications, 86; salaries, 90–91; sessions, 85–86, 87–90; standing committees and, 94; terms and term limits, 72, 73–74, 93; territorial, 35–36; voter registration and, 60–61; Web site, 97; women in, 50. See also Nevada State Assembly; Nevada State Senate

Leslie, Sheila, 74

lgbt (lesbian, gay, bisexual, and transgender), 51–53

license fees, 149

lieutenant governor: as acting governor, 101, 104, 111; chairmanship of Tourism commission, 112; duties of, 111–12; executive branch line of succession and, 104; impeachment trials and, 101, 103; party affiliations, 106; in "plural executive" system, 99; as

president of the senate, 91, 101, 111–
    12; term, 72, 101
limited liability corporations (llcs), 66
Lincoln, Abraham, 19, 25, 29, 32, 115
Lincoln County, 136, 172
line-item veto, 96
List, Robert, 102, 104, 146–47
List of Excluded Persons, 164
"Little" Winnemucca, 36
live entertainment tax, 145, 149, 150,
    153
livestock owners, 171
llcs (limited liability corporations), 66
lobbying: effective techniques, 78–79;
    gaming industry and, 76, 80–82, 83;
    growth in, 78, 79; labor unions and,
    81, 82; mining industry and, 75,
    76–77, 82; overview of, 77–80; rail-
    roads and, 75, 157–58; regulation of,
    79–80
local governments: cities, 137–38;
    counties, 135–37; powers of, 134–
    35; school districts, 139; separation of
    powers and, 135; significance of, 134–
    35; special district governments, 139–
    40; townships, 135, 137
Locke, Powhatan B., 31, 117
Lockwood, A. J., 27
Los Vegas Rancho, 10
lotteries, 145–46
Lovelock, 138
Luxor Hotel, 168
Lyon County, 12, 136, 170

Macao, 173
Mack, O. H., Ms., 160
Mackay, John W., 156
magnesium, 163
mail-in primaries, 63
Mandalay Bay Hotel, 168
Manifest Destiny, 5, 6, 8
Manoukian, Noel, 117–18
March, Debra, 50
marriage: same-sex, 52, 53

Marshall, Kate, 113
Martin, Anne, 48, 160
Marvel, John, 74
Mason Valley News, 77
Masto, Catherine Cortez, 113
Mathews, Bernice, 74
mayors, 41, 50, 70, 72–73, 138
McCarran, Pat, 76, 162, 168
McCarran International Airport, 168
McCloskey, Jack, 77
McGinness, Mike, 74
McMillan, James, 41
McMullen, Sam, 81
media power brokers, 77
Medicaid, 176
megaresorts, 168
Mendoza, John, 131
mental health spending, 175–76
mercury, 165
Mesquite, 138, 168
Mexicans, 44, 45, 46, 47
Mexican War, 6, 8
Mexico, 3, 6, 7, 8, 44, 172
mgm Grand, 168
MGM Resorts International, 42, 52, 66
military bases, 163, 170
militia, 36, 171
Millennium Scholarship, 88
Miller, Robert J. "Bob," 65, 100, 102, 105,
    111, 112, 172
Miller, Ross, 66, 70, 73
mine inspector, office of, 160
Mineral County, 12, 126, 136, 146
Mineral County Independent, 77
mineral prices, 76, 165
mineral resources, 157, 165
mining industry: Bank Crowd domi-
    nation of, 156; Chinese immigrant
    labor and, 38; colonialism and exploi-
    tation in, 174; Comstock Lode, 17–18,
    19, 31, 44, 156; depression of 1864,
    24, 30; federal monetary policies and,
    159; Hispanics and, 44; in World War
    II and beyond, 163; judicial disputes,

115–17; lobbying and political influence, 75, 76–77, 82, 172; royalties and, 157, 171; Silver Purchase Act of 1934, 161; since the 1980's, 165; taxation and, 21, 22–23, 26, 27–28, 30, 82, 141, 148–49, 150, 157; Tonopah-Goldfield boom, 159–60
minorities, protecting, 173
Mint Act, 159
Mirage Hotel, 52, 168
Miranda, Tony, 46
missionaries, 10
Moapa Reservation, 37
Modified Business Tax (mbt), 148–49, 153
Mojave Desert, 38
Mojaves, 3
Mondale, Walter, 58
Morara, Gabriel, 3
Mormon Church, 50
Mormons: judges, 115; missionaries, 10; non-Mormons, relations with, 11, 12–14, 15, 16, 18; settlement of Nevada and, 7–8, 9; Utah War, 13–14
Mormon Station, 9, 10, 11, 12
Moroni, 7
Mothers Against Drunk Driving (madd), 83
motor vehicles and highways: general fund appropriations, 152
Mott, Gordon N., 115, 116–17
Mowbray, John, 118
Muddy River, 172
Mueller, John, 76
municipal corporations: cities as, 137
municipal courts: appellate jurisdiction of district courts and, 127; as courts of limited jurisdiction, 121, 128; filling vacancies in, 133; functions of, 128, 129; recording of proceedings, 127; selection of judges, 129
Murdock, Nelson E., 34–35
Murphy, Martin, 6
Musser, Col. John J., 16–17, 19

National Automobile Museum, 154
National Mining Act of 1866, 157
National Women's Law Center, 49
Native Americans: attacks against, 5; civil rights and, 36–38; gaming, 150, 173–74; missionary work with, 10; Spaniard dealings with, 3
Naval Ammunition Depot: at Hawthorne, 162
Neal, Joe, 96
Nellis Air Force Base, 163
Neustadt, Richard, 105
Nevada: early attempts to establish government in, 11–16; economic diversification and, 173–74; explorers and immigrants, 5–7; federal lands and, 171; future of, 165–73; history of, 155–73; naming of, 15, 16, 21, 26; population growth, 142, 150, 165, 167, 173; relationship with and attitudes toward the federal government, 170; requests to be annexed by California, 11, 13; settlement of, 7–10; statehood, 7–8, 21–32, 117, 135, 156, 171; water needs and, 172–73. See also Nevada Territory
Nevada Association of School Boards, 139
Nevada Association of School Superintendents, 139
Nevada Association of Student Councils, 139
Nevada Code of Judicial Conduct, 130, 133
Nevada Commission on Judicial Selection, 119, 132
Nevada Court of Appeals, 121, 124–25
Nevada Enabling Act, 25–26, 28, 29, 71–72, 171
Nevada Equal Rights Commission, 52
Nevada Gaming Commission, 164
Nevada Mining Association, 165
Nevada National Guard, 50, 110
Nevada National Security Site, 163

Nevada State Assembly: apportionment, 84–86; Democratic Caucus, 65; executive branch impeachments and, 101; majority leader, 89, 93; minority leader, 93; speaker of the assembly, 93, 104; standing committees, 94; terms, 86; Ways and Means Committee, 90

Nevada State Constitution: amending, 32, 65, 71–72, 89, 100–101; balanced budget requirement, 120, 141–42; bonds and, 151; civil liberties, 54–55; counties and, 136; Declaration of Rights, 34, 52, 53, 54–55, 84; election laws and, 70; eligibility to vote and, 60; history of, 26–32; lawmaking and, 93–95; overview of, 32–33; revising, 71–72; taxation and, 143, 145, 146

Nevada State Education Association, 82

Nevada State Prison, 20

Nevada State Senate: apportionment, 84–86; executive branch impeachments and, 101; lieutenant governor as president, 91; majority leader, 91, 93; minority leader, 91; presiding officer, 91; standing committees, 94; terms, 86

Nevada Supreme Court: appellate jurisdiction, 123; campaign finance and, 64; cases, prosecuting before, 112; chief justice, 101, 123; controversial elections, 110; as court of last resort, 121; filling vacancies in, 132–33; justices in (see supreme court justices); original jurisdiction, 123; overview of, 122–24; pay raise controversy, 119–20; public opinion concerning, 117–21; recall elections and, 70; on "school support tax," 146; size of, 122; terms and term limits, 72, 123; 2001 legislative session and, 85, 88; Whitehead controversy, 118–19, 129–30; workload, 122, 123–24, 127, 130

Nevada Supreme Court Task Force for the Study of Racial and Economic Bias in the Justice System, 43

Nevada System of Higher Education, 73, 139, 154

Nevada Tax Commission, 161, 163, 164

Nevada Taxpayers Association, 82

Nevada Territory: attempts to establish territorial status, 16–18; Carson City as capital, 21; constitution of 1859, 16–17; constitution of 1863, 21–25; constitution of 1864, 25–32; establishment of, 19; judiciary, 20, 30–32, 115–17; legislature, 35–36; map of, 29; mining depression of 1864, 24, 25, 30, 159; territorial governor, 19–20, 99, 141; transition to statehood, 7, 21–32

Nevada Test Site, 163

Nevada Transcript, 31

New Deal, 161, 165

New Mexico Territory, 8–9, 10, 99

news media, 77

New York: Nevada's 1863 constitution and, 22, 32

Nineteenth Amendment (U.S.), 48, 60

"none of these candidates" option, 63–64, 118

nongermane amendments, 94–95

North, John W., 22, 23, 25, 31, 116–17

Northern Paiutes, 36, 37

North Las Vegas, 138

North Las Vegas City Council, 48–49

notaries: public, 114

Nourse, George A., 27, 28, 35

nuclear waste repositories, 174

Nye, James W., 19–20, 21, 22, 24, 32, 99, 102, 141

Nye County, 12, 136, 170-2

Obama, Barack, 57, 103

O'Brien, William S., 156

O'Callaghan, Mike, 42, 77, 102, 120

Oddie, Tasker, 102, 160, 161, 162

Oddie-Colton Act of 1930, 162

Ogden, Peter Skene, 4

Old Spanish Trail, 5–6, 10

"one person, one vote," 68

ore mills, 156
organized crime: gaming industry and, 81, 163–64, 165
organized labor: lobbying and, 81, 82
Ormsby County, 27, 28, 135
Ormsby House Hotel, 21
Orr, James L., 15
Overland Hotel, 41
override: of gubernatorial vetoes, 96–97, 110

Paiutes, 10, 36, 37
pardons, 107
Paredes, Ignacio, 44
parking fines, 149
Parks, David, 96
Parnell, Bonnie, 74
parole, 175
Parole Commission, 104
Patient Protection and Affordable Care Act, 176
Peck, A. S., 32
People's Party, 58
per capita income, 143
Perkins, Richard, 169
"permanent commission," 133
Pershing County, 126, 135, 136
petitions, 67–68, 69–70
Pittman, Key, 159–60, 161, 162
Pittman, Vail M., 102
plan (Progressive Leadership Alliance of Nevada), 47–48, 65
"plural executive," 99–100, 105
pocket veto, 96
political action committees (PACs), 65, 66
political machines, 75–76, 161
political parties: campaign finance, 64-5; chief function of, 59–60; decline in importance of, 75; general characteristics of, 59–60; historical periods of electoral dominance, 59–60; relative independence of candidates, 59. See also individual parties

Polk, James K., 8
poll tax, 61
poor: health care and, 176; social services and, 83, 143; taxation and, 147
population. See demographics
"pork barrel" projects, 153–54
Potosi Mining Company, 117
Potter, William, 130–31
poverty, 49, 175–76
prescription drugs, importation of, 88
presidential elections, 57, 58–59, 61, 62–63
presidential primaries, 62–63
president of the senate, 91, 101, 111–12
president pro tempore of the assembly, 46
president pro tempore of the senate, 91, 104
press, 77
primary elections, 60, 62–64, 65-6, 160
prison system, 20, 107, 174–75
Pro, Philip, 65, 68
Proctor, Francis, 23, 26
Progressive Era, 67, 160–61
Progressive Leadership Alliance of Nevada (plan), 47–48, 65
property taxes, 21, 22–23, 146, 147–48, 157, 170
Proposition 13 (Calif.), 146
"pro se" representation, 128–29
provincial governors, 99
public land, court rulings concerning, 171
public land, state laws, enforcing on, 171–72
public land: "patenting," 157
public safety, 152, 152, 154
Public Works Board, 104
public works projects, 162–63
Puerto Ricans, 45, 47, 47
Pyne, George D., 96
Pyramid Lake, 7
Pyramid Lake Reservation, 37
Pyramid Lake War, 36

Question 6, 146–47
Question 10, 65

racial discrimination, 35–36, 41
racial diversity, 35
Radical Republicans, 25
Raggio, William, 67, 89, 91, 93, 96
Railroad Commission, 160–61
railroads: Chinese immigrant labor and, 38; Hispanic labor and, 45; Interstate Commerce Act and, 158; lobbyists and lobbying, 76, 157–58; between Los Angeles and Salt Lake City, 44–45; Nevada land given to, 157; overcharging customers, 157–58; in politics, 76, 174; regulation of, 159; state-supported bonds and, 141
Ralston, Jon, 81
Ralston, William C., 156
Ramsey v. City of North Las Vegas, 131, 132
ranching industry, 26, 44, 75, 103, 171, 172
Reagan, Ronald, 57
real property transfer tax, 153
reapportionment plan of 2001, 85, 88
recalls, 67, 69–71, 101, 112, 131, 160, 173
recessions, 142
Red Rock Resorts, 42
Reese, John, 9
referendum election, 67, 69, 160, 173
referendum petition, 69
Reid, Harry, 57, 93, 103
relief projects, 162
relief tax, 146, 169
Reno: Chinatown, 39; divorce bill, 1931 and, 162; gaming in, 168, 173–74; government of, 137, 138; migration to, 172; representation, 85
Republican Assembly Caucus, 65
Republican Party: control of legislature, 92, 93; first Nevada state elections and, 32; issues important to, 59;

Nevada governorship and, 103, 106, 107; in Nevada politics, 56, 57; since 1980, 165–66
reservations, Indian, 37
responsible parties, 59
retirees, 57, 170
revenues: biennial budgeting and, 141–42, 151; bills, 94; gaming taxes, 142, 145–46, 149–50; overview of, 143–50; recessions and, 142; sales taxes, 142, 146–47, 150, 169; by source, 144, 153. See also taxation
Reynolds, Donald, 77
Reynolds v. Sims, 85
Rhoads, Dean, 74
"riders," 94
riots, 41
roads: federal assistance for, 161–62
Rocky Mountain Fur Company, 4
Roe v. Wade, 69
Rogich, Sig, 82
Roop, Isaac, 17, 18
Roop County, 135
Roosevelt, Franklin D., 57, 161, 162
Rose, Robert, 119
Rowland-Workman party, 5
Russell, Charles H., 100, 102, 104, 164

Sadler, Reinhold, 102
Sagebrush Rebellion, 171
Sagebrush II, 171
Sahara Casino, 168
sales taxes, 142, 146–47, 148, 149, 150, 153, 169, 170, 176
same-sex marriage, 52, 53
Sampson, Dewey, 96
Sandoval, Brian: business tax created under, 149; campaigning, 66, 82; county home rule approved by, 135; educational background, 104; education measures by, 139, 153; as first Hispanic governor, 113; Great Recession, response to, 109; judges

appointed by, 121, 124; lieutenant governor, work with, 112; Medicaid expanded by, 176; political party, 103; redistricting plans vetoed by, 88–89; term served by, 102; veto power exercised by, 110

Sands Hotel, 164

San Francisco, 27

San Gabriel Mission, 3, 4

Sawyer, Grant, 41, 76, 100, 102, 104, 111, 164

Sawyer v. District Court, 111

Schieve, Hillary, 50

school boards, 139

school districts, 139

school support tax, 146

Scrugham, James G., 102

secretary of state, 99, 101, 104, 106, 113–14

segregation, 41-42

Senate Democratic Caucus, 65

Senate Finance Committee, 90

Senate majority leader, 91, 93, 96

Senate minority leader, 91

Senate Republican Leadership Conference, 64–65

senators, state, 72, 86

senators, U.S., 32, 159

senior citizens, 62, 170

separation of powers, 84, 135

September 11, 2001 terrorist attacks, 142, 173

Sequinata, Chief, 36

Seventeenth Amendment (U.S.), 32, 62, 160

Seward, William H., 19, 20, 24

sexual orientation, 51–52

Sharon, William, 156, 158

Shearing, Miriam, 118, 119, 131

Sherman Silver Purchase Act, 159

Shoshones, 36, 37, 38

Silver-Democrat Party, 56, 159; Nevada governorship and, 103, 106

Silver Legacy Hotel, 168

Silver Party, 56, 58, 103, *106*, 159

Silver Purchase Act of 1934, 161

silver/silver mining: Comstock Lode, 17–19, 44, 156; Hispanics and, 44; in Las Vegas Valley, 10; ore, discovery of, 159; Sherman Silver Purchase Act, 159; Silver Purchase Act of 1934, 161; since the 1980's, 165, 174; Tonopah-Goldfield boom, 159–60; U.S. monetary policies and, 159; in World War I, 161

Sinatra, Frank, 164

Singapore, 173

sit-ins, 41

slot machine tax, 145, 150

SLS, 168

small claims court, 128–29

Smith, Jedediah, 4, 5

Smith, Joseph, 7

Smith, William "Extra Billy," 15, 16

social services, 83, 147, 175

social welfare policies, 83

Southern Paiutes, 10, 36, 37

Southwest airline, 168

Sparks (city), 129, *138*, 170

Sparks, John, *102*

speaker of the assembly, 93, 104

speaker pro-tempore of the assembly, 50

Spearman, Patricia, *96*

special charters, 137

special district governments, 139–40

special education, 153

special interest, appropriations for, 153–54

special purpose agencies, 89–90, 152

specialty courts, 127–28

Spring Valley, 169

Stanford, Leland, 158

Stardust Casino, 165

state budget: appropriations, 141, 150–4; proposals, 108–9, 150; requirement to be balanced, 120, 141–42

State Ethics Commission, 67

state governments, powers of, 134-135

state income tax: prohibition on, 143, 145

State of Nevada Employees Association, 82

State of the State address, 108

state party conventions, 63

Station Casinos, 42

statutes: initiative process and, 67–68, 69

Stead Air Force Base, 163

Steele, John, 10

Stevens, Elisha, 6

Stevenson, Charles C., 102

Stewart, William M.: mining taxes fought by, 22; 1863 constitution supported by, 23, 24, 25; North, Justice, conflict with, 116–17; territorial judges opposed by, 31; territorial judges undermined by, 115; as U.S. senator, 32, 157, 158

Stiglich, Lidia S., 131

Storey County, 12, 136

Styles, George P., 12

suffrage, 35, 48, 61, 159, 173

suicide, 156, 175–76

Summerlin South, 169

superintendent of public instruction, 99

supermajority votes, 95

Supreme Court Commission on Law Libraries, 120

supreme court justices: controversial election campaigns, 117–18; eligibility of, 125; as members of the Board of Pardons Commissioners, 107; midterm appointments, 133; pay raises, 119–20; public attitudes toward, 115, 117–19; recall process, 70; terms and term limits, 72, 122

surveyor general, 99

Sutter's Mill, 8

Switch, 167

Tao, Jerry, 131

taxation: business, 148–49; decisions, future on, 176; excise, 149; gaming, 142, 145–46, 149–50, 153; mining industry and, 21, 22–23, 26, 27–28, 30, 82, 141, 148–49, 150, 157; overview of, 143–50; property, 21, 22–23, 146, 147–48, 170; proposals, 120–21; public opinion concerning, 142–43; recessions and, 142; regressivity, 147; sales, 142, 146–47, 148, 149, 150, 153, 169, 170; sources, 153

tax bills, 94, 95, 148

Taylor, Zachary, 9

teachers' unions, 76, 82

Teamsters, 164

television: state legislature and, 97

"temporary commission," 133

Tenth Amendment (U.S.), 33, 84, 134

term limits, 72–74; executive branch and, 72, 100–101

Territorial Act, 1861, 20

territorial judges, 116–17

Tesla, 167

"13-counties" rule, 67–68

Thirteenth Amendment (U.S.), 25, 32, 40, 173

Thomas and Mack Center, 145

Thompson, Charles, 117–18

Thorrington, William "Lucky Bill," 15

Timbisha Shoshones, 38

Titus, Dina, 96

Tonopah, 159

Tonopah-Goldfield boom, 159–60

Tourism Commission, 112

tourism industry, 150, 163, 168, 173

Townsend, John, 6

Townsend, Randolph, 74

townships, 128, 135, 137

traffic cases, 129

traffic fines, 149

transgender individuals, 52

Treasure Island Hotel, 168

treasurer, state, 99, 100–101, *106*, 114
Treaty of Guadalupe Hidalgo, 7, 8
Treaty of Ruby Valley, 38
Tropicana Casino, 165
Truckee Meadows, 9
Trump, Donald, 58
"truth squad" law, 67
Turner, George, 31, 115, 117
Twenty-second Amendment (U.S.), 100
Twenty-sixth Amendment (U.S.), 60

underperforming schools, funding for, 153
Union Party, 23-6, 116
unwed parents, 175
U.S. Constitution: amending, 50–51 (*see also under individual amendment*); Bill of Rights, 53, 54; Nevada State Constitution compared to, 54–55, 93–95, 101, 103; "one person, one vote" mandate, 68; size of, 33; state constitutions and, 71–72; state powers addressed in, 134
U.S. Court of Appeals for the Ninth Circuit, 64, 68, 171
use taxes, 144, 150, 153
U.S. Forest Service, 171
U.S. Supreme Court: abortion and, 69; appeals to, 121; apportionment and, 85; *Barron v. Baltimore*, 53; cases, prosecuting before, 112; incorporation, 54; same-sex marriage and, 53; term limits and, 72; voting eligibility and, 60
Utah Territory: creation of, 8–9; government, 11, 12, 17, 18, 115; governors, 99; judiciary, 115; maps, *29*; secession from, 15–16, 19
Utah War, 13–14

Vassiliadis, Billy, 82
Vega, Valorie, *131*
Vegas Golden Knights of the National Hockey League, 167
veto, 95–97, 107, 109–10, 157

veto override, 96–97, 109
Victory funds, 153
videoconferencing, 97
Vietnamese, *39*
vigilantes, 15
Virginia and Truckee (v & t) Railroad, 75, 154, 156, 157, 158
Virginia City, 18, 21, 31
Virginia City Territorial Enterprise, 27
voter turnout, 61–62
voting rights, 34–35, 41, 60–62, 159, 160, 173
Voting Rights Act of 1965 (U.S.), 41

Wagner, Sue, *113*
Walker, Joseph, 5, 6, 36
Walker-Bonneville party, 5
Walker-Chiles party, 6
Walker Pass, 5
Walker River, 7
Walker River Reservation, 37
Wallace, Charles "Black," 75, 158
Warm Springs Hotel, 20
Washington, Maurice, 74
Washoe, State of, 21
Washoe County, 12, 135, *136*, 169, 170
Washoe County Board of Commissioners, 50
Washos, 36, 38
water, 172–73
water projects, 159
Weir, Jeanne, 160
welfare, 83, 175–76
Wells, *138*
Western Emigration Society, 5
Western Shoshones, 37
West Wendover, *138*
Whitehead, Jerry Carr, 118–19, 129–30
White Pine County, *136*, 160, 172
Whittemore, Harvey, 81
Williams Station, 36
Wilson, Woodrow, 96
Wingfield, George, 75–76, 159–60, 161

Winnemucca (city), 137, *138*

Winnemucca (Paiute chief), 36

Wolfskill, William, 4–5

women: business ownership, 48-9; economic equality and, 49; Equal Rights Amendment, 50–51; in poverty, 49; socioeconomic status of, 48–51; in state politics, 50–51; voting rights and, 34, 48, 60, 159, 160, 173

workman's compensation, 160, 173

Works Progress Administration (wpa), 162

World War I, 161

World War II, 45, 162–63

Worthington, H. B., 32

Wynn Resorts, 52–53, 66

Yerington (city), *136*

Yerington, H. M., 75, 158

Yosemite Valley, 5

Young, Brigham, 7–8, 9, 10, 11, 13, 14, 19

Young, Cliff, 117–18, 119

Young, Ewing, 4–5

Yount, George C., 4–5

Yucca Mountain, 174

Zoom funding, 153